Improving
Goat Production
in the
Tropics

A Manual for Development Workers

Christie Peacock

Illustrated by
Mandefro Haile-Giorgis

Oxfam (UK and Ireland)
in association with FARM-Africa

To the memory of
Professor Joseph Peacock
and
Wagaye Ayele

Contents

Contents

3 Assessing goat-production problems

6 Goat health

Contents

9 Management of large goat farms

10 Processing and marketing goat products

11 Goat-improvement programmes

List of tables

List of illustrations

Acknowledgements

The book has greatly benefited from the suggestions of Bill Forse, David Hadrill, Nick Honhold, David Little, Alemayehu Mengistu, Alan Mowlem, Emyr Owen, Clare Oxby, Dick and Stephen Sandford, David Sherman, and Alan Wilson.

Many extension staff read early drafts of the book. The comments of Gezu Bekele, Teferra Gebre-Meskel, Getenet Lemma, Nima Lepcha, Teferi Seifu, Feleke Tadele, Sisay Takele, and Kettema Yilma have been particularly helpful.

I am very grateful for the support and encouragement of David Campbell of FARM-Africa, Chris Mason and Liz Stone of Oxfam (UK and Ireland) in Ethiopia, and my mother.

Catherine Robinson edited the text, and Paul Kendall designed it. All line illustrations were drawn by Mandefro Haile-Giorgis.

Most of the photographs were taken by Jenny Matthews or myself, but some have kindly been provided by David Little, Alan Mowlem, John Petheram, Peter Roeder, Alan Walters, Trevor Wilson, and the International Livestock Research Institute (ILRI).

Financial support during the writing of the book was provided by FARM-Africa, through a generous grant from the Baring Foundation.

FARM-Africa

FARM-Africa specialises in agricultural development in Africa. Established in 1985, it is committed to helping the smallholder farmers and herders of Africa to help themselves, thereby breaking the cycle of famine and bringing new prosperity to neglected marginal communities. In partnership with local people, FARM's projects pioneer new strategies and techniques in crop and animal husbandry, aiming to produce more food and income in a sustainable way that does not damage the environment. Current projects cover dairy goats, pastoralist development, farmers' research, community forestry management, and general rehabilitation and resettlement projects. FARM currently operates in Ethiopia, Kenya, Tanzania, and South Africa.

FARM-Africa is the recognised development organisation of the United Kingdom's agricultural community, and provides a channel through which supporters can give direct assistance to rural people in Africa.

Oxfam (UK and Ireland)

Oxfam (UK and Ireland) was founded in 1943 to send relief supplies from British people to starving civilians in Greece during World War II. Now working in over 70 countries in Africa, Asia, the Middle East, the Caribbean, Latin America, and Eastern Europe, Oxfam provides assistance and training to support people's efforts to build secure and productive lives for themselves and their families. Its staff work with local counterparts in fields as diverse as emergency relief, health, human rights, capacity building, and agricultural production.

Oxfam's funds are derived from a wide range of sources, including individual donations, trading activities, the British government, the European Union, and international agencies.

Oxfam believes that every man, woman, and child has a basic right to a life free from misery and want. Poverty is not inevitable: it can be tackled and must be ended.

CHAPTER 1

Introduction

1.1 Historical background

Goats have helped people to survive and thrive for countless generations. The goat (*Capra hircus*) is thought to have been the first animal to be domesticated for economic purposes. Evidence suggests that domestication took place about 7,000 BC in south-west Asia, on the borders of present-day Iran and Iraq, where agriculture was already advanced. From there goats spread into all the tropical zones and most temperate areas. Now there is hardly a climate zone without goats.

Immediately after domestication, physical differentiation into breeds and types began. Early physical changes affected the ears, horns, colour, and hair type. These changes arose from natural mutation and from selection by goat keepers within the environment in which goats were reared, usually in relative isolation. Early goat keepers must also have selected for the production charact-eristics which were appropriate to their needs. New blood probably entered goat populations when people migrated for economic reasons or in times of conflict. There is a huge range of size, colour, and hair type among modern breeds of goats.

1.2 Current status

There are now estimated to be about 592 million goats in the world. Goats have shown themselves to be extremely adaptable animals and now are found as far north as Scandinavia and as far south as South America. They can be found at very altitudes. The long-haired Pashmina goats can live in the high Himalaya, while dwarf goats are able to thrive in the humid forests of West Africa.

Table 1.1 shows that the vast majority of goats (more than 90 per cent) are found in the developing countries of Asia, Africa, and South America. Goats in developed countries are really of minor agricultural importance. There are dairy goat industries in France and Switzerland which specialise in cheese-making, but otherwise goats are kept by enthusiasts, partly for profit, but also for pleasure. However, in developing countries goats are of very great importance. Large flocks, of several hundred, are kept by the pastoralists of Asia and Africa, and millions of farmers keep goats in small numbers on small farms.

Table 1.1 Goat population estimates

Area	Population (million)	Percentage of total population
Asia	359	60.6
Africa	172	29.1
South America	23	3.9
Europe	14	2.4
North America	16	2.6
Former Soviet Union	7	1.2
Oceanic	1	0.2
Total	592	100

1.3 The role of goats in developing countries

The contribution of goats to the people and economies of developing countries is obscured by several factors combining to give an underestimate of their true value. Firstly, estimates of goat numbers are usually inaccurate. Most goats are kept in developing countries which often cannot afford to carry out a regular livestock census and so they are rarely, if ever, directly counted. Cattle are more likely to be counted, but goat numbers are often mere guesses. Goat products seldom enter a formal marketing system, and so the goat's contribution to the rural and national economy tends to be grossly underestimated. In addition, goats are usually kept by poorer people, often tended by women, who seldom have a voice in national discussion. For all these reasons goats, and the people who keep them, are accorded a low status and given a low priority in national development. They are thought of as representing an old, primitive, low technology. What people want is new, sophisticated, high technology. In many countries there is even propaganda against goats. They are wrongly accused of destroying the environment, and prejudice has built up against them. As a result, little attention has been paid to goats by politicians, policy-makers, development administrators, and researchers.

Table 1.2 Goat products and services

Products	Services

Meat
  raw
  cooked
  blood
  soup
 	
Milk
  fresh
  sour
  yoghurt
  butter
  cheese
 	
Skins
  clothes
  containers
  tents
  thongs
 	
Hair
  cashmere
  mohair
  coarse hair tents
  judges' wigs
  fish lures
 	
Horns
 	
Bones
 	
Manure for
  crops
  fish
	Pack transport
	
	Draught power
	
	Medicine
	    meat and soup for a range of
	      conditions
	    milk for ulcers, allergies and
	      lactose intolerance
	    butter for wounds
	    aphrodisiacs
	
	Cosmetics
	
	Control of bush encroachment
	
	Herding guide for sheep
	
	Cash income
	
	Security
	
	Gifts
	
	Loans
	
	Religious rituals
	
	Pleasure

Goats provide their owners with a vast range of useful products and services. Some of them are listed in Table 1.2. They can be regularly milked for small quantities of milk. In harsh environments, goats often produce milk when cattle have dried up. Goat milk is highly nutritious and has a similar nutritional profile to human milk, containing 4.5 per cent fat, 4.0 per cent lactose, and 3.0–4.0 per cent protein, depending on the goat's nutrition, breed, and stage of lactation. The higher proportion of short- and medium-chain fatty acids, compared with the milk of other livestock species, allows goat's milk to be digested easily by infants and those with digestive problems. Milk is an excellent source of calcium and phosphorus for growing children and can also provide a vital supply of vitamin A, which is often deficient in the diets of infants in developing countries. Goats' small size makes them ideal to slaughter for a few people at family celebrations or during religious holidays.

In addition to providing milk, meat, skins, and hair, goats have several important economic functions. They are relatively cheap to buy. Flocks can be built up until they contain many goats, which spreads the risk inherent in livestock ownership. It is not sensible for a family to put all its savings into one valuable cow or buffalo, when several goats could be purchased with the same money. Goats are often used as a first step up and out of poverty. Once the family has acquired additional resources, part of the goat flock can be sold and replaced by a large ruminant.

In marginal cropping areas, farmers will often try to keep livestock as an insurance against crop failure. If all or part of the crop fails, cattle or goats can be milked, or sheep or goats sold or exchanged for grain. Such mixed farming is an important drought-survival strategy. However, in some drought-prone parts of Africa this strategy has been used to the limit and has now broken down. Selling the last animal leaves families vulnerable to the vagaries of the weather. Many of Africa's famines arise when this dual strategy irreparably breaks down.

Goats reproduce very fast. Most tropical breeds regularly produce twins and sometimes triplets. A small flock can quickly expand until it forms a major part of the family's capital assets. Goats can regularly and easily be sold for cash and can either be part of a regular cash income or be sold in times of urgent need, such as sickness, death, or the payment of school fees. Goats, being small, can be looked after by young children.

Goats are kept in a wide range of different production systems. Most of the important systems are described in Chapter 2. At one extreme they are kept in large numbers, in extensive systems, by pastoralists grazing common pastures; at another extreme they may be intensively managed, permanently housed in specially-constructed houses, fed by supplies that are cut and carried to them, as in Java, Indonesia. Their hardiness means that they are often kept by people living in marginal agricultural areas, where they are particularly important.

1.4 The environmental question

There has been much propaganda against the goat, and the animal has frequently been used by politicians and bureaucrats as a convenient scapegoat for the environmental degradation caused by human activity. Goats are often blamed for the destruction of vegetation, when the real culprits are people and the overuse they make of vegetation in fragile environments, through tree-felling and over-grazing by all species of livestock. The goat is often found in degraded environments, because it is the only species able to survive in such conditions. Found at the scene of the crime, it is blamed for it, with little thought given to the complex impacts of different species (including humans) over the preceding 20–30 years. The simplistic thinking which blames the goat does little to solve the underlying problems of environmental mismanagement.

Many of the goat's characteristics, in fact, mean that it makes little impact on the environment. It is small and light and moves quickly, compared with cattle and sheep. Cattle, grazing hillsides, are likely to cause much more damage through trampling and overuse of paths, which leads to gully erosion. Goats prefer to browse, which tends to even out the pressure on mixed-species vegetation stands. Sheep often pull out grass by their roots when grazing in sandy soils, causing the loss of valuable ground cover and quickly leading to soil erosion. The goat's natural preference for browse means that they must be controlled, along with other livestock, in areas where young trees have been planted or recently cut forests are regenerating. Young trees can be eaten by hungry cattle and sheep, as well as by goats. The emotive language used against the goat indicates that some appear to believe they can cut down mature trees! People are solely responsible for this, and must take the blame and live with the consequences.

Goats turned loose and left to themselves in a confined, fragile environment (which has occurred on a few small islands) are sometimes too good at surviving and reproducing and may damage the environment in the process. However, this can happen with all species, placed in a similar situation. People must take responsibility for properly managing all their domestic livestock and keeping them in balance with the environment.

1.5 Research and development

Largely as a result of prejudice and ignorance of the importance of goats to farmers in rural areas, there had been little research on goats in developing countries, until about 20 years ago. Scientists in a few developed countries carried out research to support the intensive dairy-goat industries of Europe and North America, but little research was done on goats in developing countries.

Having begun to realise the informal, and normally unquanti-fied, contribution of goats to the rural economy, governments and donors, from the early 1970s onwards, began to fund research and development projects on goats in Africa, Asia, and Latin America. Over the last 20 years a considerable body of knowledge has accumulated on this previously neglected species. There are now regular national, regional, and international research meetings and information networks on goats. The best known is the 'International Conference on Goats' supported by the International Goat Association, which is held in a different continent every five years.

1.6 The potential role of goats in development programmes

Mahatma Gandhi, the great Indian leader, rightly described the goat as 'the poor man's cow'. But the goat is much more than this. The range of products and services it provides is vast. The goat could justly be called 'the poor person's bank', or 'the poor family's insurance policy'. Goats, of course, can serve rich and poor alike. But many of their characteristics (Table 1.3) lead them to play a special role in alleviating the poverty of the poorest in many developing countries. Goat-development programmes provide an opportunity for development agencies to assist some of the poorest families, in developing countries, through their goats.

Table 1.3 Some advantages and disadvantages of goats

Advantages	Disadvantages
Efficient use of fibrous feeds	Susceptible to predators
Preference for vegetation unused by other species	Small value makes formal credit systems uneconomic
Efficient use of water	Small value makes formal insurance systems difficult to administer
Wide climatic adaptation	Susceptible to broncho-pneumonia
Cheap to purchase	Susceptible to internal parasites
Spread risks	
Fast reproductive rate quickly builds up flock	
Fast reproductive rate allows early returns from investment	
Small size allows easy and quick movement of household when necessary	
Easy for women and children to handle	
Few facilities required	
Lack of religious taboos against goat meat	
Small size allows easy home slaughter	

The philosophy underlying this book is that farmers and pastoralists in developing countries are capable of improving their own lives with very little outside assistance. Many of the suggestions in the book cost little, if anything, to adopt. The emphasis is on making more efficient use of the resources already available, through reducing losses and wastage, and introducing outside inputs to enhance production only when appropriate.

1.7 The aim of this book

There are now many goat-development projects in the developing world supported by governments, bilateral and multilateral agencies, and non-governmental organisations (NGOs). Government and NGO staff are expected to serve in government extension services or on projects without, in most cases, any training, either academic or in-service, specifically on goats. Agricultural colleges in developing countries tend to present sheep and goats together; because most textbooks are about sheep, extrapolations are made, often wrongly, to goats.

This book is written for development workers who do not necessarily have any formal training in livestock production. It explains the theory underlying goat production and how this can be used to design simple improvements. It contains many practical suggestions for how to improve goat production, together with suggestions for how they might be implemented in development programmes. It is written in the belief that technical solutions cannot be divorced from the social, economic, and organisational context into which they are introduced. It is not enough for development workers to know the technology — although they must; they also need to understand the context in which that technology must function. This book attempts to put goat technology in this development context.

Further reading

Chambers, R. (1983) *Rural Development: Putting the Last First*, Harlow, UK: Longman
Devendra, C. and M. Burns (1983) *Goat Production in the Tropics*, Farnham, UK: Commonwealth Agricultural Bureau
Gall, C. (ed) (1981) *Goat Production*, London: Academic Press
Mason, I.L. (1984) *Evolution of Domestic Animals*, Harlow, UK: Longman

CHAPTER 2

Common problems of goats in the tropics

2.1 Introduction

Goats are kept in many different systems of production in the tropical world. Different ways of feeding, breeding, and using goats have evolved in response to factors such as the climate, needs of the owner, economic environment, and level of technology available. Within each system of production, goat keepers have developed their own method of looking after goats, according to their own particular circumstances.

If goat-production systems are to be improved, they must be accurately described and their problems properly analysed. This chapter describes the main goat-production systems of Africa, Asia, and South America, classified according to the main agricultural system of which each is part, and the major climate zone in which it is found.

Until about 20 years ago there was very little written information about goats in the tropics, but now there is sufficient research and development experience to be able to predict with reasonable accuracy some of the common problems most likely to occur in the main systems of production. However, most of the difficulties confronted in the field are not simple problems, but are caused by a complex set of factors which all contribute to creating the situation. For example, if many kids die before weaning, which is a problem common to many systems of production, there is rarely any single cause of death that can be simply identified and remedied. Poor nutrition of the dam may cause her to produce little milk, which undernourishes the kid and makes it susceptible to diseases. Although it is a helpful start to know the common problems of the system in which you are working, it is not enough. Each village, district, or region is likely to have its own particular problems, which must be identified before any sensible course of improvement can be followed. Chapter 3 describes how to identify the specific problems of goat production in a village or district. You can make a start by trying to identify the system closest to the one in which you work, using the descriptions below.

2.2 Africa

2.2.1 Pastoral systems: arid and semi-arid

Pastoral systems are found in arid and semi-arid areas of Africa, where low rainfall causes varying degrees of nomadism among the local inhabitants. The system is characterised by a marked seasonality in feed supply; typically there is only one wet season. Annual rainfall may vary from 700 mm to a level as low as 200 mm. Goats may be kept in large flocks, and may, or may not, be mixed with sheep or other species. Goats are kept for meat, milk, and cash, as well as fulfilling various traditional cultural obligations. They are valued for their ability to survive periods of drought better than cattle or sheep. There is likely to be marked variability in production from year to year, because of the highly variable rainfall.

Figure 2.1 African pastoral system
GEOFF SAYER/OXFAM

Typical problems found in pastoral goat flocks in Africa :

- high mortality rates in kids before weaning, typically as high as 30 per cent, or higher in periods of drought;
- long parturition intervals, up to two years;
- occasional epidemic diseases, such as contagious caprine pleuropneumonia (CCPP), causing mortality rates of up to 100 per cent.

Factors contributing to problems

There is a marked seasonality in the quantity and quality of forage consumed. During the dry season, low protein levels and high fibre content limit production and may cause weight loss and low milk production. Goats are able to take advantage of a pre-rains flush of growth in browse species which often occurs. There may be occasional mineral deficiencies. Water is scarce, causing infrequent watering and further reducing milk production. Occasional epidemic diseases, particularly contagious caprine pleuropneumonia (CCPP) and peste des petits ruminants (PPR), may have devastating consequences. Internal parasites can be a major cause of kid mortality and loss of milk production. External parasites, particularly ticks, may transmit diseases such as heartwater. Mange can also cause high levels of mortality and morbidity.

There is often a breeding season in pastoralists' goat flocks. This may be due to green flushes of pasture and browse, triggering oestrus and subsequent mating, or because the pastoralists themselves exercise some control through the use of a leather apron or other device. Having many kids born at the same time can cause kid-management problems, especially if there is a shortage of labour at that time. Kids may require special attention and even bottle feeding. If weak kids do not get this care, they may die. Kids weaned into a long dry season may have problems.

Main opportunities for improvement

Kid mortality can be reduced through better health care, particularly parasite control, and management. Large flocks mean that selection within a breed is possible. Pastoralists could group together to organise group breeding schemes, such as an Open or Closed Nucleus Breeding Scheme, for traits such as growth rate. This could take place within one flock, provided that it is large enough (more than 200). Vaccination against epidemic diseases is recommended where possible.

2.2.2 Agro-pastoral systems: semi-arid

Agro-pastoral systems are found on the margins between areas of cultivation and pastoral areas. The emphasis is on keeping livestock to provide the bulk of the family's food and income. Crops supplement this to some extent. Livestock keepers may grow an opportunistic crop or a regular crop during the wet season and then may move all or part of their stock away during the dry season. The Fulani ethnic group in West Africa are typical agro-pastoralists, but many of them are taking up a more settled existence.

Common problems of goats in agro-pastoral systems:

- high pre-weaning mortality rates;
- occasional epidemic diseases.

Figure 2.2 Typical agro-pastoral system, with the remains of crop residues (millet stover) on the ground
INTERNATIONAL LIVESTOCK RESEARCH INSTITUTE

Factors contributing to problems

As in pastoral systems, there is a marked seasonal variation in the quality and quantity of feed available. High fibre and low protein levels cause low productivity, particularly in the dry season. This is partly improved by access to crop residues in the dry season. As in pastoral flocks, negative selection for growth may have occurred.

Main opportunities for improvement
Kid mortality should be reduced through better health care, including parasite control, and vaccination of dams. Group breeding schemes to select for fast growth rates would be possible.

2.2.3 Mixed farming: humid

Mixed farming systems in the humid tropics of Africa, for example in Nigeria, Benin, Togo, Ghana, Côte d'Ivoire, and Cameroon, may be divided into those involving cereal and root crops and those predominantly using tree crops. Annual crops may include maize, beans, and rice. Common root crops are cassava, sweet potatoes, yams, and taro. Tree crop systems may include cocoa, oil palm, rubber, plantain, and fruit trees. Goats are normally kept in small numbers, which may range freely and combine with goats from other households to form a village herd scavenging for food. Goats may be tethered or penned during the crop-growing season to prevent crop damage. There is typically a low labour input into this system of goat keeping. Goat breeds in the humid tropics tend to be small but prolific, such as the West African Dwarf goat. In most humid areas of Africa, trypanosomiasis is a problem. Human population pressure is high and increasing in the humid tropics, which is leading to the year-round confinement of goats, and the need to develop cut-and-carry systems of feeding. This will be a continuing trend.

Common problems in goats kept in the humid tropics:

- high pre-weaning mortality from internal parasites and PPR;
- high adult mortality rates, mainly from PPR (especially in the wet season);
- high morbidity rates from sarcoptic mange, internal parasites, and foot-rot.

Factors contributing to problems

The high moisture content of forage can limit feed intake. Some in-breeding in village herds can occur. Communal herding means that there is little selective mating. Increasing human and livestock populations increase the incidence of disease. Internal parasites are a year-round problem. Seasonally-confined goats are more susceptible to disease and compete for labour during the cropping season.

Main opportunities for improvement

The main opportunities for improvement include vaccination against PPR, drenching, improved housing, and the promotion of cut-and-carry feeding in densely populated areas. Forage development, especially using leucaena and glyricidia fodder trees, may also allow the expansion of flock sizes and extend goat ownership. Improved marketing would also increase the rate of off-take.

2.2.4 Mixed farming: sub-humid

The sub-humid zone lies between the humid and semi-arid zones of West and Central Africa and has rainfall of 1,000–1,500 mm per year. Sorghum and maize are the main crops grown, with

Figure 2.3 Goats in a dry sub-humid system

INTERNATIONAL LIVESTOCK RESEARCH INSTITUTE

some root crops near the humid zone. The zone may be split into the dry sub-humid, inhabited by pastoralists such as the Fulani, and the wetter sub-humid zone, inhabited by settled farmers. Trypanosomiasis is a problem in the latter zone. Goats may be kept in transhumant (seasonally moved) pastoral flocks which may graze on crop residues in the dry season, returning to grazing lands during the wet season. Some of the pastoralists in these areas may be called agro-pastoralists. Settled farmers keep smaller flocks of goats, which are normally herded with sheep and may be allowed to roam freely during the dry season, but are tethered during the cropping season. They are normally kept in the family compound at night.

Common problems of goats in sub-humid zones:

- high pre-weaning mortality rates;
- adult mortality from PPR near the humid zone.

Factors contributing to problems
Seasonal fluctuations in feed-supply restrict production. Increasing human population is placing a strain on feed resources. Internal parasites are also important in areas of high stock numbers.

Main opportunities for improvement
The development of forage crops can make a major contribution. Vaccination against PPR and drenching for internal parasites are important health interventions.

2.2.5 Mixed farming: highland

Goats are kept in small flocks throughout the highlands of Africa. They may be found as high as 4,000 metres in Ethiopia, where they frequently grow long hair. Typical crops grown on highland farms are maize, wheat, barley, oats, *teff*, and potatoes. Goats may be fed on crop residues as well as grazing on steep hillsides. They may be seasonally tethered, or confined throughout the year in very densely populated areas. Goats are kept for milk, meat, and skins, as well as serving as a source of cash. Their manure provides a small but valuable source of fertiliser for the thin, infertile highland soils.

Common problem syndromes among goats in the highlands of Africa:

- high pre-weaning kid mortality rates;
- poor reproductive performance;
- low milk production.

Factors contributing to problems

The low intake of poor-quality feed, often crop residues, limits production. Small flock sizes lead to poor conception rates and the possibility of in-breeding. There are several serious disease problems, such as internal parasites (including gastro-intestinal parasites and liver fluke), mange, abortion, and external parasites in lower altitudes.

Opportunities for improvement
The small farm sizes, owing to an increasing human population, encourage the intensification of this production system. This may be achieved through forage development, parasite control and, in some cases, the use of improved breeds.

2.3 Asia

2.3.1 Mixed farming: humid (irrigated)

Arable crop production under irrigated conditions implies that there is a high human population pressure. Rice is the main crop irrigated, with occasional short-season legumes or cash crops, such as sesame. Goats, if kept at all, are normally housed or tethered in some way, and fed with crop residues and by-products. Forage may be cut from rice bunds, or goats may be tethered by roadsides. Countries where this system of production may be found are Indonesia, the Philippines, India, and Malaysia. Goats are kept mainly as a source of cash, but may also be slaughtered at home for special occasions. They may, occasionally, be milked. Goat breeds kept in these systems tend to be prolific. Goats can be an important source of income for landless labourers, who may graze goats on rice bunds or roadside verges.

Common problems of goats in irrigated rice systems:

- high pre-weaning mortality rates (25 per cent);
- low reproductive rates;
- low growth rates.

Factors contributing to problems
Production may be constrained by low feed-intake rates, owing to the high moisture content of cut forage and/or the high fibre content of crop residues. The small flock sizes, when combined with confinement, lead to poor conception rates. Farmers may not always own a buck, and so oestrus detection can be difficult, particularly if the goats are housed. If a buck is owned, in-breeding may occur unless bucks are regularly replaced through purchase, exchange, or loan. The humidity and the presence of irrigation lead to a year-round problem with internal parasites.

Opportunities for improvement

Human population pressure and a strong urban demand for animal products make these systems appropriate for intensification. Feed-intake rates can be improved through selection of palatable forage species, improved trough designs, supplementary feeding, provision of salt, and better water supplies. The design of goat houses can be improved to enable easy oestrus detection. Bucks should be regularly rotated with neighbours' bucks. Internal parasites can be controlled through drugs, or by wilting forage before feeding. The use of improved breeds may be appropriate.

2.3.2 Mixed farming: humid/sub-humid (rain-fed)

This is perhaps the most common system in which goats are kept in South and South-East Asia. A wide range of systems of production is practised, from full confinement in specially-constructed houses to free grazing on hill sides and crop-stubble fields. Many systems would fall between these extremes. Typically, rain-fed crops would include rice, maize, cassava, yam, taro, sweet potato, and other vegetables. Goats would mainly be kept for sale to generate cash, meat, and manure. Some cultures may milk their

Figure 2.4 Housed goats in Java

Jeremy Hartley/Oxfam

goats. Goats in rain-fed mixed farming systems are generally more important to their owners than those of the relatively wealthier farmers living in irrigated systems.

Typical problems of goats in humid rain-fed systems:

- low growth rates;
- low reproduction rates;
- high pre-weaning mortality rates.

Factors contributing to problems

Low rates of feed-intake are due to the high moisture content of forage and high fibre content of crop residues. There are generally low levels of energy in feeds. Small flock sizes mean that breeding males cannot always be kept. If this is combined with confinement, it often leads to poor reproductive perform-ance and in-breeding. Internal parasites are a major problem.

Opportunities for improvement

Human population pressure and a large and expanding urban demand for animal products encourage intensification of this system, particularly if close to urban market centres and sources of feed supplements. In-take rates can be improved by selection of forage species, improved trough design, feeding of energy supplements, and provision of salt and water. Forage development is an important option. Conception rates can be improved through better oestrus detection (by allowing bucks better access to does), or through more alert management. Rotating bucks with neighbours' bucks reduces in-breeding. Internal parasites can be controlled by use of anthelmintics or by wilting forage before feeding. The use of improved breeds could be considered.

2.3.3 Extensive systems: semi-arid (high altitude)

Extensive goat-raising systems are found in the arid and semi-arid areas of Pakistan, India, Bangladesh, and Nepal. Nomadism is practised to varying degrees. Flock movement tends to follow a transhumant pattern, with goats grazed at higher altitudes during spring and summer returning to lower altitudes during autumn and winter. Flocks may graze crop-stubble fields at the lower altitudes during the winter. Kidding is seasonal, taking place mainly in the spring. Kids are fattened on the high-altitude summer pastures. Does are normally milked, and male kids fattened for sale. Cashmere-fibre production and processing is often an important by-product. The coarse hair may be used for making rugs and rope.

Common problems of goats in extensive grazing systems:

- high pre-weaning mortality rates;
- slow growth rates.

Factors contributing to problems
Seasonal fluctuations in quality and quantity of grazing, combined with a general decline in available grazing areas, are a major source of problems. A shortage of labour may lead to problems in kid management during the peak kidding season.

Opportunities for improvement
Higher off-take is probably the most important intervention. Improving marketing and possibly encouraging the development of specialised fattening systems at lower altitudes would be useful. There are few nutritional interventions which do not involve lowland cultivators in some provision of better winter feed. Appropriate vaccination should be encouraged.

2.4 Central and South America

2.4.1 Extensive systems: semi-arid

Goats are kept in extensive grazing systems throughout the semi-arid areas of Central and South America. Small flocks of 2–10 goats may be allowed to graze freely, often with other species. These small flocks are often owned by agricultural labourers working on large estates or cattle ranches. Larger flocks of 20–50 may be herded by family or hired labour. They are mainly kept for meat and skins, which may constitute up to 30 per cent of the value of the goat. In many cultures kids, 2–6 weeks old, are consumed as a delicacy. There is a trend towards the greater home consumption of goat milk and dairy products in many countries. Grazing is a mixture of grass, herbaceous plants, and trees, known as *caatinga* in Brazil, which is often vegetation regenerating after deforestation of the area for ranching or cash-crop production. Goats have proved to be relatively drought-tolerant and are the last species sold during severe droughts.

Common problems among goats in extensive systems:

- high pre-weaning kid mortality;
- poor-quality skins;
- low milk production.

Figure 2.5 A mixed flock of sheep and goats in Bolivia

17

Factors contributing to problems

Seasonal fluctuation in feed supply restricts milk production and increases kid mortality. Skins are often damaged through poor flaying and preservation methods.

Main opportunities for improvement

Supplementary feeding of lactating does, improved health care, and better skin processing are some possibilities. The increasing interest, among both rural and urban populations, in goat milk and dairy products might lead to the further intensification of goat production and the possibility of breed improvement.

2.4.2 Mixed farming: sub-humid

Goats are often kept tethered or housed in more intensive systems in the sub-humid zones of Central America, including the West Indies, and northern margins of South America. Goats form part of a more intensive mixed farming system. Natural vegetation, including a wide variety of tree leaves, such as *Erythrina* spp, makes up most of the diet, which may be cut and carried to housed goats. This diet may be supplemented by tree legumes, such as glyricidia, as well as cultivated grasses such as *Panicum* spp, and crop by-products such as banana stems, and other fruit and arable crop by-products. The main products are meat, including kid meat, skins, and cheese. Goats are a significant source of cash income, as well as being an important form of savings.

The main problems of goats in intensive systems are listed below:

• high pre-weaning mortality rates among kids;
• low milk production;
• some evidence for high abortion rates;
• respiratory problems in some housed goats.

Factors contributing to the problems

There are fluctuations in the quality and quantity of the diet, and internal parasite problems. The main causes of abortion are thought to be poor nutrition and brucellosis.

Main opportunities for improvement

There is great potential for the intensification of this system through forage development to reduce the seasonal fluctuations in feed supply, through improved health care, and through the use of improved breeds.

2.5 Minor systems

2.5.1 Perennial tree-crop systems

Goats in many of the humid and sub-humid parts of Asia, the Pacific Islands, and to a lesser extent in Africa may be grazed underneath perennial tree crops such as cocoa, coconuts, oil palm, and rubber. There are two main systems of production. Large flocks may be kept by estate owners, primarily to keep down the vegetation under the trees and so improve tree growth and facilitate harvesting. Shade-tolerant legumes may be grown to protect the soil and to provide high-quality fodder to the goats. Tree crops such as oil palm and rubber also produce effluent from processing factories which can be used to fertilise improved pastures for goats or other ruminants. Tree-crop processing may also provide by-products which can be used as feed supplements, for example palm-kernel cake and palm-oil sludge. In rubber-tree plantations there is a risk of goats disturbing the latex-collection cups. Goats may also be kept by landless estate workers as a valuable source of cash. A small herd may be tethered in the estate or beside estate roads.

2.5.2 Urban goat-keeping

The sight of goats scavenging in urban areas in tropical countries is relatively common. Being of such an independent character, goats easily adapt to looking after themselves in what would appear to be an alien environment. Goats may also be kept

Figure 2.6 Urban goats in Addis Ababa
JENNY MATTHEWS/OXFAM

19

confined in backyards, and feed collected or even purchased for them. Their relatively small feed requirements make them more convenient than cattle in providing members of the urban population with a source of milk, meat, and cash. The problems of urban goat-keeping are finding sufficient feed and, in scavenging goats, digestive disturbance from the consumption of plastic bags!

2.6 Which system is closest to the one in which you work?

Think about the goat-keeping system in which you work. Which of the systems described above is closest to the one you know? What characteristics made you decide? What differences are there between your system and the one described that you think is closest to it?

Further reading

Gall, C. (ed) (1981) *Goat Production*, London: Academic Press
Wilson, R.T. (1991) *Small Ruminant Production and the Small Ruminant Genetic Resource in Tropical Africa*, Animal Production and Health Paper 88, Rome: FAO

CHAPTER 3

Assessing goat-production problems

3.1 Introduction

The start of any development initiative is the time to ask
fundamental questions about the situation to be improved, and
about what is an improvement. Often what is thought to be an
improvement by outside 'developers' is very different from
farmers' own ideas. Farmers have many reasons for keeping goats,
and unless these are understood it is impossible to develop
appropriate improvements. For example, scientists commonly
suggest methods of improving the growth rates of goats. This is
appropriate when farmers are trying to maximise their cash profit
and where the costs of inputs are carefully related to the levels of
output. However, most farmers and pastoralists in the tropics have
many different objectives in keeping goats, and trying to avoid
losses and reduce risks may be more important than maximising
profits. Before any practical steps are taken, the existing situation
must be assessed, and the farmers concerned must be consulted.
Unless they actively participate in evaluating their existing
situation, defining their problems, and expressing their
aspirations, the development initiative is doomed to fail.

The objective of this chapter is to give the reader the tools to be
able to identify the specific problems of goat production in a
village, district, or region, in order to develop, with farmers and
pastoralists, the means of improving goat production.

3.1.1 Methods to identify specific problems of goat production

The common problems of goat production in different systems in
the tropics have been described in Chapter 2, which may be used as
a starting point in identifying the likely problems of goat-keeping
in an area. The next step is to investigate the particular problems
of a specific area, district, or village in order to identify the

purposes of the farmers in keeping their goats, and to identify their problems and opportunities for improvement.

Many methods have been developed by agricultural scientists for evaluating farming situations, identifying problems found in the system, and developing solutions. The methods range from the quicker methods such as Rapid Rural Appraisal (RRA) or Participatory Rural Appraisal (PRA) techniques to more complicated Farming Systems Research (FSR) methods requiring the collection of a great deal of information about the agriculture of an area. These methods can broadly be divided into those that require only a few visits to an area and those that require the long-term monitoring of the situation in question.

Two procedures will be described in this chapter. The first is for the extension/development worker working in a remote area, possibly alone or with a small group of people. It is envisaged that this worker has little assistance from outside and would not have access to facilities such as laboratories to carry out feed analyses or disease investigations. What low-cost methods can be used by such a person with little or no external support, to identify problems of goat production?

The second approach to problem identification is for an individual, or more likely for a team, engaged in a goat project or programme, possibly with external donor funding, or at least with government support. It is imagined that this person or team would have access to specialists, laboratories, libraries, and perhaps computers, to assist in a detailed analysis of the problems. What can be done with this higher level of external support?

The steps followed and techniques used in each approach are outlined in Table 3.1.

3.2 Low-cost methods of assessing goat-production problems

It is assumed that a development worker wants to help a village or district with goat production and that in this case goats are already kept by at least some members of the community. The questions to ask when considering the introduction of goats into communities that have not previously kept them will be discussed in Chapter 11.

The methods of assessment discussed below are methods that focus specifically on goats and the people who keep them, and the physical and social contexts in which they are kept. The methods described require nothing more than a pencil and paper, although access to a photocopier or stencil machine would save time. Many development workers feel unable to initiate development activities

Table 3.1 Procedures to identify problems of goat production

Low-cost methods Individual at village/district level	Higher-cost methods Project planning team

Define objectives
Secondary information
↓
RRA Techniques
↓
Public meeting
↓
Group discussion
Feed calendars
Disease calendars
Problem ranking
↓
Individual interviews
Flock structure
Progeny histories
Interview
Direct observation
Expert interview
↓
Maps and walks
↓
Community consultation
	Define objectives
	Secondary information
	↓
	RRA Techniques
	↓
	Public meeting
	↓
	Group discussion
	Feed calendars
	Disease calendars
	Problem ranking
	↓
	Individual interviews
	Interview
	Direct observation
	Expert interview
	↓
	Maps and walks
	↓
	Community consultation
	
	Monitoring (minimum 1–2 years)
	Select sample
	Initial flock inventory, including flock
	  structures, progeny histories and weight
	Ear-tag all goats, start regular recording of:
	  productivity
	  disease
	  feed
	  management
	  marketing
	
	On-farm trials of improvements

Outputs Some specific problems of goats identified. Farmers' needs and aspirations identified. What constitutes an improvement? How can it be achieved?	**Outputs** Detailed problems of farmers and goats identi- fied, including seasonal dynamics of problems. What constitutes an improvement? How can it be achieved?

without some sort of external help from a donor agency. This need not be so. There are many improvements to goat production that do not require anything to come from the outside and can be achieved with simple practical modifications to the existing system. See what you can do in your area.

3.2.1 Secondary information

Start by finding out what is already known about the area in which you work. Secondary information is information on an area or topic that may already exist in government reports, research papers, newspaper articles, and maps. Often this information is hard to obtain, and in a remote area may be impossible. However, it is important to try to find out what information is already known about the area in which you are working, so that you do not waste time collecting it again.

3.2.2 Public meetings

The involvement and active participation of goat keepers themselves in identifying their own problems is the key to obtaining an accurate picture of the current situation and developing solutions that farmers truly want.

At the start of any information-gathering exercise, it is usually a good idea to hold a public meeting, involving the whole village or community, at which the objectives of collecting the information are clearly explained. This provides an early opportunity to build up trust, as the community is able to question your credentials. Explain the sort of cooperation you need. Choose a time and place that is convenient for the farmers and not just for you, perhaps on a holiday or at night after work, or in a less busy season.

Start by introducing yourself, and then clearly explain the objectives of collecting the information. If you come from a government organisation, explain how the information will be used. Be honest about your resources and the limitations on your ability to assist the community. It is important at the first meeting that you are open to questions. In some societies farmers are not used to questioning outsiders at public meetings, particularly if they come from the government; but they should be encouraged to do so, to reduce suspicions. Make it clear that you have come to learn and help them to solve their problems, and improve the benefits that they get from their goats. Make it clear that you do not have all the answers to their problems, but that together with them you will try to help them as best you can and with the resources at your disposal. Don't make empty promises.

Explain the timetable of the data collection and whether you would like to talk to people individually or in groups. This is also a good moment to let those attending the meeting identify individuals who are recognised experts, whom you can question later on.

In some cultures it is not possible to have meetings where men and women can sit together and where women feel comfortable speaking in public. If this is the case, try to organise a separate meeting for women in a situation when and where they feel comfortable to question you and freely respond to your questions.

Many approaches can be taken after the initial meeting. You and your team can start talking to individuals, groups, or experts. This may be in the week or two following the original meeting, or during a couple of days a week for the following few weeks. Make a programme for data collection that is convenient for the community.

3.2.3 Approaching interviews and discussions

There are many ways of carrying out interviews and discussions in rural communities. They range from the formal questionnaire survey of individual households to unstructured group discussions. Each method has certain advantages and disadvantages; the choice depends on the purpose of the interview and the sort of information you hope to obtain from the community.

The most important precondition for any discussion, whether with an individual or group, is that there is some degree of trust between those asking questions and those answering. It is always better if the interview can take the form of a dialogue rather than a long list of questions. The quality of the information received will be immeasurably better if the goat keepers have confidence in those asking the questions. This may be hard to achieve, if you are coming to a new area where you are not known. In this case, try to obtain the help of a local extension person from the area, who is already well known and respected by the community.

It is important that the purpose of the interview or discussion is clearly explained, so there is no misunderstanding. If you are an outsider arriving for the first time, people may have expectations of assistance associated with you. Be aware of this and never make promises you cannot keep, or your credibility will be lost.

3.2.4 Group discussions

Discussions held with groups of goat farmers, for one or two hours, can be a very useful method of obtaining qualitative information very quickly. A range of opinions can be obtained from the different members of the group and a consensus can be reached about what normally happens in that particular area. Listen to the way farmers discuss issues and argue about them among themselves. A group discussion is also a useful forum to cross-check with the group any queries that may arise from other group discussions or individual interviews.

The main disadvantage of a group discussion is that normally the information is exclusively qualitative. It is hard for the group to calculate mortality rates over the last year, for example, whereas this is relatively easy for an individual farmer to estimate for his or her own flock. The group may give you an estimate of how many goats in the village died from a recent epidemic, but this is only an estimate and is likely to be exaggerated. You should treat such group estimates as a figure used to show you the severity of the epidemic.

The group discussion should be organised according to the principles for the public meeting. The farmers should be comfortable and undistracted. The meeting should be organised at a convenient time and place and should not last too long. The size of the group should be such that everyone in it has a good chance of contributing to the discussion. If it is too small, you won't get the breadth of experience that you are seeking. Probably a group of five–ten is ideal. Do not allow one or two individuals to dominate the meeting.

It is not always possible to select the knowledgeable farmers to join the group, but you should try to choose the people who are likely to have the knowledge you need. Women are often responsible for looking after goats, so they must be involved in group discussions, either with the men or separately. It is often revealing to discuss the same issues with women that were discussed with the men, to obtain their different perspectives on the issue.

Do not rely on the results from one discussion. Several group discussions should be held, often covering the same issues. In this way a more accurate picture of problems can be built up and investigation begun of the factors contributing to these problems.

What information is best collected from a group discussion? Such a meeting can give a quick picture of goat production in the area, which is a useful start to further investigations. Specifically, it should enable you to do the following:

- compile feed calendars
- compile disease calendars
- rank problems
- identify improvements
- identify farmers' aspirations.

3.2.5 Feed calendars

In most systems of production in the tropics, the supply of feed to goats varies according to the season. This is the case whether the goats are grazing or feed is cut and carried to them. The main sources of feed (hillside grazing, swamp grazing, crop residues, feed supplements, etc.) and the methods of feeding them (herding, tethering, housing, etc.) are likely to vary through the year, and it is crucial to understand this variation.

If you are working in a different culture from your own, first name the months of the year according to the local names. Then group them into seasons. Sometimes it is easier for farmers to think about a specific year, say last year, and talk about that. However, if you do use a specific year, be careful. If a season didn't come (the rains failed), then farmers might miss out that season altogether, because it didn't happen! Next, go through each season and ask what is fed to goats in that season and how it is fed. You can further refine this technique by asking about the quantity of feed in each season and the times when there are particular problems in finding enough feed. You may draw a line on the ground to represent the year and get farmers to put leaves or stones on the months when there is a lot of feed.

If you are in a mixed farming system, it is important to understand the links between the cropping system and the goat system. Try to get a picture of the cropping system and link feed supply to the seasonal cropping pattern. The method of feeding should also be linked to the labour demands for crop production, in order to identify the busiest times of the year, and when goats are most likely to compete with crop production for labour. It is important to identify which members of the family are responsible for the various tasks involved in goat-keeping. Seasonal calendars can be constructed for each task, indicating the age and sex of the person involved during each season. Remember that farmers may keep other livestock which compete with goats for feed.

Figure 3.1 shows an example of a seasonal feed calendar for a mixed farming system.

3.2.6 Disease calendars

The seasonal pattern of disease incidence can be described in a similar way as for feed. First identify the common diseases of goats. Farmers will use their own local names, so ask them to describe the symptoms clearly, so that you are able to make a reasonable identification of the disease. Ask which sorts of goat are affected (kids, adults, males or females) and then ask when each disease is most prevalent. It may occur all the year round or only in the wet season. Ask the farmers to describe the effects of the disease (such as *sick but recovers, immediate death*, etc.), so that at the end of the session you are able to identify the most important diseases and when they occur. If farmers keep other livestock, it may also be important to describe their diseases, as there may be transmission of diseases between species. An example of a disease calendar is given in Figure 3.2.

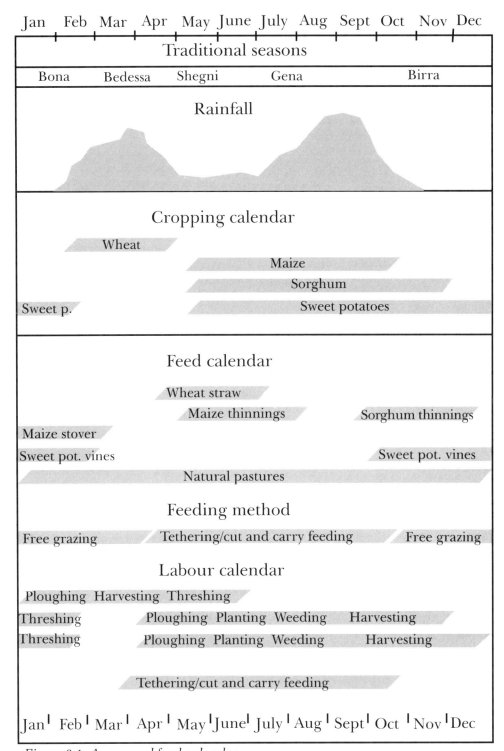

Figure 3.1 A seasonal feed calendar

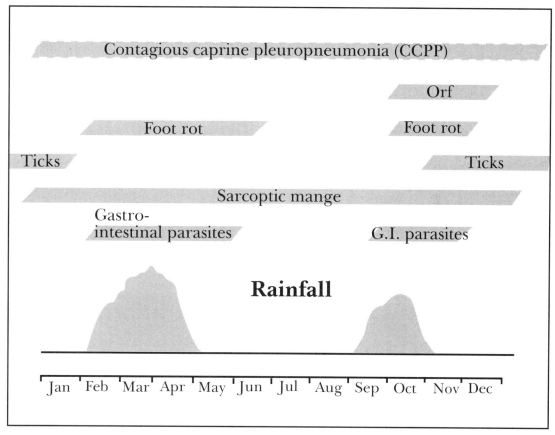

Figure 3.2 Disease calendar, Konso, Ethiopia

3.2.7 Problem ranking and identification of improvements

The group discussion is an excellent forum to ask about the major problems of goat-keeping and to hear what farmers think would be an improvement. You need to take great care to focus the group on issues that you and they can actually solve together. If you ask any group of farmers what their problems are, they are likely to list many things that are indeed problems, such as low goat prices or lack of water, but which cannot be solved without a lot of money or by a change in government policy. Explain again who you are and what sorts of things you and your organisation are able to help the community with. Talk through the problems that farmers have identified, and begin to work towards identifying problems that can, realistically, be solved by the farmers themselves. Table 3.2 sets out a simple format that might be used with a group to specify more fully a problem identified in the discussion.

Get the group to list their problems and reach a consensus, by vote perhaps, on which is the most important problem, the second most important problem, and so on. Try to include a wide range of

Table 3.2 Guide to problem specification

Questions	Problem 1	Problem 2	Problem 3
What is the problem?			
Where is it a problem?			
When is it a problem?			
Who has this problem?			
What **evidence** is available?			
Additional evidence required?			
Class of problem?			

views here. Men may easily say that their goats don't produce enough kids because they are not fed well enough, but the women who cut and carry the feed to the goats may say that their problem is the amount of time it takes to collect the feed, taking them away from other important tasks. These are both feeding problems which could be overcome by the introduction of improved forages. When different viewpoints emerge in response to the same problem, it is sometimes helpful to draw a simple diagram setting out the causes of the problem and linking them together into a network of factors affecting the problem of concern (Figure 3.3). These chains can be developed for several different problems; it may emerge later that several problems share a common cause, and these chains can be linked together to make a larger problem tree. This will be discussed below in 3.2.13.

What constitutes an improvement in any situation is largely influenced by the purpose for which goats are kept, and any improvement programme is doomed to fail if the proposed improvements are not in keeping with the purposes of the goat owners. Goats may be kept for manure production, or merely to have a goat for sale in times of trouble. Farmers may be more concerned with reducing risk than with increasing production, if that will increase the risks. It is of fundamental importance that you clearly understand the reasons for which goats are kept, so that you are able to help farmers achieve their objectives better. This is not to exclude the possibility that farmers may not change their objectives over time. It is often found in goat-improvement programmes that, in order to gain the interest of farmers, programmes should be designed to meet traditional objectives, but that, once farmers start to learn about new technologies, their objectives may change to take advantage of the new technology.

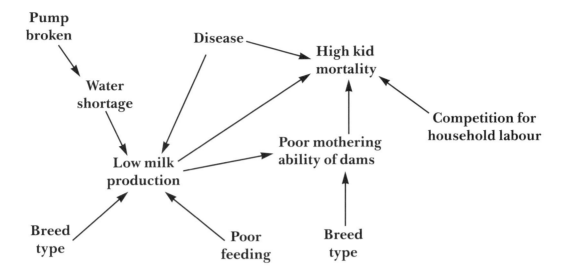

3.2.8 Rapid flock-appraisal method

Figure 3.3 Low milk production: a causal chain

The information obtained in group discussion tends to be of a rather general nature, so it is important to obtain more specific information about individual flocks, their performance and management. A surprising amount can be learned from one visit to a family and their goats. Through a simple field technique it is possible to find out the flock size, flock structure, the reproductive performance of breeding females, and the fate of their offspring. The owner and the owner's family can be interviewed to find out their individual management practices and the problems they face in keeping goats.

Flock size
Knowing the sizes of the flocks in an area helps one to understand

- the relative economic importance of goats (if the importance of other farm enterprises is known);
- the labour required to look after the goats.

When a flock's age and sex composition (known as the flock structure) is determined, it can provide a picture of the flock at one point in time. This is the most basic information about the flock. But flocks are dynamic: goats are born, sold, given away, consumed, bought, borrowed, and lent. So any flock structure represents a snapshot of the flock — the past events — as well as the future intentions of the owner. It represents:

- the past events in the flock (the birth and death rates, as well as levels of off-take);
- the owner's objectives in keeping the flock (whether the purpose is meat or milk or both).

It is very easy to combine a rapid study of flock structures with collecting information on the reproductive performance of breeding females and the fate of their offspring.

Sample size and selection

It is usually impossible to visit every goat keeper in the village or district. A smaller group or sample of households has to be selected, representing as closely as possible the characteristics of the population of interest. The use of statistical sampling procedures will indicate, for a measurement, the size of sample that will accurately represent the whole population from which it is selected. These procedures cannot be applied unless the size of the population is known, together with the degree of variability within the selected village or district. In practice, of course, in developing countries, very little information of this nature exists. In some countries where censuses are carried out, a list of households in the village may be available and can be used to select a sample. But in order to use statistical sampling procedures, the amount of variability and the precision of information required should also be known; this, however, is rarely possible.

In reality, practical considerations become more important than considerations of statistics. Common questions to answer are listed below:

- How much money is available to collect the data?
- How many people can be employed or released from other work to carry out the assessment?
- How much time is available?
- Are there vehicles available?
- Is there enough stationery?

Once these questions have been answered, the next question is: with the resources available, how many goats/households/villages/districts can be covered in the time available? The basic rule is that the more households the better: the bigger the sample, the more precise will be the results.

When you have decided how big a sample you can afford with the resources you have available, you need to think what sorts of goat keeper should be in the sample. Do you want to get a representative picture of the total population, or do you want to focus only on particular types of goat farmer, such as the poorer ones, or only those with larger flocks, or only goat farmers who house their goats?

If the sample is supposed to give a picture of all goat farmers in the area, it is important to try to avoid many of the biases that can creep in and distort the picture. If you are new to the village, the first people you will meet will probably be the village leaders, who will want you to meet the best, most progressive goat farmers in the community — who are probably some of the wealthiest. You may then have to make a special effort to meet the poorer farmers. Perhaps you can go to the communal watering point and chat to people there and observe the goats as they come to water. If you are in a hurry, beware the temptation to visit only the most accessible farms, close to the road. This is especially likely in the wet season, when the roads may be bad or even impassable. A number of small biases, when combined, can give a very distorted picture of reality. Unless you make a special effort, you will find yourself dealing primarily with men rather than women, and confident people rather than shy ones. This is why the group discussion is particularly useful in providing cross-checks within the community, to give a clearer, more balanced picture.

Field method

1 Prepare a data-collection form which is easy to fill in quickly. Test the form while collecting information on a few flocks. An example is found in Figure 3.4. You may like to adapt it for use in your own area. Prepare enough forms for the anticipated number of goats and flocks. It is irritating to run out of forms when you are in a remote area.

   At least two people are required for the job, one to handle the goats, the other to record the information on the form. In larger flocks it is more efficient to have more than one person handling the goats, as the recorder can note down information from at least two goat handlers and possibly more. The quicker the data are collected the better, so the owner is less inconvenienced.

2 The owner of the flock should be politely approached and the objectives of looking at the flock should be clearly explained. Most owners are happy to allow their animals to be handled, provided they are handled gently, and the owner is not inconvenienced too much in the process. However, in some areas taxes on livestock are collected, which may make the owner reluctant to allow the flock to be visited and counted, and may also lead the owner to give misleading information concerning progeny histories. Clearly explain the purpose for collecting the information and give assurances that it will be kept confidential.

3 Agree a time and place that is convenient for the owner and the owner's family. If the flock goes out grazing all day, you may

Figure 3.4 Form for recording goat flock structures and progeny histories

Owner's name		Village		District		Recorder		Date	

Sex: male female castrate	Tooth age: MT suckling MT weaned 1 pair 2 pairs 3 pairs 4 pairs Worn	No. of parturitions	No. of kids	Still in flock	Dead	Sold	Lent	Gift	Exchange	Lost	Aborted	Remarks (milked, sick, etc.)

MT = milk teeth

have to visit very early in the morning or in the evening, when the animals return from grazing. If the flock has to walk a long way to grazing, they may leave and return in the dark, in which case torches will be needed. Alternatively, it may be more convenient to handle the flock at a water point or dip, where they may be in one place for several hours.

4 Each goat in the flock should be physically handled and a record made of its sex (male, female, castrate, hermaphrodite) and age by dentition (suckling, milk teeth, one pair, two pairs, three pairs, four pairs, worn) recorded. The owner is then asked its age and origin (born in flock, bought, borrowed, given). In some societies goats may be owned by different members of the family, who might have different rights of use over their goats. This may be important to record. If the goat is kept under some sort of sharing arrangement with another family, the arrangements should be understood. For females of breeding age, you should record the number of times they have given birth, and what has happened to each animal born:

still in flock	given away
sold	aborted
dead (cause)	exchanged
lent	lost

It is also useful to ask the owner the cause of death, and even the season in which the goat died. This can be very helpful in building up a picture of the seasonality of the causes of mortality, which can be very important; but collecting this extra information will slow down the procedure.

As goats are often tended by women or children, you will often get more accurate information if you ask them the questions, particularly about deaths and abortions. However, in some cultures male extension workers may not be allowed to talk directly to women. You need to exercise sensitivity in such a case .

The goat should then be marked in some way, such as with a special waxed marker crayon or simply a water-based paint, to ensure that it is not handled again. Or it should be removed from the pen and kept with the goats that have already been handled.

How to age goats by their dentition

Goats are born with small milk teeth, which they will keep until they are 14–19 months old, when one pair of permanent incisors will replace the central pair of milk teeth. Thereafter further pairs of these permanent teeth appear either side of the previous new teeth, roughly every six months, until they have a full set of four permanent pairs of incisors (Table 3.3 and Figure 3.5). Teeth do

Figure 3.5 Sets of teeth at different ages

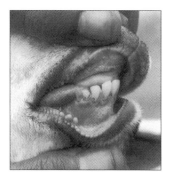

(a) Milk teeth
CHRISTIE PEACOCK

(b) One pair of permanent incisors
CHRISTIE PEACOCK

(c) Two pairs of permanent incisors
JENNY MATTHEWS/OXFAM

not appear at fixed intervals. There will always be a range of ages at which particular teeth appear, because the speed of teeth-growth will vary according to the health and nutrition of the goat. If a goat is well fed and healthy, teeth will erupt earlier than in poorly fed, unhealthy goats. Likewise, teeth age and become worn at different rates in different systems. In extensive pastoral systems where the forage may be very fibrous for long periods, teeth will wear faster than in the humid tropics, where feed is lower in fibre.

Although it is not possible to identify the exact age of a goat from its teeth, it is a useful guide which can be used, to some extent, to evaluate the performance of goats. If, for example, you want to know how well a female goat is breeding, you can check its age from its teeth and if you see, say, three pairs of permanent teeth, you know that the goat is roughly two and a half years old. You can then ask the farmer how many kids it has had in its lifetime. If it has had two kids, then you know that it is fertile and a good breeder. If it has had one or none, then you should be aware that there is a reproductive problem which probably should be investigated.

Table 3.3 The age of goats as shown by dentition

Age (months)	Type of teeth
0 - 14	Milk teeth
14 - 19	One pair of permanent incisors
19 - 24	Two pairs of permanent incisors
24 - 30	Three pairs of permanent incisors
30 +	Four pairs of permanent incisors

How to interpret the data
The data can be analysed using a pencil and paper. A simple pocket calculator is helpful, but not essential. Do some analyses while still in the field, so that any queries can be checked immediately.

1 First calculate the average size of goat flocks in the area investigated, and the range in sizes. It is sometimes helpful to make a bar chart of this information, so that the degree of variability in the size of the flock is very clear (Figure 3.6).
2 Next, using all the data collected, make a table of the flock structure for all goats sampled. The table might be presented in the form of Table 3.4. What can be learned from such a

Figure 3.6 Flock size distribution by household

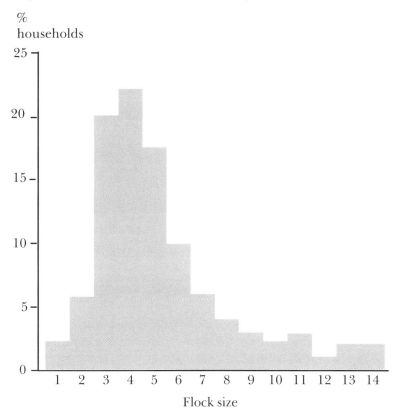

%
households

Flock size

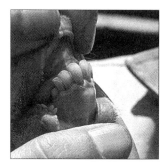

(d) Three pairs of permanent incisors
JENNY MATTHEWS/OXFAM

(e) Four pairs of permanent incisors
JENNY MATTHEWS/OXFAM

table? If there are a lot of very young suckling kids with their lactating mothers, it may be that there is a seasonality to the breeding of the goats. Reckoning backwards, it is possible to calculate the peak season of conception. This seasonality in breeding may be controlled by the owner, or it may occur naturally because a flush of good feed initiates oestrus and conception. Find out which applies by asking the owner.

If there are a lot of goats being milked but few kids suckling, then it looks as though significant numbers of kids have died recently, and it would be worth trying to find out why. This is usually fairly obvious while the flock is being recorded, so the owner can immediately be asked what happened to the kids.

The ratio of breeding females to males can be calculated to make sure that there are enough breeding males. If certain males are castrated (this varies from culture to culture), it would be worth finding out the age at which they are castrated and the reasons for castrating those particular males. Is it because they were fast-growing and needed for sale, or because they were slow-growing and the owner did not want them to mate with the females?

Table 3.4 Sex and age structure of Maasai goats in Kenya (expressed as a percentage of the total)

Age (months)	Entire males	Castrated males	Total males	Females	Total
0 - 6	4.5	0.0	4.5	7.2	11.7
6 - 14	2.9	2.3	5.2	5.2	10.4
14 - 19	1.0	7.4	8.4	9.4	17.8
19 - 24	0.1	1.5	1.6	4.5	6.1
24 - 30	0.05	4.3	4.3	6.7	11.0
30 - 60	0.4	9.3	9.7	32.9	42.6
> 60	—	—	—	0.4	0.4
Total	8.9	24.8	33.7	66.3	100
n =	122	335	457	899	1356

Figure 3.7 Age pyramid of a goat flock

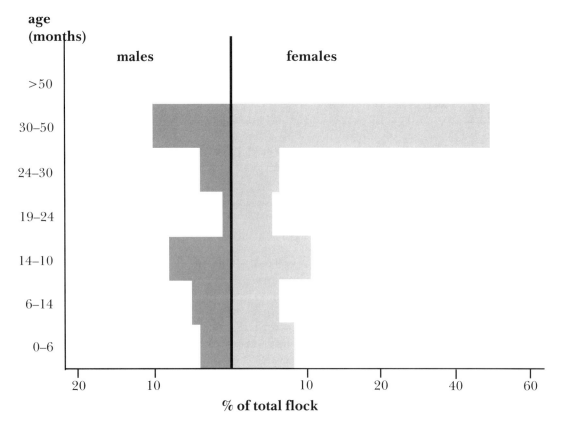

If there is a missing kid crop, i.e. a very low or non-existent number of goats between the ages of for example 14 and 24 months, then it might indicate a drought or disease that affected the young kids between one and two years ago. The effects can still be seen in the flock. What caused this?

3 A simple age pyramid (Figure 3.7) may also be revealing. It may show any missing kid crops, the age at which most males are sold, etc.

4 From the information on progeny histories, it is possible to calculate the number of births per breeding female, and the approximate age at first parturition. Set out the table headings shown in Table 3.5. Place each breeding female in the correct age group and write down the number of times she has given birth, as reported by the owner. Add up the totals for each age group category as in Table 3.5, and a total for each birth number category. Finally convert these totals to percentages, as in Table 3.5.

Table 3.5 Parturition histories

Age group of female (months)	Number of births reported by owner									No. of females
	0	1	2	3	4	5	6	7	8	
10-14	36									36
14-19	109	5								114
19-24	37	14	7							58
24-30	45	38	6							89
> 30	35	87	135	73	52	17	12	6	2	420
Total	262	144	148	73	52	17	12	6	2	717
%	36	20	21	10	7	2	0.8	0.3		100

From this table it is clear that there are reproductive problems in the goat flocks in this area. Having 36 per cent of the potential breeding females non-productive is a tremendous waste. If they have not given birth by 24 months of age, either they are infertile or there is a major mating/nutrition problem, which should be investigated. Age at first parturition also seems to be rather delayed, which reduces the total productive life of the goat.

5 It is also possible to make a rough estimate of an annual reproductive rate. This can be done by assuming that the ratio of

males to females is 1 : 1. Then multiply by 4 the number of females in the age class 0–6 months, to arrive at the total number of births in a year, excluding deaths. Apply a reasonable mortality rate by deducting 10–20 per cent from this figure. Now divide the result by the number of potential breeding females (those that have reached 12 months). From Table 3.4 the annual reproductive rate is 66.6 per cent, which is very low.

> Approximate annual reproductive rate =
>
> $$\frac{4 \times \text{Total 0-6 mths} \times 100 - \text{Mortality (\%)}}{\text{Total potential breeding females}}$$

Table 3.6
Off-take methods

Method	%
Remain in flock	51
Dead	36
Sold	7
Abortion	4
Gift	2
Lost	0
Slaughtered	0
Exchanged	0

6 Finally a table showing the methods of off-take from the flock can be prepared, such as Table 3.6.

3.2.9 Individual interviews

If the owner has the time, and is willing, a good moment for an interview is after you have examined the flock for the structure and progeny-history data, and it is obvious that you have a genuine interest in the goats. This can form a bond between you. Otherwise make another appointment at the owner's convenience.

Unless it is just a casual visit to a family for a chat about their goats, it is best to have at least a checklist of questions you would like to ask them. If you lack confidence in talking to farmers, or need more quantitative survey data, then use a questionnaire. You can train recorders to administer the questionnaire on your behalf, so enabling you to question many more farmers than you can by yourself. If you do use inexperienced recorders to do a survey, keep the questions simple, so that accuracy is maintained. You cannot expect these recorders to ask probing follow-up questions. Keep the questionnaire simple and short. Long questionnaires are boring for all involved. Avoid sensitive matters, such as direct questions about income. The accuracy of the information will not be very high if the farmer is bored, embarrassed, or suspicious about the questions.

For more information on survey and questionnaire design, see *Social Survey Methods* and *Choosing Research Methods*, both published by Oxfam (UK and Ireland).

3.2.10 Key informant interviews

There are often farmers in a community who are recognised experts in keeping goats or in some particular aspect of goat husbandry such as treatment of diseases. These people can provide a wealth of information on different aspects of goat production in the area, the long-term trends, and a perspective on the degree of variation between years. When was there a bad epidemic? How often do they occur? How did goats perform during a major drought?, etc.

Local experts may also be helpful in describing different husbandry practices and why they are carried out in the way described; for example, care of newly-born kids or local treatments for disease.

3.2.11 Direct observation

It may seem strange to include observation as a separate method of collecting information, but people do not use their eyes and other senses enough. Close observation of the way in which people manage their goats is very important and can lead to more relevant questioning of the farmer. Sometimes unobservant recorders may be conducting an interview and writing down an answer that directly contradicts what is happening in front of them. This may not mean that the farmer is not telling the truth (although it may!), but could just mean that the question needs to be expanded and asked in more detail. Perhaps under certain circumstances a practice like supplementary feeding is done in one way and in other circumstances done in another way. Or perhaps one member of the family, for example the wife, does it one way and others in another. This is why it is necessary to question the relevant person involved in goat management within the family. Observation can help in cross-checking farmers' responses with reality.

3.2.12 Maps and walks

It is useful to gain an understanding of the physical arrangement of the village or locality. It may be important to know the distances to grazing and water points, particularly in pastoral systems, where the grazing and water resources are under communal ownership and where the goat owners' main management strategies are concerned with manipulating the use of grazing, water, and house location.

A group or individual can be asked to draw a simple map of the village or locality on a piece of paper, or on the ground with a stick. Important areas for goat production can be entered on the map. These may include areas of grazing/browsing particularly suited to goats, places where goats get sick, places in the river where goats can be watered, local mineral licks, the site of a dip tank, and places where farmers may wash their goats. Gradually a picture of the physical environment emerges; this impression can be matched to, or drawn on, a published map, if available. Once these places have been identified, you should visit them on foot to learn more.

3.2.13 Problem analysis and objectives analysis

By now you should have a considerable body of information about goat-keeping in the area. Some of it will be qualitative information from group discussions and interviews, complemented by quantitative information on individual flocks, their size, structure, and performance. It is helpful to draw this information together in the form of a diagram or series of diagrams to illustrate core problems. This is sometimes known as **problem analysis**. Problem analysis helps to:

- analyse the existing situation affecting a general problem of goat-keeping;
- identify the major problems;
- define the core problem(s) of a situation;
- visualise the cause–effect relationships in a diagram or problem tree.

First identify the major problems of goat-keeping in the area. The causal chains developed in the group discussions (3.2.7) could be the starting point, but information from all the sources should be used to build up the most thorough possible picture of goat-production problems. Try to identify one core problem and focus on it. If you are not happy to identify only one problem, add one or two more; but you are likely to find that they are linked anyway. Write down the causes of the problem and then write its effects. Draw a diagram showing the cause and effect relationships in the form of a problem tree. The causal chains may form the branches of the problem tree. This could be done with farmers and/or a group of colleagues. It is always better if a small group develops the problem tree. This will give it greater validity and completeness. An example of a simple problem tree is given in Figure 3.8. At this point you may find that multiple core problems are linked together: perhaps one is the cause of another, or possibly the effect. Try to concentrate on one important core problem and tackle that one wherever possible.

Next consider how these problems might be tackled by individual farmers, the community, and/or development agencies. This is sometimes known as **objectives analysis**. It helps to describe the future situation and to identify potential alternatives for a project or programme. Objectives analysis simply restates all the problems into objectives, i.e. positive, desirable, and realistically achievable conditions. The cause–effect relationships become means–ends relationships. Check that they are valid. At this point additional objectives can be added which might not directly solve

Figure 3.8 Problem analysis: low milk production

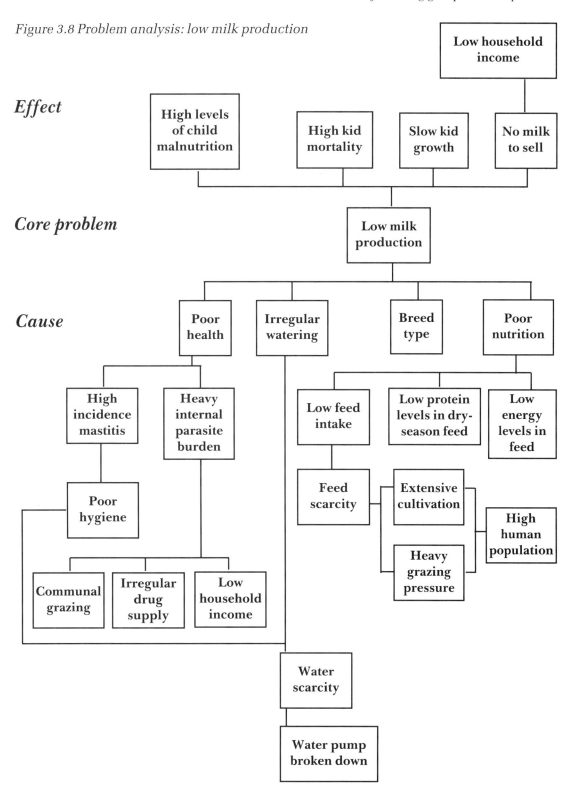

an identified problem but may be an additional opportunity for improving the situation. In the example in Figure 3.9, forage development is introduced not as a positive aspect of something negative, but as a new opportunity to improve the situation.

The objectives analysis can form the basis for planning a programme or project. This will be discussed in Chapter 11, when alternative technical and organisational options are considered and methods of participatory planning discussed.

3.2.14 Reporting

It is helpful to record the information you have collected into some sort of report, either handwritten or typed, for circulation to your colleagues for comment. The report might take the title 'A Profile of Goat-keeping in ...' and could adopt the following structure:

- **Introduction**
- **Objectives**
- **Physical background** of area, probably from secondary data collection and direct observation, including rainfall, roads, markets, maps, general description of the farming system
- **Methods** used in field; dates, timing, personnel
- **Results**
    General description of goat-management system
    Goat ownership, distribution within community, flock sizes
    Flock structures
    Progeny-history results
    Feed calendars
    Disease calendars
    Economic uses of goats
- **Conclusions**
    Major constraints on goat production identified with the community
    Possible interventions
    Areas for further study

Such reports are important documents, because they record the information that led to the initial actions taken. Information will constantly be added, but it is important to take the time to write an accurate report, including all the diagrams developed during the course of the investigation. The report will be referred to in the future and may form the basis for planning and funding a project.

3.2.15 Community consultation

Once you have spent time with the community learning about their goat-keeping and have collated the information into a simple report, you should return to the community as soon as

Figure 3.9 Objectives analysis to increase milk production

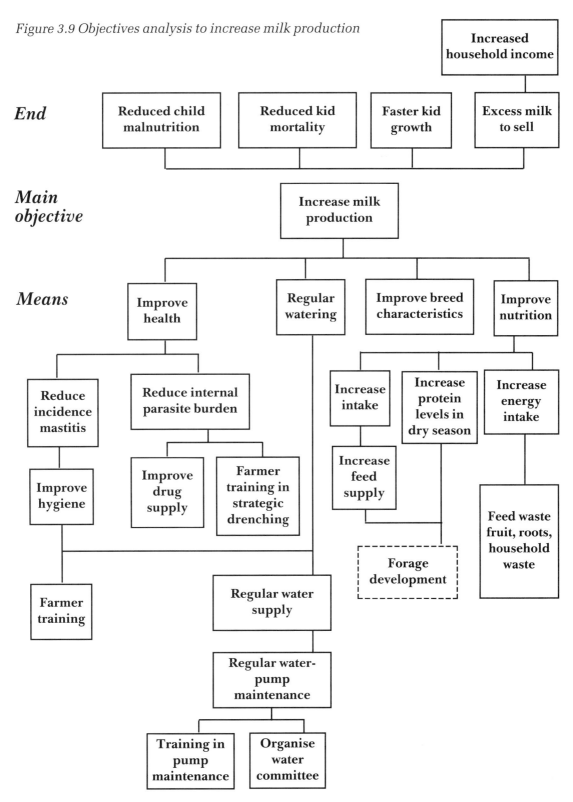

possible and present your results and conclusions to them for their comments. This might be done at a public meeting, where wider issues raised during the RRA can be discussed. It might also be done at group discussions. Learning never ends, and you should not be afraid of admitting that you do not know things and that you need to learn more. However, we also learn by doing, and at some point the community will expect some action and should not be disappointed! Once a real problem has been identified, however trivial, if it can be solved it should be tackled without delay. You will learn more about the problem by trying to solve it than by continuing passive research.

3.2.16 Have a go!

We have looked at the sorts of information that can be collected with few resources other than a pencil and paper. A lot can be learned from these simple techniques. This should encourage you to have a go at goat development, even if you do not feel that you have many resources to help you.

3.3 Higher-cost methods of assessing goat-production problems

The Rapid Rural Appraisal (RRA) techniques described in 3.2 provide a quick way of taking a first look at goat production in an area. They require very few resources, and can be done at village level by one person or at district level by a small team. The information acquired is largely qualitative, and indicates some of the problems of goat production.

However, RRA techniques may not always provide accurate diagnoses of all problems. For example, a disease calendar may give a picture of the main diseases, perhaps using local names, and the seasons during which they are most prevalent. But this may not lead to an accurate identification of the disease. In order to develop an effective control programme, blood or faecal samples may need to be taken, possibly at different seasons, for an accurate diagnosis of the disease and a record of its seasonal incidence. Likewise, if farmers complain of a shortage of feed in the dry season, it might be helpful to analyse the feeds in a laboratory to assess their digestibility or estimate any protein deficiencies. In addition, weighing a sample of lactating females at the start of the dry season and again at the end will accurately show their weight loss, and the effects of this on milk production as well as the effect on kid mortality. RRA techniques provide a one-shot view of a situation, but are less accurate in describing the seasonal dynamics of that situation. For this, a longer-term monitoring study is needed.

What can be done, if external support is available, to diagnose problems of goat production accurately? Table 3.1 outlines a procedure for monitoring goat production. It should be kept as simple as possible. Regular monitoring of aspects of production will provide more accurate information on the technical constraints on goat production. Where relevant, the procedure, ideally, would involve technical specialists. They might include a veterinarian with access to a diagnostic laboratory, an animal nutritionist with access to a feed-analysis laboratory, and finally someone to help analyse the productivity data with access to a computer and appropriate software. You do not need these specialists all the time, but should draw up a work-plan with them and involve them as required. The procedures described do not form a complete livestock-systems research procedure, which is a specialist activity requiring a lot of resources (ILCA, 1990, p. 399). The procedure proposed could be followed by a livestock extension officer with access to laboratories able to carry out fairly basic analyses. Many donor-funded projects now include a flock-monitoring component during project preparation and implementation (see Chapter 11).

If you are working with particularly needy communities, you may find it morally and practically difficult to carry out a longer-term monitoring study of goats without doing something practical for the community at the same time. There is no reason why you cannot simultaneously initiate some practical improvements, based on the results of the RRA, and also carry out a long-term study of goat production. However, you should be aware that the interim intervention may affect the results of the monitoring.

Research scientists like to try to keep monitoring and intervention as separate activities, but in practice it is hard to do so, and they can be complementary. By regularly visiting a goat flock, outsiders are already making an impact on it. If a practical intervention is introduced, much can be learned by monitoring the impact of the intervention on the goats, the farmer, and the farmer's family. This will improve the efficacy of the intervention itself. There is always concern that the effect of the intervention on the goats cannot be measured if the performance of the goats before the intervention is unknown. In fact, it is known by the farmer. The farmer is the best judge of an intervention, because, if the intervention is not perceived to be an improvement by the owner, it has little value. It is vital that the farmer and his or her family are involved in evaluating any improvements made. How to involve farmers in evaluation will be discussed in more detail in Chapter 11.

3.3.1 Selection of sample sites

There is little point in carrying out a monitoring study of goats in order to identify the problems of goats in only one village. It is assumed that you are concerned with more than one village and most likely a district or region. There are a number of questions to consider:

- How much environmental variability is there within the area?
- How much economic variability is there?
- What resources (personnel, money, transport) are available?
- How long can the monitoring last?

Classify the main goat-production systems of the district, however crudely. There may be, for example, a section of highland where crops are grown and goats are mainly tethered, and a lowland area where agro-pastoralism may be practised. Refer to your original objectives and select areas and flocks that meet them best. Focus your resources on monitoring flocks that come from the most relevant production systems of interest to you.

3.3.2 RRA procedures

Section 3.2 described the procedures to follow in acquiring a quick general picture of goat production in an area. Follow the steps outlined in that section: the results from the RRA will help in planning the monitoring study. It is important that public meetings and group discussions are held at the start of a longer-term monitoring study. The rapid flock-appraisal visit can be used to set up the monitoring study.

3.3.3 Setting objectives

Having had discussions with the community and with smaller groups of farmers, you should by now be able to identify particular areas of interest that require further study. Clearly define your objectives. This is very important in deciding what information you need to collect, how often it should be collected, and who is able to collect this information with an acceptable level of accuracy. There is so much information that could be collected about a goat flock and its management and productivity, but to make efficient use of your resources you must focus on key topics.

3.3.4 Sampling size and recording frequency

If you plan to set up a long-term study of flock performance, the selection of households willing to cooperate in the study is essential. The same principles of selection of sample size and composition apply here as were described in 3.2.8. In addition the following points need to be considered when deciding sample size and composition for a monitoring study:

- average number of goats per household;
- arrangement of households: in village, dispersed, nomadic;
- number of staff, local recorders;
- transport needed and available;
- desired frequency of data collection;
- management system: housed or herded (all/part of day);
- degree of farmer cooperation.

3.3.5 Farmer participation

It is essential, in a long-term monitoring study, that you have good cooperation from farmers throughout the recording period. It is a waste of resources to start recording a flock, only to lose access halfway through the study because the farmer gets bored or angry with the frequent visits. Keeping farmers involved and interested in the study is essential. There are many ways of doing this. The purpose of the study has to be clearly explained to the farmer and any suspicions allayed. Make clear what cooperation you need from the owner's family. Do they merely have to allow access to the flock every month, or does someone have to report if any goats get sick? Make this clear and then ask if they still agree to the study. In some cultures, livestock staff have found it necessary to offer some sort of incentive to farmers to get and maintain their cooperation. This should not be necessary in the context of a development programme, where the farmer and the community should receive some tangible benefits from the results of the work. If the study is purely for research purposes, with fewer practical benefits at the end, then incentives might have to given. These may take the form of veterinary treatment for the flock, small gifts of hoof trimmers, buckets, etc., or even money. However, if gifts are made, it is very easy for the relationship with the farmer to turn quickly from one of mutual collaboration to one of paternalistic intervention. This should be avoided.

3.3.6 Setting up the monitoring study

Once the objectives of the monitoring study have been clearly defined and the resources available for the work are known, the data to be collected and the frequency of collection need to be decided.

At the core of any monitoring study is the collection of basic data on the productivity of the goat flock. These data can be collected fairly easily during regular visits to the flock. So how often should you go? The more frequently you visit, the more accurate will be the information, particularly in larger flocks where there are many births and deaths. A monthly visit is probably adequate for most purposes, but more frequent visits would be even better and are

*Components of flock
productivity*

Reproduction:
number of kids born
frequency with which dams give birth
proportion of potential breeding does actually giving birth

Growth and weight changes:
growth rates of young animals
seasonal weight loss and gain of adults

Mortality:
number of deaths
age at which goat died
cause of death
season of death

Morbidity:
incidence of sickness
age of sick goat
cause of sickness
season of sickness

necessary to record the incidence of disease. A two-level recording system is often a useful approach to take: a local person, even a member of the family, records daily events such as births, deaths, and diseases, and a monthly visit is made to the flock by a team with a weigh-scale, when records are up-dated and checked.

Weighing the whole flock can take some time and requires the use of weighing equipment, and a means to transport it. It may not be necessary to weigh the whole flock every month. You can reduce the frequency of weighing and the animals to be monitored by weighing a sample from the flock at strategic seasons. For example, the growth-rate of kids is a good indicator of the milk production of the dam. If milk is an important product, then kid growth should be measured at least until weaning. If there are marked wet and dry seasons, seasonal changes in weight can be an important factor, especially in breeding females. If they are losing weight, they may not be able to conceive; or if they are losing weight during lactation, the kid may get little milk, making it weak and susceptible to disease and death. Kids and breeding females are usually the goats most in need of supplementary feeding. It is important to find out if they do have problems. You will have to decide if it is easier to weigh only particular goats at particular seasons, rather than the whole flock every month.

A similar form to that used for the flock structures and progeny histories can be used to start a monitoring study, with the addition of columns for the following:

* tag number
* colour
* presence of horns/toggles/beard
* weight.

The field method is the same as for the rapid survey, with the addition of tagging or marking each goat and weighing the flock.

3.3.7 Goat identification

It is of vital importance that each goat to be recorded can be accurately identified in the flock and in all the records. Ideally each goat would have a number on it. In small flocks, where farmers might give their goats names, it might be possible not to number the goats but to rely on names and convert the names to a number for analysis, but this is not ideal. There are several ways to identify goats:

* ear-tags (plastic or metal)
* collars (chain or leather)
* tattoos (in ear or under tail)
* brands (hot or freeze brands)
* ear notching.

Each method has certain advantages and disadvantages. Tattoos, brands, and ear notching are permanent, but may be disliked by farmers. Metal ear-tags are preferred over plastic ones, which can easily be removed, and often are, by children for toys or jewellery (Figure 3.10). However, some farmers do not like ear-tags at all. If ear-tags cannot be used, a small collar might have to be used.

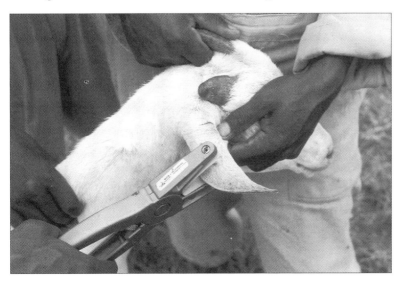

Figure 3.10 Applying an ear-tag in the correct position
Christie Peacock

51

*Figure 3.11
Initial format for
goat monitoring*

Owner's name				Village					Recorder					Date	
Tag no.	Sex Male Female Castrate	Tooth age: MT suckling MT weaned 1 pair 2 pairs 3 pairs 4 pairs Worn	Colour	No. of parturitions	No. of kids	Still in flock	Dead	Sold	Lent	Gift	Exchanged	Lost	Aborted	Remarks Milked, sick, etc.

These are not very reliable, as they can easily be removed, but may be useful in certain circumstances; they have the advantage that they can be made from local materials.

It is important to record a physical description of each goat (colour, presence/absence of horns, toggles, beard, mane, etc.), in case its ear-tag or collar is lost.

3.3.8 Weighing goats

The simplest method of weighing a goat is to use a canvas or leather sling and a spring balance. The spring balance can be hung from a tree or suspended from a metal tripod. The dimensions for a sling and tripod are shown in Figures 3.12 and 3.13. Small pocket spring balances can be used to weigh kids.

There are other, more expensive, methods of weighing; they include a special mobile crush and weighing platform or the use of load-cells underneath a platform with a digital read-out. Really sophisticated weighing machines can even be linked to a data-logger for direct transfer to a computer, but these are very expensive and not always reliable.

Goats should be weighed at the same time of day every time they are weighed. In one day they can eat and drink a weight equivalent to 15 per cent of their body-weight, so it is best always to weigh them early in the morning before they go out grazing or are watered, to obtain a standardised weight. Regularly check the accuracy of the scales against a known weight, to make sure they are giving you accurate readings.

In some countries scientists have developed equations that allow the measurement of the chest of a goat, known as heartgirth, to be converted into an estimate of its liveweight. Table 3.7 presents a table for conversion of a heartgirth measurement (cm) into a weight (kg). The goat should be standing square and a simple tailor's measuring tape put around its chest, just behind the front legs. This method gives only an estimate of the goat's weight. It can be combined with condition scoring to provide a more accurate picture of changes in the weight and condition of a goat.

The body condition can be assessed by the look and feel of the area around the backbone behind the last rib and the area around the tail area. These are good places for estimating the relative amount of fat carried by the goat, which gives an indication of its condition. It is quite a simple technique, but it is a subjective method that relies on the opinion of the recorder. It is best if the same animals are always assessed by the same recorder, in order to reduce the subjective element in the technique. Condition scoring can provide only relative measures of the body condition of the goat and so is best used to make a rough assessment of the effect of seasons on the goat's body condition. However, it is hard to compare scores between flocks recorded by different people.

Table 3.7
Table for conversion of heartgirth measurements to weight

Heartgirth measure- ment (cm)	Weight equivalent (kg)
63	20.0
65	22.5
68	25.0
70	27.5
72	30.0
76	35.0
80	40.0
84	45.0
88	50.0
91	55.0
95	60.0
98	65.0

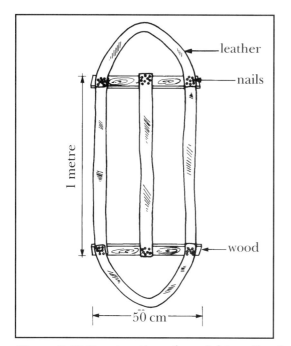

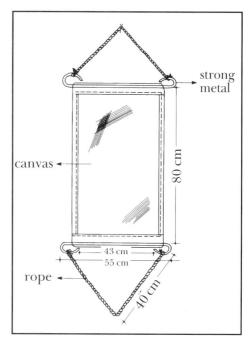

Figure 3.12 Construction of a weighing sling (canvas and leather)

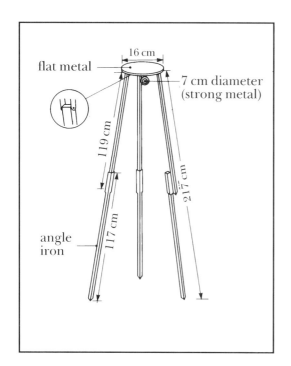

Figure 3.13 Construction of a tripod

Figure 3.14 Weighing a goat with a sling and a spring balance

Table 3.8 Body-condition scores for goats

Score	Backbone	Tail area
1	Backbone very sharp and prominent; fingers easily pass under the ends of the top of the vertebrae, which are sharp. NO FAT COVER	Very bony pelvis, with a deep hole either side of the tail
2	Backbone still prominent, but ends of the top of the vertebrae are rounded; fingers can still pass under them with a little pressure. MINIMUM FAT COVER	Pelvis still bony, but holes either side of tail filling
3	Backbone well covered and smooth; ends of vertebrae tops not felt unless firmly pressed. MODERATE FAT COVER	Pelvis os more rounded, with hip muscles developing
4	Backbone not visible. Back well rounded. End of vertebrae tops cannot be felt. THICK FAT COVER	Pelvis well rounded and hip muscles well developed

3.3.9 Continuous monitoring

After the initial visit to record flock structure and progeny history and tag the goats, a simple register of the flock can be made. Every goat in the flock should be checked against the register, to determine presence or absence in the flock. If it is absent, questions can be asked about the reason (death, sale, etc.); any new goats found in the flock, but not on the register, can be added to the register and the reason for their presence given. A flock register is the only way to keep track of events in the flock. It is essential in large flocks and helpful in small ones.

A regular timetable of visits to the flocks in the area should be drawn up and agreed with the owners. Time and place should be at the owner's convenience and create as little disturbance to the family's routine as possible.

Design the formats to be used so that they are easy and accurate to complete by the recorder in the field. They should also be weather-proof and goat-proof. Always make a copy of the record taken at every visit, in case the original copy is lost or eaten by goats (it has happened!). Some people find printed cards are strong and hard to lose; others like bound record books. Some basic formats are shown in Figure 3.15 as a guide.

3.3.10 Milk measurement

If milk is an important product, it should be measured as accurately as possible to gain a good understanding of the

Figure 3.15 Some formats for monitoring goat flocks

Flock inventory								
District			**Village**				**Owner**	
Tag no.	Sex	Teeth	Birth date	Physical description Colour | Horns |Toggles			Exit date	Exit reason
								.

Additions to flock: Births and abortions									
Village				**Owner**					
Date of birth	Tag no.	Sex	Breed	Dam no.	Sire no.	Physical description Colour | Horns | Toggles			Remarks

Additions to flock: Purchases, gifts, loans, etc.									
Village					**Owner**				
Date of birth	Reason for entry	Tag no.	Sex	Breed	Teeth	Physical description Colour | Horns | Toggles			Remarks

Removals from flock: Death			
Village		**Owner**	
Date of death	Tag no.	Cause of death	Remarks

Removals from flock: Sales, gifts, loans, etc.					
Village		**Owner**			
Date of removal	Reason for removal	Tag no.	Price	Place	Remarks

dynamics of its production. The milk output per day and the length of the lactation must be known, if you want to calculate the total milk output per lactation. It is relatively easy to measure milk off-take, but much harder to measure the total milk production of the dam when a kid is suckling part of the milk. Various techniques can be used to estimate the amount of milk suckled by the kid, none of them very accurate.

Weighing before and after suckling: suckling animals are weighed on a sensitive scale, before suckling and again after suckling. The gain in weight is assumed to be equivalent to the amount of milk consumed. Care needs to taken to measure the kids quickly after suckling, before they urinate or defecate. This technique requires close supervision and a lot of labour.

Bottle feeding: the dam is milked out completely by hand, and the kid is bottle-fed. This is an unnatural situation and it is unlikely that the dam will let down all her milk as she would if she was being suckled. This method is therefore likely to give an underestimate of total milk production.

Partial suckling and liveweight equivalents: by knowing the growth rate of the kid, it is possible to estimate how much milk was consumed to produce that growth. A useful equation is shown in the box on the next page.

Total milk yield for first 6 weeks' lactation =

$$\frac{\text{Weight of kid at 6 weeks} - \text{birth weight} \times 1.2}{0.13}$$

(based on a milk : growth conversion ratio of 1.2, and assuming there are 13 per cent solids in the milk)

This method can be used only during the first few weeks of lactation, when virtually all the kid's nutrients are obtained from the milk. Once the kid starts nibbling at other feeds and developing an active rumen, this method will not be accurate.

The milk that is taken for human consumption can be measured by weight or volume. Weight is generally considered to be more accurate than volume, but volume is usually easier to measure in the field. It is best if the recorder is present at milking and can observe the methods used. Is the kid present? Is it suckling at the same time as milking? Does the kid always suckle one teat, and the milker always milk the other teat?

After milking, the milk should be measured before it is mixed with milk from other goats. Some farmers will pour their milk only into their own container. Many farmers and pastoralists treat their calabashes or gourd containers in some way, smoking them for example, and do not like milk to be poured first into a plastic measuring jug. In this case it will be easier to weigh the milk by weighing the container before and after milking. Some goat keepers will milk into a container of known volume, a tin can for example, and this can be used for measuring the milk. You may also find traditional units of measurement which can be used to estimate milk volume, provided that the unit is the same on all farms.

3.3.11 Investigating and monitoring disease

The purpose of disease investigation and monitoring is to find out if disease is a constraint on goat production in the area, and whether cost-effective measures can be taken to control the main diseases. There are three steps to this.

- Identify the main diseases and their causes.
- Identify which goats are affected.
- Quantify the effects of the main diseases.

Diseases can affect goats by killing them (mortality) and by making them sick (morbidity). Diseases can be regularly found in a region (endemic), or occur at a much higher rate than normal (epidemic). Goat health is covered fully in Chapter 6. At this stage it is important to think about designing a study that enables the recording of mortality and morbidity rates for both epidemic and endemic diseases. There are basically two approaches that can be taken: a one-shot disease survey, or a more extended disease-monitoring study.

One-shot disease survey

A one-shot disease survey covers a large number of goats, and uses the RRA techniques of group and individual interviews with farmers, together with sampling of blood, faeces, skin scrapings, external parasites, etc. This can give a picture of the prevalence of diseases at one point in time. Goats can be physically examined and samples taken from them for analyses. If this is combined with interviews with individual farmers and group discussions, a reasonably informative disease picture may emerge. The main weakness is that it gives an accurate indication of disease incidence at one point in time only, and so the seasonal dynamics of diseases, which can be very important, are not understood. The survey can be repeated at different seasons, in which case a more dynamic view will be obtained. However, if a productivity-monitoring study is being undertaken, it is relatively cheap and simple for a disease-monitoring study to be incorporated.

Extended disease monitoring

A disease-monitoring study of the incidence of disease in a small number of goats over at least one year should record the name of the disease (including local names), the symptoms, treatment, and outcome; there might be regular sampling of blood, faeces, and external parasites, as well as sampling at the time of disease and death. It is relatively simple to add to a basic productivity-monitoring study a few simple steps that record disease incidence, morbidity and mortality. You can use the local name of the disease, combined with a description of the basic symptoms, whether any treatment was given, and the outcome of the disease. However, this sort of information is not sufficient to make a definitive diagnosis.

It should be possible to group the diseases into disease types (respiratory, intestinal, skin, etc.). This will give a basic picture of disease incidence and whether any deaths were caused by disease or non-disease factors. Appropriate samples should be taken to provide more specific identification of diseases.

Sample collection

Samples taken from the body of a goat can provide an accurate picture of the past and present incidence of disease. As the collection and preservation of samples can be expensive and difficult in the field, collect only the samples that you really need, and ensure that they are sent to a reliable laboratory, able to do the tests you want. Always find out what tests can be done by the laboratory to which you will send the samples, and take only the samples that are appropriate for those tests. There are three categories of sample that can be collected:

- serological samples: blood-serum samples to analyse antibodies and determine the goats' previous exposure to diseases;
- samples to identify disease agents such as viruses, parasites, bacteria, etc. that are on or in a goat;
- indicator samples, to show the likely cause of a disease or its severity; for example, the Packed Cell Volume (PCV) will indicate if there are any blood-sucking parasites in the goat's body, but not which parasites.

The regular or seasonal sampling of faeces, blood, or external parasites can be extremely helpful in understanding the seasonal incidence of diseases of major importance. Goats are particularly susceptible to internal parasites, and the regular collection of faeces for examination in a laboratory can be helpful in building up a picture of the seasonal incidence of different parasites. This can be used to design a strategic, cost-effective drenching regime (see 6.4.1). Likewise the seasonal collection of ticks to identify the major species at different seasons can be useful, if combined with a quantitative estimate of tick incidence, for predicting the seasonal incidence of tick-borne diseases. In deciding which samples to collect, you should be guided by the experience of local veterinarians, combined with information from the farmers themselves.

The design and management of the sampling should be supervised by an experienced veterinarian, who would be responsible for ensuring the proper laboratory analyses of the samples. Sensitivity needs to be exercised with farmers when sampling, particularly in taking blood samples. Some farmers will simply refuse to allow their goats to be bled. Others may allow it once but not regularly — as would need to be done in monitoring trypanosomiasis. Explain clearly why you are taking the samples and that it will do no harm to the goat. Report results quickly and explain them to the farmer, so that it becomes a joint process of learning about the health of the flock. Do not push too hard if the farmer is reluctant. You can lay yourself open to being blamed by a disgruntled farmer for deaths and diseases in the flock for which you are not responsible.

Practical sampling techniques and proper handling of samples are described in Chapter 6.

Sampling at time of disease or death
To obtain an accurate diagnosis, it is ideal for an experienced veterinarian or veterinary assistant to see the goat and take

appropriate samples at the time when it is actually sick. In order to achieve this, it is necessary for the veterinary professional to be alerted to the sickness and be able to travel quickly to the goat. This responsiveness is not always possible to organise.

It is also ideal if an experienced person is able to undertake a post-mortem examination of a goat that has recently died. If this is done and samples are taken to a competent laboratory, it should be possible to establish a definitive cause of death. Post-mortems can be carried out by anybody, and the procedure to follow is described in 6.6.2. If a more experienced person is not available, it is better for the farmer or extension staff to do the post-mortem than that it is not done at all.

What to do with the data
After at least one year of disease monitoring and sampling, you should be able to estimate

• morbidity rates by disease type, goat age/sex, season;
• mortality rates by goat age/sex, season.

These will tell you

• the most important diseases;
• the seasonal incidence of these diseases;
• which goats are most affected by which diseases.

This information can then be combined with the productivity recording (milk, growth, reproduction). It is hard to define the exact causal relationship between a disease and its effect on production. Diseases often have indirect effects on productivity. For example, internal parasites in a lactating dam will considerably reduce milk production, which in turn will lead to malnourishment in the suckling kid, possibly causing it to die. That is an indirect effect of parasite burden on kid mortality. It can be hard to quantify the effect of disease on production in order to put a monetary value on the cost of the disease.

Once the important diseases are known, it should be possible to sit down with a veterinary professional and design disease-control strategies for the most economically significant diseases. Diseases do not always have to be controlled by the use of drugs. Often it is small improvements in management which can be the cheapest way of controlling disease. Strategies for the control of major diseases of goats are discussed in Chapter 6.

3.3.12 Feed monitoring

The proper feeding of goats is of fundamental importance to successful production, but the quantity and quality of feed actually consumed by a goat can be very difficult to measure in the field.

Measurement is much easier in systems where goats are housed or tethered, and feed is cut and carried to them. If they are free-grazing or tethered to graze, then it is very difficult and expensive to make any sort of estimate of their intake rates and quality of the diet consumed. Ideally feed monitoring would record feed intake (dry matter consumed) and diet quality (protein and digestibility) for different classes of goats and at different seasons.

Housed goats

If goats are housed, it is relatively easy to measure the amount of feed they eat. The quantity left over, subtracted from the quantity offered, tells you the quantity consumed.

Samples of offered and left-over feed should be taken and analysed for digestibility, where possible. Care needs to taken in collecting a representative sample of the feed. Fresh forage should be weighed to obtain its fresh weight (FW). If it cannot be transported to a laboratory on the same day, it should be placed in a porous bag (paper or cloth will do) and dried in the sun. Once it reaches the laboratory, it should be dried in an oven at 65°C to a constant weight. This is the weight of dry matter (DM). The dry matter can then be analysed, using laboratory techniques. The advantages and disadvantages of different methods of laboratory analyses will be discussed in Chapter 4.

If you are taking feed samples from a stack of crop residues or hay, take care in your sampling procedures to obtain representative samples from the pile. Take from the middle and edges as well as the top and bottom.

Grazing goats

Measuring the amount of feed consumed by grazing goats and the quality of the diet selected is very difficult. The most sophisticated technique is fistulation, whereby a hole is made in the oesophagus and/or rumen of the goat, and samples of feed actually consumed are taken at different stages (see 4.6). Fistulation has been carried out very rarely on goats on research stations and even less often in the field.

Grazing observations can be carried out to estimate the amount of time spent grazing and the distance covered by the flock in the course of a day. The distance covered by pastoral goat flocks in the dry season can be considerable, up to 10–15 km/day. Walking long distances can have a significant impact on production.

3.3.13 Management monitoring

There are many aspects of goat management in addition to the basic requirements of feeding and health. The RRA discussions might perhaps highlight one or two aspects of management for special, detailed study. For example, it may be relevant to record the time spent by various members of the family in looking after their goats. Or a breeding problem might have been identified, perhaps a shortage of breeding bucks, and it might be necessary to record from where the breeding male is obtained. Special formats and procedures should be developed for each activity.

3.3.14 Marketing studies

It might be considered necessary to study the marketing of goats and goat products in an area. Prices could be monitored at a weekly market over several seasons to determine the terms of trade for goat keepers of livestock for grain, or the trading margins of traders. Milk, butter, or cheese prices may also be monitored for seasonal fluctuations and profit margins of traders. Be careful when interpreting the data. Because a trader makes a profit does not mean that he or she is exploiting the farmer, although it may! Traders perform many useful functions for farmers which might be difficult for farmers to do for themselves.

3.4 On-farm trials of improvements

Once problems have been identified and solutions to those problems designed, it is best if innovations are tested with a small group of farmers before they are disseminated to a larger number. There are many types of trials that can be carried out on farms, from highly controlled, statistically analysed exercises to simple trials with a few farmers giving their opinion on the innovation. Statistically valid trials on livestock are notoriously difficult to organise and should be left to research organisations. They require a relatively large number of goats and/or farms to be involved, precision in the application of the treatment, and the control of any external factors which may affect the results of the trial. In the real world, these conditions are hard to achieve and the trial will require many resources to supervise and record it accurately.

Simple trials using a small group of farmers willing to try out an innovation can be carried by development-orientated organisations. The effect of the innovation can be evaluated jointly by the farmer and extension staff. The farmers can also modify the innovation and make their own improvements to it. Farmers' perception of the effect of the new method is all-important, because that will determine the likelihood of its being adopted by other farmers. Innovations such as the use of feed supplements, the use of anthelmintics, or improved goat-house designs can all be tested with a few farmers before wider distribution to many.

Further reading

Amir, P and H. C. Knipscheer (1989) *Conducting On-farm Animal Research: Procedures and Economic Analysis*, Winrock International Institute for Agricultural Development, USA and International Development Research Centre, Canada

IIED (International Institute for Environment and Development) (1994) *RRA Notes* (Number 20): Special Issue on Livestock, London: IIED

ILCA (International Livestock Centre for Africa) (1990) *Livestock Systems Research Manual*, Working Paper 1, Vol. 1, Addis Ababa: ILCA (now known as the International Livestock Research Institute)

Nichols, P. (1991) *Social Survey Methods: A Fieldguide for Development Workers*, Development Guidelines No. 6, Oxford: Oxfam (UK and Ireland)

Pratt, B. and P. Loizos (1992) *Choosing Research Methods: Data Collection for Development Workers*, Development Guidelines No. 7, Oxford: Oxfam (UK and Ireland)

CHAPTER 4

Basic nutrition

Introduction

Feeding goats well is of fundamental importance to the success of the whole goat enterprise. Good nutrition is a prerequisite for good health, good reproduction, high milk yields, fast growth rates, and a successful goat system.

Most textbooks on goat production and animal nutrition in the tropics approach the improvement of nutrition in a classical European way, by itemising the nutritional requirements of goats in terms of energy, protein, vitamins, minerals, and water at different stages of their life: pregnant, lactating, or growing. After listing what the goat should ideally eat, these books proceed to formulate rations composed of several different feeds which will provide the identified nutrients. This approach implies that farmers in the tropics are able to follow 'demand-driven' recommendations for goat feeding in the same way as a farmer in Europe or the USA is able to, by buying different feeds and making a ration from them. Unfortunately most farmers who keep goats in the tropics are not in a position to pick and choose the feeds they give to their goats according to the energy or protein content of each feed.

Farmers keeping goats in the tropics make use of the natural grazing and crop by-products that are available, and try to feed their goats as best they can with what they have. This might be termed 'supply-driven' feeding, as goats are fed according to the supply of feeds available, over which the farmer may have little control. Farmers can be helped to make more efficient use of the available feeds and to increase the supply of feeds by growing forage crops; but encouraging the use of a formulated ration is not helpful in most situations.

This chapter takes a very practical approach to feeding goats. You do not have to be a highly qualified nutritionist to be able to feed a goat properly. A basic understanding of the contents of different feeds, how the goat likes to eat, and how it digests different foods can provide sufficient understanding to make the best use of the feeds available. Guidance is given on making simple calculations of need which provide a practical framework of reference, and how to make the best use of the feeds available. Consideration is also given to the special needs of lactating does, kids, and fattening stock.

The next chapter describes how the feed supply itself can be improved to match the demands of the goats through the year, by planting forage crops, controlling livestock, and conserving and storing feed. It is possible to read Chapter 5 first for ideas on how to feed goats better. But for a better understanding of many of the interventions suggested in that chapter, this chapter should also be read.

4.1 The feeding habits of goats

It is important to understand the feeding habits of goats, so that when they are cared for by people, particularly when confined in a house, their natural habits can be copied as closely as possible, and they are comfortable and healthy.

Figure 4.1 A goat browsing on its hind legs

Jenny Matthews/Oxfam

The goat, being a ruminant, is able to live and be productive on fibrous vegetation of relatively poor quality. The goat is a natural browser, feeding by preference on tree leaves, flowers, and seed pods, when it can. Goats are able to eat quite woody stems of trees and bushes. They are very active when they eat, moving rapidly round a tree, picking off the best parts, and quickly moving on to the next tree or bush. Goats naturally prefer to eat at a height 20–120 cm above the ground. They can stand on their hind legs for long periods, and even climb into trees in order to reach some particularly delicious part of the tree (Figure 4.1). Goats find it difficult to eat directly off the ground, normally bending down on their knees to do so (Figure 4.2). They have a very mobile upper lip and tongue, allowing them to consume leaves between thorns. When left to themselves, goats are able to find a diet of reasonable quality by making a selection of the plants, and the parts of plants, which they eat. In the same environment goats will consume many more species of plants than sheep, grazing the same area. Goats have wide-ranging tastes in food and can adapt to eating unusual foods, such as tree bark and cloth, in extreme conditions.

Figure 4.2 Goats kneeling to eat from the ground
Jenny Matthews/Oxfam

Figure 4.3 Feeding heights (in centimetres above the ground) of sheep, goats, cattle, and camels

Sometimes it is thought that, because goats eat so many things, they will eat anything. This is not true. They will refuse even lightly soiled feed. They prefer to be selective and are easily bored by having to eat the same feed every day, unless it is one they particularly relish, such as alfalfa or desmodium. If feed is of uniformly low quality, goats may spend a lot of time trying to select high-quality material and in the process not eat very much.

The goat's preference for consuming browse can be put to good use in the control of bush species invading grassland. Keeping a mixture of grazers and browsers can maintain rangeland grazing areas as grassland, rather than allowing them to become overgrown with bushes. Goats have been used in Australia by graziers to control blackberries. The mixed species of livestock kept by many pastoralists in Africa have the same effect. Pastoralists usually keep several species, enabling them to exploit several ecological niches at the same time. In arid environments, keeping camels allows the exploitation of vegetation above the browsing range of goats, so there is no competition between them and an even pressure is maintained on the scarce vegetation.

4.2 The feeds available to goats, and their characteristics

Goats consume many different types of feed in the tropics and are allowed by their owners to eat those feeds in many different ways. Goats may browse and graze freely throughout the day (and sometimes the night), or they may be completely confined in specially constructed houses, with feeds cut and carried to them. These are the two extremes, but there is a huge range of feeding systems that fall between the two. The method by which goats are fed may also vary through the year. Goats may be restrained by tethering or housing for part of the year, perhaps while crops are in the field, and then allowed to graze freely after the crops have been harvested in the dry season.

It is important to know the main types of feed in the area in which you are working, and the characteristics of those feeds in terms of nutritional quality.

4.2.1 Natural bushes and trees

There are so many species that goats will browse in any particular grazing area or that may be collected by farmers for their goats that it is hard to characterise them. They may be green throughout the year, or may lose their leaves during some part of the year. Trees that are evergreen give goats an advantage over grazing animals during the dry season. When chemically analysed, they tend to show high protein levels and good digestibility; however, in reality, much of the actual protein digestibility is reduced by the presence of anti-nutritional factors such as polyphenolic compounds, tannins for example, in the leaves. This is the reason why goats often perform worse than might be predicted from a simple chemical analysis of their feeds.

In the humid tropics, leaves from shrubs and trees can have a very high moisture content, which can actually depress intake. In the arid and semi-arid areas of the tropics at the end of the dry season, there is often a flush of growth on trees as the humidity rises before the onset of rains. Goats can take good advantage of this flush of green leaves, gaining weight before the start of the rains. They may then be able to start breeding earlier than sheep. In addition, the seed pods of native trees can be a valuable dry-season feed for goats. Pods may be eaten off the ground or shaken down by herders for their flocks. Pods of species such as *Acacia tortilis* or *Acacia albida* can be stored for later supplementary feeding.

4.2.2 Natural grasses

Natural grasses can be highly digestible when in a young stage of growth during the wet season, but tend to become stemmy and indigestible quickly during the dry season. Goats will eat grasses when there is no alternative. In pastoral areas the grass will quickly dry out and become what is known as standing hay. Although goats do not prefer this dry grass, they will eat it if there is nothing else available, so it can provide essential feed during the difficult dry season.

4.2.3 Crop weeds and thinnings

Weeds collected from cropland during the crop's growing period, or grazed just after harvest, can be a valuable source of highly digestible feeds. Farmers in many countries have developed their own methods of using their growing crops for animal feed. Picking the leaves from growing maize or sorghum is one. Crops such as cassava, jackfruit, and banana can supply a high-quality feed for goats.

4.2.4 Crop residues

Crop residues include the stover of maize, sorghum, and millet, and the straws of rice, wheat, barley, oats, legumes, and oil crops. Generally they have a high fibre content, which makes them relatively indigestible to goats. Crop residues can be treated to make them more digestible, but they are basically unsuitable feeds for goats. The exception to this is the sweet-potato vine, which is a highly digestible and valuable feed.

4.2.5 Planted legumes

Legumes are planted to improve the quality of feed available to goats. They are normally rich in protein and highly digestible but, like natural trees, may have high levels of anti-nutritional factors, such as tannins, which reduce their digestibility.

4.2.6 Planted grasses

Grasses are normally planted to improve both the quality and quantity of the goat's feed. If they are regularly cut or grazed, they can supply relatively high-quality feed which, with some supplementation, can be used as a basic diet.

4.2.7 Crop by-products

Crop by-products include rice or wheat bran, cassava chips, peanut cake, sunflower cake, linseed cake, and sugar-cane tops. These feeds can provide useful low-cost feed supplements for goats.

4.2.8 Crops

Crops such as maize, barley, oats, and sweet potatoes may be fed directly to goats in intensive systems of production.

4.3 The composition of feeds

It is important for extension staff and farmers to know the quality of different types of feeds and to know their characteristics and role in goat feeding. Feeds can be described at various levels of precision: simply as roughage or a supplement, for example. This may be useful in certain circumstances, but may not be accurate enough in others. At the other extreme, feeds can be analysed for the exact amount of protein in the feed or the precise amount of a mineral such as sodium, or the micro units of a vitamin. This level of accuracy is very high. In developed countries printed tables of feed analyses show the composition of feeds. This information is not available for many of the tropical feeds consumed by goats. However, it is useful to be able to read and understand printed tables of feed analyses. In order to do this, the composition of feed needs to be understood.

All food consists of the components shown in Figure 4.4. Food is first divided into water and dry matter (DM). The dry matter (DM) component provides all the nutrients necessary for life: energy, protein, vitamins, and minerals. It is on a dry-matter basis that foods are evaluated, because the quantity of water in

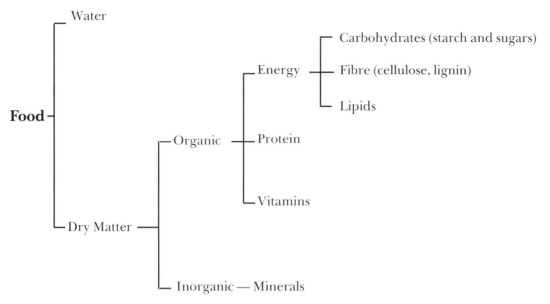

Figure 4.4 The main components of food

food varies greatly according to food type, season, stage of growth, etc. So the starting point is to know the proportion of dry matter in a feed, because it is that part which contains the vital nutrients.

Carbohydrates

'Carbohydrate' is a general term which includes simple sugars such as glucose, more complex sugars such as sucrose, and highly complex substances such as starch, cellulose, and lignin. There are big differences in the ease with which each can be digested, and thus in the availability of the energy they contain. Glucose, sucrose, and starch can all be digested easily, and in the rumen cellulose can be degraded and digested. However, lignin is indigestible and unfortunately it is often combined with cellulose, making it hard for the goat to digest the cellulose part.

Lipids

The important lipids are fats and oils which are broken down to monoglycerides and fatty acids, absorbed by the goat, and used as a source of energy or stored as fat. Most tropical forages contain little fat. Any fat that is deposited in the body may be mobilised later, in the dry season for example, as a source of energy. Goats deposit less fat in the body than sheep.

Protein and non-protein nitrogen
Proteins are vital to the goat: they form soft tissue, enzymes, hormones, antibodies, and genes. Proteins are made up of amino acids. Fortunately, the goat is able to make all the amino acids it requires out of proteins in its diet, and also from non-protein nitrogen compounds such as urea.

Vitamins
Vitamins are essential substances that are required in very small quantities. Some vitamins can be made by the goat itself (vitamin A, B complex, C, D, K), but others are required in the diet. A free-grazing goat should not have any problems obtaining most of its vitamin requirements for itself, but a stall-fed goat or a high-producing goat may face difficulty. Vitamin deficiencies can cause severe metabolic problems (see 6.5.9).

Minerals
Several minerals are essential for proper metabolism: calcium, phosphorus, sodium, chlorine, magnesium, potassium, sulphur, iron, iodine, copper, molybdenum, zinc, manganese, fluorine, cobalt, and selenium are all required in some quantities. Mineral deficiencies can cause metabolic problems. Goats observed to be eating soil are likely to be deficient in one or more minerals. Certain areas are well known for specific mineral deficiencies; for example, the Rift Valley in East Africa is known to be deficient in copper, zinc, manganese, and cobalt (see 6.5.9).

Water
Water is vital for life. It is used by the goat as a solvent in which nutrients are transported around the body and in which waste products are excreted. Many important chemical reactions take place in water. The evaporation of water is also used by the goat as a cooling method. Water evaporated from the skin, lungs, nostrils, and mouth helps to keep down body temperature. The goat obtains water from three sources: drinking water, water in food, and water released as a by-product of certain metabolic processes.

4.4 Methods of feed analysis

Feeds can be analysed to find out the amounts of the different nutrients they contain. Many feeds have been analysed in the past and there are standard feed-analysis tables for several thousand feeds, including many tropical feeds. By far the most common method of making a basic analysis of a feed is known as **proximate analysis**, which was developed over 100 years ago. In this method the food is broken down into the parts or fractions shown in Table 4.1.

Table 4.1 Feed components of proximate analysis

Fraction	Components
Moisture	Water
Ash	Minerals
Crude Protein (CP)	Proteins, amino acids, B-vitamins
Ether Extract (EE)	Fats, oils, vitamins A, D, E, K
Crude Fibre (CF)	Cellulose, hemicellulose, lignin
Nitrogen-Free Extractives (NFE)	Cellulose, hemicellulose, lignin, sugars, tannins, water-soluble vitamins

There are problems in interpreting the results of proximate analysis. Important food components are split between two fractions; carbohydrates, for example, are split between the crude-fibre fraction and the nitrogen-free extractives fraction. The crude-fibre fraction should indicate the proportion of the feed that is indigestible; but it does not, because it contains both cellulose and hemicellulose, which can both be digested, depending how closely they are associated with lignin. Despite its weaknesses, this method of analysis is widely used in the tropics, and results from it are still the most commonly available sources of information on feeds. A typical feed-analysis table will look like Table 4.2.

Table 4.2 Proximate feed analysis for Leucaena leucocephala

Plant part	Dry matter %	As % of dry matter				
		CP	CF	Ash	EE	NFE
Fresh leaves	30.7	24.2	24.2	8.9	2.7	40.0
Pods	91.0	35.8	11.4	4.4	7.5	40.9

This table shows the amount of dry matter in the different parts of *Leucaena leucocephala*. It can be a helpful starting point when estimating how much dry matter a goat will receive from a feed. It also gives an indication of the amount of protein, but the crude-protein figure does not show how much of the protein is digestible by the goat. As a result, proximate-analysis results should be viewed as an initial, rather crude, guide to the potential value of a feed. The real value of the feed to the goat is, as we shall see, affected by many factors.

Another problem with proximate-analysis results is that in the tropics goats tend to eat many different species of vegetation, either when out grazing and browsing, or when feed is cut and carried to goats. Goats tend to eat mixtures of feeds, with a wide range of nutritional characteristics. It is perhaps more practical to think about the general characteristics of the different feed types — grass, tree legumes, crop residues — rather than the specific characteristics of any particular species. This is discussed in 4.10.2.

Proximate analysis has been criticised for being imprecise and therefore unhelpful in guiding feeding. A better method of feed analysis is the Van Soest method, which has replaced proximate analysis in some laboratories. The Van Soest method divides the feed into different fractions from those employed in proximate analysis. The term Acid Detergent Fibre (ADF) may be seen in some tables; it is a good indicator of the indigestible fibre content of feeds. If fibre is indigestible, the amount of energy a goat can obtain from the feed is low.

Feed-analysis methods are improving all the time. However, it takes time for these new methods to be available in the developing world, and for tropical feeds to be evaluated using these new methods. In the mean time, goats must be fed, using any available information to best effect.

4.5 Digestion in the adult goat

It is now time to examine the goat's digestive system and see how it can be manipulated to improve the nutrients it absorbs. The goat, like all ruminants, has a specialised series of organs, in which the huge quantity of fibrous feeds it eats is broken down into food components that it can absorb and actually use. This breaking down of foods is done for it by a collection of bacteria and protozoa, known as micro-organisms, to which the goat plays host. The goat provides the micro-organisms with a nice warm environment and a steady supply of food. The goat benefits from this arrangement, because it obtains food which has been partially broken down and which the goat itself can directly digest. The goat can also digest both dead and living micro-organisms when they pass out of the rumen, providing the goat with valuable nutrients. So when feeding a goat, it is important to think not just about the goat itself, but also how to make the micro-organisms active and able to multiply, by supplying them with the nutrients they need.

Feed enters the stomach through the mouth, where it is mixed with saliva. After passing down the oesophagus, it enters the rumen. The rumen is composed of four compartments: the omasum, abomasum, reticulum, and rumen proper. Once in the rumen, the food is broken down by physical means through the movement of the rumen and during rumination, when the food is regurgitated and chewed again by the goat. This normally happens twice. The rumen is home to micro-organisms which secrete enzymes that act on the food and break it down. Carbohydrates (fibre, starch, and sugars) are converted into Volatile Fatty Acids (VFA) and methane. The VFAs can be absorbed through the rumen wall by the goat, while the methane is released through belching. During the process of breaking down food, a substantial amount of heat is also released. The goat has to get rid of this heat through panting, sweating, and simple convection. This heat source can be a huge advantage to it in a cold climate, but a burden in hot climates.

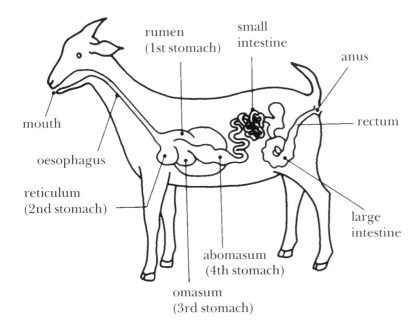

Figure 4.5
The digestive system of the goat

VFAs are the main direct source of energy for the goat's maintenance and growth. The goat is also able to convert them into milk. Three main types of VFA are produced in the rumen: acetic acid, propionic acid, and butyric acid. The proportions in which they are produced are determined by the type of feed consumed. For example, the balance between fibre and starch/sugars can have an effect on the quality and quantity of milk yield. Starch/sugars largely determine total milk production, while increasing fibre increases the fat content of milk. Feeding food rich in starch and sugars, such as sweet potatoes or whole grains, can have a dramatic effect on milk yield, but you have to careful. The break-down of starch and sugars happens very quickly, producing large quantities of methane, which must be removed quickly if a bloating of the rumen is not to occur. Bloat can be fatal. Fibre is broken down much more slowly and helps to maintain efficient conditions for digestion in the rumen. Fibre should always be fed with foods such as grains.

Proteins are broken down by the micro-organisms in the rumen into peptides, amino acids, and ammonia. These are then used by the micro-organisms themselves, when they reproduce and multiply. Micro-organisms are continuously multiplying and dying. Living and dead microbes, when they move out of the rumen, constitute microbial protein, which together with amino acids is digested by the goat in the abomasum and the first part of the small intestine (Figure 4.6). It is important to understand that only proteins and amino acids which actually manage to reach the small intestine are of direct use to the goat. It is much more efficient for the goat to digest protein for itself in the small intestine, than to wait for the microbes to break down and digest a protein and convert it into microbial protein — which the goat then has to break down again for itself. Protein is often the scarcest, most expensive, component in the diet, so it is important to think about how to use most efficiently the protein that is available.

Urea can be absorbed directly by the goat, which recycles it through its saliva; or it may be converted into micro-organisms and then microbial protein for later use by the goat. This clever feature of rumen physiology means that microbial organisms in the rumen of the goat can be encouraged to develop, by feeding urea in the diet as a source of non-protein nitrogen. Non-protein nitrogen is usually a cheap source of nitrogen. The urea must be fed with a source of easily fermentable energy; molasses is commonly used, but others may serve this purpose. The urea might come from simple urea fertiliser. This is a feature that can be exploited to achieve cheap improvements in goat feeding.

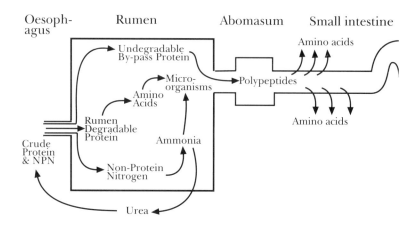

Figure 4.6 Protein digestion in the rumen and small intestine

4.6 Manipulation of digestion in the rumen and small intestine

By now it should be clear that one option to improve the nutrition of goats is to manipulate the proportions of energy (fibre, starch, and sugars) and protein (amino acids and non-protein nitrogen), so that the rumen micro-organisms are well fed to do their job, and so that some protein escapes the rumen and provides a source of protein directly, and efficiently, to the goat through the small intestine. Protein that is broken down in the rumen is called Rumen Degradable Protein (RDP), which supplies a source of nitrogen to the microbes in the rumen. Protein that goes through the rumen and is digested in the small intestine is called Undegraded Dietary Protein (UDP), or simply 'by-pass protein'. Different feeds contain different proportions of RDP and UDP (Table 4.3).

Table 4.3 Degradability and by-passability of proteins from different feeds

Food	Degradability	By-passability
Grass hay	0.9	0.1
Wheat	0.8	0.2
Soya bean meal	0.6	0.4
Fish meal	0.4	0.6
Blood meal	0.3	0.7

Source: adapted from Chesworth (1992)

The amounts of RDP and UDP in any feed are measured by using the rumen bag technique. In this technique a hole, or fistula, is made in the rumen of an animal. The hole is kept open by a rubber ring with a plug, called a cannula. Samples of the feed to be investigated, which have already been analysed for protein content, are put into the rumen in small nylon bags with tiny holes in the bag. Enzymes from rumen micro-organisms digest the feed samples in virtually the same way that they would digest normal feed. The bags are suspended in the rumen and tied to the cannula, so they are not lost inside the rumen. In order to determine the simple digestibility of the feed, the samples should be left in the rumen for at least 24 hours. To estimate the amount of protein in the feed that will be degraded in the rumen, samples should be removed at 12, 24, 36, and 48 hours and analysed, as different proteins are degraded at different rates. The rumen bag technique gives a simple, quick, and useful assessment of the nutritive value of a feed in the rumen.

Unfortunately this technique has not been extensively used in goat-nutrition studies. Ideally, locally available feeds would be screened in this way to determine the proportions of UDP and RDP, and feeding strategies could be designed accordingly. Some of the more common tropical legumes are starting to be screened in this way and results from these studies are becoming more widely available. How can we use this knowledge to make sure the goat gets the best balance of nutrients?

The first question should be: does the current diet contain a source of carbohydrates that can be used easily by the rumen micro-organisms? This might be derived from grass or better sources such as bananas, banana peelings, or bread fruit. In addition to energy, the goat's micro-organisms need a source of protein or non-protein nitrogen, so that they can multiply and build up a source of microbial protein for the goat. A diet that satisfies the rumen micro-organisms, and thus indirectly the goat, is likely to be sufficient for the basic needs of the goat. However, protein made by micro-organisms will not be enough if high levels of production are expected. In this case, a source of by-pass protein will be needed to supply higher levels of protein directly to the goat. This approach to feeding is shown in Figure 4.7.

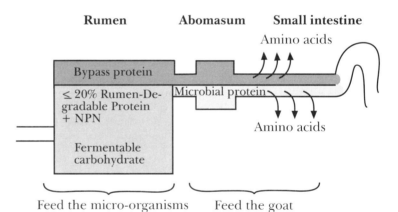

Figure 4.7 Rumen and small intestine feeding

The principles of rumen manipulation are clear, but how can it be used in practice? It is important to know the characteristics of the current diet, identify their deficiencies, and try to rectify them as best you can.

For example, a typical diet of goats in the tropics has a high proportion of roughage, which is high in indigestible fibre and low in protein. What can be done to improve this diet? The most important deficiencies here are protein and energy to enable micro-organisms to build themselves and be active to attack the fibrous feed and break it down. The micro-organisms will lack either RDP or non-protein nitrogen (NPN), which are required to enable them to grow, multiply, and break down the fibre in the diet. In this situation, a source of protein is required to supplement the diet. For example, feeding green-legume supplements to a diet consisting of crop residues, such as maize stovers, can improve the digestibility of the fibrous part of the diet and so speed up digestion in the rumen and allow the goat to eat more.

If, on the other hand, you have planted legumes to improve the protein levels, is there sufficient energy for the micro-organisms to use that protein effectively? If not, is there a source that farmers can afford to use? A common source is molasses, but other sources could be grains, bananas, or other fruit or fruit peelings.

If a goat is expected to produce a lot of milk or grow fast, feeding needs to be further refined to consider sources of by-pass protein. Many legumes contain high levels of by-pass protein.

It is clear that the rumen is a remarkable organ that can be manipulated to improve the supply of nutrients to the goat. Understanding the feeding habits of the goat and some of the functions of the rumen can improve the way in which goats are fed.

4.7 Digestion in the kid

The kid is born to drink milk and not to digest fibrous feeds, and so at birth it has only a partially developed rumen and reticulum. The kid digests milk with a well-developed abomasum. Food is directed to the abomasum through a tube formed after a reflex closure of the oesophageal groove, found in the wall of the rumen. This reflex closure ensures that milk goes directly to be digested in the abomasum and small intestine, and does not enter the rumen, where this valuable food would be broken down by microbes for themselves. The reflex is triggered by the suckling action of the kid. If it is weak and unable to suckle, digestive problems will be created by forcing milk down its oesophagus. If available, a feeding tube should be used to feed very weak kids and ensure that it receives adequate nutrients.

Soon after birth, the kid will start nibbling at grass and other vegetation. Although at this stage it is of little direct benefit to the animal, by eating such food the kid acquires the rumen micro-organisms it needs for an active rumen. Unfortunately this is when the kid is most vulnerable to infections acquired by indiscriminately eating contaminated food or drinking dirty water. Ideally the kid should be confined, and from the age of 2–3 weeks it should be given a small amount of highly digestible, clean feeds such as tree leaves or green grass, which it can nibble and so acquire rumen micro-organisms. As the quantity of dam's milk declines, the kid will want to eat, and be able to eat, more vegetative material. Kids are very vulnerable to malnutrition at the time of weaning, unless they are weaned on to high-quality feeds. The rumen is still poorly developed, so high-quality feeds such as sweet-potato vines, together with clean water, should be provided to ensure a good supply of nutrients to the kids through this critical period of weaning. In harsh environments, weaning can be a time of high mortality, particularly if it takes place in the dry season. Abrupt weaning is unnatural and should not be encouraged, because, unless high-quality feeds are provided, high mortality is likely to result.

4.8 Digestibility

Although the potential value of a food can be roughly determined by proximate analysis, the actual value of the food to a goat, what is digested and absorbed, cannot be calculated unless the digestibility of the food is known. Digested food is the part of the food that is consumed and not excreted as faeces. It is commonly expressed in terms of dry matter. There are two main methods of calculating digestibility, using live animals (*in vivo*) and in a laboratory (*in vitro*).

How to calculate digestibility

If a goat consumes 1.5 kg of DM as feed and excretes 0.3 kg DM, the apparent digestibility of the feed is:

$$\frac{\text{Intake} - \text{Output}}{\text{Intake}} \times 100$$

$$= \frac{1.5 - 0.3}{1.5} \times 100$$

$$= 80\% \text{ digestibility}$$

Coefficients for digestibility can be calculated for each fraction of the proximate analysis of dry matter. This method of calculating digestibility is not strictly accurate, as there are other losses of nutrients apart from the loss through faeces. Nutrients are lost in sweat and gases, for example, but these are very difficult to measure. Moreover, not all the material in faeces comes directly from the food just eaten; it could also have come from the body of the goat itself, in the form of dead micro-organisms from the rumen, for example. Estimates of digestibility tend to lead to underestimates of true digestibility and are normally expressed as estimates of **apparent digestibility**.

The higher the digestibility of a food, the higher the quality of that food. Low-quality feeds that take a long time to be digested in the rumen will take up space and prevent more food from being consumed, reducing the total amount eaten. Feed that has a high dry-matter digestibility, such as young green grass or young leaves of leucaena, is high-quality food. Feeds such as older stemmy grass or rice straw have low digestibility, because there are high levels of lignin, making most of the cellulose indigestible to the goat.

The digestibility of any particular feed can vary according to many factors, including the following:

- **Stage of growth and part of plant:** the stage of growth of a forage species can affect its digestibility; similarly, the part of the plant, whether it is the growing point or older more lignified material, affects the quality of the feed.

- **Species of animal:** goats are thought to be more efficient at digesting fibrous feeds than sheep, particularly at low levels of crude protein.

- **Physical characteristics of the feed:** if the feed is chopped or ground, it may pass through the rumen so quickly that its digestibility is actually reduced.

- **Level of feeding:** an increase in the quantity of food can cause an increase in the rate of passage through the rumen and digestive system, so the food is exposed to digestive enzymes for a short period, reducing digestibility.

4.9 Feed in-take

The more food a goat eats, the better. This is true unless feed is very scarce and needs to be carefully rationed over a particular period, as in the dry season. The amount of food a goat eats will affect its health and production: the more the better. But eating is essentially a voluntary activity; it is hard to force a goat to eat something it does not want to eat! So it is important to understand the factors that affect the amount of food a goat eats, and how these influences can be manipulated so that the goat can be encouraged, and in some cases tricked, into eating as much as it can.

The amount of feed actually eaten by goats (the voluntary feed in-take) is possible to measure only in stall-fed goats. The amount eaten by grazing goats can only be guessed at. The quantity of feed consumed is determined by factors relating to the goat and factors relating to the feed, and the way the goat has access to that feed (Figure 4.8). This is true whether the goat is free-grazing or stall-fed, although obviously there is more scope, and need, for manipulation in stall feeding than if the goat is out grazing and allowed to express its natural preferences.

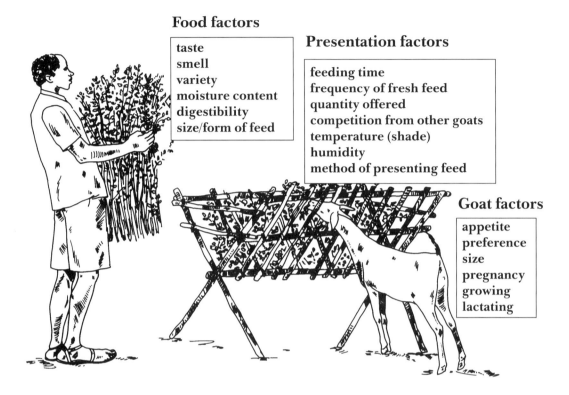

Food factors

| taste |
| smell |
| variety |
| moisture content |
| digestibility |
| size/form of feed |

Presentation factors

| feeding time |
| frequency of fresh feed |
| quantity offered |
| competition from other goats |
| temperature (shade) |
| humidity |
| method of presenting feed |

Goat factors

| appetite |
| preference |
| size |
| pregnancy |
| growing |
| lactating |

Figure 4.8 Factors affecting feed in-take

An objective of the farmer should be to 'trick' the goat into eating cheaper, lower-quality feeds such as crop residues, rather than the more attractive, more digestible, foods.

The taste, smell, and physical ease with which the goat can eat the feed are important. If it is contaminated, smells bad, tastes bad, and is difficult for the goat to reach, or the feed is presented low down on the ground so that it has to bend down to eat, then the goat will not eat very much. Ideally long coarse grasses or crop residues should be chopped. This can be done with a machete knife. If straw and stovers are fed, the goat will need access to clean water. These coarse feeds, with a high dry-matter content, need to soak up water in order for them to be digested.

If the feed is highly digestible, it will be degraded and absorbed quickly and pass through the goat's digestive system quickly. This in turn stimulates appetite, because the goat will quickly feel empty. Conversely, in some parts of the humid tropics, moisture content may be very high, in which case the goat may quickly fill up with watery feed and be unable to eat until it has excreted the excess water as urine.

If a feed is not liked by the goat, it will be very selective in what it eats. If a lot of feed is offered, the total amount eaten will be more than if it had only a small amount from which to select.

Mixing new feed with left-over feed, provided that it still smells and looks good, can trick the goat into thinking it is being offered a large quantity of new feed from which it can make its selection.

If the feed is liked, it is best to feed it little and often to avoid wastage. Goats are unable to be too fussy and selective in their feeding if they have only a small amount of feed; they will be forced to eat a higher proportion of feed on offer than they would have done if they had been offered a large quantity at one time.

In very hot and/or humid climates, the heat and humidity can reduce the amount that goats eat. In the process of digestion a great deal of heat is produced, which must be lost if the goat is not to overheat. Most of this heat is lost through sweating, which is less effective in humid environments. During the hottest part of the day goats may stop eating, not because they are full, but because they will have great difficulty in keeping their body temperatures down to a tolerable level if their rumens are very actively digesting feed and producing heat. In this situation goats will more actively feed at a cooler time of day, early in the morning and late in the evening. Allowing goats to go out grazing early in the morning and stay out late in the evening can significantly increase the amount eaten in hot environments.

In stall feeding, with many goats eating from the same feed rack, there needs to be enough space for all the goats to have easy access to the feed. Small, weak, sick goats may have trouble coping when there is competition for space and they have to fight over feed. In this case it is probably best to feed them separately.

4.10 The feed requirements of goats

Feed serves many different purposes, including the following.

- **Maintenance**: The normal activities of staying alive, breathing, blood circulation, digestive processes, etc., all require nutrients.

- **Reproduction**: Pregnancy and delivery make demands on the dam which have to be met from her feed, if she is not to lose weight. The foetus increases in size quickly during the last two months of gestation, drawing on the body reserves of the dam.

- **Growth**: Any growth requires nutrients; during the main period of growth between weaning and attaining the mature body weight, the goat requires large quantities of energy and protein.

- **Lactation**: Producing milk either for one or two kids or for human consumption requires high levels of energy and protein and good access to water.

- **Mohair production**: Energy and protein are both required for fibre production, but significant responses have been obtained from protein supplements. However, a very high level of feeding does not produce a profitable response.

- **Extra activity**: Goats in pastoral systems have to be very active, particularly in the dry season, walking long distances searching for food. Goat flocks may walk 10–15 km each day, which requires a great deal of energy.

So far, we have considered the quality of the diet needed by a goat and ways of improving the balance of nutrients reaching the rumen and small intestine. In addition, particularly when stall-feeding goats and cutting and carrying feed to them, it is useful to have some estimate of the quantity of feed a goat needs. We need to convert the known nutritional needs of goats into quantities of real foods found on the farm.

How can we calculate the quantity of feed needed by a goat in order for it to meet its requirements?

4.10.1 How much dry matter?

At the simplest level, the goat has a basic requirement for a quantity of dry matter each day, regardless of its quality. To start with, this dry matter has to supply nutrients for maintenance, in order to keep the goat alive. Once the requirements for maintenance have been met, the goat will have other food needs: for growth, for lactation, etc. So it will have to eat more feed. This is where the problem arises with bulky low-quality feeds such as hay and crop residues, because — even when they are available in large quantities — the goat simply cannot eat enough of them to meet more than its basic requirement for maintenance. This is why it is important to try to improve the quality of the diet, so that the goat only has to eat smaller quantities of higher-quality foods.

In the tropics, goats eat about 2–3 per cent of their body weight in dry matter each day. The smaller meat-type goats (West African Dwarf, Small East African, Kambing Katjang) probably eat 2.5 per cent, while the larger, milk-type goats (Jamnapuri) eat about 3 per cent of their body weight. Dairy goats imported from temperate countries will need higher in-take rates, of about 4.5 per cent. In their home countries they might have in-takes as high as 6 per cent. For tropical goats, to be safe, it is probably best to slightly overestimate a goat's needs and so use 3 per cent as a guide.

In order to know the actual weight of food which the goat should be fed, we now need to know the amount of dry matter in the food it is eating. If possible, take a sample and weigh it fresh, then dry it in an oven and calculate its dry-matter content for yourself. You may be able to refer to feed-analysis tables and calculate a rough average dry-matter content for the mixture of feeds which the goat eats (see Table 4.7). As a rough guide, most tropical grasses contain about 25–30 per cent dry matter, depending on stage of growth. After calculating the amount of fresh feed needed, round up the figure to the nearest kilo or half kilo.

A sample calculation
An adult goat weighs 28 kg and will consume 3 per cent of its weight in dry matter per day.

28 x 0.03 = 0.84 kg dry matter per day

0.84 x 3.33 = 2.79 kg fresh feed required per day

So a 28 kg goat needs about 3 kg of feed per day.

How heavy is 3 kg? Find something that you know weighs 3 kg and try to remember how heavy this feels in your hand. As a guide, a newborn kid normally weighs about 3 kg.

Results from this calculation show the amount of feed the goat must actually eat after it has selected the bits it likes and left the rest. Allowance must be made for goats being very selective in what they eat. They need to be fed a lot more feed than 3 kg each, unless it is something they particularly like.

4.10.2 How much energy and protein?

It is possible to refine our estimates of the quantity needed and start to think about the *quality* of the diet, and whether it provides enough energy and protein to allow the goat to produce what we want it to.

The energy value of a feed is expressed in terms of Metabolisable Energy (ME), which is the energy actually available in the feed to be used for metabolism by the goat. There are several different energy units used in different countries. Most countries use the joule as their unit of measurement. ME requirements are quoted in megajoules (MJ). The amount of energy in a feed is expressed in MJ of ME per kg dry matter, because it is the dry matter that contains the energy. The amounts of energy required by the goat for different purposes are shown in Table 4.4.

Estimates of the requirements for protein are normally presented as digestible crude protein (DCP) requirements in grams per day. The DCP requirements for maintenance, growth, and pregnancy are shown in Table 4.5.

When considering feeding for milk production, remember that in addition to the considerable extra energy and protein which the doe requires, she will also need additional water, calcium, and phosphorus. If she does not have enough water, her production will be severely reduced. If the doe does not get sufficient calcium

Basic nutrition

Table 4.4 Total energy requirements (MJ ME per day) for goats

Live-weight (kg)	Mainten-ance	Mainten-ance + some activity	Mainten-ance + a lot of activity	Mainten-ance + growth (50 g/day)	Mainten-ance + growth (100 g/day)	Mainten-ance + growth (150 g/day)	Mainten-ance + pregnancy
10	2.3	2.8	3.2	4.0	5.8	7.5	5.1
15	3.2	3.8	4.4	—	—	—	6.9
20	3.9	4.7	5.5	5.5	7.3	9.0	8.5
25	4.6	5.5	6.5	—	—	—	10.0
30	5.3	6.4	7.4	6.8	8.6	10.3	11.5
35	5.9	7.1	8.3	—	—	—	13.0
40	6.6	7.9	9.2	8.0	9.8	11.6	14.3
45	7.2	8.6	10.1	—	—	—	15.6
50	7.8	9.3	10.9	9.0	10.8	12.6	16.9
55	8.3	10.0	11.7	—	—	—	18.2
60	8.9	10.7	12.5	10.3	12.0	13.8	19.4

Source: adapted from Devendra and McLeroy (1982)

Table 4.5 Digestible crude protein requirements for maintenance and growth (grammes per day)

Live-weight (kg)	Maintenance	Maintenance + 50g/day	Maintenance + 100g/day	Maintenance + 150g/day	Pregnancy
10	15	25	35	45	30
20	26	36	46	56	50
30	35	45	55	65	67
40	43	53	63	73	83
50	51	61	71	81	99
60	59	69	79	89	113

Source: NRC (1981)

and phosphorus, she will have to draw on her body reserves and may develop metabolic disorders such as milk fever (see 6.5.9).

Typical nutritive values of common types of feed consumed by goats are shown in Table 4.7. A range of values is presented in the table, because each feed type contains several different feeds, of different nutritive values. The values in the table can be used as a starting point.

The amount of dry matter in **grasses** increases with age, while the amount of protein and the degree of digestibility decline. The concentration of energy in grass is not high. **Crop residues** have quite a high concentration of potential energy, but unfortunately most of this is in the crude-fibre fraction, which tends to be indigestible. It is hard for animals to eat enough bulky straws and stovers to obtain sufficient energy for maintenance; crop residues are also very low in protein (2–4 per cent), which also tends to be relatively indigestible.

Table 4.6 Energy and protein requirements for one kg milk

Breed	ME (MJ/day)	DCP (g/day)
Tropical	5.0	45
Temperate dairy	5.2	50

(ME = metabolisable energy;
MJ = megajoules;
DCP = digestible crude protein)

Table 4.7 General nutritive value of common feed types

Type of feed	Dry matter (%)	Crude protein (%)	Digestibility of protein (%)	Crude fibre (%)	ME (MJ per kg of DM)	Energy concentration (MJ ME/kg feed)
Grasses						
Young	15	15-20	50-70	20-35	8-10	1.2
Old	25	5-10	40-50	25-35	8-9	2.0
Crop residues						
Straw	80-90	2-4	20-30	30-40	7-8	5.6
Stover	80-90	2-4	20-30	30-40	7-8	5.6
Green leaves (fresh)						
Legumes	20-30	20-30	60-70	15-25	10-12	2.0
Non-legumes	20-30	15-25	40-60	20-30	7-12	1.4
Grains and oil cakes						
Legumes	90	40-50	70-80	5-10	10-12	9.0
Cereal	—	10-15	70-80	2-10	13	10.8
Roots	30-50	2-8	40-70	1-10	12-13	3.6
By-products	70-90	5-30	40-70	2-15	10-13	7.0

Tree leaves vary tremendously in quality. Leguminous trees tend to have high protein contents. However, much of this protein is associated with anti-nutritional compounds such as tannin. Much tree-legume protein is 'protected' from digestion in the rumen and may be classified as 'by-pass protein'. Tree legumes should ideally be fed with another source of rumen-degradable protein for best effect. Non-leguminous trees include a wide range of tree species. They tend to have lower levels of protein than tree legumes.

Oil cakes made from legumes such as peanut cake or soya-bean meal tend to be high in both fats and proteins. The high fat content gives them a high concentration of energy. They can make a useful protein and energy supplement. Other feeds in this category include fishmeal, linseed meal, and coconut cake. They tend to be high in fats.

Cereal grains such as maize, barley, oats, sorghum, and rice have the highest concentration of energy, mainly in the form of starch with some sugars. Protein content can be as high as 16 per cent in oats, which appear to be particularly liked by goats. Most cereals should be regarded predominantly as a source of energy. Some form of treatment to the grain increases its digestibility. This might include coarse grinding or rolling.

Root crops are low in protein, but high in energy. The concentration of energy is not as high as in grains, because roots tend to have a high moisture content. Roots, unless very small in size, should be chopped to improve intake.

By-products of food processing include a huge variety of potential feeds, including brans left over from milling, brewer's grain, sago chips, and molasses. Dry matter tends to be high and protein tends to be low.

How can this information be used to calculate the food needs of a growing goat?

A sample calculation

To calculate the amount of feed needed to supply enough energy and protein to a growing goat, let us assume that a 20 kg goat is growing at 50 g per day. From a simple calculation of dry-matter in-take, 3 per cent liveweight, it needs 0.6 kg dry matter. If it is eating grass of 20 per cent DM, it must eat at least 3.0 kg of fresh grass. The goat needs 5.5 MJ ME per day for maintenance and growth of 50 g per day (see Table 4.4).

How can this be supplied from different feeds? Using data from Table 4.7, we see that 5.5 MJ ME could come from any one of the feeds shown in Table 4.8. But remember that the goat would find it hard to physically consume forage of more than 3 per cent of its body weight, which in this case is 0.6 kg of feed (DM). It is possible to feed energy-rich cereals or oil seed cakes in very small quantities, while much more grass or tree leaves have

Table 4.8 Alternative sources of the energy requirement

Feed type	FW	DM	DMI (% LW)
Young grass	4.6	0.7	3.5!
Old grass	2.7	0.7	3.5!
Straw	1.0	0.8	4.0!
Tree legume leaves	2.7	0.5	2.5
Tree leaves	3.9	0.8	4.0!
Legume cake	0.6	0.5	2.5
Cereal	0.5	0.4	2.0
Roots	1.5	0.4	2.0

(DM = dry matter; DMI = dry-matter intake; LW = liveweight, FW = freshweight)

to be eaten. Straw appears as quite an energy-rich feed, but in reality is high in fibre, so much of the energy is indigestible and cannot be used. But more importantly, in order to grow at this rate, a goat needs more than energy: it also needs protein.

From Table 4.5 we see that the goat also needs 36 g of digestible crude protein. Table 4.9 shows how this protein can be supplied from these same feeds. Compare the quantities of the same feed needed to supply enough energy and protein to the goat. Which are the best-balanced feeds? Which are the worst-balanced that would need to be supplemented to achieve growth of 50 g/day?

Table 4.9 Alternative sources of the protein requirement

Feed type	FW	DM	DMI (% LW)
Young grass	3.2	0.5	2.5
Old grass	7.2	1.8	9.0!
Straw	11.2	9.0	45.0!!!
Tree legume leaves	1.2	0.3	1.5
Tree leaves	3.0	0.6	3.0
Legume cake	0.1	0.1	0.5
Cereal	0.5	0.5	2.5
Roots	13.5	4/5	22.5!!!

Here it can be seen that straw would not after all be a good feed for a growing goat! Nor would old grass, tree leaves, or root crops. The best 'balanced' feeds for growth are young grass, tree-legume leaves, or an oil-seed cake. However, from the calculation of dry-matter in-take, it is clear that this goat would have difficulty eating enough young grass or tree legumes to achieve this high rate of growth. In reality it is hard to achieve even the modest growth of 50 g/day without feeding an energy and protein supplement, either a cereal or an oil cake.

This calculation shows how these tables can provide a rough, but practical, guide to feeding goats. Where possible, use feed analyses of specific feeds; but, if they are not available, using these simple tables can show the sorts of level and types of feed that goats need in order to live and produce to meet the needs of their owners. In reality, goats are fed a mixture of feeds. Section 5.5 shows how to calculate the right mixture of different feeds. The challenge is to match the needs of the goats with the feeds that are available, and where possible to improve the supply of the sorts of feed that can make up for any deficiencies.

4.10.3 How much water?

Goats in the tropics are second only to the camel among domestic animals in the efficiency with which they use water. However, this efficiency should not lead us to overlook their needs, and particularly the needs of lactating goats. In the wet season, or in the humid tropics, goats may eat forage composed of 70–80 per cent water. In this case, they may not need to drink water at all. However, most feed in the tropics has a lower content of moisture, and goats will need to be given water in addition to their feed. Coarse, fibrous feeds will need to be accompanied by quite a lot of water, if the goat is going to be able to digest them at all. The feed needs to have absorbed water in the rumen, if the rumen micro-organisms are going to be able to attack it at all. Ideally goats would have constant access to a supply of clean water, but in most parts of the tropics people themselves do not have such access, so it is too much to expect goats to have it.

The amount of water a goat needs depends on its breed, the climate, the type of food eaten, and the purpose for which the goat needs the water: for milk, growth, fibre, etc. Tropical breeds kept in arid and semi-arid areas may be able to drink only once every two–four days in the dry season. They have a great ability to use their rumen for water-storage and reduce water-loss in urine and faeces. Temperate breeds of goats do not have this ability to the same extent and may need twice as much water as a tropical breed in the same environment.

It is normally recommended that goats consume four times as much water as dry matter, i.e. 4 kg water for 1 kg DM feed, but they may need more than this at higher temperatures. Remember that milk is 90 per cent water, so if a goat is producing one litre of milk, she will need at least an extra litre to replace it. Normally it is recommended that an allowance of 1.3 litres of water per litre of milk produced is given to lactating goats.

Finally

Feeding animals is partly a science, but it is also an art. Close observation of the performance and behaviour of goats can lead to better feeding. It is very important that farmers closely observe their goats to look at their health and general well-being, their performance (milk yield, etc.), and preferences. The guidelines set out above may be used, but should be modified after observing the behaviour and performance of particular goats.

Further reading

Agriculture and Food Research Council (AFRC) (1993) *Energy and Protein Requirements of Ruminants*, AFRC Technical Committee on Responses to Nutrients, Wallingford, UK: CAB International

Chesworth, J. (1992) *Ruminant Nutrition*, London: Macmillan/CTA

Devendra, C. and G. B. McLeroy (1982) *Goat and Sheep Production in the Tropics*, London: Longman

Food and Agriculture Research Organisation of the United Nations (FAO) (1981) *Tropical Feeds*, Rome: FAO

McDonald, P., R. A. Edwards, and J. F. D. Greenhalgh (1988) *Animal Nutrition* 4th edition, London: Longman

National Research Council (NRC) (1981) *Nutrient Requirements of Goats*, Washington DC: National Academy Press

Preston, T.R. and R. A. Leng (1987) *Matching Ruminant Production Systems with Available Resources in the Tropics and Sub-Tropics*, Armidale, Australia: Penambul Books

CHAPTER 5

Improved nutrition

5.1 Introduction

The basic principles of goat nutrition were described in Chapter 4. The challenge for extension staff and farmers is to put them into practice in the real world. In order to improve the feeding of an individual goat, there are two courses of action:

- improve the balance of nutrients reaching the rumen and small intestine;
- increase the total amount of food eaten.

However, the farmer is seldom feeding just one goat. In a flock of goats of any size, different goats will have different nutritional needs; where feeds are scarce, the farmer may have to target those scarce feed resources to the most needy goats. In addition, farmers have to cope with fluctuations in the feeding supply with the seasons, and so they must also consider how to:

- target goats with special needs;
- reduce the seasonal fluctuation in feed supply.

5.1.1 Checklist of questions on feeding

Before any attempt is made to improve the feeding of goats in any situation, it is important to understand the current feeding practices. Chapter 2 described the feeding problems commonly found in each of the major systems of goat production. Chapter 3 outlined methods to investigate feeding practices: feed calendars (3.2.5) and feed monitoring (3.3.12). Before any action is taken, the following information should, ideally, be known:

- seasonal description of feeds fed to goats, by quantity and quality: grazing, crop residues, supplements, etc;
- seasonal description of method of feeding: free grazing, tethered, housed, etc;
- seasonal pattern of production: breeding season, family's milk requirements, special ceremonies;
- likely periods of feed deficit;
- availability of supplements, minerals, water.

This chapter will describe practical methods of improvement which can be adopted by farmers in different systems of production. It will then use three case studies as examples to show how feeding problems can be analysed and strategies designed to overcome the problems identified.

5.1.2 Common feeding problems of goats in the tropics

A wide range of feeding problems is commonly encountered in tropical goat-keeping, including:

* fibrous feeds causing low intake rates, resulting in low levels of overall production;
* seasonal fluctuations in quantity, digestibility, protein, water availability;
* low levels of protein for growth and milk production;
* specific mineral deficiencies, such as a lack of sodium in feeds with high moisture content or in a specific area;
* poor presentation of feed to confined goats;
* poor access to water;
* poor nutrition of lactating dams, leading to low milk yields and poor rates of growth and survival among kids;
* poor quality of feeds for kids at weaning, causing a sharp drop ·in weight and possible death.

5.1.3 What practical options are available to farmers?

The main options for improving the quantity and quality of feed available, and the amount of feed consumed by goats in different feeding systems, are shown in Table 5.1.

5.2 Improving feed supply: grazing management

Owners often have to graze their goats on communal grazing areas, either supervised by a full-time herder, or left to roam by themselves. Often children herd goats, but in some systems a herdsman is employed to look after large flocks. Goats are adept at looking after themselves, and in several systems, such as village goat-keeping in humid West Africa, or forest goat-keeping in western Ethiopia, they are allowed to go out by themselves, following a leader goat, and returning home by themselves at night.

The communal ownership of grazing resources leaves few options to an individual goat owner acting alone to improve the amount consumed by his or her goats. There are more options if all livestock owners act together.

Table 5.1 Options to improve feed supply, nutrient balance, and quantity of feed consumed

Options	Feeding system		
	Free grazing	**Tethered**	**Stall-fed**
Feed supply (Quantity and nutrient balance)	Select grazing area	Select best site	Select quality feeds
	Develop forage crops	Develop forage crops	Mix feeds
	Supplement diet with energy protein minerals	Supplement diet with energy protein minerals	Develop forage crops
			Supplement diet with energy protein minerals
Treatment of feed	Conserve feed	Chop unpalatable feeds	Chop unpalatable feeds
		Wilt wet feeds	Wilt wet feeds
		Mix feeds	Mix feeds
		Treat with urea	Treat with urea
		Conserve feeds	Conserve feeds
Presentation	Increase total grazing time	Ensure comfort and safety of tether	Feed at correct height
	Allow time for ruminating	Move frequently	Present feed in an accessible manner
	Ensure presence of shade	Ensure presence of shade	Ensure adequate space for all goats
	Select best time to graze		Feed little and often
			Clean up waste feed
Water	Allow frequent access	Allow frequent access	Allow continuous access

In herded systems the herder is likely to have a fairly limited choice of places to graze within walking distance of the house. However, herders quickly learn what their goats like to eat and will normally allow them to linger in places supporting the preferred vegetation. In very hot climates, goats will seek shade in the middle of the day and should be allowed to rest and ruminate there during the hottest period. However, this resting time will cut down the time which goats have for grazing; so, to compensate, they should be taken out early in the morning and returned home late in the afternoon, to allow sufficient time to seek food. This is especially important during drier seasons, when vegetation is scarce and goats need much time to seek and eat enough feed, even to satisfy their maintenance requirements.

Goats need water in order to digest fibrous feeds, but valuable grazing time is lost during watering. In arid and semi-arid environments, herders have to decide how frequently to water their goats. Vegetation around watering points is usually over-grazed, so time must be spent in walking from the water point to better grazing; thus grazing time is lost. Goats in arid areas may be watered only every three–four days.

In societies which rely on communal grazing, the community has usually developed traditional ways of managing the grazing resource, to allow equal access to it, and to try to prevent its over-use. It is always important to try to understand the traditional systems of grazing management and find out if they still exist, or whether they have died out. In many pastoral societies in Africa and the Middle East, traditional management systems are under great pressure from increasing human and livestock populations using diminishing grazing areas. In many places these traditional systems have broken down altogether.

Most communal systems of grazing management function to limit the number of owners using the grazing, and allow the preservation of grazing for dry periods. Often particular groups, clans, or relatives may claim traditional rights over a defined grazing area and will try to exclude others from its use. Traditional grazing rights may be fiercely protected.

Community agreement controlling when, and where, livestock may graze can allow the regeneration of vegetation for future use in more difficult periods such as the dry season. This community agreement can be used as a basis for establishing a more formal management plan for the grazing area, which may also include some forage development such as establishing banks of high-quality forage for use in the dry season. Up-grading the vegetation of communal grazing areas is discussed in the section on oversowing communal grazing areas (5.3.7).

Herding goats requires a great deal of labour. Often this task is carried out by children, usually boys, which prevents them from attending school. As governments become more strict about compulsory school attendance, it will become increasingly difficult to find the labour needed to herd goats all day. In most societies the education of male children is given priority over that of their sisters. As a result, in many parts of the tropics, there is a trend towards girls taking on more responsibility for herding livestock. The long-term viability of many goat-herding systems must be in doubt, because of the shortage of labour, together with the reduction in grazing lands from encroaching cultivation.

Traditional grazing organisation of the Maasai of southern Kenya

The Maasai traditionally used to divide their grazing land into residential areas, areas set aside for calves, grazing areas for the early/mid dry season, and distant areas for the end of the dry season. Groups of households, associated with particular reserved grazing areas, do not have exclusive rights to that grazing but do, collectively, decide when livestock may enter an area for grazing. When disputes arise about the time of entry, collective action may be taken against any person who uses the reserved grazing prematurely. Owners of large herds are discouraged from taking up residence in a neighbourhood.

This system of controlling the rate at which grazing resources are used existed widely before the 1960s, but has since declined with the introduction of group ranches. The system still exists in pockets, but is under great pressure.

5.3 Improving feed supply: forage development

5.3.1 Forage for what?

The development of forage crops is one way of making affordable improvements to the quantity and quality of feed available to goats. Forage crops can

- improve the total supply of bulk feed available to goats;
- improve the quality (digestibility and protein) of feed;
- compensate for seasonal fluctuations in quantity and quality.

In addition to the advantages for the goat, growing forage crops can have many beneficial side effects for the farmer, his or her family, and the environment. For instance, it may

- reduce soil erosion;
- provide a source of green manure for food crops;
- provide firewood and building materials;
- reduce the labour required to feed goats;
- provide shade.

Before a decision is made on what to grow, and where and when to grow it, the current feeding problems must be considered. Do the goats need more bulk feed? Do they need a source of protein? Do they need better feed in the dry season? Do particular goats, such as weaners and lactating does, need special feeding?

Apart from improving the quality and quantity of feed, developing forage for cut-and-carry feeding systems can ease the burden of the person responsible for collecting feed for the goats.

This task may take several hours each day. Often this job is done by women or children, and it takes time away from their other work on the farm or in the household.

When the needs are clear, a forage strategy can be planned and species to meet those needs can be selected.

Experience of introducing forage growing to farmers in the tropics has shown that it is most successful in systems of production that offer a good monetary return. If farmers are already making money from their goats, there is a great incentive for them to feed them better and make more money. In this case they are much more likely to put effort into developing forage. This issue will be discussed again when the implications of forage development for extension are considered (5.3.10).

5.3.2 When and where can forage be grown?

Women involved in a dairy-goat project in Ethiopia were encouraged to plant some forage crops for their local goats, which were yielding very little milk. Most planted a small area, helped in many cases by their husbands, but they did so mainly because they were expected to, in order to participate in the project. When these same women received a cross-bred goat each, yielding 1–2 litres of milk per day, every woman planted much more forage. Some women started to sell milk, while others gave it to their children. The women marvelled at how much their cross-bred goats ate, wondering if they had a second stomach! But they all appreciated how much milk the goats gave and realised the need to have more feed, of a higher quality.

Ethiopia: women plant forage for goats

Growing trees, grasses, and bushes to feed to goats is often a very new technology for farmers, and careful consideration should be given to the question of how the forage species fit into the existing farm. Often too much time is spent testing which species or cultivar best suits a particular environment, but what is much more important to the farmer is not so much the species themselves but the strategy for growing them: where, when, and how.

Forage crops, whether they are perennial trees, bushes, grasses, or annual legumes, need a place to grow and a time to be grown. A few simple questions can quite quickly pinpoint the opportunities — in space and time — for growing forage on the farm. Once the opportunities have been identified, a suitable strategy can be designed, and species found that will best fit into that strategy in that particular environment. Look at the farm and discuss with the

*Forage instead of coffee
in Tanzania*

In the foothills of Mount Kilimanjaro in Tanzania, farmers have very small farms. In the 1960s and 1970s they planted a lot of coffee, but when the price fell, some farmers changed to dairy farming of cows or goats. Some farmers have been pulling up their coffee trees and planting forage crops, because they can make more money from forage than coffee.

farmer where and when a forage crop could be grown without taking land away from food crops (Figure 5.1). If growing forage is new to the farmer, it is always best to show what improvements can be made without disturbing the existing cropping pattern. Later, if the farmer gets real benefits from the forage, he or she may decide to allocate more land to forage production and even use crop land; but a start can be made by using 'spare' land.

Consider farmer's objectives and current feeding practices.
What are the major deficiencies?
Identify nutritional needs.

*Figure 5.1 A forage-
development strategy*

Seek land and time slot free for forage.
Select forage strategy.

Consider environment (rainfall, temperature, soils, etc.).
Select available species for strategy.

Promote strategy and observe outcome.
Adapt strategy and species as needed.

The areas that might be considered for forage production are:

- the area immediately around the house;
- along the edge of fields, including bunds in rice fields;
- a strip of land in the field area;
- underneath an established annual crop;
- underneath a perennial crop;
- communal grazing areas.

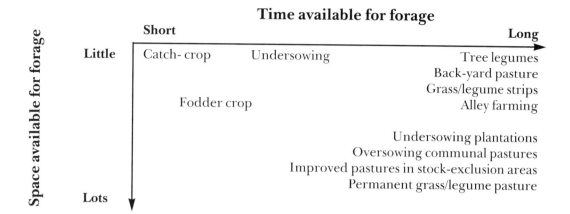

Figure 5.2 The forage strategies appropriate for different slots of space and time

Discuss how long these areas will be available for forage. Can they be permanently allocated for forage production, in which case a perennial species can be planted? Or is it possible to plant a forage crop for a short time only, for example until the next crop has to be planted? Look for these slots of space and time when forage can be planted (Figure 5.2).

Very often the land that is found to be available, which a farmer is prepared to set aside for growing forage, will be some of the worst, most infertile, and otherwise unusable land. It may be a challenge to grow anything on it successfully! If forage growing is being introduced for the first time, the results in such unpromising areas can be disheartening for all concerned. In this case, select good pioneer species: ones that are easy to establish and grow quickly. In this way farmers are encouraged and will allocate more of their better land for forage in the future.

A communal grazing area is more difficult to improve, because it requires the agreement of the whole community to control their livestock and work together in improving the vegetation of the area.

5.3.3 What species to use?

Once the forage strategy has been agreed, the species to use in that strategy must be selected. The major deciding factors in selecting suitable species will be

- desired characteristics: annual/perennial; tree, bush, grass, creeping;
- availability of planting material: seed, cuttings, splits;
- rainfall;
- temperature;
- soils.

Improved nutrition

Table 5.2 Key features of the major forage types

Forage type	Quantity	Digestibility	Protein	Other uses
Tree legumes	Low	High	High	Firewood Timber Green manure Shade
Herbaceous legumes	Medium	High	High	
Grasses	High	Medium	Low	Thatching Weaving

Table 5.3 Common forage species suitable for different climates

Type of forage	Humid Rainfall 1000 mm+	Sub-humid Rainfall 700-1000 mm	Semi-arid Rainfall 400-700 mm	Highland Rainfall 500-1000 mm, frost
Tree legumes	Leucaena Glyricidia Calliandra Sesbania	Leucaena Glyricidia Sesbania	Sesbania Leucaena	Tree lucerne Sesbania
Herbaceous legumes	Centrosema Axillaris Desmodium Stylosanthes Desmanthus Calopo Lablab	Pigeon pea Axillaris Desmodium Stylosanthes Desmanthus Glycine Siratro Lablab	Pigeon pea Stylosanthes Axillaris Siratro Lablab Cassia	Clover Alfalfa Vetch Medics
Grasses	Elephant grass Rhodes grass Green panic Para grass Setaria Phalaris	Elephant grass Rhodes grass Guinea grass Green panic Para grass Setaria Phalaris	Elephant grass Forage sorghum Buffel grass	Rye grass Tall fescue Cocksfoot
Multi-purpose	Sweet potato Banana	Sweet potato Banana	Sweet potato Banana	Fodder beet Oats

Many extension staff assume that exotic forage species are the only species to use. While the well-known forage species have been cultivated for years and selected for high yields, they may not always perform better than local species. Consider the forage species currently eaten by goats and the ones particularly liked by them, and consider whether these species can be more widely grown and promoted in forage strategies. For example, *Erythrina* spp is a family of leguminous trees, indigenous to many parts of the tropics, easy to establish by seed or cuttings, and often used as a living fence. Goats appear to relish the leaves of most species of *Erythrina*, and it could be much more widely used as a forage tree. However, if the indigenous species are difficult to propagate, or they are not very productive, then try exotic species, but do not immediately rush to use exotic species without first considering indigenous ones.

A major problem with exotic species of forage is obtaining the seed in sufficient quantities for an extension programme. Several of the more common species, such as leucaena, sesbania, glyricidia, and calliandra, are now quite widely available; but others, such as axillaris, desmodium, or centrosema, are more difficult to obtain and may even have to be imported. Always be sure you have a good supply of the seed for the farmers with whom you work. In the long term, farmers should produce their own seed, or planting material. Later we will consider how this can be organised in order to make forage-development sustainable.

Once the type of forage desired and the strategy in which it will be grown are agreed, the species that best fit the farmer's particular needs can be selected. Consider the rainfall and temperature pattern of the area. What is the total rainfall? How long is the dry season? Are there ever frosts? What sorts of soil are there? Do they ever get waterlogged, or are they very sandy and free-draining?

The key features of the different types of forage species are shown in Table 5.2. Legumes, being able to trap atmospheric nitrogen in the soil and convert it into vegetative material, produce forage with relatively high levels of protein. Grasses produce lower-quality bulk feed, which needs to be supplemented with legumes to make a balanced diet.

The common exotic improved forage species used in forage development are listed in Table 5.3. The major climatic zones in which they perform best are also shown. Each species will have several cultivars or varieties, each with slightly different characteristics and adaptabilities. The agronomic characteristics of the common forage species are summarised in Table 5.4.

Table 5.4 Characteristics of common forage crops

Common name	Scientific name	Minimum rainfall (mm/yr)	Seeding rate (kg/ha)
Tree legumes			
Pigeon pea	*Cajanus cajan*	300	20-25
Calliandra	*Calliandra calothyrus*	1,000	20-50 seeds/metre
Glyricidia	*Glyricidia maculata*	900	Cutting/seed
	Glyricidia sepium	900	Cutting/seed
Leucaena	*Leucaena diversfolia*	500	20-50 seeds/metre
	Leucaena leucocephala	400	20-50 seeds/metre
Sesbania	*Sesbania grandifolia*	600	20-50 seeds/metre
	Sesbania sesban	500	20-50 seeds/metre
Tree lucerne	*Chamaecytisus prolifer*	500	20-50 seeds/metre
Herbaceous legumes			
Calopo	*Calopogonium mucunoides*	700	1-3
Cassia	*Cassia rotundifolia*	400	2-3
Centro	*Centrosema pubescens*	900	3-5
Desmanthus	*Desmanthus virgatus*	500	1-2
Greenleaf desmodium	*Desmodium intortum*	700	1-2
Silverleaf desmodium	*Desmodium uncinatum*	700	1-3
Glycine	*Glycine wightii*	600	2-5
Lablab	*Lablab purpureus*	400	10-30
Lotononis	*Lotononis bainesii*	800	0.5-1
Siratro	*Macroptilium atropurpureum*	500	1-3
Axillaris	*Macrotyloma axillare*	500	3-5
Alfalfa	*Medicago sativa*	600	2-15
Tepary bean	*Phaseolus acutofolius*	300	n/a
Puero	*Pueraria phaseoloides*	1000	1-5
Graham stylo	*Stylosanthes guianensis*	600	3-6
Verano stylo	*Stylosanthes hamata*	500	3-6
Seca stylo	*Stylosanthes scabra*	500	3-6
Red clover	*Trifolium pratense*	600	2-8
White clover	*Trifolium repens*	600	1-4
Vetch	*Vicia dasycarpa*	400	20
Cowpea	*Vigna sinensis*	300	20

Tolerance to Drought	Tolerance to waterlogging	Tolerance to frost	Establishment method	Nutritive value
Very good	Poor	Poor	Seed	Very good
Fair	Good	Poor	Seed/seedling	Good
Fair	Fair	Poor	Cutting/seed	Good
Fair	Fair	Poor	Cutting/seed	Good
Good	Fair	Fair	Seed/seedling	Good
Very good	Poor	Fair	Seed/seedling	Good
Good	Good	Poor	Seed	Good
Good	Good	Poor	Seed	Good
Good	Poor	Very good	Seed/seedling	Good
Fair	Fair	Poor	Seed	Good
Very good	Fair	Fair	Seed	Good
Fair	Fair	Poor	Seed	Very good
Good	Fair	Poor	Seed	Good
Fair	Good	Fair	Seed	Very good
Good	Fair	Fair	Seed	Very good
Good	Poor	Fair	Seed	Very good
Good	Poor	Fair	Seed	Very good
Fair	Very good	Good	Seed	Good
Good	Fair	Fair	Seed	Very good
Good	Fair	Poor	Seed	Very good
Very good	Poor	Very good	Seed	Very good
Very good	Poor	Poor	Seed	Good
Fair	Good	Poor	Seed	Good
Fair	Fair	Poor	Seed	Good
Very good	Poor	Poor	Seed	Good
Very good	Poor	Poor	Seed	Fair
Fair	Poor	Good	Seed	Very good
Fair	Fair	Very good	Seed	Very good
Fair	Fair	Good	Seed	Very good
Good	Poor	Fair	Seed	Good

Common name	Scientific name	Minimum rainfall (mm/yr)	Seeding rate (kg/ha)
Grasses			
Signal grass	*Brachiaria decumbens*	1000	3-6
Para grass	*Brachiaria mutica*	1000	2-6
Buffel grass	*Cenchrus ciliaris*	250	1-4
Rhodes grass	*Chloris gayana*	600	1-6
Cocksfoot	*Dactylis glomerata*	500	3-6
Tall fescue	*Festuca aruninacea*	600	4-6
Perennial ryegrass	*Lolium perenne*	500	5-20
Molasses grass	*Melinis minutiflora*	1000	1-4
Elephant grass	*Pennisetum purpureum*	600	Splits
Bambatsi panic	*Panicum coloratum*	400	1-6
Gatton panic	*Panicum maximum*	750	2-6
Green panic	*Panicum maximum*	550	1-6
Guinea grass	*Panicum maximum*	900	2-6
Hamil grass	*Panicum maximum*	900	1-4
Paspalum	*Paspalum plicatulum*	900	6-10
Phalaris	*Phalaris aquatica*	400	2-4
Setaria	*Setaria sphacelata*	800	2-5
Fodder crops			
Oats	*Avena sativa*	600	70-80
Fodder beet	*Beta vulgaris*	750	5

Table 5.4 continued

5.3.4 Back-yard pasture

Back-yard pasture is the growing of forage in the area around the house. It is a relatively simple way of increasing forage production and is often a good one for farmers to start with. It is particularly appropriate for women, because they are normally responsible for looking after the house compound. The fertility of the soil around the house is usually high, so even small forage plots can be very productive.

Back-yard forage may consist of the following:

- hedges of tree legumes;
- mixed plots of perennial grasses and herbaceous legumes;

Tolerance to Drought	Tolerance to waterlogging	Tolerance to frost	Establishment method	Nutritive value
Fair	Good	Poor	Seed/splits	Fair
Fair	Very good	Poor	Seed/splits	Fair
Very good	Poor	Fair	Seed	Good
Good	Fair	Fair	Seed	Good
Good	Fair	Very good	Seed	Good
Fair	Good	Very good	Seed	Good
Fair	Poor	Very good	Seed	Good
Fair	Poor	Poor	Seed/splits	Fair
Good	Poor	Fair	Splits	Good
Very good	Very good	Good	Seed	Good
Fair	Fair	Fair	Seed	Good
Good	Poor	Good	Seed	Good
Fair	Fair	Fair	Seed	Good
Good	Good	Fair	Seed	Fair
Fair	Good	Good	Seed	Fair
Very good	Very good	Very good	Seed/splits	Good
Fair	Good	Good	Seed	Good
Fair	Good	Good	Seed	Good
Very good	Poor	Very good	Seed	Good

- highly productive legumes, such as alfalfa;
- highly productive grasses, such as elephant grass;
- annual fodder crop, such as fodder beet.

Tree legumes are particularly suitable, for several reasons.

- They can be sown around the edges of the plot and so do not compete for space with other crops.
- They can be interplanted with existing back-yard crops.
- They can improve soil fertility.
- They can provide shade for livestock and for the family.
- They can provide a handy source of firewood.

It is best to start farmers who are new to growing forage trees with a mixture of tree species. For example, sesbania, glyricidia, and pigeon pea grow very fast; farmers are usually impressed by how quickly they grow and are encouraged by this. Trees such as leucaena or tree lucerne grow much more slowly at the start, but may be more productive in the long term. Planting a mixture of tree species ensures that farmers are both encouraged and rewarded by the trees they plant.

Planting a mixture of species is also best for ecological reasons. Forage plants harbour pests, and planting large areas of one species makes the farmer vulnerable to their loss by insect, bacterial, or fungus attack. The most dramatic example of a forage pest has been the psyllid attack on leucaena in Asia and Africa. The psyllid is a tiny insect that sucks sap from the growing tips of leucaena branches. Most varieties of leucaena are susceptible to their attack and quickly die. In parts of the Indonesian archipelago, and notably the island of Timor, large areas of leucaena have been destroyed by this pest. Although some trees recover and some varieties have been found to be relatively resistant to attack, millions of trees have been destroyed. Psyllid-resistant varieties are now widely available, but much damage has already been done. Although planting a mixture of trees would not have prevented the psyllid attack, it would have reduced the increase in the psyllid population, and the other species of trees would have provided an alternative supply of forage. A hard lesson has been learned.

Establishment
It is normally best to establish tree legumes by planting seedlings, but some species such as glyricidia can be easily established by using cuttings. Sesbania can be directly seeded into the soil and

Figure 5.3 Back-yard pasture: a hedge of Sesbania sesban growing beside a house
Christie Peacock

can grow very quickly after planting in this way. Whichever way the trees are established, it is vital that they are planted as early in the growing season as possible. This may not be so important in the humid tropics, which may have higher rainfall, more evenly distributed, but it is vital in the sub-humid and semi-arid tropics, which have marked wet and dry seasons. Young seedlings will have trouble surviving a dry season unless they are well established at the start of it, or are watered through the dry period, which may be difficult.

Young trees are very vulnerable to weeds and to being damaged by livestock — particularly by the goats for whom they are planted! Young trees should be protected by, for example, thorn branches, and the family's and neighbour's livestock should be controlled.

Management and use

It is best to allow trees to become well established before starting to cut them. Exactly when to start cutting will depend on their growth, which in turn will depend on rainfall and temperature and will be different in each area and for each farm. Cutting too early can damage the tree and may even kill it, while cutting too late will encourage the development of a large trunk but few branches. The frequency of cutting will depend on the growth-rate of the tree. Farmers will quickly learn what is best for the trees around their house.

Cutting heights can be varied according to the farmer's preference. Cutting low at one metre is easier for the person cutting, but means that the new growth is within easy reach of goats and other livestock. Cutting at a height of 1.75–2.0 metres is higher than normally recommended, but has the advantage of being too high even for cattle to reach (Figure 5.4).

Tree legumes can provide a valuable source of high-quality protein. When they are planted around the house, there is unlikely to be a sufficient quantity for them to be anything other than a protein supplement. When in very short supply, legumes should be fed to the goats most in need of a high-quality protein supplement: lactating does, weaners, and fattening males.

Figure 5.4 High cutting of tree legumes

Jenny Matthews/Oxfam

When and where to promote back-yard forage

When and where to promote back-yard forage
Back-yard forage production can be promoted in the following situations:

- where livestock numbers are high and there is little grazing;
- where it is possible to control livestock;
- where there is enough space in the back yard;
- where a protein supplement is needed;
- where women are closely involved in goat-keeping.

5.3.5 Forage strips and alley farming

Forage strips are narrow lines of forage planted between arable crops. The forage strips can have several purposes:

- to provide both bulk and quality feed for a cut-and-carry feeding system;
- to prevent soil erosion;
- to provide fuel-wood;
- to provide shelter and green manure for crops;
- to improve soil fertility.

Figure 5.5 Grass strip used to feed goats and check soil erosion

JENNY MATTHEWS/OXFAM

Forage strips are particularly useful in erosion-prone areas — sloping land, light soils, etc. — and, if planted on contours, can serve as a cheap and effective method of soil-erosion control. Contour forage strips are cheap to establish and can, over a number of years, result in the formation of effective terraces. They require much less maintenance than the more conventional stone or soil terraces normally promoted in soil-conservation programmes.

Forage strips may include the following:

- grass/legume mixtures planted in a dense strip;
- tree legumes closely planted in parallel rows, forming alleys ('alley farming');
- trees planted as shelter belts around crop land;
- forage species planted on existing terraces or bunds.

A wide range of forage species is suitable for use in forage strips. On or around arable land, creeping grasses should never be used, because they can quickly become a weed in the crop and will be difficult to eradicate. Likewise if erect grasses or creeping legumes are included, they should be cut regularly to prevent them seeding near the crop-land.

Forage species suitable for use in forage strips depend on the physical context.

- **Bunds, terrace walls, and contour strips**
  Erect grasses: setaria, phalaris, panics, buffel grass
  Herbaceous legumes: axillaris, desmodium, vetch
  Tree legumes: glyricidia, leucaena, sesbania

- **Alley farming, hedges and shelter belts**
  Tree legumes: leucaena, glyricidia, sesbania, tree lucerne, calliandra

Establishment

Tree legumes may be established from seedlings, cuttings, or seeds, depending on the species. Grasses should be established from seed or splits, as appropriate. Forage strips should be established early in the growing season, to ensure their survival through the first dry season.

Tree legumes for alley farming can be planted close together, 25–35 cm apart, in areas of high rainfall (more than 1,000 mm), but should be farther apart (50 cm) in areas with lower rainfall. Likewise the spacing between the rows should vary according to rainfall, availability of arable land, type of crop grown between rows, the slope of the land, and the preference of the farmer. They could be quite close together, at 4 metres apart, if arable land is not in short supply, the rainfall is high, and the farmer wants a high proportion of forage. In areas of lower rainfall, a less intensive system should be practised, with rows farther apart, 8 or more metres. On sloping land, rows should be closer together as the slope gets steeper.

Figure 5.6 Alley farming: maize intercropped with leucaena
INTERNATIONAL LIVESTOCK RESEARCH INSTITUTE

109

Management and use

Ideally forage strips should be cut to get the best production. If goats are tethered beside strips, they should be supervised to make sure they do not over-graze the strip or trample it excessively. Regular cutting of all species is essential during crop growth, to ensure that there is no interference with the arable crop. Regular cutting results in higher-quality feed, because there will be a higher proportion of young leaves, which are easily digestible and have high levels of protein. Cutting frequency can be increased during the wet season, but must be reduced during dry periods, or the tree will suffer and might even die if it is not given time to recover.

In alley farming, trees may be cut at a height of about one metre. The farmer may prefer low cutting during the time of crop establishment, to avoid shading the emerging crop. Alley farming is often promoted as a way of supplying a cheap source of nitrogen to the crop, through cutting leaves for use as a green

Much research on alley farming in Africa has been carried out in southern Nigeria by the International Livestock Research Institute (ILRI) and the International Institute for Tropical Agriculture (IITA). In this region typical farms consist of an area of cultivated land (2 hectares) and an area of fallow land (6 ha). The main crops grown are maize, cassava, and yam. The family may consist of 6–8 people, who look after 3–6 goats. Alley farming offers the possibility of reducing the need for a fallow period, through fertilising arable land with a green mulch of tree-legume leaves. The main tree species used have been *Glyricidia sepium* and *Leucaena leucocephala*. As population pressure mounts, goats, which currently roam freely through the village, scavenging for food, will have to be confined. Alley farming offers a means of supplying high-quality feed to confined goats.

ILRI's research has shown that, in order to maintain crop yields, the trees should be cut just before the planting of the crop and the cuttings should be used as a mulch and green manure. Thereafter most (75 per cent) of the cuttings can be fed to goats without any harmful effect on crop yield.

Goats were allowed into the plots during the fallow period. Some trouble occurred when the understorey vegetation was poor and unpalatable, and the goats took to eating the bark of the trees. This can kill the trees. It is best to allow the goats into the plots only for short periods, if at all, to ensure that they never resort to debarking trees.

Source: AFNETA (1992)

In the uplands of the Philippines, the Mindanao Baptist Rural Life Centre has been working for a number of years on the problems of soil conservation. They have been promoting a strategy widely known as SALT (Sloping Agricultural Land Technology), which encourages farmers to plant double rows of leguminous trees and shrubs along contours on sloping land. In the original SALT scheme, cuttings from the trees were used exclusively for manuring crops and providing vegetative cover, conserving soil and water. SALT 2 is a similar strategy, developed specifically for goats, which incorporates a higher propor-

tion of tree legumes and sets aside blocks of land for pure forage production.

The double hedgerows consist of closely planted *Flamengia congesta*, *Glyricidia sepium*, *Desmodium rensonii* and *Leucaena diversifolia*. Napier grass is also planted between the trees. It is reported that a farm of 0.5 ha, with half of the land producing food crops and the other half producing forage for 12 Anglo-Nubian milking does, can produce an income for the family far above the income from a traditional farm in the same area.

Source: IIRR (1990)

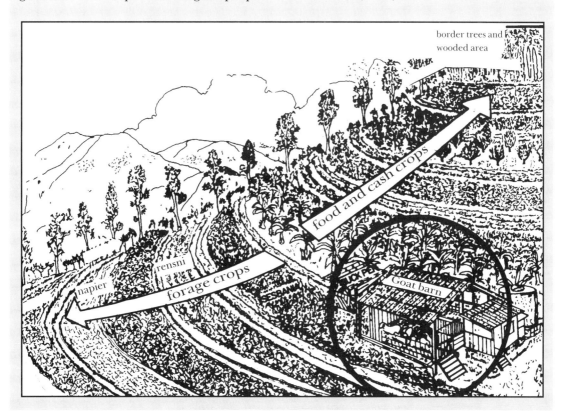

manure, as well as building up soil fertility through the decay of roots and root nodules; livestock feeding is a secondary objective. Green manure from alley farming can completely replace any previous use of chemical fertilisers and plays a part in a long-term sustainable system of crop production. However, increases in crop

Figure 5.7
Sloping Agro-Livestock Technology (SALT 2) in the Philippines

yields take several years to develop, while farmers can get more immediate benefit from the improved feeding of livestock. As a result, it is necessary to develop a balance between using the legume leaves for manure and using them for feed. In most cases, if goats are kept, farmers tend to direct more cuttings towards feeding their animals than manuring their land. However, for the system to be sustainable and crop yields to be maintained, care needs to be exercised in ensuring that sufficient nutrients are directed to the crop, and not exclusively to the goats.

In well-developed alley-farming systems, a large quantity of high-quality livestock feed can be produced and a highly productive goat system can develop as a result.

When and where to promote forage strips

Forage strips should be used

- on sloping land where soil erosion is a problem;
- where good control of livestock is possible;
- where both bulk and quality feeds are scarce.

5.3.6 Undersowing

Undersowing is the planting of forage, normally forage legumes, underneath an existing crop. The crop may be an annual food crop such as maize or sorghum, or a perennial crop such as rubber, coffee, citrus trees, oil palm or coconuts. Undersowing has a number of functions.

- It improves the feeding value of crop residues.
- It provides ground cover and protects against soil erosion.
- It improves soil fertility of the existing and/or following crop.
- If grain legumes are used, it can provide extra food for the family.
- It is one method of establishing long-term pastures.

Undersowing allows farmers to grow both food and cash crops, together with forage. It is therefore very useful in areas where land is scarce. It also serves to control erosion, because it maintains ground cover when the soil would otherwise be exposed, and helps the farmer by suppressing weeds underneath the crop and replacing them with more useful species.

Undersowing in annual crops

Forage species planted underneath an annual crop should be sown soon after the last weeding of the crop, when the maize or sorghum is well established. Planting then will not interfere with the farmer's normal cultural practices. Low seeding rates should be used in areas where soil moisture is likely to be low after the growing season. It is not the aim to have a dense sward. The forage crop will start by growing slowly, because it will be shaded by the main crop, and will not interfere with it. It will grow more rapidly after the main crop has been harvested, and go on growing well into the dry season. After harvesting the crop, the forage can either be rotationally grazed by tethering goats in a different area each day, or it can be cut, carried, and fed to stalled goats.

Undersowing can very quickly increase feed supply with little labour or management, and will leave nitrogen and organic matter in the soil for the crop in the next cropping season. This can be particularly valuable for infertile, sandy soils.

Farmers are likely to be anxious about undersowing a crop of additional 'weeds', underneath their valuable food crop. To start with it is best to plant a small area of the field, so the farmer can see if there is any detrimental effect on the main crop. Once the farmer is convinced that it does no harm, the area can be expanded the next year.

A range of legume species is suitable for undersowing beneath annual crops. The species should have the following characteristics.

- It should be deep-rooting, to allow the plants to continue growing when the rains have stopped and the main crop has been harvested.
- It should retain its green leaves, to increase the feeding value of the stubble or crop residue.
- It should be easy to establish.
- If it is a grain legume, it should need only a short period to mature.

Species such as lablab, vetch, or cowpea are ideal annuals. Species such as desmodium, axillaris, siratro, or a species of stylosanthes are perennials that might be established by undersowing.

Undersowing perennial crops

Shade-tolerant forage crops can be planted underneath perennial crops in plantations or on small farms. It is best to plant them at the same time as the perennial crop, so they can grow quickly before the crop's canopy reduces the sunlight reaching the understorey; the forage crop will protect the soil while the canopy develops. If forage is being introduced into perennial systems, shade-tolerant species, such as centrosema, should be selected. High production from forage crops planted underneath perennial trees should not be expected. Goats can graze underneath trees, or forage can be cut and carried to them. If goats are grazing under trees, they must have enough to eat, or they may resort to eating the bark of the trees. Some difficulty has been found in grazing goats under rubber, because their inquisitive nature leads them to disturb the latex-collection cups.

The key characteristic for species under perennial tree crops is that they should be able to tolerate the shade underneath the tree canopy. Legumes such as centrosema, siratro, and glycine are particularly well adapted to shady conditions. Creeping grasses such as signal grass, para grass, and rhodes grass are most suitable for planting with legumes.

5.3.7 Oversowing and improvement of communal grazing areas

Communal grazing areas in places of high livestock populations are generally over-grazed and may also be severely eroded. As the human population increases and arable land becomes scarce, farmers are forced to cultivate increasingly marginal land — which is usually the community's grazing land. As the livestock population builds up and exerts increasing pressure on the dwindling grazing areas, unpalatable species will become more dominant, because the palatable species will be over-grazed and eventually eliminated. Under severe grazing pressure, little edible vegetation is left and the community's livestock will suffer. This is a common situation in many parts of Africa and Asia.

Improving the quantity and quality of feed from communal grazing areas is not easy. It requires the coordinated effort of the whole community — which can be difficult, but not impossible, to organise. The approach adopted depends on whether or not it is possible to control the livestock currently using the land. Control can be achieved on a voluntary basis through community agreement — which is often done traditionally anyway; or it can be achieved through legislation. If livestock are excluded from the area, regeneration of the existing vegetation can take place

Hezati grazing areas, Ethiopia

In the Tigray region of northern Ethiopia, the *Hezati* system of communal grazing management is under great pressure. Traditionally farmers set aside grazing areas — hillsides or swamps — which cannot otherwise be used for crop production. The grazing is guarded and used by the community only at the end of the dry season. This is a particularly important source of feed to strengthen oxen before the ploughing season. It may also be used by sick cattle, sheep, and goats throughout the year. The *Hezati* areas are managed by a committee. Tigray suffered from famine and civil war during the 1970s and 1980s. In areas where the *Hezati* system broke down but has been reinstated, the indigenous vegetation has made a spectacular recovery. If livestock can be successfully controlled, it would be relatively easy to oversow these areas with improved forage legumes such as *Stylosanthes* spp, which would substantially improve the quality and quantity of forage available, as well as reducing soil erosion.

In parts of Tanzania, over-grazing of community grazing areas is so severe that many local councils pass laws banning the free grazing of livestock species in communal grazing areas. In several areas, livestock are not only banned but have to be confined, with feed cut and carried to them. Heavy fines are imposed on farmers who allow their animals out to graze. In the Dareda area of Babati district, several village committees have banned the grazing of livestock on the steeply sloping forested escarpment spanning the district.

Legislation banning livestock in Tanzania

and it is possible to oversow the area with improved forages. In the absence of stock control, it is much harder to establish new species, because the soil is compacted and the existing vegetation is continuously grazed. Vigorous species must be used to oversow the area lightly, or sow in strips. Heavily-used roadside grazing can also be improved in this way.

Tropical environments are remarkably resilient and have an extraordinary ability to recover from over-use. Excluding livestock from a grazing area permanently, or temporarily, will allow the (sometimes spectacular) regeneration of indigenous vegetation.

If the community do agree to control their livestock, forage species can be planted and will help to improve the regenerating indigenous species. Which species to plant will depend on whether stock can be excluded permanently, and feed cut from the area — in which case they should be highly productive species — or whether there is only a temporary exclusion of livestock — in which case hardy, resilient species should be planted.

If stock control is not possible, oversowing vigorous-growing forage species can still improve forage production and soil fertility at very low cost. It requires little labour, and little or no management. The seed should be broadcast before the start of the rainy season, to give the forage plants the best chance of establishment and survival. Encourage farmers to sow on loose soils, because it is very hard for seeds to germinate on compacted soils. Seeding rates should be low. If the species do survive, they will seed and spread by themselves. Sowing may cover the whole area, or be done in strips, or in small patches where soil has been lightly disturbed, to aid germination and establishment.

Suitable species are stylosanthes, siratro, axillaris, and calopo.

In north-east Thailand, there is such a shortage of grazing for livestock that the only grazing available is along the side of the roads. The quality and quantity of this roadside grazing has been improved by oversowing it with *Stylosanthes* species. The seed was broadcast out of the window of a moving vehicle.

Roadside seeding in Thailand

5.3.8 Fodder crops

Growing a high-yielding, normally annual, crop specifically to feed to goats is not common, but it can be done to supply feed in intensive systems of goat production where land can be set aside for it. Species used might be forage sorghum, maize, oats, and vetch, or fodder beet. Their advantage is that they produce a large quantity of high-quality feed in a short time, but they do require good cultivation and management. Fodder crops might usefully be grown at institutional breeding stations, research stations, or commercial dairy or fattening goat farms.

5.3.9 Permanent grass/legume pasture for goats

Permanent pastures are normally mixtures of grasses and legumes. They can be extremely productive over a long period, with little management, once established. However, they do require land to be permanently set aside, which may not be possible for small farmers, but might be suitable for commercial farms or institutions. Grass/legume pastures produce high-quality forage, improve soil fertility, and can support a large number of highly productive goats.

Figure 5.8 Multi-layered pasture for goats

Pastures can be grazed, but goats should be obliged to graze closely by tethering or fencing them, in order to reduce wastage from trampling and selection. Pastures can also be used in cut-

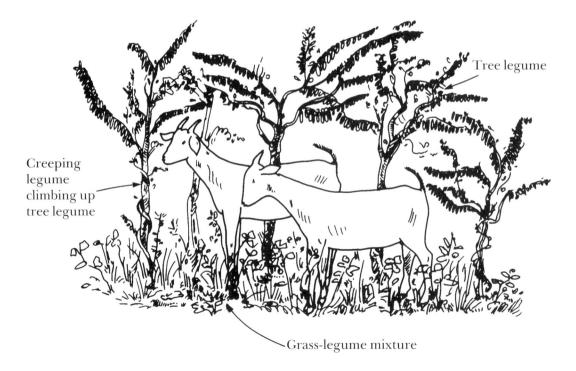

Tree legume

Creeping legume climbing up tree legume

Grass-legume mixture

and-carry systems of feeding. There has been little experience of pastures specifically designed for goats which take into account their particular feeding habits and needs. In any area there is much scope to select species and adapt management systems specifically for goats. If the pasture is to be grazed, planting tree legumes, up which creeping legumes may climb, would allow goats to browse. A multi-layered pasture made up of herbaceous legume, tree legumes, and some grasses, resulting in a high proportion of forage in the browsing zone, would suit goats extremely well (Figure 5.8).

Establishing permanent pastures can be expensive, because high seeding rates need to be used, and because during the first year weeding should be carried out to ensure good establishment. Pastures cannot be used in the first year, unless in areas of high rainfall, which is an additional cost. A well-prepared seedbed is also essential for good germination and survival. Fertiliser may be recommended, but should not be needed if there is a high proportion of legumes in the mixture.

Management of the pasture should be guided by observation of the performance of the pasture itself and the behaviour of the goats. There are no fixed rules. The aim should be to maintain high-quality (i.e. young) forage, maintaining a high proportion of legumes, little stemmy material, and few weeds. Grazing/cutting pressure should be adjusted in order to preserve the most desired species.

Suitable species in a mixture for goats might be:

- **tree legumes:** sesbania, leucaena, pigeon pea and glyricidia;
- **herbaceous legumes:** desmodium, siratro, calopo, axillaris, clover;
- **grasses:** rhodes grass, panic grasses, rye-grass, setaria.

5.3.10 Planning and implementing successful forage development

In order to achieve successful long-term forage development, there are certain conditions which have to be met, including:

- well-motivated farmers;
- initial extension support;
- selection of appropriate forage strategy;
- stock control (total or partial);
- availability of planting material.

First and foremost, farmers must be convinced of the value of forage development for their goat enterprise. Unless farmers make money from the forage, or at least derive some tangible benefit from it for their families, they are unlikely to want to expend effort on developing forage on their farms. Forage development is often a new technology, and farmers may have to gain some direct personal experience of forage growing before they are convinced of its value. Forage development nearly always requires good extension support initially. Farmers should be encouraged to start small and gain experience before expanding the area covered.

Forage extension package for highland farmers in Ethiopia

A forage extension package, consisting of a set of flip charts and guidelines for extension staff, was developed as part of a World Bank-funded livestock project implemented by the Ministry of Agriculture in Ethiopia. The package is designed to be used during a course of eight meetings involving groups of 15–30 farmers. The extension agent is given training in how to use the package as the framework of a course introducing farmers to forage development. The extension agent encourages the group to discuss their present and future needs for forage for their draught cattle, milking cows, young oxen, and small ruminants. Different ways of integrating forage on the farm as well as improving community grazing areas are described and discussed in a series of meetings.

The package has been found to be an effective way of introducing farmers to different means of forage development, and stimulating discussion about how improvement could be made on their own farms. For the package to be used effectively, the extension agent needs good communication skills and a high level of commitment to its use.

Often farmers cite lack of feed as one of their biggest problems, but may be unwilling to set aside land and labour for forage production. There may be good reason for this: perhaps they have to plant forage at the same time as the main crop, and they simply do not have the labour available to do so. Or they accord greater priority to having fruit trees around the house than tree legumes, and no other spare land is available. It is important to be sure that farmers need the forage and that the strategy selected is that one that best fits into their existing system of production.

The control of livestock for some period of time is necessary for nearly every strategy. In up-grading communal grazing areas it may be crucial; for other strategies it may be desirable for a short period only — for example, when tree seedlings have just been planted. Make sure it is possible to control all livestock, not just goats, during the relevant period, or that the new growth is effectively protected in some other way, such as fencing. Many tree seedlings are carefully grown in tree nurseries, only to be destroyed soon after planting out in the field site.

Sufficient quantities of planting materials — seed, cuttings, seedlings — should be available at the correct time. All too often, tree seedlings planted in a large nursery are ready too late, or cannot be delivered to the farmer on time because of lack of transport. This leads to disappointment for all concerned. It is preferable if farmers themselves can be closely involved in nursery management or even have their own individual nurseries. Ultimately farmers should also be responsible for growing their own seeds. This may be at the community or individual level for their own use, or on contract to a purchaser such as a project or government department.

5.3.11 Planting trees, herbaceous legumes, and grasses

There are three ways to plant forage species: by direct seeding; by seedlings; and by cuttings and splits. The choice of method will depend on the species (see Table 5.4), the planting material available, and the situation in which it is to be planted

Direct seeding
Direct seeding is used for all herbaceous legumes and most grasses, and can be used for some tree legumes. Seeds can be broadcast, sown in rows, or sown in patches. Early sowing is usually the key to successful establishment. Sowing can even take place before the rains start, because the seed can survive in the dry soil and be ready to germinate as soon as the rains arrive. This is important in strategies, like oversowing, where plants are likely to have difficulty in becoming established. Dry planting also helps the farmer who is likely to be busy with other cropping activities at the start of the rains.

In strategies such as oversowing that require only low seeding rates, or when sowing species with very small seeds, such as desmodium, it is helpful to mix the seed with sand to ensure an even distribution. When tree legumes are sowed directly into the soil, it is best to sow 2–3 seeds per hole.

When planting trees in soils of low fertility, it has been found to be helpful to roll the seed in a small ball of manure, to give it a small source of nutrients just after germination.

When using strategies such as permanent grass/legume pastures, where much seed has to be sown for the success of the strategy, it is advisable to carry out a simple test of the germination capacity of the seed. Germination declines with age, especially if the seed is stored in damp conditions. Try to keep seed dry and use it when fresh. If germination is found to be low, seeding rates should be increased to compensate.

A germination test is conducted as follows.

1 Cover the bottom of a shallow tray with blotting paper or layers of tissue paper. Moisten the paper. Do not make it too wet, or the seeds will rot.
2 Count 100 seeds of the species or mixture to be tested, and scatter them evenly on the tray.
3 Leave the tray to stand.
4 Keep the paper moist all the time.
5 Count the seeds that germinate every day.
6 After one week, most of the seeds will have germinated. Calculate how many seeds have germinated and divide by 100. This is the germination percentage.

Some legumes require a treatment in order to break dormancy and ensure more even germination. This is particularly important for tree legumes being raised in tree nurseries, where a batch of trees are sown and raised at the same time. However, for direct seeding, if rainfall is very uneven and likely to start and then stop for a long period, it is best to sow a mixture of treated and untreated seeds, to ensure that at least some seeds germinate and get established.

The following method of seed treatment is suitable for most species.

1 Boil a container of water.
2 Remove from the heat and immerse the seed in a porous bag such as a jute sack for 5–10 minutes. The length of time for soaking varies according to species. Species such as leucaena or tree lucerne need to be boiled for 3–5 minutes. Alternative treatments, such as scalding and soaking the seed for 24 hours, or manually scarifying the seed, require much labour.

Another form of treatment is called **seed inoculation**. Legumes are able to trap atmospheric nitrogen in the soil by establishing a relationship with a bacterium called rhizobium which lives in the soil. The bacterium establishes itself by developing small nodules on the roots. There are several strains of the bacterium and, although different strains can trap nitrogen to some degree, there are certain strains that are able to do this more efficiently than others. Some legumes require to be inoculated with a specific strain of rhizobium before sowing, to ensure good growth and nitrogen fixation. This is particularly important if the legume is new to the area. Inoculation simply means sticking some of the bacteria on to the surface of the seed when it is planted. In this way nodules will quickly develop on the young plant's roots and it will quickly start trapping nitrogen for the benefit of its host plant. Inoculating legumes with the correct rhizobium is the ideal method of planting them. But not all legumes require inoculation, and the rhizobium is often hard to obtain and requires cold storage when it has been procured. For all these reasons most legumes in the tropics are not inoculated before planting. In some cases this may result in a complete failure to grow (this is often the reason why leucaena does not grow well), and so either the inoculant must be obtained or use of the species should be avoided. To check if a legume is nodulating properly, simply dig it up and look at the roots and see if the root nodules exist and are full and hard. Nodules will reduce in size during the dry season, when nitrogen fixation is limited by the lack of moisture. An alternative means of obtaining an inoculant is to find a growing, healthy specimen of the species to be planted and to dig up some soil from around the tree. This soil is likely to contain the right strain of rhizobium. Mix this soil with the legume seed before planting.

If inoculation is carried out, a sticking agent is required. Common sticking agents are 40 per cent gum arabic in water or 4 per cent methyl cellulose in water. A simpler agent is to make a very concentrated sugar solution in water. Mix the inoculant and sticking agent together and then add the seeds. This mixing can be done in a strong plastic bag. Continue mixing until all the seeds are coated. Take them out and dry them in a cool place. Sow as soon as possible. Do not store the seed for more than three days; after that, the inoculation process should be repeated.

Figure 5.9 A legume root: the grass stalk points to nodulation
JENNY MATTHEWS/OXFAM

Seedlings

Tree legumes can be planted as potted seedlings or bare-root seedlings, by direct seeding, or cuttings. Seedlings grown in plastic pots or polythene bags have very high survival rates when planted out, but producing them is expensive. The plastic containers have to be obtained, much labour is involved, and it may be difficult to transport them to their planting sites. Ideally the nursery would be close to the final planting sites, so that farmers can transport their own seedlings. Unfortunately large government nurseries are often far from the community.

Bare-root seedlings are grown in a large bed. Before planting out, the leaves should be stripped off and the seedlings carefully lifted out of the bed. They are planted in the same way as potted seedlings, but they are much cheaper to produce and easier to manage and transport. Unfortunately their survival rates are lower than potted seedlings. Once lifted out of the bed, they should be planted out quickly.

The major advantage of planting tree legumes as seedlings is that it gives the trees an early start in the growing season. Trees may be two–three months old at planting time, which should be at the start of the wet season. This gives them a good chance of surviving the first year and getting well established.

Tree seedlings can be grown in government/NGO nurseries; community nurseries; and individual nurseries. The management

Figure 5.10 Bare-root planting: sesbania seedling
JENNY MATTHEWS/OXFAM

of a large government or NGO nursery is beyond the scope of this book. However, nurseries managed by communities or by individual farmers in their own house compounds should be encouraged in goat-development programmes. If farmers become involved in preparing their own tree seedlings, they will feel responsible for the trees' future care.

Konso, Ethiopia: a tree nursery run by women

Women involved in a goat project in Konso, south-west Ethiopia, were encouraged by local extension staff to plant leucaena trees around their houses and in their fields. The local NGO had a tree nursery near one village and ran the nursery, giving tree seedlings free to any farmer who wanted them. One year the NGO supplied tree seedlings late, towards the end of the rains. Most of the seedlings died. Some seedlings survived, because the women carried water to them throughout the dry season. Frustrated, the women asked if they could take over one of the nursery beds and raise their own trees. The NGO agreed and supplied them with seed and polythene tubes. The next year the trees were ready in time for the start of the rains, and the NGO found the women to be so efficient that some of them were employed full-time in the nursery.

Community tree nurseries

Members of the community involved in goat development may decide to get together and run their own tree nursery. This may be on a voluntary basis, or they might be paid in food, or cash, for the work they do. All that is needed is a small level area, close to a water source and protected from livestock. A source of good soil for the beds is also important and protection against wind may also be necessary. Bed-width should be about one metre (about one pace) wide, with 0.5 metre walk-ways in between. Lengths can vary according to the size of the site. A bed one pace wide and three paces long is big enough for about 100 seedlings. If plastic containers are not used, sink the beds below the surface of the soil, so that they hold the water given to the seedlings. If the sun is very strong, a simple shade should be constructed over the beds so that the seedlings do not wither (Figure 5.11).

Seedlings may be distributed free to those who worked in the nursery and sold to those who did not. Either way a value has been placed on the tree, which is important in order for people to appreciate them fully.

It may also be beneficial to get schools involved in raising trees. Helping a school establish a small tree nursery can have a long-term impact on tree planting in a community. Children can work in the nursery and take home forage and fruit trees. Perhaps

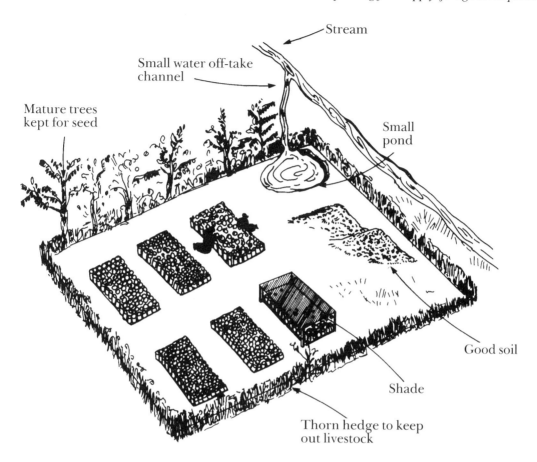

Stream

Small water off-take
channel

Mature trees
kept for seed

Small
pond

Good soil

Shade

Thorn hedge to keep
out livestock

*Figure 5.11 The key
features of a
community tree nursery*

prizes can be given for the pupil, or class, achieving the best tree-survival rates. Children can quickly learn the value of trees for their family and can even help to educate the other members of their family.

Individual nurseries

A farmer and his or her family can develop their own small tree nursery close to the house (Figure 5.12). This is often a good project for children to take part in. A small plot, even as small as 1 m x 1 m, is enough to start. The soil should be well cultivated and seeds directly sown into the plot. It is more convenient if the bed can be raised slightly and water seepage prevented by wooden barriers around the edge of the plot, but this is not essential. In this way it is easier to lift out the seedlings for planting. If wooden battens are not available, the plot should be level with the soil surface, so that water is retained. This is very important, because in most back-yard nurseries water has to be carried to the seedlings, and so it must be used efficiently.

Figure 5.12 A woman weeding sesbania in her own tree nursery, Hararghe, Ethiopia

JENNY MATTHEWS/OXFAM

It is a good idea in individual nurseries to start by using tree species which are very easy to grow. This encourages those involved.

Cuttings

Cuttings are an easy and cheap way of propagating some forage species, particularly glyricidia and some grasses, such as elephant grass.

Tree legumes: Cuttings from tree legumes should be taken from mature branches. Cut woody sections 30–50 cm long, about the length of an arm and about the thickness of a thumb. The sections should be cut at a 45-degree angle. Do not allow the cuttings to dry out: plant them quickly into a moist site. Trees planted from cuttings tend to develop a very superficial root system, which may make them vulnerable to periods of drought. Trees planted from seedlings develop a deeper root system and can better withstand dry periods.

Grass cuttings and splits: Elephant grass is propagated by cutting the mature stem and planting sections 20–30 cm long at an angle in the soil. If the soil is moist, survival rates can be excellent. Elephant grass cuttings should not be planted straight down during the rainy season, or the rain may rot the cutting before the nodules have sprouted. At least half the cutting must be below the surface at an angle, with a nodule just visible. Planting too high may cause the cutting to dry out (Figure 5.13).

Figure 5.13 Planting elephant grass with the cut face angled towards the ground, to prevent it from trapping rain-water and rotting

JENNY MATTHEWS/OXFAM

Many erect grasses, such as guinea grass and phalaris, can be propagated by splits. Cut the grass low, then dig it up carefully and separate it into splits and plant. Creeping grasses can be planted using runners. Cut a section with at least three nodes and bury it so that only a very small part is exposed.

Seed supply

Once forage growing becomes a firmly established practice, the supply of planting material must be ensured. Plants may age and die and need to be replanted; farmers may want to expand their forage area; new farmers are likely to become interested in forage growing and will need a source of seeds, seedlings, and cuttings. In some countries there is a well-developed structure for supplying seeds through extension staff or commercial retailers. These countries have their own seed farms and may even export forage seeds. In most countries in the tropics, forage crops are not widely grown and it is hard for farmers to obtain planting material. But once they are introduced to forage species and convinced of their value, provision must be made to maintain a supply of seeds and other planting material. How can this be done?

A government or NGO project promoting forage development should be able to organise the contract production of seed, seedlings, cuttings, and splits, either for sale to the project for subsequent delivery to farmers, or for sale directly to farmers. If a good price is offered, farmers will become interested in growing forage for seed and it can become a valuable cash crop. Guidance should be given on how to grow the species for seed, and a price should be guaranteed for production of seed of a clearly specified quality.

On individual farms, the farmers should be able to multiply their own forage species without external help. A farmer might set aside two or three trees for tree-legume seed-production, for use in his or her own tree nursery. Elephant grass can be allowed to grow and cuttings can be taken from it to expand the area on the farm. Community nurseries may leave a few trees around the edge of the nursery and allow them to flower and set seed for collection and use in the nursery. In this way whole communities can become independent of outside seed suppliers.

Some of the herbaceous legumes and grasses may be difficult for farmers to grow for seed, and the seed may have to be obtained from outside the community; but farmers should be encouraged to become as self-sufficient as possible in the forage species they need.

5.4 Feed conservation

In most parts of the tropics, the supply of feeds fluctuates through the seasons. Preserving surplus feed in the wet season for use in the dry season is one method of making the supply of feed to goats more evenly distributed through the year. There are two main methods of preserving feed: drying and making silage.

5.4.1 Drying

For use in the dry season, crop residues are commonly preserved, either in the field or in the farmer's house for storage. But natural and improved grass, herbaceous legumes, and tree legumes can also be dried and stored for later use.

Grass can be cut, wilted, dried, and stored in a stack or tied in a bundle or bale of hay. In order to make high-quality hay, the grass should be cut quite young. If it is left to grow past the flowering stage, a greater quantity of hay will be harvested, but it will be of lower quality. In order to balance quality and quantity, a compromise is to cut the hay when about half the grass has just flowered. It should be cut on a dry day and left in the field. It should be turned over at least once to ensure even drying. It will probably take about two days to dry sufficiently for storage. Unfortunately, in the tropics, the time of year when grass is growing is also the time of year when it is raining, so the cut hay is quite likely to get wet. This reduces the quality slightly, but efforts to dry it should continue. If the rain is very heavy, it is not worth trying to make hay. Hay-making should not be attempted until the end of the wet season, when the rain is stopping. Once made, the hay must be stored in a dry place. If the hay cannot be kept under a waterproof roof, a tightly packed stack will keep most of it dry. Ideally the stack would be raised off the ground, but this might not be possible. In some places farmers use a hay box to make a tightly packed bale, tied with string (Figure 5.14).

In places with a long severe dry season, tree legumes may lose their leaves during the driest period. Rather than being wasted, the leaves can be collected, dried, and used as a protein supplement. Herbaceous legumes such as desmodium can also be dried and stored. High-quality hay, relished by goats, can be made from desmodium. It should be cut and carried to the place of storage when green, to avoid losses from the shattering of leaves. Once dry, leaves tend to fall off the stems and can be lost completely if left in the field — although goats can be put into the field to eat fallen leaves off the ground. Once collected and dried, legume hay can be stored in a stack. Tree-legume branches should be cut and the leaves allowed to dry on the branch. They can then be easily

Figure 5.14 Hay-box construction

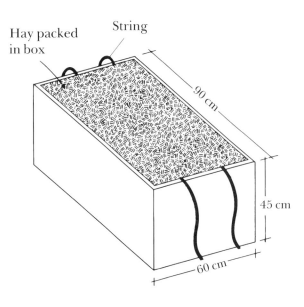

Hay packed in box

String

90 cm

45 cm

60 cm

stripped off the branch and stored in a sack as a protein supplement for later feeding.

Cutting, turning, transporting, and storing hay requires much labour and should not be attempted except in the absence of any alternative feed source in the dry season.

Grass can also be left standing in a field or grazing area to dry. If livestock are excluded, this standing hay can be a useful dry-season feed. It has a much lower digestibility and lower protein content than cut hay, because the stem becomes increasingly lignified as it dries out. Standing hay can be a useful feed and it takes no labour to preserve. Leaving standing hay in grazing areas is a common method used by pastoralists for preserving feed for the dry season.

5.4.2 Silage

If green feed is allowed to ferment in the absence of air, it can be preserved in a good state for later feeding. The product made is called **silage**. This technique is much used in temperate countries. The process of making silage requires bacteria to produce lactic acid, increasing the acid content of the feed and preserving it. If the acid content is high enough, unwelcome micro-organisms cannot grow and the feed is preserved. In order for this to happen, the bacteria need a source of energy. Some crops such as whole maize plants, which have developing grain in their immature cobs, can supply energy, and can be ensiled by themselves. Other tropical forages will need the addition of a source of energy, such as molasses, in order to ferment successfully.

The green feed should be packed very tightly into a pit, or in bags in a pit, and sealed so that no air can enter. Ideally a plastic sheet and stones, or banana leaves and stones, should be placed on top of the pit to seal it, and then people should jump up and down on the contents.

Very little high-quality silage is made in the tropics. Silage making requires the quick cutting of all the forage to be ensiled, and so demands much labour or machinery. The silage pit requires good sealing and possibly the addition of molasses. Rather than risk wasting the feed altogether and making unpalatable silage, rejected by selective goats, it is probably best to make lower-quality hay with any excess feed. Large farms and institutions might be able to make good-quality silage, but it is a difficult, labour-intensive, technology for small farmers.

5.5 Improving the quality of feed and the quantity eaten

In nearly every goat-production system in the tropics, goats will have to eat, at some time of the year, feeds that contain a lot of fibre

Table 5.5 Typical nutritional values of some fibrous residues

Feed	Dry matter (%)	Crude protein (%)	Crude fibre (%)	Digestibility of crude fibre (%)
Cereal crop residues				
Maize stover	85	7.0	34	65
Wheat straw	90	3.6	42	61
Sorghum straw	85	6.0	33	74
Barley straw	92	4.2	35	55
Rice straw	91	4.6	36	60

(Table 5.5). These feeds may be coarse grass, crop residues such as maize stover or rice straw, or legume crop residues such as peanut stover. All these feeds have a lot of indigestible fibre in them, making it difficult for the goat to digest them and release the nutrients they contain. Goats will struggle to eat these feeds and, once inside them, the feed has to remain in the rumen for a long time before it is digested sufficiently to move out of the rumen and allow more feed in. These feeds thus create double trouble for the goat, supplying it with few nutrients and also reducing the amount it is able to eat. It is common, when fed only these low-quality feeds, for goats to lose weight and condition, produce little milk, and even have difficulty breeding.

There are two methods of increasing the quality of these fibrous feeds and so increasing the amount which the goat eats:

- to treat the residues physically or chemically, to make degradation by rumen micro-organisms easier;
- to supplement the residues with energy and protein to enable the rumen micro-organisms to be very active in breaking down the fibrous feeds.

5.5.1 Treatment of fibrous feeds

Three main treatments can be applied to residues such as straws: chopping; treatment with sodium hydroxide; treatment with urea.

Chopping
When goats are stall-fed, chopping residues, such as rice straw or maize stovers, can improve the amount they are able to eat. The

goat, being a small animal, has a small mouth, and prefers to pick its own feed from a tree or bush using its agile jaws, rather than having to chew its way through large quantities of coarse, unpalatable, feed. When faced with a feed like maize stover, they can commonly be seen struggling to bite an edible mouthful off a stalk, sometimes even resorting to standing on one end of the stalk in order to have something to pull against, and biting off part of the stalk. If residues have to be fed, it will help the goat if they can be chopped into small, mouth-sized, pieces which can be easily eaten. Chopping some of the coarser green feeds such as elephant grass will also increase the amount eaten. This chopping can simply be done by a machete knife. There are also special manual or motor-driven choppers which are very efficient (Figure 5.15).

Treatment with sodium hydroxide

In some parts of the world, the finer straws from rice, wheat, or barley are treated with an alkali such as sodium hydroxide (NaOH) or caustic soda. Alkalis attack the cellulose in the straw, making it easier for the micro-organisms to attack them in the rumen. Unfortunately, strong solutions of sodium hydroxide can be dangerous when spilt on the skin or eye, so special clothes and gloves have to be worn and great care taken. Because of this it is a technology that is appropriate only for farmers who are used to handling chemicals.

Treatment with urea

A much safer chemical treatment of straws is to use urea. Urea has many advantages over sodium hydroxide. It is easier to obtain, it is not toxic, and it also supplies some nitrogen for use by the rumen micro-organisms. The effect of urea treatment on rice straw is shown in Table 5.6. It is clear that the effect is quite small and is the result of a combination of increased digestibility and increased intake. The effect may be significant in some systems. If there are no tree leaves or grass available, urea treatment may be an option for some goat keepers. It might be suitable in intensively cultivated irrigated rice systems, where there is little room for forage growing, but where there is a copious supply of rice straw which is normally burned and wasted. In some parts of the Sahel, millet

Figure 5.15 Using a manually operated chopping machine. Chopping by hand would be cheaper and more appropriate for a small flock.

Jenny Matthews/Oxfam

Table 5.6 The effect of urea treatment on rice straw

	Before treatment	**After treatment**
Crude protein	3–5%	7–10%
Digestibility	40–50%	45–55%
In-take		+20–40%

stover is even collected from fields and sold in town for dry-season feed. For the effect to be best appreciated, the goat should be offered as much treated straw as it can eat. Ideally if any production above a maintenance level is desired, a protein and/or energy supplement should also be fed.

Urea treatment procedure
Straws can be treated either in a stack or in a pit in the ground.

1 The straw is stacked or put into a pit. The bottom of the stack should be on waterproof plastic sacks, or plastic sheeting. The pit should be lined with plastic sheeting.
2 The urea solution should be poured over the straw at 40 g urea in 900 ml water per kg straw (i.e. 200 g/4.5 litres/5 kg) to make a feed of 50 per cent moisture. Using a watering can or knapsack sprayer to apply the urea solution ensures an even distribution throughout the straw.
3 The stack or pit is then sealed with plastic and left for three weeks.
4 After three weeks it should be opened and allowed to ventilate. A strong smell of ammonia will be released; this smell must fade before feeding the treated straw.

Farmers should always use the best-quality straw available and store it in a stack before treatment. It is best to treat small batches of straw, because it will not keep for long, once treated and opened to the air.

5.5.2 Supplementation

The physiological principles behind supplementation have been described in Section 4.6. It is important first to identify the deficiency in the current diet. Most tropical feeds have a high fibre-content. When thinking about supplementing any fibrous feed, think about how to feed the rumen micro-organisms with the nutrients they need to be active, and then think about directly feeding the goat. Fibrous feeds contain low levels of protein.

Table 5.7 Ranking of common supplements

	Energy	Protein	Cost
Legume leaves			
Leucaena	•	• •	•
Glyricidia	•	• •	•
Sesbania	•	• •	•
Desmodium	•	• •	•
Cereal by-products			
Rice bran	• •	• •	• •
Wheat bran	• •	• •	• •
Brewers' grain	• •	• •	• •
Oil by-products			
Peanut cake	• • •	• • •	• • •
Linseed cake	• •	• • •	• • •
Cotton seed meal	• • •	• • •	• • •
Coconut cake	• •	• •	• •
Fruit and vegetables			
Cassava whole	• • •	•	• •
Cassava leaves	• •	• •	•
Sweet potato (whole)	• •	•	• •
Sweet-potato vines	• •	• •	•
Banana peelings	•	•	•
Sugar-cane tops	•	•	•
Molasses	• • •	•	• • •
Animal origin			
Fish meal	• •	• • •	• • •
Poultry manure	•	• • •	•

Micro-organisms require both energy and protein to multiply and enable them to attack the fibrous feed and break it down.

There are many feeds in the tropics that can be used as supplements. Table 5.7 lists some of the common supplements and rates them as sources of energy and protein. There are very few energy supplements that are not consumed directly by people as well as by goats. Whole grains or roots or sweet fruit are the best sources of energy that can easily be used by micro-organisms. Obviously they should be used only where there is an unwanted surplus of these foods which humans also consume. Otherwise there are few energy-rich supplements, apart from the by-products of 'human' foods such as oil cakes or by-products from milling. Obtaining these will cost the farmer money and they should not be used unless it is clearly profitable to do so.

Purchasing protein supplements is expensive. Avoiding expenditure on supplements is an important reason for growing forage legumes whenever possible.

Mineral supplements

Mineral deficiencies are often hard to detect, because their only effect may be to lower production — which can be caused by several different factors, such as poor nutrition or poor general health. Once mineral deficiencies become pronounced, they are easier to identify, because the symptoms are obvious (see Table 6.15). Kids may be born with bone deformities or muscle stiffness, or hair starts to fall out. In almost every goat system there is likely to be a deficiency of one or more mineral, and goats would benefit from supplementation. In some areas there are well-known deficiencies, such as copper deficiency in the Rift Valley in East Africa.

Ideally goats would receive a specially-formulated mineral supplement in the form of a mineral lick, but in practice this can seldom be achieved. Supplements are not manufactured in every country in the tropics; even if they are, they are seldom widely distributed, except to high-yielding dairy cows near urban centres. In practice, farmers have to rely on locally available minerals, which are likely to be just as deficient as the vegetation. Locally-mined minerals are sometimes traded and find their way to more remote markets. It might be useful to try them, to see if there is any response. Plain cooking salt should be fed where possible: in hot climates, goats will be losing salts all the time and would undoubtedly like, and benefit from, a salt supplement. The mineral nutrition of lactating goats requires special attention. Legumes of all sorts are richer in minerals, particularly calcium and phosphorus, than grasses or stovers.

Internal parasites

All goats in the tropics carry a burden of internal parasites, which rely on their host for nutrients, either (like *Haemonchus contortus* and *Bunostomum spp*) by sucking blood directly, or (like *Moniezia* spp) by actually consuming partially digested food in the intestinal tract. They place a burden on the goat, which has to support these parasites as well as itself. If farmers decide to put resources, whether labour or money, into supplying food supplements, they should also be encouraged to relieve the goat's parasite burden and spend extra money on anthelmintic drugs (see section 6.4.1). Otherwise the goat will not benefit from the extra nutrients, and farmers will be wasting money.

5.5.3 Improving feed intake: methods of feeding goats

The method of physically presenting food to goats is crucial, yet it has received little attention from researchers. It is important, because it can affect the amount a goat eats, as well as the amount it wastes. If feed has been specially grown, or collected, it is a great waste not to feed it as carefully as possible.

When designing a feeding method, take account of the following factors.

- Goats like to browse, so raise the feed high off the ground.
- Goats are very selective feeders and can waste much of what is offered to them. Ways must be found either to reduce waste feed or to keep fallen feed from being trampled and contaminated.
- There must be enough space at the feeder for all goats to be fed easily without fighting. Young goats should be fed separately from older goats, to avoid competition and trampling.
- If the place where the goats are to be fed is hot and exposed to the sun, the animals' appetite will be depressed. Goats will eat more in a cool and shady place than in a place exposed to direct sunlight.
- The floor must be clean and dry. If goats have to stand for hours on wet and dirty ground, they are likely to develop foot problems. If the ground is clean under the rack or net, then any feed that drops down is more likely to be acceptable if offered again than if it is immediately made dirty by mud and faeces on the ground.
- Think about what materials are available for constructing the feeder. Is there timber, metal or rope?

Bundle and net

The simplest way to feed a small amount of forage is to tie it in a bundle and suspend it from a tree, or from the roof of the farmer's house. The bundle needs to be tied as tight as possible, because goats will pull quite hard. A better method is to make a simple rope net, pack the feed into it, and then suspend the net. The net reduces wastage considerably and is easy to make.

Figure 5.16 A tied bundle of leucaena

INTERNATIONAL LIVESTOCK RESEARCH INSTITUTE

Feed rack

Feed racks can be made from wood or metal. The wood does not have to be cut timber: tree branches will do nearly as well, provided that they are smooth. The height of the rack will depend on the height of the goats. It should be high enough for them to have to reach up and pull the feed down, but not so high that they decide it is less tiring to climb into the rack to eat! Young goats, especially, finding it tiring to eat from an adult-height rack, are prone to jump on top of the rack, and may trap and even break a leg in the gaps between the bars.

Take a goat of average size and extend its head and neck upwards until it is at full stretch. This height should be half-way up the feeding section of the rack. The width between the bars will vary according to the size of the goats and the sort of feed being fed. Fine grass will quickly fall through gaps designed to trap desmodium. Experiment until the gap is the right width for the goats and the feed in question.

The rack may be free-standing or attached to a wall for support. Ideally a tray or second rack would be placed underneath, to catch smaller bits of feed that fall through and prevent them from being soiled on the ground. This feed can be collected and mixed in with fresh batches.

Feeding supplements

Goats can be given feed supplements in various ways: wet or dry, with or without salt, rolled or ground. Farmers should experiment, to find the best method of feeding different supplements, to ensure that they are eaten and not wasted. Goats, like most ruminants, seem to like eating supplements as a gruel rather than as a dry feed. A wooden or clay bowl can be used. Ideally it should be raised and supported, to stop it being knocked over.

Feeding chopped feeds such as elephant grass is difficult with a rack. They should be fed on a tray or in a bowl.

Introduction of new feeds

It is a common misunderstanding that goats will eat anything! This is not true. If goats are allowed to graze freely, they will select a wide-ranging diet, but they can be very fussy when confined and presented with new feeds. Although goats can be persuaded to eat most feeds, they can remain resolute in their rejection of some. It is a common complaint that when glyricidia is introduced for the first time, goats initially reject it, and may take several weeks to get used to it. Some oil cakes have a strong smell, which goats may take time to get used to. If it smells or tastes disgusting to you, it will not be acceptable to the goat.

Provided that the feed is clean and uncontaminated, goats can learn to eat most feeds. There are various stratagems that can be used. Always present the new feed to them when they are hungry. Mixing the new feed into a favourite feed will normally oblige them to eat a little of the new feed inadvertently. Mixing the new feed with something much liked, such as molasses or salt, will also encourage them to eat it. If all else fails, simply force them to eat it or go hungry. If they have not eaten at least part of it after one or two days, they never will!

Figure 5.17 A simple feeding rack
JENNY MATTHEWS/OXFAM

5.6 Feeding special goats

In situations of scarce feed resources, or when spending money on feed supplements, it is sensible for the farmer to target scarce or expensive resources on goats that will bring the most reward. The engine of the flock is the breeding female. If she is expected to produce healthy kids regularly, she must be fed enough to do so. If she is also expected to supply milk for human consumption, she will need special feeding to do so. Likewise kids, once produced, deserve special care, because they are vulnerable to poor nutrition and may quickly die because of it.

Fattening young males for sale is an income-generating option for many goat farmers in the tropics. If supplements are purchased, they should be used to their best economic benefit.

5.6.1 Feeding the doe

The doe needs food for maintenance, activity, gestation, lactation for kid(s), lactation for humans, and recuperation.

In addition to looking after herself, the doe needs extra energy and protein to produce young ones, and then to produce milk to feed them. This is a huge nutritional demand. If, in addition to feeding her kid(s), she is expected to produce excess milk for human use, then this is a large extra burden. During lactation, unless very well fed, the doe will have to use her own body reserves and so will lose weight. After lactation she will need a period of recuperation before producing more offspring. In extreme conditions, if the doe is under-nourished she may not show signs of oestrus and so cannot be mated until she has regained weight. For an efficient goat system, does should kid regularly if possible, but in order to do so they need good feeding.

Figure 5.18 Energy and protein demands of a doe during pregnancy and during lactation

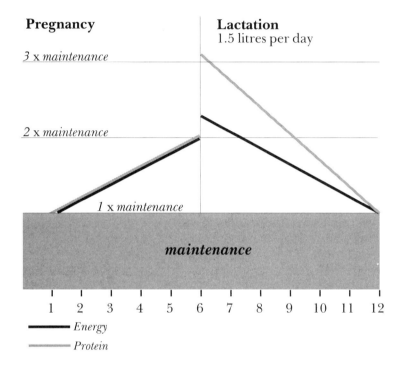

Figure 5.18 shows the energy and protein requirements of a 30 kg doe that is mated in month 1, becomes pregnant, kids in month 6, and starts her lactation by yielding 1.5 kg milk, which declines to zero in month 12. This figure is presented to indicate how much more energy and protein a doe requires for a successful pregnancy and productive lactation. It also indicates how much she will have to take out of herself if the extra feed is not provided. By the end of the pregnancy the doe has doubled her protein and energy requirements. Lactation starting at 1.5 kg trebles the goat's requirement for protein and doubles its requirement for energy.

Based on the data in Tables 4.4, 4.5, 4.6 and 4.7, Table 5.8 shows the quantities of different feeds needed by a 30 kg doe in order to meet her requirements for maintenance, pregnancy, and lactation. It is considered unrealistic to expect the doe to eat more than 4.0 per cent of her liveweight.

Table 5.8 Quantity of different feeds required by a 30 kg pregnant and then lactating doe yielding 1.5 kg milk/day

Requirements	Maintenance		Pregnancy		Lactation	
	Energy 5.3 MJ ME/day	Protein 35 g DCP/day	Energy 11.5 MJ ME/day	Protein 67 g DCP/day	Energy 12.8 MJ ME/day	Protein 102.5 g DCP/day
Young grass						
Dry matter	0.7	0.5	1.4	0.9	1.6	1.4
Fresh weight	4.4	3.1	9.6	6.0	10.7	9.0
Intake (% liveweight)	2.3	1.7	4.6!	3.0	5.3!	4.6!
Legume leaves						
Dry matter	0.5	0.3	1.2	0.6	1.3	0.8
Fresh weight	2.6	1.5	5.7	2.8	6.4	4.3
Intake (% liveweight)	1.7	1.0	4.0	2.0	4.3!	2.7
Roots						
Dry matter	0.5	1.4	1.1	2.7	1.2	4.1
Fresh weight	1.5	4.2	3.2	8.1	3.6	12.3
Intake (% liveweight)	1.7	4.6!	3.6	9.0!	4.0	13.7!!

In order to calculate the balance of feeds required for a specific requirement, Pearson's square can be used. The box on the next page shows how to calculate the protein requirement estimated at 103 g/day, from a combination of young grass and legume leaves.

It is a good idea to practise using the tables given in Chapter 4, to calculate the energy and protein requirements of a doe at different times of her life and to consider how these might be met from the feeds available. Think how long she will have to suckle her kid; and, if she is going to be milked, how long she can be milked. Once the lactation length is decided, a simple seasonal calendar of feed demand can be estimated. Is there a deficit? How can this be overcome?

An alternative to altering the feed supply to meet the demands of the goat is to manipulate the feed demand of the doe to match the available feed supply (Figure 5.19). Breeding can be controlled

Balance of young grass and legume leaves needed to supply 103 g protein for lactation

On the left side, write the protein content of the two feeds, obtained from Table 4.7 (lower values); in the middle, write the target protein requirement. For each feed, calculate the difference between its protein content and the target, e.g. 120 — 103 = 17. Write the difference on the opposite side of the target figure. The ratio of these differences indicates the balance of these two feeds that must be eaten to supply the needed protein.

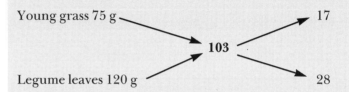

Young grass 75 g ⟶ **103** ⟶ 17

Legume leaves 120 g ⟶ **103** ⟶ 28

In this case, 17 parts young grass should be fed to 28 parts legume leaves; in other words, for every 1 part of young grass fed, 1.6 parts of legume leaves should also be fed.

in most systems of production, and many goat farmers in different parts of the world do control the time of mating so that kids are born when the feed supply is at its best (see section 7.2.2). For example, the Maasai in Kenya use a leather apron to control mating, and there are other devices that can be used. But remember that, although the kid may be born at the best time of year, it may be weaned, three to four months later, at a very difficult time of year.

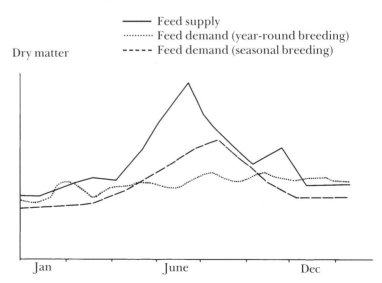

Figure 5.19 Breeding season matched with feed supply

In addition to feed, the dam has a high requirement for water during lactation. If she does not receive enough water, her milk production will be restricted and the kid may suffer and even die.

A dam should receive 4 litres of water for every kilo of dry matter that she eats, and 1.3 litres for every litre of milk she produces.

How much water?

A 30 kg doe eats 3 per cent of her body weight in dry matter = 0.9 kg DM per day.

She requires 4 litres of water per kg DM eaten = 4 x 0.9 = 3.6 litres

and 1.3 litres of water per litre of milk produced.

If she produces 1.5 litres of milk per day, she needs 1.95 litres of water.

Rounding up these figures, we can say that the TOTAL water required = 3.6 + 2.0 = 5.6 litres of water per day.

5.6.2 Feeding the kid

The kid is born with a partially developed rumen and needs milk or a milk substitute for the first few weeks of its life, while its rumen develops to digest fibrous food. If the kid and dam were in their natural state, the kid would be following its mother as she grazed, suckling on demand. The dam is producing milk all the time, and the kid is able to suckle only a small amount of milk at one time. Its natural rhythm is to suckle a little, sleep a little, follow its mother and suckle again. When goats are domesticated, this natural rhythm is disturbed. The goat keeper may want some of the milk for the family and may have to restrict the amount taken by the kid. Dairy-goat farms in developed countries will rear female kids on a purchased milk-replacer diet, and may slaughter unwanted male kids at birth, to ensure that all milk produced is sold.

If the doe is milked, then the kid should be allowed to suckle at least twice a day. The presence of the kid at milking encourages the doe to let down all the milk in her udder. The kid may be allowed to suckle one teat, while the other is milked (see 10.1.1). The teat milked and the teat suckled should be changed from morning to evening milking. The kid should be allowed to suckle out both teats at the end of milking, to avoid mastitis (see 6.4.9).

If the doe is not milked, the kid may be allowed to suckle regularly. If the doe is housed all day, the kid could be with the dam continuously, unless the doe is feeding with other goats which may knock over the kid. A way around this is to have a kid box which only kids can get into, or a second pen for kids, separated by a wall with a gap at the bottom through which kids may creep and suckle and then return to the other pen. If these arrangements do not work, the kids should be kept separately in a draught-free place, out of excessive heat or cold, and put with their mothers three or four times per day.

If the dam is out grazing all day, the kid should be allowed to suckle on its mother's return and be allowed to stay with its mother all night. Ideally the dam would return in the middle of grazing to allow the kid to suckle, but if the dam is far away, this may be difficult to arrange. Suckling only twice a day will reduce kid growth and make the kid susceptible to malnutrition and disease.

The kids will start nibbling on bits of vegetation one week after birth. They should be encouraged to do so, because this is how the rumen micro-organisms are acquired. However, kids are very susceptible to infections and to picking up parasites when they are very young; so they should be provided with high-quality clean feed, such as sweet-potato vines or tree legume leaves or natural tree leaves (Figure 5.20).

Figure 5.20 Sweet-potato vines hung to feed recently weaned kids

Christie Peacock

If kids' suckling time is restricted, they may also need additional water, particularly in very hot climates. If they are allowed to wander freely, they will search for water and may pick up infections from drinking in dirty puddles. Provide a source of clean water for the kid.

Kids may be able to go out grazing with their dams when about six weeks old, provided that they do not have to walk too far. Weaning should take place when the kid has reached about three times its birth weight. In most tropical breeds, weaning takes place naturally, because milk supply declines abruptly after two–three months of lactation, and the kid is able to feed on vegetative material.

5.6.3 Feeding for fattening

In most developing countries there is a steady rise in the demand for meat in towns and cities, as population increases and people move into urban areas. As people become richer, they are able to afford more animal protein in their diet. Farmers who have access to urban markets may be able to take advantage of these markets and fatten goats for sale. Goats can also be fattened for specific religious holidays, when prices rise. Farmers may fatten stock which they have reared themselves or buy young males for fattening and sale.

There are very few reports of commercial goat-fattening enterprises in the developing world; some reports indicate that it is probably not economic to spend money on concentrate feeds for indigenous tropical breeds of goats unable to respond to the high level of feeding. It is doubtful whether a large-scale feedlot system, with intensive feeding of batches of goats for slaughter, would be profitable with indigenous breeds of goats. However, the less intensive fattening of goats on low-value feeds is an option for small-scale farmers who have access to cheap agricultural by-products or high-quality forages.

In intensive dairy-goat systems using temperate breeds of goats such as Saanen, Toggenburg or Anglo-Nubian, large numbers of male kids will be produced which would be more responsive to intensive feeding than indigenous goats. A more intensive fattening system might be appropriate, using crosses (or pure) temperate breeds.

The age of fastest growth is between weaning (3–4 months) and acquiring the first pair of permanent incisors at 14–15 months. It is probably not economic in most circumstances to feed a goat very intensively for one year after weaning. The semi-intensive fattening of goats for 12–18 months after weaning, using high-quality forages or crop by-products, might be profitable.

Chapter 4 showed how to calculate the nutrient requirements of different goats, and showed how different feeds were able to supply different nutrients. When fattening a goat, it is likely that several different feeds will be used, some of which may be purchased. If the farmer is going to spend money on purchased feed supplements, it is important to know if the supplementation really does result in a cash profit. This can be calculated by using a partial budget.

How to prepare a partial budget in order to calculate the profit/loss of a small change

The following information is needed:

Costs	**Benefits**
Extra costs	Extra returns
+	+
Reduced returns	Reduced costs
= Total costs	**= Total gain**

Total gain – Total costs = Profit/Loss

It is useful to calculate a partial budget in the following circumstances.

- Small changes are made to one enterprise.
- The change made is not linked to an input or output of another enterprise.
- The inputs are easy to measure and value.
- The farmer is interested in a cash profit.
- The fixed costs on the farm do not change .

Simple calculations can help to clarify whether the farmer is receiving real benefits from the change made in the management of the goats.

How to calculate the benefit of supplementation

It is assumed that supplementation increases the growth rate of the goat, resulting in a larger goat sold, in a shorter period, which will reduce the other costs associated with keeping goats.

Costs	**Benefits**
Cost of supplement	Higher price because larger goat at sale
Cost of transporting supplement	Reduced labour because of shorter period
Cost of feeder construction	
Total costs	**Total gain**

Total gain – Total costs = Profit/loss

The total cash costs of buying, transporting, and feeding the supplement should be easy to compute. It may be harder to estimate the additional benefits, unless records were kept of performance before the change was made.

Partial budgets are suitable only in situations where farmers have a clear objective to make money from their goats. Once farmers start spending money on inputs (feed supplements, drugs, etc.) for goats, then closer scrutiny of the real benefits of the inputs should begin. There are, of course, many intangible benefits from keeping goats, which cannot easily be costed.

5.7 Case studies

In order to show how to apply nutritional principles to improve the feeding of goats in real systems, three case studies from widely different systems will be described.

5.7.1 Housed goats in Java, Indonesia (mixed farming: humid tropics)

Java is a very densely populated island in Indonesia, where land is very intensively cultivated. The staple crop is rice, which may be irrigated or grown on upland slopes. A multitude of fruit, vegetable, spice, and cash crops are also grown. Around their houses farmers plant several layers of crops, ranging from tall timber trees, to coffee trees and fruit trees, down to spices and herbs and root crops under the ground. Rainfall in the west is as high as 4,000 mm per year, but may fall to 1,000 mm in some parts of the east; humidity is high all the year round. There is no room for any livestock to graze freely, so they are all restrained in some way. Buffaloes and cattle may be tethered in rice-stubble fields when not working, or kept in a small pen close to the farmer's house. Sheep and goats may also be tethered, but are often kept in specially constructed houses. The houses are made of bamboo, with thatched or tiled roofs, and are normally raised off the ground. Feed has to be cut from roadsides and rice bunds and carried to the goats in the house. They are normally fed from a small trough attached to the outside of the house (Figure 5.21).

Goats are kept for the family's security and to generate some cash when needed. They are rarely milked. Farmers are trying to keep as many goats as they can on the very limited land available. They like goats to twin and for mortality to be as low as possible. Most people in Java are Muslims, so the price of goats rises sharply at the time of Muslim holidays; good money can be made if goats are sold at this time. Generally the price of meat is increasing, as

Figure 5.21 Traditional goat house, Java, Indonesia

JOHN PETHERAM

143

demand rises from the expanding urban population. There is a need to intensify goat production, to make the most efficient use of the limited feed resources, and there is scope for some farmers to engage in the profitable fattening of goats.

A rapid survey of goat production was carried out in two villages in west Java. The rainfall pattern, cropping pattern, and seasonal feeding practices are shown in Figure 5.22.

Farmers rely heavily on crop residues such as rice straw, cassava leaves, sweet-potato vines, legume straws, and rice bran in feeding their livestock, as well as cutting grass (*Axonopus compressus* and *Ischaemum timorense*) from roadsides, rice bunds, and under the many clove trees grown in the area. A few tree legumes such as leucaena and calliandra are cut as feed, and there are several other tree leaves such as jackfruit and banana. The samples of the mixture of feeds were collected and analysed, first

Figure 5.22 Rainfall, cropping, and feed calendar, west Java

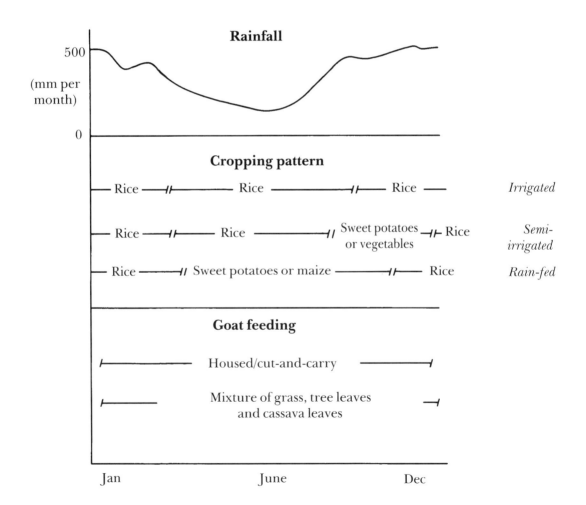

for simple dry-matter content. The fodder cut to feed goats contained 15–30 per cent DM, herbs 13–20 per cent DM, and tree leaves 20–40 per cent DM. Grasses made up 40–60 per cent of the diet, herbs 20–30 per cent, and tree leaves about 10 per cent. This indicates that not only are farmers carrying a lot of water in this cut-and-carry system, but they are feeding forage with a high water content. This was thought to be reducing the amount the goats were eating.

When proximate analysis was carried out, the crude protein content of grass was found to be 8–20 per cent, for herbs it was 15–30 per cent, and for tree leaves it was 15–25 per cent. The fibre content was quite low, so it would be anticipated that digestibility would be quite high. In addition the feeds were analysed for sodium.

The following conclusions on the quality of the diet were drawn.

- Dry-matter intake-rates were low, because the feed had a high moisture content.
- Protein levels were adequate.
- Levels of energy were not adequate to make use of the protein.
- Levels of sodium were low.

Apart from looking at what feeds were cut and carried to the goats at different seasons, the method of presenting the feed was observed. The feed was collected once a day and given only once a day, in a big load placed on top of the old feed. By the time the new feed was given, the old feed was starting to rot in the high temperature and humidity, and it smelt bad. As the old feed had already been rejected by the goat, it was pointless to keep it in the trough. However, it was not very easy for the farmer to clean the trough, because it was high up and rigid. Cleaning it out would have been easier if it was hinged, so that it could swing down and allow the rejected feed to fall to the ground. Once on the ground, it could be put under the house and mixed with the urine and faeces which fall through the slatted floor. This is a good method of trapping valuable urine to enrich the composted waste feed and faeces. Compost in Java rots very quickly and can be used to fertilise crop-land or forage.

It was obvious that herbs and tree leaves were particularly liked by goats, while the grasses were avoided.

The following conclusions on the method of feeding were drawn.

- Some species were obviously particularly liked by goats and could be fed in greater quantities.
- Most of the feed was liked, but it was fed in one lump, allowing goats to be wastefully selective. More would be eaten if the goats were fed little and often.
- The left-over feed quickly rotted and became unpalatable. It

would be better if the trough was cleaned every day and the waste feed composted.

The following nutritional improvements were suggested to goat farmers in the village.

1 Construct a hinged feed trough to help cleaning. Cleaning should be carried out every day and the waste feed should be put under the house to trap urine, and mixed with the manure to make high-quality compost.
2 As most of the feed is liked by goats, feed it in small amounts regularly through the day (three–four times a day), to increase in-take.
3 Feed more of the forage species particularly liked by the goats.
4 If possible, feed a source of energy that rumen micro-organisms can use, to make good use of the crude protein already in the diet.
5 Supply salt to the goats in a simple bamboo container.

Near the village are several sources of by-products suitable to feed as a supplement. There is a rice mill where rice bran can be purchased, a cassava-processing factory producing a waste called 'onggkok', and a soyabean-processing factory supplying waste from 'tahu' processing. Most of these products contain some amount of starch and are quite cheap to buy. They could be fed as energy supplements to selected goats, for example young bucks being fattened for a particular Muslim holiday, or does suckling twins.

Figure 5.23 Improved house design

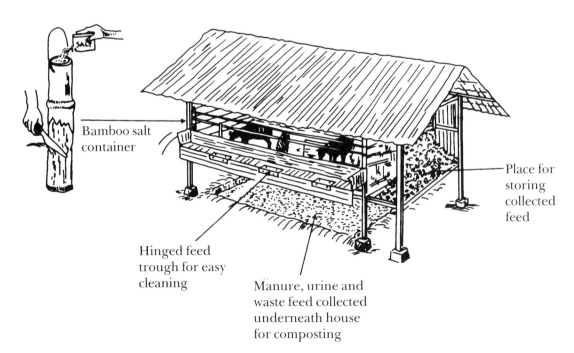

Bamboo salt container

Place for storing collected feed

Hinged feed trough for easy cleaning

Manure, urine and waste feed collected underneath house for composting

The supplements should be fed every day in a form which the goat finds easy to eat. For example 'onggkok' is very hard and should be soaked in water to soften it before feeding. Adding salt to supplements makes them more palatable. When starting to encourage farmers to purchase supplements, the health of the goats, particularly their intestinal parasite burden, must be considered. Although goats in this area of west Java were housed, because of the humidity they were still picking up parasites' larvae from their cut feed. Research found that parasite larvae can even live for some time attached to the bamboo poles of the house. Goats were often observed licking the poles of the house, in order to acquire salt, and might pick up parasites in the process. When encouraging farmers to spend money on supplements, they should also be encouraged to spend money on drenching their goats, in order to get the full benefit of the supplement.

5.7.2 Tethered dairy goats in the highlands of Ethiopia (mixed farming: highland)

Goats are kept throughout the highlands of Ethiopia on small mixed farms. Some parts of the highlands are very densely populated, and farms are as small as 0.5–0.25 ha per family. The main crops are sorghum, maize, sweet potatoes, and the narcotic bush and cash crop, 'chat' (*Catha edulis*). Rainfall is low, 500–800 mm, and fluctuates from year to year. There are occasional severe droughts. Soil erosion is a serious problem. There is an increasing shortage of livestock feed for the cattle, goats, sheep, and donkeys kept. Communal grazing areas are under pressure from their increasing cultivation, from erosion, and from increasing numbers of livestock.

Poverty and malnutrition are major problems in most areas. With the rainfall available and the small size of the farms, it is very difficult for farmers to feed their families, let alone produce excess for sale. A few cash crops such as coffee or chat may be grown by some farmers. Livestock are an important source of income.

One or two cattle are kept by some farmers for ploughing and milk, and in some areas for fattening. Goats are kept in small flocks of 2–5 animals. The main reasons for owning goats are for family security, for sale, and in some places for the small amount of milk they produce. They are normally housed or tethered during the crop-growing season and may be released to graze in stubble fields or hillsides during the dry season. The price of meat is continuously rising, due to the increasing demand from urban centres, especially before the many religious holidays. Some farmers specialise in fattening cattle, sheep, and goats for sale during these holidays, when high prices can be obtained.

Figure 5.24 A goat tethered at the edge of a field to feed on a strip of forage

Jenny Matthews/Oxfam

There is an increasingly important role for both goats and sheep in the highlands of Ethiopia, as farms become too small to need, or support, cattle for cultivation or milk. A small intensive goat system fits in well. The question is: how to intensify the feeding of goats when food for humans is so scarce?

A non-governmental agency started a dairy-goat project in the south and east of Ethiopia with the intention of developing a more intensive dairy-goat system. A group of students from the local college carried out a rapid survey of current goat-feeding practices, by interviewing some of the women involved in the project. The seasonal feed calendar they produced is shown in Figure 3.1.

From the descriptions of the feeds available, there are some obvious problems in both quantity and quality of feed. During the growing season, farmers are able to provide a diet of reasonable quality, by feeding weeds from their farm-land, and maize and sorghum-leaf pickings from growing crops. In the dry season the situation changes and quality deteriorates rapidly, unless the goats are able to graze bushy hillsides freely, in which case they can probably select a reasonable diet for themselves. But in some areas goats may have only fibrous maize or sorghum stover, and their condition rapidly deteriorates. There is some scope for using sweet-potato vines in places where they are grown.

The project realised that feed supply was going to be critical to the success of the project, as the aim was eventually to introduce a cross-bred, high-yielding goat on each farm. This goat would need a lot of high-quality feed for it to perform well. The supply of feed had to be ensured.

It was obvious that there were virtually no by-product supplements available, either on or off the farm, to improve the diet, and that any improvement would have to come from improvements on the farm itself. There was, however, potential for integrating forage crops into the cropping system, without affecting the main crop. Growing forage was a new technology for the farmers, so the project started by insisting that they planted a small area of forage around their houses, before they received goats on credit.

The women and their husbands were trained in appropriate forage strategies, in this case backyard pasture, undersowing, and forage strips for forage and erosion control. Farmers started to plant grass strips on contours in their fields. They also planted tree lucerne, sesbania, and leucaena around their houses and in contour strips, and along paths and as fences. A few farmers sowed vetch under their sorghum crop. Some even planted forage under their valuable chat bushes.

Most farmers developed their own back-yard tree nurseries, growing sesbania and leucaena. As soon as the cross-bred goats were distributed, there was an upsurge in interest in growing forage crops in order to feed the goats well.

The cross-bred goats are kept tethered throughout the year. Women try hard to feed them as well as they possibly can, because they know that the next day they will be rewarded with extra milk. In the dry season, sweet-potato vines and small, poorly formed potatoes are fed. Small quantities of left-overs from maize grinding may also be fed. Leucaena and sesbania are regularly cut, and dry-season bulk feed comes from elephant-grass strips.

The cross-bred goats are performing better than expected. As farmers get more benefit from their goats, they are planting more forage to feed them.

5.7.3 Goat herding by the Maasai in Kenya (semi-arid pastoral)

The Maasai are pastoralists who inhabit the semi-arid grazing lands of southern Kenya and northern Tanzania. Rain falls in two seasons, leaving a long and a short dry season. The long dry period may last for five months. The Maasai are renowned for keeping large herds of cattle and milking them for most of their staple food. In fact the area inhabited by the Maasai is diminishing in size, so it is difficult for the expanding Maasai population to live exclusively off their cattle. They have kept sheep and goats in mixed flocks for centuries, but are increasingly relying on them, as over-grazing and recurrent droughts reduce cattle numbers more than sheep and goat numbers. The ability of sheep and goats to survive droughts has led the Maasai to increase their dependence on them, although cattle are still important. Livestock are regularly traded for grain and other commodities.

The Maasai are nomadic to varying degrees. Some are now settled, but most still move their cattle and sheep and goats, even though they may maintain a house (*boma*) near schools or shops. The grazing land has always been communal, but is now being broken up into areas owned by groups. Goats are kept in flocks with sheep. Total flock numbers may be as small as 5 or as large as 400. The mean flock size is about 120, usually half goats and half sheep. Goats are mainly kept for family security, and for sale in times of need. They are also used as currency in social transactions such as marriages, or to cement a friendship. They may be slaughtered at ceremonies and are highly prized for their medicinal properties. It is thought that, because goats eat so many different species of vegetation, they must possess the ability to cure illness. They may be milked in the dry season, if the cattle have dried up.

Goats are herded the whole day (8–10 hours) by young children or women. In the dry season they walk 8–15 km per day while out grazing. The Maasai try to keep their goats in more favourable bushy areas, rather than grassland areas, which are reserved for cattle. In the dry season they lose weight, as much as 25 g per day, quickly regaining it in the wet season. Goats are able to take advantage of the green flush of new growth immediately before the start of the rains. There are areas known as *enkusero*, specially reserved for sheep and goat grazing. These *enkusero* are

Figure 5.25 Near Garfarsa, Kenya: shaking high-protein seed pods from an Acacia tortilis tree
Jeremy Hartley/Oxfam

normally areas of poorly drained black-cotton soils where bush vegetation, such as *Acacia mellifera* and *Acacia nubica*, tends to grow. In some parts of the Maasai territory there are large areas of *Acacia tortilis*. These trees, once mature, produce large quantities of protein-rich seed pods during the long dry season. If the labour is available, flock owners will move their sheep and goats to the *A. tortilis* areas during the dry season and feed their flocks on the pods. Herders use long poles to shake the pods down from the trees, and the flock follows on to pick up the pods.

The environment in which the Maasai live is harsh, and they have to cope with a great deal of variability in the supply of grazing. Rain falls in marked seasons; the amount that falls varies from year to year and from place to place. There is no doubt that being able to move cattle, sheep, and goats to areas of good rainfall is of fundamental importance in ensuring healthy and productive livestock. In this situation of low rainfall and communal ownership, it is very hard for a Maasai goat owner to increase the quantity of feed available through, for example, planting forage crops. All that can be done is to move to good vegetation when possible and make the best of the grazing that is there.

In order to feed their goats well, Maasai goat-keepers have to manipulate the following factors.

- **Movement**
  The location of the flock
- **The grazing day**
  The frequency of watering
  The direction of movement
  The speed of movement
  The total time spent grazing

A family's ability to move their livestock is mainly determined by the supply of suitable labour available for herding cattle, sheep, and goats as well as for looking after school-children, old people, and other dependants. In the dry season, households may split into three units: a school-children's *boma* with some milk cows, a far-away cattle *boma*, and possibly a sheep and goat *boma*, perhaps in an area of *A. tortilis* or some other area suited to sheep and goats.

Once in a particular place, the herder has to decide how often to water the goats. In the wet season this will be easy, because there are surface water ponds. But in the dry season, although the herder knows that the goats will be able to eat more if they have water, the watering place is likely to be well used by other flocks, and will be over-grazed in the area immediately surrounding it. Watering takes time away from grazing time, and for that day may result in the flock eating little from the over-used vegetation. On non-watering days the herder is better able to pick the bushy places most suitable for goats, and allow the flock to linger there.

It is clear that there is little a goat owner can do to improve the total supply of feed available, but he or she could manipulate the seasonal demands of the flock by controlling breeding so that kids are born during the most favourable seasons. This, in fact, is what the Maasai do. Mating is controlled, so that most kids are born during the short wet season, which is followed by a short dry season before the long wet season. This is the best time of year for them to be born; but if the short rains fail, the kids are born at the end of a very long dry season. There are risks associated with this practice.

The results of a monitoring study showed that kids are very vulnerable at the time of weaning, particularly if this takes place in the long dry season. There might be scope for storing some of the *A. tortilis* or other pods, and using them as a supplement for weaners, or for goats suckling twins. Suckling kids also need special care.

Much of the Maasai grazing lands are in or near the Rift Valley, which is known to be deficient in copper and other minerals. The Maasai use natural salt licks, but investigation is needed into whether these natural licks offer an adequate supply of supplementary minerals.

At an aggregate level the Maasai, in any particular area, can coordinate their grazing, so that some is left as standing hay for the dry season, rather than large herd owners moving ahead of smaller families and monopolising the grazing. There is evidence that this coordination was a traditional practice which is now dying.

Further reading

AFNETA (1992) *The AFNETA Alley Farming Training Manual* (Volumes 1 and 2), Addis Ababa: IITA/ILRI

Blair, G.J., D. A. Ivory, and T. R. Evans (1986) *Forages in Southeast and South Pacific Agriculture: Proceedings of an International Workshop Held at Cisarua, Indonesia, 19-23 August 1985*, ACIAR Proceedings Series No. 12

Chesworth, J. (1992) *Ruminant Nutrition*, London: Macmillan/CTA

IIRR (1990) *Agroforestry Technology Information Kit*, Cavite, The Philippines: IIRR

Food and Agriculture Research Organisation of the United Nations (FAO) (1981), *Tropical Feeds*, Rome: FAO

Preston, T.R. and R. A. Leng (1987) *Matching Ruminant Production Systems with Available Resources in the Tropics and Sub-Tropics*, Armidale, Australia: Penambul Books

CHAPTER 6

Goat health

6.1 Introduction

Maintaining goats in a state of good health is obviously of great importance to the owner. Sick goats are less able to supply products and may eventually die; the economic impact on the owner's family could be considerable. Some epidemic diseases can kill an entire flock, leaving the family destitute. For all these reasons, owners must take steps to keep their goats healthy. Keeping goats healthy does not involve the use of expensive drugs and highly trained veterinary staff. In most situations, the majority of the important diseases can be controlled through simple preventative (prophylactic) measures such as good feeding, clean, well-ventilated housing, vaccination, drenching, spraying/dipping, and foot trimming. In some countries these measures have been estimated to control 80 to 90 per cent of the diseases of economic importance. Efforts should be focused on controlling these diseases, rather than worrying about the less common diseases which may only occasionally affect a small proportion of goats. The emphasis of this chapter is on preventing and controlling the diseases of economic importance to the farmer or pastoralist.

This chapter is written for people who do not have veterinary training. In most countries in the tropics there is a chronic shortage of all levels of veterinary staff, from highly qualified veterinarians to animal-health assistants and vaccinators. These staff are often poorly equipped with transport and drugs. As a result, few farmers have easy access to veterinary services. Because of these conditions, everyone involved with goats — farmers, *all* extension staff, as well as the veterinary staff — must take responsibility for keeping goats healthy and helping them to recover if they do get sick. Do not be afraid of tackling problems of goat health because you are not a veterinarian. The purpose of this chapter is to help you

- to help farmers to prevent disease;
- to investigate health problems;
- to carry out simple treatments of sick goats.

6.1.1 The goat, its environment, and defence mechanisms

Goat diseases may be caused by a variety of living organisms which exist in the environment. These agents of disease are classified as bacteria, viruses, mycoplasma, chlamydia rickettsia, fungi, protozoa, and parasites (external, internal, and blood).

These disease agents may enter the goat directly, for example through the consumption of grass contaminated with infective parasite larvae. Disease agents can also be transmitted by a vector such as a tick or biting fly; for example, the heartwater rickettsia (*Cowdria ruminantia*) is transmitted by the tick *Amblyomma* spp.

In addition, goats may become unhealthy through nutritional problems such as a deficiency of vitamins or minerals, or poisoning from plants or chemicals, or through physical damage.

The goat lives and reproduces in an environment that may contain several of these disease agents and their vectors, either permanently or seasonally or occasionally. The presence or absence of disease agents in a particular place will be determined by several factors:

- climate (temperature, humidity, etc.);
- vegetation (grassy, bushy, swamp);
- the presence of other livestock and wildlife;
- husbandry methods.

In order to prevent these agents from causing disease, the goat has a number of defence mechanisms which either protect it from attack or help it to reduce the effects of attack when it does occur. There are five main defence mechanisms.

- **The skin** is the first defence against invasion by agents of disease. Infective organisms may invade only if the skin is broken or penetrated by a biting vector such as a tick or fly.

- **The acidity of the abomasum** can destroy some invading micro-organisms that may have entered the goat with the food it ingested.

- **Mucous lining of the respiratory tract** can trap some invading organisms in the air breathed by the goat.

- **Macrophage cells in blood** consume invading micro-organisms.

- **Immunity** may be acquired through antibodies in the blood which inactivate invading bacteria and viruses. If a goat is infected with relatively low levels of an organism, large numbers of antibodies are produced to fight off the infection during the process of recovery. If the goat is infected again, even with high levels of the same organism, it already has antibodies available to inactivate it. By this process the goat develops naturally acquired immunity. Immunity can also be acquired artificially. This is done by purposely challenging the goat, either by injecting it with low levels of the infective organisms, as with vaccines (artificial active immunity); or by injecting the goat with antibodies from another immune goat, as with anti-serum or anti-toxin (artificial passive immunity). Antibodies can also be acquired passively by the kid through drinking colostrum — the milk produced immediately after birth, which is rich in antibodies and provides the kid with natural passive immunity.

It is of course impossible to keep goats in a disease-free environment. The goat's environment is never constant; conditions which favour or disfavour the presence of disease organisms are always changing. Likewise the goat's own condition is also changing; its defence mechanisms are sometimes put under great pressure, while at other times they are able to defend the goat effectively.

It is the job of the goat's owner to minimise the disease challenge faced by the goat, and to ensure that the goat has healthy defence mechanisms at all times. There will be times when the defences of even the healthiest goat are broken down by a massive attack, such as the outbreak of an epidemic disease; but, under normal conditions, the goat should be given the best chance possible of fighting attack. Factors predisposing the goat to succumb to disease have to be present for disease to appear. There are four main predisposing factors.

- **Poor nutrition:** a well-fed goat has a much better chance of fighting off disease through its active defence mechanisms.

- **Stress:** any stress placed on the goat will reduce its ability to fight disease and make it more susceptible. Stress includes a wide range of factors such as kidding, fatigue from walking or being transported long distances, poor housing, excessive cold (particularly when combined with damp), excessive heat, high humidity, and dehydration.

- **Lack of tolerance**: goats in some areas may be tolerant of certain diseases through their close association with the causative agent over generations. Goat breeds have different levels of tolerance to different disease organisms. Temperate breeds may lack the tolerance which some tropical breeds show to some tropical diseases. Goats have evolved as browsers and show poor tolerance to intestinal parasites which are acquired from grazing infected pastures close to the ground. Tolerance shown by breeds should not be confused with immunity, which can be developed by individuals.

- **Lack of immunity:** it is very important that the goat's immunity levels are maintained. Where appropriate, immunity must be acquired through vaccination and, for the kid, through suckling colostrum immediately after birth. The lack of immunity to infection makes the goat vulnerable to attack. Kids are particularly susceptible to disease, because they have no antibodies of their own, only those acquired from their mothers. Consumption of colostrum provides them with some immunity for their first few weeks of life. Thereafter they must make their own antibodies, a process which can be assisted with vaccination.

A disease may appear dramatically as a set of rapidly develop-ing symptoms. This is known as the *acute* form of the disease. Diseases are often slow and long-lasting, indicating a *chronic* infection. Chronic infections may develop into an acute form of the disease, but not always. Chronic infections of goats with intest-inal parasites are common and may remain in the chronic form, never appearing as an acute disease unless the goat is very weak.

6.2 Assessing health and disease in goats: the clinical examination

Chapter 2 explained that the problems most commonly found in various goat-keeping systems are not due to one simple cause, but to a combination of several management and disease factors. This is nowhere more true than in matters of health, where several factors contribute to ill health. Bad management is usually the main cause of disease.

Chapter 3 described methods of carrying out disease surveys and investigations in order to describe

- the incidence patterns of disease syndromes;
- the syndrome type and age/sex of goats affected;
- the effect of disease: morbidity, mortality;
- current husbandry and preventative treatment practices.

In goats, several disease problems are commonly encountered in the field. Once the problems in a particular system have been identified, it is important to identify the specific diseases and environmental factors that are influencing the disease. During the course of a disease survey, or while carrying out extension work, it is important for extension staff to be able to obtain an accurate description of a health problem. This is called 'taking a case history'. It might be a description of an existing problem or a past problem. Learning how to take an accurate history will help in identifying the disease and will enable extension workers to discuss health problems with professional veterinary staff later.

Case histories can be taken in the field at the time of an illness or after an illness. In order to be able to identify abnormalities, the normal behaviour and physical condition of a goat must be known. Make a point of observing the behaviour of normal goats, so that you are quickly able to identify any abnormalities.

It is important to be able to describe disease incidence in a systematic way that allows you to consult either a veterinary professional or textbook.

6.2.1 Observations to make of a sick goat

General
- Is the goat by itself, or with the rest of the flock?
- Is it alert, or dull and unresponsive?
- Is it breathing normally?
- Is it coughing?
- Is it shivering?
- Is it eating and drinking normally?
- Is the rumen bloated?
- Is it ruminating normally?
- Is it standing up or lying down?
- Is it lying normally?

Head
- Is the head held normally, or drooping or bent round?
- Are the eyes bright, clear, and shiny; or are they red, opaque, or weeping?
- Are the ears alert or drooping?
- Is there a discharge from the eyes or nose?
- Is there frothing at the mouth or an excess of saliva?
- Are mucous membranes around the eye pale, yellow, blue, or dark red?

Skin
- Is the coat shiny or dull?
- Are there bite or lick marks on the coat?
- Is the skin loose or tight, soft or hard?
- Are there patches of hair missing?
- Is there a swelling (oedema) under the jaw?
- Are the lymph nodes swollen?

Legs and movement
- Are the legs stiff?
- Is the goat lame?

Faeces and urine
- Are the faeces normal or abnormal (is there diarrhoea, mucous, or blood)?
- Is the urine pale yellow, brown, or red?
- Does the goat strain to pass urine or faeces?

Recognising pain
- Is the goat bleating?
- Is the goat restless?
- Does it grind its teeth?
- Is it grunting?
- Is it licking a lot?
- Is it kicking itself and, if so, where?

Lactating goats
- Are either or both teats inflamed, swollen, and tender?
- Are the teats injured?
- Does the milk contain milk clots?
- Is the milk blood-stained?
- Has the milk yield fallen?

6.2.2 Physical examination

Five major physical measures can be taken.

Respiration rate: count the number of chest movements made per minute when the animal is at rest (Figure 6.1a). Normal values for goats are 10–20 per minute. Young and old goats have slightly higher respiration rates than normal.

Pulse: place a hand over the heart area, just under the left elbow, and count the heart beats; alternatively there is an artery that can be felt on the inside surface of the thigh (Figure 6.1b). Measurements must be taken when the goat is at rest. Normal values for goats are 60–80 per minute.

Temperature: the thermometer should be inserted through the anus into the rectum in a slightly upwards direction, and held there for at least one minute (Figure 6.1c). The normal temperature range for goats is 38.0–40.5°C.

Mucous membranes: observe the lining inside the eyelids and mouth. If it is pale, the goat is anaemic, probably from gastro-intestinal parasites or blood parasites. If it is yellow, there is a liver problem.

Rumen contractions: important for assessing general health and gastro-intestinal function. Place the palm of your hand firmly in the depression behind the last rib on the left and leave it for two minutes. Normal contractions can be felt at a rate of 1–2/minute.

6.2.3 History of disease

In addition to observations and a physical examination of the sick goat(s), a full history of the disease in the flock should be obtained from the owner. Key factors are listed on page 160.

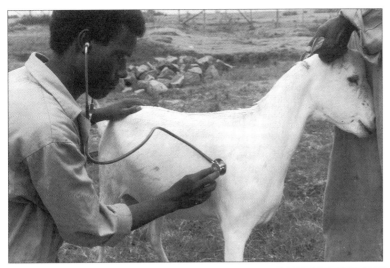

*Figure 6.1 (a)
Measuring the
respiration rate*
CHRISTIE PEACOCK

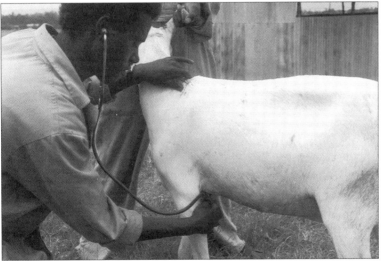

*Figure 6.1 (b) Taking
the pulse*
CHRISTIE PEACOCK

*Figure 6.1 (c) Taking
the temperature*
INTERNATIONAL LIVESTOCK
RESEARCH INSTITUTE

159

- Age/sex of goat(s) affected.
- The first symptoms (loss of appetite, unusual behaviour, diarrhoea, difficulty breathing, colour and consistency of any discharges).
- Proportion of flock affected.
- Action taken by farmer. Effect of action.
- Development of the disease after the first signs (depression, lying down, straining, diarrhoea, changes in colour and consistency of any discharges).
- Further action taken by farmer.
- Outcome of disease (death, complete recovery, partial recovery).
- Similar symptoms in other goats in flock/area.
- History of vaccination.
- Description of feeding practices.

In addition to making observations during a physical examination, it may be appropriate to take samples (faeces, urine, skin scraping, and blood) for laboratory examination. In addition, making a post-mortem examination soon after the death of a goat can be of great value. A simple post-mortem procedure is described in 6.6.2.

6.2.4 Taking samples

In order to investigate a disease problem and make an accurate diagnosis, it is sometimes useful to take samples from living or dead goats in order to identify the cause of a disease, the health of a goat, or the cause of death. The chronic shortage of veterinary staff in the tropics means that it is important for all extension staff to be able to take relevant samples from both living and dead goats for later analysis by a veterinarian or laboratory. Samples may be taken as part of a disease survey or monitoring study, or might be taken as the need and opportunity present themselves.

In order for laboratories to carry out diagnostic tests on the sample, it should either be very fresh or be preserved in some way. If the sample cannot be properly presented to the laboratory, it is probably not worth trying to collect it.

Always remember when collecting samples to record the following information:

owner's name	date
ID of goat	place
age	preservant (formalin, alcohol)
sex	reason for sample collection

Ideally all this information will be written on the sample container itself; but, if there is not enough room, a number may be written on the sample and the information recorded separately.

The correct procedures for taking samples may be found in the following sections of this chapter:

faeces	6.4.1
skin scraping	6.4.2
blood	6.4.1
ticks	6.4.3

6.3 Common disease problems

Tables 6.1–6.10 show the main disease problems of goats, together with the likely causes of the problem. They have been adapted from a useful publication entitled *Goat Health Handbook* (Thedford, 1983). These tables should be used to diagnose the disease after making a physical examination or taking a case history. Often, if extension staff make irregular visits to a flock, they will miss seeing the sick goat, because it has either died or recovered. In this case, close questioning of the farmer and members of the family can give a reasonable picture.

If a specific diagnosis of the disease cannot be made, indicating a specific treatment, the symptoms shown by the goat should be alleviated where possible. In addition, action should be taken to prevent the spread of the problem to other goats in the flock or to goats in neighbouring flocks. Suggestions are made for the management of the disease problems described.

6.3.1 Kid death (with or without diarrhoea)

The death of kids before they are weaned is perhaps the single biggest cause of loss experienced by goat farmers. It is a tremendous waste for a kid to be born only to die in the first few weeks of life. It is all too common when visiting goat flocks to see a weak kid, often with diarrhoea, standing listlessly apart from other goats. Kids very quickly become too weak to suckle, and at this point they will quickly die. The causes are usually complex. Predisposing factors may include lack of colostrum at birth; poor nutrition of the dam, leading to low milk production; dirty housing and pen areas, which allows a build-up of infective agents; dirty water; and failure to vaccinate the dam appropriately. These factors lead to a weak kid which is open to infection from bacteria or parasites. Kids should be kept apart from the rest of the flock with their mothers. The mother should receive good feed and clean water. Dirty bedding should be removed and disposed of safely. (See Table 6.1.)

Kids may also disappear from a flock through predation by wild animals, including birds, or simple theft.

Table 6.1 Likely causes of kid death

Disease	Causative agent	Symptoms
Coccidiosis	P	Diarrhoea, sometimes bloody. Sudden death may occur without diarrhoea. Normally in housed goats.
Colibacillosis	B	Dry mouth. Stomach full of gas. Fever. Quick death unless treated. Responds well to antibiotics.
Colostrum deprivation	M	Dry mouth. Fever. Severe weakness. Most die.
Enterotoxaemia	B	Sudden depression. Drunken appearance. Lies on side when close to death, paddling legs. May have watery diarrhoea.
Internal parasites	P	Sudden death. May have swelling under chin, anaemia, and weakness. PM reveals parasites in intestines, esp. *Haemonchus contortus* in abomasum.
Suffocation		No physical signs of disease. Can occur if many kids and adults are kept together, esp. in cold climates.
Malnutrition	M	Weakness, no stomach fill. Check dam for milk and kid for access to dam.

Key:　P = parasitic　B = bacterial　V = viral　M = metabolic

6.3.2 Diarrhoea and loss of condition (adults)

Adult goats may suffer from chronic diarrhoea and weight loss or, in some cases, acute diarrhoea. Predisposing factors include poor or unbalanced nutrition; dirty house or pen; lack of anthelmintic use; and lack of appropriate vaccination. Goats with acute diarrhoea should have constant access to clean water and feed, and may be treated with oral or injectable antibiotics. (See Table 6.2.)

6.3.3 Respiratory problems and fever

Respiratory diseases are common in goats, particularly in large flocks of housed goats with inadequate ventilation. Occasional epidemic diseases such as contagious caprine pleuropneumonia (CCPP) may occur in specific areas where the disease is endemic.

Table 6.2 Likely causes of diarrhoea and loss of condition (adults)

Disease	Causative agent	Symptoms
Acidosis	M	Full stomach, watery contents. Diarrhoea (watery, bad smell). Very weak. No rumen movement. Recent dietary change.
Bloat	M	Full stomach with gas or froth. Distension on left side behind ribs. Laboured breathing.
Coccidiosis	P	Acute diarrhoea, often with blood. Severe straining.
Enterotoxaemia	B	Full stomach. Fever. Sudden death is common.
Internal parasites	P	May have swelling under jaw, anaemia. Weakness, weight loss. May die before signs of diarrhoea.
Nairobi sheep disease	V	Fever. Depression. Bad-smelling, blood-stained diarrhoea and nasal discharge.
Peste des petits ruminants (PPR)	V	Fever. Raw, red areas around mouth.
Rift Valley Fever	V	Fever. Sores on cheeks and tongue. Unsteady gait. Abortion.

Predisposing factors include poor ventilation; large numbers of goats in close proximity; lack of appropriate vaccination; introduction of new goats into flock; or mixing at a watering place. Respiratory problems are often highly infectious, so affected goats should immediately be separated from the rest of the flock and placed in a warm, dry, well-ventilated place. (See Table 6.3.)

6.3.4 Skin diseases and swellings

Skin diseases (Table 6.4) may not seem important, but they can, if untreated, kill goats, cause major economic loss (mange), or develop into a recurrent, chronic problem (caseous lymphadenitis). Predisposing factors include lack of appropriate vaccination (goat pox); close contact with goats from other flocks; or introduction of infected goats into the flock. Poor condition worsens the infection.

Table 6.3 Likely causes of respiratory problems and fever

Disease	Causative agent	Symptoms
Anthrax	B	Bloody nasal discharge and bleeding from body openings. Death within 24–48 hours.
Contagious caprine pleuropneumonia (CCPP)	V	Nasal discharge. Rasping sound from lungs. Fever. Death in most cases, sometimes 24 hours after first signs.
Lungworm	P	Breathing difficulties, coughing leading to pneumonia.
Melioidosis	B	Symptoms vague. Coughing, weakness, respiratory distress. Sometimes thick yellow nasal discharge. Sometimes lameness. Death after 1–8 weeks.
Nairobi sheep disease	V	Nasal discharge with blood-stained, foul-smelling diarrhoea, and fever.
Peste des petits ruminants (PPR)	V	High fever. Raw patches in and around mouth. Clear nasal discharge at first, then thick, blocking breathing. Diarrhoea after 2–3 days. Commonly develops pneumonia. Death after one week.
Pneumonia	B, V, P	Rapid, laboured movement of ribs with rasping sound. Grunting, groaning, and grinding of teeth from pain.
Goat pox	V	High fever, nasal and eye discharge. Pimples appear after 24 hours, forming itchy scabs after one week. Death may occur.

6.3.5 Poor condition, anaemia, pale mucous membranes

It can be hard to pinpoint the cause of the generalised poor condition of a goat. Parasitic diseases often cause chronic diseases and should be suspected. Predisposing factors include poor nutrition; presence of vector (ticks, tsetse fly); dirty pens; and lack of anthelmintic use. (See Table 6.5.)

Table 6.4 Likely causes of skin diseases and swellings

Disease	Causative agent	Symptoms
Caseous lymphadenitis	B	Small lumps under the skin, located at lymph nodes, developing into large abscesses. Usually in adults. Chronic form shows wasting.
Streptothricosis	B	Large spots commonly on face, ears, and legs, exuding clear serum. Spots may merge into large scabs, causing hair to stand erect.
Goat pox	V	Fever. Nasal discharge. Spots appear after 24 hours on mucous membranes inside and outside body. Spot becomes itchy scab.
Mange	P	Sarcoptic mange shows rough, hard, itchy, wrinkled skin on back of legs and between front and rear legs, gradually spreading to mouth. Demodectic or follicle mange causes small hard itchy lumps all over body.
Orf	V	Thickened areas around mouth, on gums and teats. Often affects kids.
Ringworm	F	Roughly circular areas of missing hair, leaving rough, scaly skin
Warts	V	Growths appear on the skin, starting small but sometimes growing and spreading to affect a large area. May affect any area, including udder and teats.

Key: F = fungus

6.3.6 Lameness

Lameness can be a serious problem in grazing goats: it can limit or even prevent their ability to graze with the main flock. For this reason it should be treated seriously and prevented whenever possible. Predisposing factors are mainly overgrown, untrimmed hoofs. In tick-infested areas, a common cause of lameness is the attachment of ticks to the sensitive skin between the claws of the feet, resulting in inflammation and severe lameness. Lameness can also be a side-effect of other important diseases such as foot and

Table 6.5 Likely causes of poor condition, anaemia and pale mucous membranes

Disease	Causative agent	Symptoms
Anaplasmosis	P	Poor condition and severe anaemia.
Babesiosis	P	Bloody diarrhoea and dark red urine. Poor appetite, listless with fever. Most recover, but some die, showing nervous symptoms including paddling.
Coccidiosis	P	Acute bloody diarrhoea. Weak. Severe straining.
Internal parasites	P	Good appetite, but poor body condition. Sometimes diarrhoea. In severe cases, swelling under jaw ('bottle jaw').
Teeth problems	P	Weak or damaged teeth.
Trypanosomiasis	P	Poor body condition, poor appetite. Chronic weight loss. Swollen lymph nodes.

mouth disease or melioidosis. Good nursing, and cutting and carrying feed to the goat, are very important if the goat is lame and unable to graze for itself. (See Table 6.6.)

6.3.7 Nervous diseases

Goats show nervous symptoms — circling, convulsions, and head pressing — in the course of several important diseases. Unfortunately in many diseases nervous signs are shown only towards the end of the disease, when the goat is close to death. Lying down and making paddling movements with the front legs is a common sign before death from many diseases. (See Table 6.7.)

If rabies is suspected, very great care must taken in dealing with the goat, as this a highly infectious and fatal disease in humans (see 6.5.8).

6.3.8 Female and male infertility

A doe's inability to breed can be caused by many factors, acting together or separately. Management problems should be investigated first, to check that oestrus is being shown; if it is shown, is it being detected by the buck, or, in the absence of a buck, observed by the owner? If oestrus is shown and mating takes place without

Table 6.6 Likely causes of lameness

Disease	Causative agent	Symptoms
Akabane disease	V	Kids born with rigid joints, often blind as well.
Caprine arthritis encephalitis	V	Young kids show weakness in hindlegs and finally cannot rise. Death usually follows. In adults, swollen joints develop slowly (2 years). Difficulties in walking.
Contagious agalactia	B	Hot, painful, swollen joints that may rupture as an abscess.
Foot and mouth	V	Small blisters between claws of feet, causing lameness.
Foot rot	B	Lameness in one or more foot. Affected foot appears ragged and rotten, with bad smell. Often occurs in wet season, or in dirty conditions.
Mastitis	B	Does with inflamed udder may show a straddling walk.
Melioidosis	B	Joints, testicles, and lymph nodes sometimes swollen.
Mineral deficiencies	M	Kids born with deformed joints because of calcium:phosphorus imbalance or deficiency.
Navel ill	B	Inflamed navel and hot painful joints in kid.
Ticks	P	Tick attachment between claws of feet. Inflammation of skin at site of attachment.
Physical injury		
Vitamin deficiencies	M	See Table 6.16.

conception, the possibility of infertility in the buck must also be investigated. Female infertility may be caused by the presence of another disease which suppresses oestrus in the female, or by a condition such as lameness which prevents the buck from serving. Congenital physical deformities of the reproductive organs occasionally occur. There are very few diseases that directly cause infertility. (See Table 6.8.) Problems of infertility are described in more detail in 7.3.

Table 6.7 Likely causes of nervous diseases

Disease	Causative agent	Symptoms
Caprine arthritis encephalitis (CAE)	V	In addition to lameness, often head tremors, blindness, jerky movement of eyeballs, and circling.
Copper deficiency	M	Muscle tremors and nodding or shaking of head.
Enterotoxaemia	B	Star gazing, convulsions, teeth grinding, pitiful cry of pain. Paddling movements and throwing back head just before death.
Heartwater	R	Circling movement. Convulsions, twitching eyelids. Depression.
Listeriosis	B	Facial paralysis, resulting in drooping eyelids and ears. Circling and head pressing.
Melioidosis	B	Sometimes staggering, jerky movement, or paralysis, with swollen joints.
Navel ill	B	Convulsions may occur in kids when close to death. Enlarged navel stump is a critical symptom.
Pregnancy toxaemia		Inability to stand, poor balance during late gestation.
Rabies	V	Staring eyes, eating unusual objects, confusion, drooling saliva, strange bleat.
Scrapie	V	Only in adults. Uncoordinated limbs, especially. hind legs, high-stepping fore-legs. Salivation.
Tetanus	B	'Rocking-horse' straight-legged stance. Usually 2 weeks after wound.

Key: R = rickettsia

Table 6.8 Likely causes of female and male infertility

Disease	Causative agent	Symptoms
Brucellosis	B	Swollen testicles (orchitis), causing infertility in buck.
Intersex	H	Mixture of male and female reproductive organs.
Metritis	B	Dark, sticky, smelly discharge after giving birth indicates metritis. If left untreated, may develop into chronic problem and infertility.
Physical damage		Physical damage to penis or testicles may result in male infertility.
Sperm granulomas	H	Sterility. Small, hard tumour at top of unusually small testes can eventually be felt.
Trypanosomiasis	P	Inflammation/degeneration of testes.

Key: H = hereditary

6.3.9 Abortion

Spontaneous (non-infectious) abortion is slightly more common in goats than in other species, because the foetus is entirely dependent on the corpus luteum throughout gestation. However, there are several infections which can cause abortions. If aborters are not culled, abortion may spread and build up into a serious problem in the flock. Investigating a problem of abortion can be difficult, even with the support of a competent laboratory. It is simplest to cull goats which abort twice consecutively. Any disease that raises the body temperature of a pregnant goat may result in abortion. Predisposing factors are poor nutrition; stress; and shock (gunfire has been found to trigger abortion!). (See Table 6.9.)

6.3.10 Udder problems

A doe's udder problems (Table 6.10) can jeopardise her kid's life, because the doe may be so uncomfortable that she cannot bear the kid to suckle. Mastitis will affect total milk production and quality.

Table 6.9 Likely causes of abortion

Disease	Causative agent	Symptoms
Brucellosis	B	Abortion in last 50 days of the 150-day gestation. Possibly swollen joints.
Chlamydial abortion	B	Abortion in last 50 days of gestation. High proportion of herd will abort.
Foot and mouth disease	V	Abortion at any time of gestation, early in course of disease. Sores on tongue, in mouth, and between claws of feet.
Listeriosis	B	Abortion in last 70 days of gestation. May have drooping ears and eyelids. Tongue may hang out. Fever, depression, and nervous symptoms.
Malnutrition	M	Abortion at any time during gestation, but especially in last 50 days if short of energy.
Nairobi sheep disease	V	Abortion at any time of gestation, if goat survives disease.
Poisoning	M	Abortion at any time of gestation, as side-effect of poisoning.
Rift Valley fever	V	Abortion at any time of gestation during the course of the disease. Affected goats are feverish, vomit, and stagger. Sore on tongue and cheeks.
Salmonellosis	B	Abortion in last 50 days of gestation. Fever, no appetite, diarrhoea.
Shock and stress		Abortion at any time during gestation, usually 2–4 days after shock or stress.
Toxoplasmosis	P	Abortion in last 50 days of gestation. Rare.
Trypanosomiasis	P	Abortion during acute disease.

Table 6.10 Likely causes of udder problems

Disease	Causative agent	Symptoms
Mastitis	B	Heat, pain, and swelling of udder. May become bright red. Udder black and cold if gangrenous.
Orf	V	Small, scabby, painful sores on udder. Doe will not allow kid to suckle.
Physical damage		Physical damage such as tears, tick damage, thorn damage can make udder sore and affect milk production. Can lead to infection.
Warts	V	Small warts may grow on teat and persist for several months.

6.4 Common diseases of goats

The set of diseases that are important to any flock of goats will vary from place to place. The economically important diseases must be identified, in order to establish cost-effective control measures. The diseases that have been found to be of most common importance to goats in different systems are described in detail below. This is not a definitive list. It may be that in a particular place a relatively uncommon disease becomes of overwhelming importance, perhaps because the goats have no immunity, or the symptoms are unknown to veterinary staff, or suitable control measures cannot be taken.

6.4.1 Internal parasites

Internal parasites are of universal importance in goats, although the species will vary according to the climate, management system, and breed of goat. It seems that goats are more susceptible to internal parasites than sheep and cattle are. This is perhaps because they are browsers by nature: they naturally consume vegetation above the height at which infective parasite larvae exist. Under natural feeding conditions, their exposure to parasites is low and their natural tolerance of them is also low. Internal parasites become a problem in goats when they are forced to graze close to the ground because they have no browse to eat. Sheep, being natural grazers, appear to have developed more tolerance to internal parasites than goats have. Goat farmers all over the world have found that the economic control of the internal parasites encountered in their area is one of the key determinants of successful goat production.

There are three main types of parasite that may live inside goats, excluding blood parasites:

- gastro-intestinal parasites in the rumen, abomasum, small intestine, and large intestine;
- flukes in the liver;
- worms in the lung.

Gastro-intestinal parasites

The main gastro-intestinal parasites can be divided into four groups:

- Nematodes (*Haemonchus contortus*, *Ostertagia* spp, *Trichostrongylus* spp, *Nematodirus* spp, *Strongyloides* spp, *Oesophagostomum* spp, *Trichuris* spp).
- Cestodes (*Moniezia* spp).
- Trematodes (*Paramphistomum* spp).
- Protozoa (Coccidia, including *Eimeria* spp).

Figure 6.2 Location of main parasites in the goat

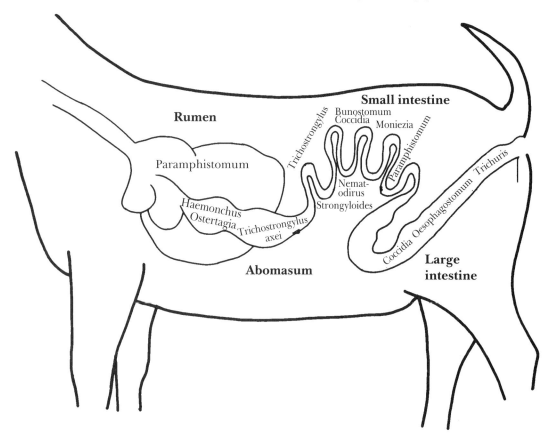

Of all the gastro-intestinal parasites that affect goats, *Haemonchus contortus* is by far the most important species. In the adult form it is a small worm, 1–3 cm long, which may be found attached to the wall of the abomasum or swimming in its contents. The male is red, while the female has red and white stripes in a spiral up its body, giving it the common name 'barber's pole worm'. Twenty adults can suck 1 ml of blood per day from a goat. If parasites are thought to be a problem, *Haemonchus contortus* should always be suspected first.

Investigating parasite problems

Identification of the parasites affecting goats, together with a quantitative assessment of the parasite burden in an area, can be made by using three methods:

- Examination and culture of parasite eggs in the faeces, together with a faecal egg count.
- Post-mortem examination of adult parasites in gastro-intestinal tract, including, if possible, a total worm count.
- Estimates of the Packed Cell Volume (PCV) of the blood.

Faecal egg counts

Faeces are collected in order to identify the parasites currently inside the goat. This can be achieved by

- microscopic examination to differentiate nematodes, cestodes, trematodes and protozoa;
- larval culture from nematode eggs to differentiate nematode species.

Defecation should be induced by inserting a moist finger into the rectum to collect a small sample of faeces. At least 3 grammes of faeces are required for analysis. This is equivalent to 6–8 faecal pellets in adults, and 10–12 pellets in kids. The sample should be placed in a small, clean container with a lid. Special bottles can be bought for this purpose; otherwise a small clean glass jar or similar container can be used with equal success.

If a faecal egg count is required, the sample should be either fresh or refrigerated. Without preservation, the eggs will start developing and the sample will be spoiled within 12–24 hours of collection. Refrigerated samples can be kept for longer periods.

If the sample is taken simply in order to identify the species of parasite, it can be preserved for long periods if submerged in 5 per cent formalin or in a concentrated saline solution, made by dissolving 400 mg salt in one litre of water, or by simply adding salt to a quantity of water until the salt stops dissolving.

The number of eggs per gramme (e.p.g.) of faeces is counted by using the McMaster Counting Technique. E.p.g. counts provide an indication of the severity of parasite infection with nematode parasites only. However, this is only an indication, because eggs per gramme may vary according to the season, the quantity of feed consumed and thus the volume of faeces produced, and the species and stage of growth of the parasite. The effect of a parasite burden also varies between breeds and between individuals within a breed. Some individual goats are able to tolerate higher parasite burdens than others, and some breeds appear to withstand higher levels of parasites than others.

Table 6.11 provides a rough guide to help interpret the results of faecal egg counts. Generally, for any parasite species, egg counts that fall into the 'medium' severity category should be considered as an important problem requiring action. Egg counts in the 'heavy' range must be considered a critical problem, particularly for *Haemonchus contortus*.

Table 6.11 A guide to the interpretation of faecal egg counts

Species	Light	Medium	Heavy
Haemonchus	100-1,000	1,000-4,000	4,000+
Trichostrongylus	100-1,000	1,000-2,000	2,000+
Nematodirus	50-100	100-600	600+
Oesophagostomum	100-800	800-1,600	1,600+

Adapted from Hansen and Perry (1990)

Post-mortem parasite counts

The most accurate method of estimating the parasite burden is to count the number of adult parasites in the intestinal tract after the death of a goat. The adult and larval parasites are washed out of the intestinal tract, from the abomasum to the rectum, identified, and counted for each species. This should be done by a veterinarian or animal-health assistant who has been properly trained.

Packed Cell Volume

Anaemia, a reduction of the number of red blood cells, is one of the main effects of parasites. An assessment of the degree of anaemia can be made by estimating the Packed Cell Volume (PCV) of blood from goats suspected of having a parasite burden; this procedure can indicate the severity of the burden. Blood samples from the jugular vein should be collected by a trained person. Blood samples for PCV estimates should be collected in a plain vacutainer.

The life cycle of nematode gastro-intestinal parasites (roundworms)

In order to design an effective control programme, it is important to understand the life-cycles of the parasites of major importance. The nematodes all have similar life-cycles, which do not involve an intermediate host. Adult nematodes live in the gastro-intestinal tract, where they mate. The female then produces eggs, which pass out of the goat in the faeces. The eggs, once on the ground, develop into larvae which, if they are on grass eaten by goats, will reinfect the animal, and so the cycle proceeds (see Figure 6.3). The time taken by the larvae to develop from eggs to infective larvae depends on the climatic conditions and species of parasite. If it is warm and wet, they may become infective after 7–10 days, but they will take longer if it is colder.

In order for the eggs to develop and the larvae to survive long enough to be consumed, the environment must be warm and wet. Desiccation will quickly kill the larvae. Once they have developed, infective larvae, in order to survive, may have to migrate to moist shady areas at the base of the grass sward. This dependence on moisture can follow a diurnal pattern, with the larvae moving

Figure 6.3 Life cycle of Haemonchus contortus

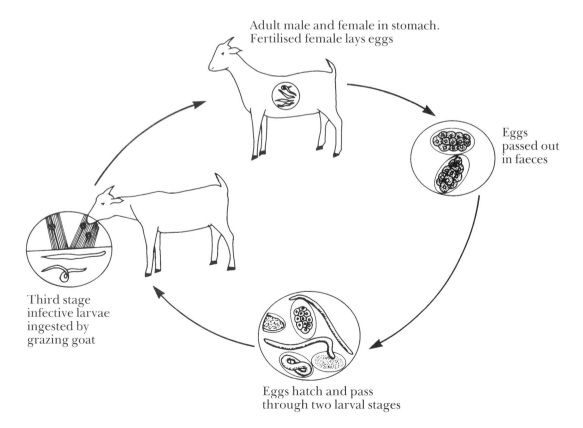

Adult male and female in stomach.
Fertilised female lays eggs

Eggs passed out in faeces

Third stage infective larvae ingested by grazing goat

Eggs hatch and pass through two larval stages

higher up the grass during the cooler, damper, period at night, and migrating down to the base of the grass when the sun rises. Larvae seldom rise higher than 5–10 cm above ground-level. They can also be washed into drinking water and infect it. Eggs can survive for long periods inside faeces, protected by the outside crust. For all these reasons, most internal parasites are picked up by goats during the wet season. In the humid tropics, environmental conditions favourable to nematode parasites may exist for most of the year. A prolonged dry season does break the cycle of infection for a while; but, with the onset of rain, conditions will immediately become favourable for larval development. Goats in even quite arid environments, such as the Sahelian zone, can suffer greatly from the effects of nematode infestations, like *H. contortus*, at the beginning of the wet season. Even in quite arid environments, local sites of infection can persist through the dry season around water points and along irrigation canals. At all times of the year, potentially highly infective sites can build up around the farmer's house, where goats may spend time during the day. Kids kept at home may nibble on infected grass around the house and quickly build up a worm burden. Be aware of the potential sources of infection.

Effects of internal parasites on goats

The effects of nematode infestations in goats may be clinical or sub-clinical. Kids are particularly susceptible to parasite burdens and often die from them. The effect on the goat will depend on the numbers of parasites and on its nutritional status. There is also some evidence that individual goats have different degrees of susceptibility to intestinal parasites, some being able to cope with relatively large burdens, while others show clinical signs at quite low levels of infection. Researchers are investigating the possibility of using this genetically-controlled resistance in breeding programmes, to breed goats with genetic resistance to intestinal parasites.

The main symptoms of parasite infection are weight loss, reduced feed intake, reduced milk production, pale mucous membranes from anaemia, diarrhoea, and sometimes death. Infection with parasites which suck blood, such as *H. contortus*, or liver damage from flukes often result in a swelling (oedema) around the jaw, known as 'bottle jaw' (see Figure 6.4). Parasite infections will dramatically reduce milk production, which can have a drastic effect on suckling kids. If the dam is infected, the chances are high that the kid will also become infected. If the kid is already weak from lack of milk, it will have a poor chance of survival. This combination of factors is one of the main causes of death among kids.

The effects of cestodes (tapeworms), such as *Moniezia* spp, are relatively minor, except in kids. Kids infected with tapeworms are

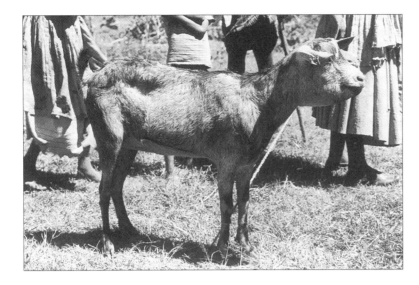

*Figure 6.4 A case of
bottle jaw*
CHRISTIE PEACOCK

also likely to carry other parasites, with the result that they grow
slowly and possibly develop diarrhoea. Tapeworms in adult goats
are not thought to be a problem.

Trematodes, such as *Paramphistomum*, are found in two sites in
the goat. Adults inhabit the rumen and are not thought to cause
any problems, even in quite large numbers. Young immature
trematodes attach themselves to the mucous membrane of the
small intestine and in large numbers may cause diarrhoea and
sometimes death.

Protozoan parasites such as coccidia, mainly of the *Eimeria*
family, inhabit the mucous membrane of the small and large
intestines. Once the goat is infected, the coccidia multiply rapidly
and damage the mucous membrane of the goat's intestine. Adults
usually develop some immunity, but continue to shed coccidia
eggs. Kids are very susceptible to coccidia, which may cause bloody
diarrhoea. Heavy infections may kill kids. Coccidia tend to be a
problem in housed goats if many animals, adults and kids, are kept
in close proximity in damp conditions. Bedding and dirty floors
can become contaminated.

Developing treatment and control strategies
The objective of a parasite-control strategy is not to permanently
free all goats of parasites, because that would be impossible. A
parasite-control strategy should aim to reduce the challenge to
kids by controlling the parasite burden of adults; and to reduce the
rate at which pasture is reinfected.

There are two approaches that should, ideally, be taken
together to control internal parasites in goats: improved management, and strategic intervention with drugs (anthelmintics). It is
wasteful to rely entirely on expensive anthelmintics to control

parasites. In many situations where drugs are not available, or are too expensive, improved management is the only option open to farmers. So what can be done?

In order to design an integrated control strategy, we need certain key pieces of information:

• rainfall pattern
• grazing-management practices
• flock-management practices
• species of parasite
• labour availability.

First, look at the rainfall pattern to see in which months conditions exist to allow larval development. Describe the current grazing practices: are goats grazing on communal land with other goats and other species of livestock or wildlife? Describe how the flock is divided for grazing: are all ages grazing together, or are young kids kept separately? What are the important species of parasite? Do you know their life-cycle? Where are the goats most likely to be picking up infective larvae? If goats are all grazing together, is there labour available to split them into two flocks? When these questions have been answered, a control strategy can be planned — with or without the use of anthelmintics.

Parasite control without drugs
Before considering the use of drugs, think about what can be done without them. There are actions that can be taken to control parasites by reducing the ingestion of infective larvae.

• Safe, larvae-free pastures should be used when possible, such as pastures ungrazed by cattle, sheep, or goats for at least three months in the humid tropics or one–two months in the semi-arid tropics; or land used for hay, or crop-stubble fields.

• If labour is available to split the flock, kids should be grazed ahead of adult goats.

• In the wet season, the grazing day should start after the sun is up and the grass is dry.

• When possible, wet areas (water points, irrigation channels, etc.) should be avoided. If this is impossible, flocks should not be allowed to linger around them.

• Goats should not be grazed intensively; they should not be forced to eat close to the ground; bushy areas should be selected when possible.

• The farmer should consider adopting cut-and-carry feeding, and wilt wet forage before feeding.

Parasite control with improved management and anthelmintics

Anthelmintics are drugs that kill internal parasites. For the most economical use, these expensive drugs should be used in combination with improved management and used at strategic intervals. In order to design a strategic anthelmintic regime, the basic rainfall pattern of the area must be described. A basic strategy for anthelmintic use must reduce the parasite burden carried into the dry season by drenching at the end of any wet period; and reduce the parasite burden of kids during prolonged wet periods.

Figures 6.5 and 6.6 show examples of high-cost and low-cost drenching strategies in a bi-modal rainfall pattern (two wet seasons each year) and a mono-modal rainfall pattern (one wet season each year). These basic drenching strategies should be combined with the management improvements described above.

Not all anthelmintics will kill all parasites, or all stages of the parasite, so check carefully before buying an anthelmintic, to ensure that it will control the parasites you want it to. There are no anthelmintics developed specifically for goats, so those developed for sheep or cattle must be used. Anthelmintics can be purchased in many forms:

liquid drench	powder
bolus	injection
paste	pour-on

Liquid drenches should ideally be applied with a special drenching gun, but this is expensive for owners to buy. Instead, a rubber teat could be attached to a Coca-Cola bottle, or something similar. The teat can be made from an old inner tube, if a baby's feeding teat is not available. A syringe can also be used. Paste also needs a special applicator. Boluses can be given with a simple plastic gun (often given free with the drug), or simply by hand; this is probably the cheapest method for a farmer to use. Boluses are harder to give at correct doses. It is not possible to give any dose other than a whole or half bolus, which may under-dose or over-dose the goat. Injectable anthelmintics, such as Ivermectin, have a wide-ranging activity, controlling external as well as internal parasites. This multiple action makes the drug expensive, but in some circumstances it may be cost-effective. See 6.6.1 for guidelines on the use of injectable drugs. Likewise some drugs that are poured along the back of the goat will be effective against both internal and external parasites. In places where dips or sprays do not exist, or water is difficult to procure, multiple-action drugs may be recommended against external parasites, controlling internal parasites as a beneficial side-effect.

If purchasing drugs from overseas, consider the weight of the drug and the cost of transport. Liquid drenches are quite heavy

Goat health

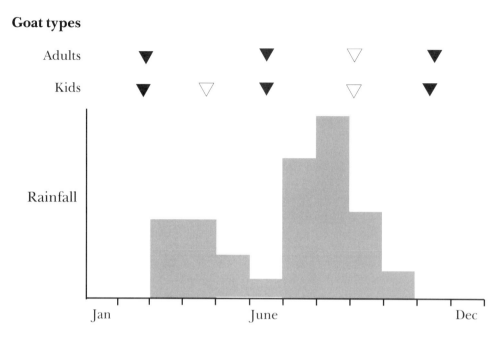

Figure 6.5 (above): Drenching regime: two wet seasons
Figure 6.6 (below): Drenching regime: one wet season

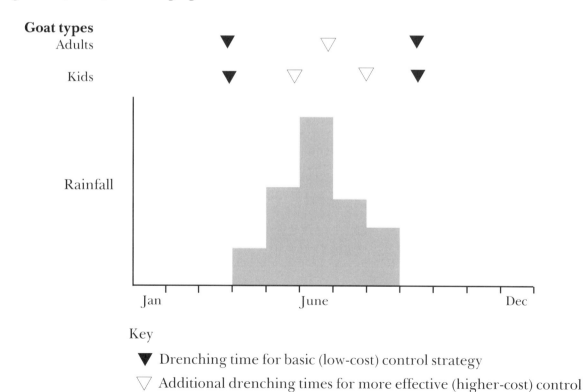

180

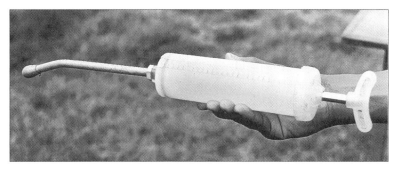

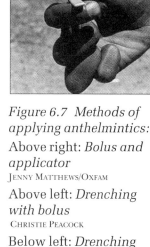

Figure 6.7 Methods of applying anthelmintics:
Above right: *Bolus and applicator*
JENNY MATTHEWS/OXFAM

Above left: *Drenching with bolus*
CHRISTIE PEACOCK

Below left: *Drenching gun for liquid drench*
CHRISTIE PEACOCK

per unit of active ingredient. Lighter drug types, such as boluses or powders, would probably be cheaper.

The methods of applying anthelmintics are shown in Figure 6.7. When using liquid drenches, care should to be exercised to ensure that the anthelmintic enters the digestive system and not the respiratory system. Pneumonia can be caused by the bad administration of anthelmintics.

The common anthelmintics for use in goats are listed in Table 6.12. In most places, only one or two types of drug will be available, if at all, so farmers will have little choice. It is important that the drug selected is effective against all the forms of the parasites that are a problem. The parasite problem itself can be made worse if the owner believes the drug to be effective when it is not; what is more, the owner's money is wasted.

Most modern drugs will effectively control a wide range of parasites, but it has been found that the repeated use of one drug can lead parasites to develop resistance to it. The anthelmintics are grouped in Table 6.12 into their drug 'families'. Drugs in the same family have a similar mode of action; so to avoid resistance, use a drug from one family and then change to a drug from a different family. It is best to change the chemical group of drug, either every year or after every four treatments, so that resistance does not develop. Anthelmintic resistance has been reported in many countries and it can develop into a serious problem. Resistance can also develop from the use of sub-standard drugs such as generic drugs made locally.

Under-dosing of goats is common, because farmers tend to under-estimate the weight of their goat, and because most dosage rates given on the drug label are for sheep, which are more resistant to internal parasites. Slightly higher dosages, 1.5 times the sheep dose, are recommended for goats. It is best to divide a large flock into groups of roughly the same weight, and calculate the dose according to the needs of the heaviest goat in each group.

If resistance is known to be a problem in a flock, care should be taken to make sure that goats carrying resistant parasites are not purchased.

Liver fluke

The liver can be infected with two main types of fluke: *Fasciola hepatica* and *Fasciola gigantica*, both of which have a snail as an intermediate host (Figure 6.8). *F. gigantica* is widely distributed in Africa and Asia; *F. hepatica* is widespread in the highlands of Africa and Asia. In certain areas, where conditions are favourable for the snail, it can be one of the biggest problems of keeping goats. Marshy, poorly-drained pastures and grassland beside irrigation channels are common sources of infection for goats. These areas may be too wet to graze during the wet season, but may be an important source of dry-season grazing. For this reason, infection often occurs during the dry season, when the ruminant host is at its weakest.

Eggs shed from goats or from other hosts (sheep, cattle, and wild ruminants) hatch and produce cysts able to swim and infect their intermediate snail host. While in the snail, they further develop into cysts that are able to infect their major host. This form of the fluke is able to survive, separate from any host, for one year. The snail host requires a warm wet environment. Adult snails cannot survive desiccation, but immature snails can remain dormant through a dry season. So even if a swampy area dries out during the dry season, do not exclude the possibility of later infection from these areas.

Once ingested, the larvae penetrate the intestinal wall and develop further in the liver, which may become severely damaged. This causes the acute phase of the disease. The final maturation of the fluke occurs in the bile ducts.

Table 6.12 Anthelmintics for goats

Generic name	Common commercial name (examples)	Dosage (mg/kg)	Spectrum of activity			
			GI	L	T	F
Benzimidazoles						
Albendazole	'Valbazen'	5-10	+	+	+	+
Febantel	'Rintal'	5-10	+	+	+	-
Fenbendazole	'Panacur'	5-7.5	+	+	+	-
Mebendazole	'Telmin'	12.5	+	+	+	-
Oxfendazole	'Synanthic' 'Systamex'	5	+	+	+	-
Oxibendazole	'Widespec'	10	+	-	-	-
Thiabendazole	'Thibenzole'	44	+	+	-	-
Thiophanate	'Wormalic'	50	+	+	-	-
Triclabendazole	'Fasinex'	10	-	-	-	+
Imidazothiazoles						
Levamisole hydrochloride	'Nilverm' 'Citarin' 'Ripercol' 'Nilzan' 'Nilvax'	7.5	+	+	-	-
Levamisole phosphate		8-9	+	+	-	-
Tetramisole		15	+	+	-	-
Salicylanides						
Rafoxanide	'Ranide'	7.5	+	-	-	+
Niclosamide	'Seponver'	53	-	-	+	-
Closantel	'Superverm'	7.5	+	-	-	+
Oxyclozanide	'Zanil'		-	-	+	+
Tetrahydropyrimidines						
Morantel	'Exhelm'	10	+	-	-	-
Pyrantel tartrate		25	+	-	-	-
Miscellaneous						
Avermectin	'Ivermectin'	0.2	+	+	-	-
Nitroxynil	'Trodax'		+	-	-	+

GI = Gastro-intestinal nematodes
T = Tapeworms
L = Lungworms
F = Liverfluke

+ = effective - = ineffective

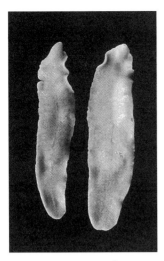

Figure 6.8 Fasciola hepatica (right) and immature Fasciola gigantica (left). F. hepatica has broader shoulders than F. gigantica.

Infection with liver flukes can produce an acute and a chronic disease. Acute fascioliasis can cause sudden death, due to massive liver destruction during migration of the larvae through the liver tissue. This is common in *F. gigantica* infections, where even light infections can cause death. Chronic fasciolosis causes weight loss, anaemia, and facial oedema ('bottle jaw', illustrated in Figure 6.4). The nutritional state of the goat is of great importance, as well-fed goats are able to tolerate higher burdens of flukes than under-nourished ones.

The drugs effective against adult flukes are indicated in Table 6.12. Few drugs are effective against immature flukes; the best available is triclabendazole ('Fasinex'). If swampy areas are grazed for a specific period, such as the dry season, drenching at the start of grazing and again at the end would be a minimum control strategy. If goats have to graze an infected area, acute fascioliasis can be avoided only by an intensive drenching strategy, drenching every 8–10 weeks; but this will be expensive. Snail-control programmes can also be considered at a community level, either by chemical control of the snail, or by draining the swampy area, or by biological control through the use of snail-eating birds such as ducks. It is difficult to control the snail completely, because it can produce vast numbers of infective cysts. Excluding livestock from the infected area is probably a more effective approach, either by fencing off swampy areas or simply by avoiding grazing those places. Unfortunately the lack of alternative dry-season grazing may make this approach difficult for farmers to follow. Delaying the grazing of swampy areas until well into the dry season, so that a lower challenge is faced, will also help.

Lungworms

Most lungworm infections of goats are caused by *Dictyocaulus filaria*. Lungworms are found mainly in the tropical and sub-tropical highlands. They inhabit the airways of the lung. Males may be 3–8 cm long, females 5–10 cm. Eggs are laid in the lungs and are coughed up and digested, passing out in faeces. Once outside the goat, the larvae take 6–7 days to develop and become infective. Infection is by ingestion of larvae on herbage. After consumption, the larvae penetrate the intestinal wall, entering the lymphatic vessels, then blood vessels, and eventually the lungs. The larvae develop in the air passages of the lung. Once in the lungs, worms cause parasitic bronchitis. Symptoms are coughing and difficulty in breathing; they may eventually predispose the goat to secondary infection, resulting in pneumonia. The cause of this pneumonia is often, mistakenly, thought to be only pasteurella, and thus the lungworms go untreated. Secondary infections with pasteurellosis may occur in goats infected with lungworms. Coughing with a fever will indicate a likely bacterial, or viral, infection, while coughing without any fever is most likely to indicate lungworms. The disease is important in kids. Treatment using anthelmintics for gastro-intestinal parasites is effective: see Table 6.12. Control measures are the same as for the nematodes.

6.4.2 Mange

Mange is a skin disease caused by tiny mites. Most mite species burrow deep into the skin, provoking severe itching, and sometimes causing the skin to break and infections to enter. There are three main species of mite which affect goats in the tropics: sarcoptic mange (*Sarcoptes scabei*), demodectic mange (*Demodex folliculorum*), and chorioptic mange (*Chorioptes caprae*). Sarcoptic mange is by far the most important mange of goats in the tropics; in some systems it can be the most important cause of death.

Sarcoptic mange

Sarcoptic mange is caused by the female mite burrowing into the skin, forming tunnels in which she lays eggs. In a few days, larvae hatch and may wander in the tunnels or on the surface of the skin. Nymphs develop from the larvae in the tunnels, and the disease can be spread by contact with either larvae, or nymphs, or adult mites. The burrowing and feeding of the mites cause intense itching and scratching. Crusts form on the skin, thickening and wrinkling it. Loss of hair is common (Figure 6.9). Typically, the disease in goats starts in the less hairy areas around the udder and the abdomen, and between the front legs. Tethering goats can predispose them to the disease, if the rope rubs away the hair on the back of the neck or leg, and thus makes the mite's penetration of the skin easier.

Figure 6.9 A case of sarcoptic mange
CHRISTIE PEACOCK

Once the disease takes hold and spreads over the body, the goat will start to lose weight, because the skin around the mouth becomes hard, making feeding difficult. Once the goat has reached this point, it will quickly lose condition and die. High mortality can ensue from the disease, and so it is very important either to try to prevent the disease, or at least to spot it and treat it in its early stages. Early signs include

- bite marks on flanks where the goat has turned its head to bite and scratch itself (this can also be a sign of fleas);

- hardening of the skin around the udder, abdomen or chest area, together with hair loss, which is a definitive sign of mange.

185

Confirmation of the disease should be made by taking a skin scraping (see below for the method) and looking for the mites under a microscope. However, in practice it is rare to have the luxury of a nearby laboratory to make a definitive diagnosis. Rapid early treatment is important in mange, and waiting for laboratory confirmation may lead to the loss of the goat.

There are acaricide chemicals available to treat mange, but they are only really effective in the early stages. The poor penetration of externally applied chemicals can be improved by washing and vigorously scrubbing infected goats by hand. Some of the chemicals available are amitraz, quintiofos, flumethrin, diazinon or permethrin; of these, amitraz has been found to be the most effective. Care must be taken when using these chemicals (see 6.4.3).

There are also drugs which have a systemic action; they are injected or poured on the skin, and are able to move through the goat from their point of application and attack the mange mites in the skin. The injectable 'Ivermectin', and pour-on chemicals such as trichlorphon and phosmet, act in this way and may be useful; but they are quite expensive.

The castor bean plant (*Ricinus communis*) is a very common perennial, growing in a very wide range of environments in the tropics. It contains an insecticidal chemical, ricin, in the leaves and stems. Being water-soluble, ricin can be extracted from the leaves and stems, using a simple water-extraction process. A quantity of chopped leaves and stems should be added to 50 times its weight in water. The mixture should be heated to just below boiling point. The residue should be pressed to extract the liquid. The liquid can be used to wash goats, but be careful: **ricin is very**

Figure 6.10 (b) Boiling castor bean leaves

Jenny Matthews/Oxfam

Figure 6.10 (c) Scrubbing a goat with castor bean wash

Jenny Matthews/Oxfam

Figure 6.10 (a) The castor bean plant   Jenny Matthews/Oxfam

poisonous. Under no circumstances should it be consumed. Great care must be taken in handling this chemical. Children should be carefully supervised during the extraction process and during its use. Washing with all chemicals should done away from the home and away from water supplies for humans.

The goat should be thoroughly washed with one of the recommended chemicals. It must be remembered that the mange mites are buried deep within the skin, so it must be rubbed very hard for the chemical to come into contact with the mites. Pinpricks of blood will be seen if the washing is done properly.

If the case is very severe, wash every 2–3 days until signs of improvement can be seen. If it is not so severe, washing every 5–6 days is probably enough. It can be helpful to wash the skin with soap and water before using the chemical, as this softens up the skin and helps the chemical to penetrate it.

Demodectic mange

Demodectic mange (Figure 6.11) is caused by a mite which burrows into the hair follicles and sebaceous glands of the host. Eventually small pustules (tiny abscesses) form; if squeezed, they exude yellow pus. This is very characteristic of this form of mange. The same treatment as for sarcoptic mange should be given.

Chorioptic mange

Chorioptic mange is not common, but may be seen in housed goats. It is known commonly as 'heel mange' for its propensity to attack the backs of the legs. It may also be seen under the tail. This mange is not so severe as the other mange diseases and can be treated easily with any of the chemicals recommended for sarcoptic mange.

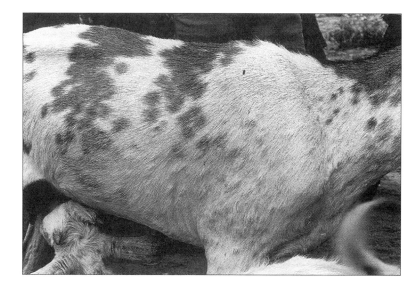

Figure 6.11 Demodetic mange: note the small bumps all over the body
Jenny Matthews/Oxfam

Figure 6.12 (a)
Amblyomma variegatum
(male, unfed)

<small>ALAN WALTERS</small>

Figure 6.12 (b)
Amblyomma variegatum
(female, unfed)

<small>ALAN WALTERS</small>

Figure 6.12 (c)
Amblyomma
variegatum (female,
engorged)

<small>ALAN WALTERS</small>

Prevention of mange

It is often thought that only malnourished goats succumb to mange, but experience has shown that this is not true. Seemingly healthy, well-fed goats can develop mange. Demodectic mange, particularly, can develop very slowly, making it hard to trace the original point of infection. Basic hygiene is important and separation of uninfected goats from those known to be infected is also important. Farmers must be trained to be alert to the start of the disease, because it is relatively easy to treat in the early stages, but becomes very hard to control once it is widely spread on the goat's body.

If there is a skin problem, a scraping of the skin may allow a laboratory to identify the cause. Use a razor blade, or sharp knife, to scrape the skin until pinpricks of blood appear. Scrape around the edge of the affected area. Use a slide, if available, to collect the scrapings. Ideally smear a layer of Vaseline on to the slide so that the scrapings stick to it; or sticky tape will do. If a slide or tape is not available, scrape on to a piece of paper and fold it. If mites are in the skin scrapings, the scrapings may move on the paper.

6.4.3 Tick-borne diseases and tick control

There are four diseases of goats that are transmitted to them by ticks. They are heartwater, anaplasmosis, babesiosis, and Nairobi sheep disease.

In addition to transmitting disease, ticks can cause physical damage to the goat. Their blood sucking causes anaemia. Tick bites can damage sensitive areas of skin (teats, vagina, eyes, etc.) and also reduce the final quality of the skin after slaughter. Tick attachment between the claws of the feet may cause severe lameness. For all these reasons, cost-effective tick-control strategies need to be developed in each situation.

Heartwater

Heartwater is probably the most important tick-borne disease of goats. It is caused by a rickettsia, *Cowdria ruminantium*, leading the disease to be known also as cowdriosis. The rickettsia is transmitted by *Amblyomma* ticks, most notably *Amblyomma variegatum* (Figure 6.12). It is a common disease in Africa and has been reported in the Caribbean. Goats reared in an environment of infected ticks are able to develop some resistance to the disease. Goats that have not been exposed to the disease will be susceptible to it when challenged with it. For this reason, goats brought into a heartwater-endemic area will be at risk unless adequate tick-control measures are taken. Exotic breeds of goats will, inevitably, be susceptible to heartwater, although they can develop resistance to the disease if reared in a heartwater-endemic environment.

Symptoms of heartwater are pronounced in adult goats, but kids show few signs. The disease starts with a rapid rise in temperature. Sometimes this is the only sign of the disease, until the goat is close to death, when nervous signs are shown: circling, lip-licking, eyelid-flicking, and a high-stepping walk. Once these signs are shown, the goat will soon be unable to stand and will die on its side, its legs paddling in the air. Post-mortem examination will show a clear fluid trapped around the heart, the characteristic sign which gives the disease its name.

Heartwater responds well to antibiotics, such as tetracyclines, if they are administered during the very early stages of the disease. However, heartwater can be difficult to spot early, unless there is a history of the disease in the area and it is expected by veterinary staff. The clearly visible nervous signs are shown so late in the course of the disease that treatment given at this time is rarely effective. If there is a sudden outbreak of the disease in a large flock, surveillance of body temperatures should be considered, together with prophylactic (preventative) antibiotic treatment.

The manufacture of an effective heartwater vaccine has been sought for many years for cattle, as well as for sheep and goats. Immunity can be induced by injecting infected blood into a goat and treating the ensuing disease. This exposure may result in immunity for up to four years, even without any subsequent challenge; but it is a risky procedure and should be carried out only by experienced veterinary personnel. Tick control is still the main method of controlling the disease (see below). Care should be taken when moving goats. Tick-infested goats and cattle should not be introduced into 'clean' areas; likewise, susceptible stock should not be introduced into infested areas, unless adequate precautions have been taken.

Babesiosis

Babesiosis is a disease caused by protozoan parasites such as *Babesia ovis*. It is widespread in most tropical and sub-tropical countries. The disease is mainly transmitted by ticks of the *Rhipecephalus* family, which introduce the organism into the host's bloodstream while feeding. The protozoa invade and break down the red blood cells. It is not so severe in goats as it is in cattle. Goats reared in an endemic area are normally immune to babesiosis, while those introduced into an endemic area are susceptible.

There is a range of symptoms: sudden death; the severe symptoms of the acute form, including blood in the urine, anaemia, and jaundice; and the more common mild form, which shows few symptoms.

Treatment, if required, involves the use of quinuronium sulphate ('Acaprin') at 0.5–1.0 mg/kg or diminazene aceturate ('Berenil') at 3 mg/kg. Control measures should try to maintain an equilibrium by allowing a low-level disease challenge to stimulate immunity continuously (this is known as 'enzootic stability'). Tick-control regimes that are too rigid will leave goats susceptible to the disease. Moving susceptible goats into an endemic area should be avoided.

Anaplasmosis

Anaplasmosis is caused by a rickettsia, *Anaplasma ovis*, which invades red blood cells and causes anaemia. Anaplasmosis is common in Africa and Asia. The disease may be transmitted by ticks, biting flies, and contaminated needles and equipment. Severe anaemia is the most common symptom, causing poor condition and performance. Stress may cause a goat carrying the disease to develop it, but it is rare in goats reared in the presence of the disease. Susceptible goats introduced into an anaplasma area should be carefully monitored.

Nairobi sheep disease

Nairobi sheep disease is a tick-borne virus disease of sheep and goats. The main vector is the tick, *Rhipecephalus appendiculatus* (Figure 6.13). This tick is distributed throughout East Africa and as far west as Zaire. Goats reared in tick-infested areas seldom show any clinical symptoms, but goats that have not been exposed to the disease, and enter an infested area, will normally show marked symptoms and high rates of mortality (15–100 per cent) and abortion (10–20 per cent). The main symptoms are fever, depression, bad-smelling and blood-stained diarrhoea, and nasal discharge. The discharge will form a crust, restricting breathing. Affected goats are likely to die 4–6 days after showing these symptoms. Pregnant females will normally abort.

Outbreaks normally occur on movement of susceptible goats into a tick-infested area. The tick thrives in dense vegetation after rainfall and may temporarily extend its normal range considerably, retreating as the vegetation dries up and dies. Even small movements of susceptible goats outside their normal grazing areas may trigger the start of an outbreak. Movement of pastoralists' flocks, at different seasons, can set up the necessary exposure of susceptible goats to the tick. Immune flocks may carry the ticks into new areas, infecting susceptible goats; or susceptible goats may be obliged to graze tick-infested areas during a drought. Control of the disease therefore involves restricting the movement of susceptible goats, and particular vigilance and tick control during movements away from normal grazing areas. There is an effective vaccine for Nairobi sheep disease, but no effective treatment. In tropical regions where Nairobi sheep disease does not occur, peste des petits ruminants is the condition which appears most similar (see 6.4.5).

Figure 6.13 Rhipecephalus appendiculatus (male, unfed)
ALAN WALTERS

Sampling of external parasites

External parasites such as ticks, fleas, or lice may remain in good enough condition for identification for several days. In order to identify a tick species, samples should be detached from the goat with their mouth-parts intact. Ticks have to be irritated to detach their mouth-parts from the skin. A hot metal or glowing cigarette can be used. Several ticks should be taken, in case some are not intact. Indicate on the container from which part of the goat the ticks were taken and how severe the infestation was. Ticks can be stored in any container with a lid, such as an old film case or glass jar. If the ticks are to be kept for a long time before reaching a laboratory, preservation in 5 per cent formalin, concentrated saline solution, or even plain water will keep them in better condition and prevent mould from developing, or dehydration of the specimens.

Tick control

For most of the tick-borne diseases affecting goats, an equilibrium between the disease-carrying tick and the immunity levels of the goat can exist and is the preferred state to achieve. It is more damaging to control ticks rigorously for a period, preventing any immunity from developing, and then discontinue the rigid control, than not to control at all. In Africa, in particular, it is a common occurrence for communal dips to stop working because supplies of the chemical are exhausted, the water supply is disrupted, or the dip-bath cracks and becomes unusable. The abrupt cessation of dipping leaves livestock vulnerable to tick-borne diseases, because the earlier tick control did not allow immunity to develop.

Tick control can be achieved through chemical and physical means. If a small flock experiences a minor tick challenge, it is possible to kill them by hand, using a needle or thorn; children can be given this task, supervised by adults. A commercial tick-grease ('Py-grease') can be applied to sensitive areas such as the udder or between the legs, preventing the attachment of ticks at these sites. If there are no tick-borne diseases in the area, these simple procedures may be enough to reduce tick damage. However, if tick-borne diseases are important, and tick control is employed to control these diseases, effective chemicals, known as acaricides, should be used and applied in an effective way.

Acaricides may be applied by washing the animal by hand; by pouring them on to its body; by spraying; by injection; and by dipping.

Dipping

Pour-on systemic chemicals, such as flumethrin ('Bayticol'), and injectable drugs, such as avermectin ('Ivermectin'), tend to be expensive to purchase, but they are relatively simple and cheap to apply. Spraying and dipping require special equipment or structures which are expensive to purchase or construct, and also require much water, which may not be available (Figure 6.14). Washing by hand is effective for a small number of goats, provided that washing of the main sites of tick attachment is carefully done. As with internal parasites, the pen feeding of goats, instead of grazing, reduces their exposure to external parasites and is a useful way of controlling ticks at no cash cost.

There is a bewildering number of chemicals that can be used in dips and sprays and for washing by hand. Like anthelmintics, they can be divided into families. As with anthelmintics, ticks can develop resistance to particular chemicals through their repeated use. In some parts of Africa the resistance of ticks to the common acaricides is a major problem. Table 6.13 presents the main

Figure 6.14 (a) Spraying against ticks with a knapsack sprayer
Jenny Matthews/Oxfam

Figure 6.14 (b) Applying a pour-on acaricide along the back of a goat
Christie Peacock

Table 6.13 Acaricides for goats

Family	Chemicals
Organo-phosphates	Chlorpyrifos, Dichlorvos, Malathion, Diazinon, Phosmet, Coumaphos, Fenthion, Chlorfenvinphos, Tetrachlorvinphos (Stirofos)
Carbamates	Carbaryl, Propoxur
Pyrethrins	Flumethrin, Permethrin, Resmethrin, Allethrin, Fenvalerate, Cypermethrin
Formamidines	Amitraz
Miscellaneous	Avermectin, Sulphur

families of chemicals used to control external parasites (ticks, mange mites, fleas, and lice) on goats. All these chemicals are potentially dangerous to humans and goats if improperly used. The instructions for their use must be read and strictly followed.

The tick-control strategy adopted depends on the species of tick and its life cycle, the incidence of tick-borne diseases, the seasonal incidence of ticks and diseases, the availability of acaricides, the amount of cash available to purchase them, and the means of application.

In commercial cattle-ranching, quite precise estimates of the financial loss from ticks and tick-borne diseases have been calculated, and an economical tick-control strategy can be developed. In smallholder production, the situation is much more complicated and, unless all livestock owners act together, tick control may not be a viable option. It may be better to try to keep a balance between the disease challenge from the ticks and the goats' resistance to the challenge.

Dipping or spraying may be carried out strategically during seasons of high tick numbers. Frequency will depend on the life-cycle of the tick and the numbers of ticks attached. Certain tick species, such as *Amblyomma variegatum*, which transmits heart-water, attach themselves to the goat on the lower part of its legs. For farmers with only a few goats, it may be feasible to dip all four feet in a dip bath made from an old 20-litre oil container, or a similar container. This can be sufficient to control tick numbers and the diseases they transmit.

If lack of money is limiting acaricide use, or acaricides are simply not available, farmers could try using a number of plants found widely in the tropics that have acaricidal or repellent properties. Some of the best-tried ones are listed in Table 6.14. All local remedies should be used with as much care as commercial acaricides. Experiment on a small scale first, before recommending the widespread use of any local plant. Be aware that some drugs can become absorbed in the blood-stream and may enter the milk consumed by humans.

Table 6.14 Some natural ectoparasite control medicines

Scientific name	Common name	Part of plant	Action
Acorus calamus	Sweet flag or Sweet sedge	Rhizomes (infusion)	Repellent
Derris elliptica	Derris	Roots (powder)	Acaricide
Juglans nigra	Black walnut	Leaves (infusion)	Repellent
Mammea americana	Mammey apple	Fruit (infusion) Seeds (powder)	Acaricide Acaricide
Nicotiana tabacum	Tobacco	Leaves (infusion)	Acaricide
Ricinus communis	Castor bean	Leaves (infusion)	Acaricide
Tephrosia vogelii	Fish poison bean	Leaves (infusion)	Acaricide

Source: Matzigkeit (1990)

6.4.4 Contagious caprine pleuropneumonia

Contagious caprine pleuropneumonia (CCPP) is an acute pneumonia of goats which causes high death rates. It is caused by a mycoplasma, identified as the F38 strain. The disease is widely distributed in North and East Africa, the Middle East, Eastern Europe, and some parts of Asia. It is a highly contagious disease. Once it has entered a flock of goats, it is likely that 100 per cent will become infected, of which 60–100 per cent will die. In endemic areas, epidemics occur when goats from different places come into close contact. One infective goat in contact with un-immunised stock is enough to trigger epidemic outbreaks of CCPP. Epidemics may start from marketing goats, especially if goats from several flocks are kept together in holding yards. Movement of goats through theft, as occurs in northern Kenya, may also result in the disease. CCPP can cause significant economic losses to goat keepers, who may lose their whole flock, as well as to livestock traders, who may lose large numbers in the course of their transactions.

Symptoms
In the acute form, goats may die within 24 hours, showing few symptoms; but more commonly infected goats show difficulty in breathing, nasal discharge, and fever. Goats may cough and rapidly become weak and emaciated. Recovery is possible, but death is more likely.

Treatment and control
Goats treated in the early stages of the disease respond well to tylosin (10 mg/kg intramuscular (i.m.)) for three days, or long-acting tetracyclines (20 mg/kg i.m.). Quarantine of infected stock is very important. Markets may have to be temporarily closed and goat movements banned. Effective vaccines, to be given annually, are made in Kenya, Turkey, and France. It is now possible to make a heat-tolerant vaccine which could be of value in controlling the disease in more remote parts of Africa and Asia. Unfortunately the low status given to the goat has meant that relatively little research has been carried out on this important disease.

6.4.5 Peste des petits ruminants

Peste des petits ruminants (PPR) is a highly contagious viral disease of goats, similar to rinderpest in cattle. It is widespread in the Sahelian and forest zones of West Africa and has recently been identified in East Africa. It is thought to have been introduced to the Middle East through exports of live goats. It has also recently been reported in India. Devastating outbreaks can occur, with mortality rates of 70–90 per cent. PPR is the most important disease of goats in the humid tropics of West and Central Africa, where it inhibits the expansion and intensification of goat production.

Symptoms
The first sign of PPR is a fever with a discharge from the nose and eyes, sometimes with sneezing. The nasal discharge becomes thick,

Figure 6.15 A chronic case of PPR. The face is covered by a thick, smelly discharge from the eyes and nose. The area around the mouth (and inside the mouth) is covered with lesions.

PETER ROEDER

and the breath is smelly. Sores will appear in the mouth, and diarrhoea may develop after two–three days of the disease. The discharge may become dry and encrusted. Affected goats become very depressed and most die from the disease (Figure 6.15).

Treatment and control

There is no treatment for PPR. Goats that do survive will have lifelong immunity. Control is by quarantine, restrictions on movement, and vaccination. Vaccination using the cattle rinderpest vaccine has been found to be effective. It is best if this can be organised on a village basis, because a vaccine vial is normally intended for 100 goats. Goats should be three months old before vaccination. PPR outbreaks occur more often during the rainy season, so vaccination should take place before the start of the rains.

6.4.6 Pneumonia

Respiratory problems are relatively common in goats, particularly housed goats. Infection of the lungs is known as pneumonia, which can be caused by mycoplasma (as in CCPP), by bacteria, or by viruses. It is often difficult to identify the specific cause of infection. The general symptoms of pneumonia are laboured, fast breathing, sometimes a nasal discharge, sometimes coughing, and sometimes a fever. In severe cases, the goat will grunt in pain as it breathes. In kids the effect of pneumonia can be rapid, and the kid may have died before clearly defined symptoms are seen. On post-mortem examination the lungs will appear infected, purple-black in colour, but the exact cause of death may never be known.

Most pneumonia problems in housed goats are due to poor ventilation and are often triggered by some sort of stress. Pneumonia can develop in goats that are housed only at night, and it is common in large flocks of permanently housed goats. The air in a goat house must constantly change to avoid the build-up of air contaminated with bacteria and viruses. The air must always smell fresh and never smell of ammonia, a sure sign of poor air quality. There should never be any condensation on the walls or roof. Goat houses in the tropics should be simple structures that keep goats dry and protected from wild animals. Direct draughts should be avoided (Figure 6.16). If cold breezes are not a problem, houses can be almost open-sided, perhaps with a wall high enough to prevent goats jumping out. The roof

Figure 6.16 A simple goat house. The animals are protected from draughts, but have plenty of fresh air.
JENNY MATTHEWS/OXFAM

should be high. Adult goats produce much heat from their rumen and do not need to be kept warm. Kids do not have a functioning rumen and do need to be kept warm. A simple kid box or basket can keep them warm and out of draughts, while allowing the air to circulate around them.

Concentrate efforts on preventing pneumonia by ensuring that the air is always fresh. Also be aware of other causes of respiratory problems: lungworms, CCPP, PPR, melioidosis, oestrus ovis, drenching pneumonia, dusty or mouldy feed or hay. Most pneumonia is caused by *Pasteurella* bacteria or *Mycoplasma* infections. Both can be treated with antibiotics. Tetracycline is the antibiotic of choice, or sulphadimidine. Antibiotics must always be given as a full course: for five days, or at least two days after signs of recovery.

6.4.7 Caseous lymphadenitis

Caseous lymphadenitis is caused by the bacterium *Corynebacterium pseudotuberculosis*. It is a common sight in goats kept in Africa, the Americas, the Middle East, and Asia. Although it may appear a relatively unimportant disease, it can build up to be of major significance in a large flock, causing important losses of production.

Symptoms
One abscess (or more) may develop on an external lymph node, commonly under the throat, behind an ear, at the point of the

197

Figure 6.17 A case of caseous lymphadenitis
CHRISTIE PEACOCK

shoulder, in front of a hind leg, or inside the hind legs. The lump will grow and eventually burst (Figure 6.17). A more serious form of the disease involves the development of internal abscesses, often on the lungs, causing pneumonia and loss of condition.

Treatment and control

It is most important that the Corynebacterium bacterium does not infect the goat house, pens, and area surrounding the owner's house. Once these areas are contaminated, it is very difficult to eradicate the disease and it will become a chronic problem in the flock. Enlarged abscesses, with a raised soft centre, should be opened before they burst, in order to control subsequent contamination. First move the affected goat out of the goat house away from other goats; then clean the abscess with soap and water, or an antiseptic. Stick a needle into it. If blood comes out, stop immediately, because a blood vessel may have been severed. If pus comes out, continue and incise the abscess with a sharp, sterile blade, making a downward cut to allow the pus to drain out. Drain the pus on to a cloth, paper, or other material that can be burned or buried. Do not allow the pus to come into contact with the ground, or it will contaminate it. Wash the abscess with water or mild alcohol. Use dressing forceps and cotton wool to clean the inside edges of the abscess, and check for any remaining pus. Finally, wash with iodine or other antiseptic (Figure 6.18). Burn or deeply bury the pus drained from the abscess. Try to keep the goat isolated until the wound is dry and healed, before returning it to the flock.

Do not attempt to open small hard lumps, because they are not ready to be opened. Wait and see how they develop: they sometimes disappear by themselves.

Control of caseous lymphadenitis is achieved entirely through good hygiene, because antibiotic therapy is always unsuccessful.

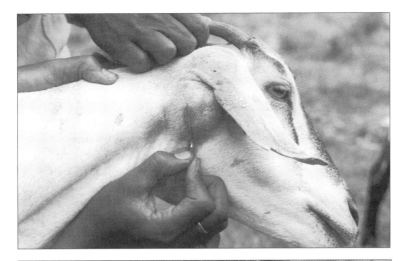

*Figure 6.18 (a) Open
the abscess by lancing
downwards in a vertical
direction*
CHRISTIE PEACOCK

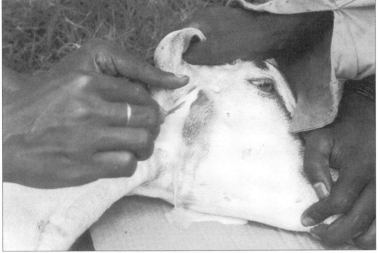

*Figure 6.18 (b) Allow
the pus from the abscess
to drain on to paper or
cardboard, which
should be burned or
buried afterwards*
CHRISTIE PEACOCK

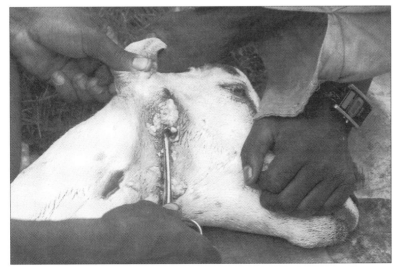

*Figure 6.18 (c) Clean
the drained abscess
thoroughly with an
antiseptic*
CHRISTIE PEACOCK

This is not a trivial disease. It can build up into one of great importance if the owner is careless and allows it to. New-born kids, if born in a contaminated area, may easily pick up the bacteria through the navel immediately after birth.

6.4.8 Brucellosis

Brucellosis in goats is caused virtually exclusively by *Brucella mellitensis*. In the presence of cattle, goats can become infected with *Brucella abortus*, but this is rare. The main effect of brucellosis is abortion, normally in the fourth or fifth month of gestation. Occasionally mastitis can be caused by brucellosis. In bucks the testicles may become swollen, causing infertility. Brucellosis is particularly serious, because it can be transmitted to humans by consumption of fresh, infected milk or by handling infected goats.

If brucellosis is suspected, a competent laboratory must carry out a blood test or preferably culture material from an aborted foetus, from the stomach of the foetus or placenta. The simple Rose Bengal or milk ring test is useful in identifying infected flocks, but does not accurately identify infected individuals. The new Enzyme Linked Immunoassay (ELISA) tests are simple to perform and 99 per cent accurate. There are two tests: the Indirect ELISA and the Competitive ELISA. The Competitive ELISA can be carried out in the field beside a goat. The lack of accurate testing facilities in many countries makes eradication difficult.

There is no treatment for brucellosis, but there is a vaccine (Rev1). Any goat confirmed to have brucellosis should be culled immediately. Great care should be taken in destroying any aborted foetus and associated material. Brucellosis should always be suspected in cases of abortion, and thorough hygienic procedures followed. Any person associated with aborting goats should, ideally, wear gloves, because these organisms can penetrate the skin. Milk should always be boiled before it is consumed by humans.

6.4.9 Mastitis

In a goat with mastitis, the udder is inflamed and becomes swollen, hot, and painful. The inflammation may be caused by several different bacteria: mainly *Staphylococcus* spp, but also *Streptococcus* spp, *Pasteurella haemolytica,* and *Corynebacterium pseudotuberculosis* (caseous lymphadenitis), as well as mycoplasma (see contagious agalactia, 6.5.6.). Mastitis may show two forms: clinical, when symptoms are visible, or sub-clinical, when infection is present but milk and udder appear normal. In either case, milk production is reduced: by as much as 25 per cent in sub-clinical cases, and as much as 100 per cent in clinical mastitis (although this is poorly documented in goats). It is more common in goats that are milked by machine or hand than in those that are only suckled by their kids. Mastitis is usually caused by milking in a dirty environment, rough handling of the udder, or forcing goats to lie in a dirty, wet environment immediately after milking. In some cases it may develop during the last few weeks of gestation.

Treatment involves the infusion of antibiotics into the teat canal (Figure 6.19). The main antibiotics used are penicillin or ampicillin for most infections. Tetracyclines may be useful for infections caused by *Streptococcus* spp or *Corynebacterium pseudotuberculosis*. Normally antibiotic applicators are available only for cattle mastitis. These applicators usually have nozzles that are too big for easy insertion into a goat's teat; if they are not used with great care, they may damage the teat. Do not drink milk for at least seven days after treatment with antibiotics. Always wash the teat with soap and water and ideally an antiseptic before inserting anything into the teat. If intra-mammary infusions are not available, and in severe cases, antibiotics should be given by injection. The teat should be milked out two–three times a day and the milk thrown away. Bathing with hot water will reduce the pain.

It is important to put effort into preventing mastitis, because for most small farmers its treatment is difficult, even impossible in the absence of antibiotics. Once it has affected a doe, she may lose the use of one or both teats; or at the very least milk production will be reduced.

All milking should be done in the cleanest possible environment. For most smallholders the purchase of a commercial teat dip is not possible. Cleaning the udder with soap and water before and after milking is feasible in most systems. Allowing the kid to suckle out

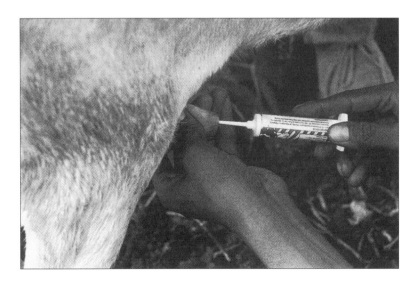

Figure 6.19 Infusing an infected teat with antibiotic
Jenny Matthews/Oxfam

both teats will also ensure that there is no milk remaining in the teat canal, which is the route of the initial infection. Feed goats in a clean dry area immediately after milking, so they remain standing until the teat canal is tightly closed.

Do not use milk from goats with mastitis for human consumption. It is usually recommended that kids do not suckle a dam with mastitis, but it may not always be feasible to insist on this.

6.4.10 Foot problems

Foot problems are relatively common in goats. Most problems are caused by bacteria infecting the foot, but the attachment of ticks between the claws of the feet can also cause severe lameness. The main pre-disposing factors to bacterial infection are prolonged wetting of the feet, making them soft and soggy, together with over-growing of the horn of the feet. A cut or tear between the claws can also allow infection to enter. Affected goats will infect the soil, from where other goats can pick up the infection. The main symptoms are lameness and a bad smell from the foot. Treatment involves trimming back the infected horn until healthy horn is found. Ideally the foot should be sprayed after trimming with an antibiotic spray, or dipped into an antiseptic solution such as formalin (10 per cent) or copper sulphate. Take care to remove and destroy all infected trimmings, because they can infect the soil and other goats. If several goats in a large flock are infected, the whole flock should be made to walk through a foot bath of copper sulphate or formalin, to prevent further infection. It is hard to design a foot bath that goats cannot jump over. Care must be taken to lead them slowly through the bath, ensuring that their feet are dipped in the solution. Make sure that they do not drink it.

Foot rot is an important disease of goats, particularly grazing goats, which may rapidly lose condition if they cannot graze properly. If they are unable to keep up with the flock, they should be kept at home and feed should be cut and carried to them.

Foot trimming

The horn of goats' feet constantly grows and will be worn down on hard, stony ground. However, not all goats walk long distances on rocky ground, so some goats, especially housed goats, need their feet to be trimmed regularly. It is easiest to trim feet with a pair of specially-made foot trimmers; if they are not available, farmers should be encouraged to use a small knife.

6.4.11 Orf

Orf is a common sight in goats, so it is included in this section on common diseases. It is caused by a virus and it is highly infectious.

Figure 6.20 (a) Trimming an overgrown foot

Figure 6.20 (b) The right-hand claw of the hoof has been properly trimmed

Figure 6.21 A case of orf
JENNY MATTHEWS/OXFAM

Orf causes sore patches around the mouth, usually starting at the corners of the mouth. An affected kid may spread it to the mother's udder. Does with painful teats will not allow kids to suckle, and these kids may die of starvation. Adult goats that are affected will not eat properly and may lose condition. There is no treatment for orf. Antibiotic sprays or powders will prevent any secondary infection from any open sores. Feeding soft feeds, such as tree leaves or sweet-potato vines, will help the goat to eat and stop it losing condition. Affected goats should be isolated, but this may not always be possible. Immunity will develop over time. Owners should be warned that humans can become affected with the sores.

6.5 Other goat diseases

The common diseases of importance to goats in the tropics have been described, together with measures that can be taken to treat, control, or prevent them. There are other conditions that can develop, either occasionally or in particular circumstances. A brief guide to these less common diseases is given below, presented according to the parts of the body most affected.

6.5.1 Diseases of the digestive system

Acidosis
Acidosis is a digestive problem caused when goats eat too much easily digestible energy (starch or sugar), such as that found in grain or root crops, without sufficient fibre accompanying it. The pH of the rumen becomes very acid. There may be bloat, diarrhoea, and great pain, shown by grinding teeth. The rumen stops functioning and, if not treated, the goat will die in one–two

days. It is rare for goats in the tropics to develop acidosis, but it can occur if goats are unsupervised and scavenge in areas where grain is stored, or when there is a sudden change in the diet due to the sudden availability of a new feed-stuff. Treatment is difficult and involves the use of a stomach tube to put oil, charcoal, and sodium bicarbonate in the rumen. Mild forms of acidosis may be called indigestion.

Bloat

Bloat is caused by the goat eating high levels of highly digestible protein, which may be found in alfalfa or clover. There is a burst of microbial activity, releasing too much methane gas, which becomes trapped in a foamy froth inside the rumen and cannot be expelled. The main sign of bloat is a swelling of the rumen on the left side. The goat will be in great pain and have difficulty breathing. **This is an emergency.** Make the goat stand and walk. In the absence of commercial remedies for bloat, force the goat to drink one cup of vegetable cooking oil. If the bloat does not respond to the oil, it is necessary to release the gas immediately by puncturing the rumen. There is a special device, a trocar and cannula, which allows this to be done efficiently. If a trocar is not available, a sterilised knife or a sharp piece of bamboo (or something similar) can be used to open and hold open a hole in the rumen to release gas. However, unless this is done very hygienically, most goats will die from later infection. Bloat is rare in the tropics, because most tropical legumes do not have high levels of digestible protein.

Bluetongue

Bluetongue is a relatively rare viral disease of goats in Africa, Asia, and the Americas. It is transmitted by a small biting midge. Most goats in areas of infection do not show any symptoms, but occasionally previously unexposed goats, such as imported exotic goats, will show signs which can be confusing. A high fever is followed by a nasal discharge, salivation, and licking. The discharge will dry and encrust the nose. The lips will swell and become tender, sometimes bleeding. The encrusted lips may look a little like orf. A swollen blue tongue may be seen. Death from emaciation may occur. Mortality rates up to 20 per cent are common, occasionally rising to 90 per cent. Control measures are seldom necessary, but consider vaccinating any exotic goats imported into an area where bluetongue is endemic.

Colibacillosis

Colibacillosis is a severe diarrhoea of young kids, caused by the bacterium *Escherichia coli*. Watery diarrhoea, dry mouth, and a stomach full of gas are the main signs. The kid quickly becomes dehydrated and will soon die, unless given fluids. Quick action must be taken to replace the lost fluids with salt, sugar, and clean water, or with oral rehydration salts (ORS), and to kill the bacteria with oral or injectable antibiotics. Kids develop colibacillosis if they have not received enough colostrum immediately after birth and are then reared in a dirty environment. This may occur because of the death of the dam or simply through poor management. Kids must be kept in the cleanest possible surroundings.

Enterotoxaemia

Enterotoxaemia is caused by a toxin produced by rapidly growing bacteria (*Clostridium perfrigens*, mainly type D) in the small intestines of kids and adults; it is usually brought on by a sudden change in diet. There are two main types of the disease. The first affects young kids and adults; the second is more commonly found in immature goats (1–12 months). Sudden death may occur without any previous symptoms. In very young kids there will be severe abdominal pain, diarrhoea, and death. Adults may have diarrhoea, may stagger, and may finally lie on their side in convulsions. The only successful treatment is to administer an antitoxin. The toxins may, in some cases, be absorbed by powdered charcoal. Only goats that are well fed are affected by enterotoxaemia. There is an effective vaccine which should be given to the pregnant doe six weeks and four weeks before she kids. Kids should be vaccinated after weaning.

Johne's disease (paratuberculosis)

Johne's disease is a chronic, progressive wasting disease, seen in goats two–five years old. They gradually lose weight, and milk production declines. The disease is caused by a bacterium, which can be picked up from the soil or by kids suckling infected milk. Stress, such as giving birth, may trigger the disease. The bacteria interfere with the absorption of nutrients. There is no treatment. To control the disease in a flock, infected goats should be culled. Imported goats should be tested for it before importation.

Salmonellosis

Infection with salmonella bacteria causes profuse diarrhoea, watery, foul-smelling, yellow to greenish-brown in adults and kids, and abortion in pregnant does. The soil of pens can become infected and may need to be replaced with clean soil. Thorough disinfection of houses or movement to a new house may be required to break the cycle of infection. Treatment with oral antibiotics, tetracyclines, or sulpha drugs is effective in most cases, together with good nursing.

6.5.2 Diseases of the respiratory system

Oestrus ovis

The nasal bot fly, *Oestrus ovis*, is occasionally a source of irritation to goats. The fly deposits larvae in or near the nostril of the goat. The larvae migrate into its sinuses and grow to 3–4 cm long, causing a thick nasal discharge, sneezing fits, and irritation. Eventually the mature larva will be sneezed out of the nasal passage and fall to the ground. There it will burrow into the ground, pupate, and re-appear as a fly. Very rarely the larva remains trapped inside the head of the goat and dies there, leading to infection of the sinus and possible death of the goat. The flies will irritate grazing goats and disturb their grazing. In most cases this condition can be ignored, provided that it does not interfere with feeding. Ivermectin, at 0.2 mg/kg, is highly effective against all stages of the larvae.

6.5.3 Diseases of the reproductive system

Chlamydial abortion

Chlamydial abortion, also known as enzootic abortion, causes abortion late in pregnancy, and still-born kids. The doe often retains the placenta, giving rise to subsequent infection. Chlamydial abortion tends to cause a wave of abortions in newly infected herds. The use of antibiotics (long-acting tetracycline at 20 mg/kg every 10–14 days) on all pregnant does can stop the spread of infection through a large flock. Control is achieved through burying aborted foetuses and other birth tissues, and separating infected from uninfected goats. There is also an effective vaccine, given one month before mating.

Dystocia

Dystocia, discussed in detail in 7.4.4, is a general term to describe any difficulties during kidding. The kid may not be in a normal position (front leg back, head back, etc.); or the doe is very young and has a small pelvis; or the kid is very large, or dead before birth.

Metritis

Metritis is the inflammation of the uterus. It may be caused by a retained placenta, by retained kids, or from trauma and infection of the uterus after a difficult kidding. The signs of metritis are fever and depression, normally with a bad-smelling vaginal discharge. A course of oxytetracycline should be given if these signs are observed after birth.

Prolapse

Sometimes, after a difficult delivery, the doe's uterus may fall outside her body; this is known as a prolapse. The rectum or vagina may also prolapse. In all cases, specialist veterinary help is required to replace the tissues inside the body. If a vet is not available, it is best to slaughter the goat.

6.5.4 Diseases of the blood, lymph, and immune system

Anthrax

Anthrax is a killer of goats. It is caused by a virulent bacterium picked up from the soil. The goat may die suddenly without any signs of disease, or it may develop a high fever and depression, with the mouth and eye becoming dark purple; there is sometimes bloody diarrhoea. After death, blood will seep from the body openings. If anthrax is suspected, **do not open the body**. If the carcass is opened, the whole area around it will become contaminated with bacteria for many years. If caught early, anthrax can be treated with penicillin or tetracyclines in large doses for five days. Normally it is discovered too late for effective treatment. There is an effective vaccine, which should be given annually in areas where anthrax occurs. Carcasses should be burned or deeply buried.

Trypanosomiasis

Trypanosomiasis is a blood parasite transmitted by the tsetse fly. It is widespread in the more humid parts of Africa and is of great economic importance to cattle. Fortunately goats are not so badly affected by trypanosomiasis as cattle are, and indigenous breeds of goats in endemic areas appear to have developed high levels of tolerance to the disease. It is still not clear whether this is because the fly does not bite goats as much as cattle, or whether there is a physiological tolerance to the blood parasite. The main symptoms are chronic weight-loss and accompanying weakness. If affected goats remain untreated, 10–15 per cent will die. There are injectable treatments for trypanosomiasis, such as 'Berenil', 'Novidium' 'Samorin', and 'Ethidium'. In areas where trypanosomiasis occurs, there is often a black-market trade in drugs, which are often bought and sometimes misused by farmers and pastoralists. The drugs are expensive, so poorer farmers are tempted to split a single dose between animals; this results in under-dosing. Repeated under-dosing in an area can render the parasite resistant to the drug, leaving livestock vulnerable to the disease.

The relative tolerance of goats to trypanosomiasis gives them an important role in livestock development in tsetse-infested areas. In some areas, goats may be the only species of domestic ruminant which can safely be kept. If tsetse-control measures are impractical, and the disease is too expensive for farmers to treat, consideration should be given to the wider use of possibly trypano-tolerant breeds of goat to supply meat and milk.

6.5.5 Diseases of the muscles and skeleton

Akabane disease

Akabane disease is a viral disease, transmitted by biting midges. It leads to the birth of abnormal kids. Infected pregnant goats may abort, give birth to stillborn kids, or deliver kids with rigid joints and wasted muscles. Kids may be blind and in some cases are brain-damaged. There is no treatment for the disease and no way to control the midges. There are effective vaccines against the disease.

Caprine arthritis encephalitis (CAE)

Caprine arthritis encephalitis (CAE) is a virus disease of goats that is distributed worldwide, with a higher prevalence in milking breeds of goats kept in confinement in developed countries. Few indigenous tropical breeds have been exposed to CAE, so all goats imported from Europe, North America, or Australia should be certified as having come from a CAE-free flock. In adults the goats show signs of arthritis, with enlarged joints causing lameness, and a gradual loss of condition. In kids of 2–4 months, CAE causes paralysis to ascend from the hind legs up the body, leading to deranged behaviour, blindness, and head tremors. Kids become infected through drinking infected colostrum and milk, so the only way of controlling the disease is to separate kids from their mothers at birth and rear them artificially.

Foot and mouth disease

Foot and mouth disease (FMD) is an important viral disease of cattle, but is much less severe in goats. Goats become dull, and develop a mild fever and blisters on the mouth and tongue and between the toes. Affected goats are lame and sometimes unable to stand. There is no treatment, but there are effective vaccines against the most common strains. Use the vaccine for the strains in your area. The local government veterinary office must be told if FMD is suspected. In some countries, affected stock have to be destroyed.

Navel ill

Navel ill, or joint ill, develops after infection enters the new-born kid through its navel. Symptoms may be seen immediately, or may be delayed for one month. The main symptoms are fever, painful joints, and a swollen, tender navel stump. If the kid is very young, less than two weeks, treatment with penicillin, tetracyclines, or sulpha drugs may be effective. In older kids, treatment will have little success. It is very important that kids are born in a clean place; ideally the remains of the umbilical cord and the navel area should be treated with an antiseptic, such as tincture of iodine.

Physical injury

Although goats are sure-footed, agile animals, they do suffer from a variety of physical injuries. They are sometimes attacked by dogs or wild animals; they may cut themselves on sharp objects while out grazing, or in their own house or pen. Goats are very prone to fractures and dislocation of their legs in feeding racks and troughs. Bucks that have not grown up together may fight to establish a hierarchy when first introduced. They can damage each other badly if they have fully-developed horns. The removal of horns and disbudding of horn buds from kids are not recommended and in most cases there is no need. Goats not kept in confinement may need their horns for protection against predators. Disbudding of kids should be performed by a veterinarian using a hot iron. It is cruel to perform this without a local anaesthetic such as lidocaine. However, inexperienced personnel may cause greater damage to the kid by the misuse of the local anaesthetic, so it is not a recommended practice unless carried out by those with experience. Adult goats, if they are aggressive, may have their horns sawn off 15 cm from the base. Do not cut any lower, or the blood supply to the horns may be severed, and severe, even fatal, bleeding may occur.

Young goats are often able to recover from broken bones if a simple splint is made to support the bone and the goat is allowed to rest and not made to walk far. Two small pieces of straight wood should be cut to the length of the whole broken bone. These splints should be strapped tightly on either side of the broken bone. Be careful not to cut off the blood supply. The splints should be removed and re-applied every week, and the broken limb checked for healing. Check the skin and soft tissues regularly, to be sure that the splint is not rubbing and damaging them.

6.5.6 Diseases of the mammary gland

Contagious agalactia

Contagious agalactia is a disease caused by *Mycoplasma agalactia*. The disease may be seen in acute and sub-acute forms. The most common form is sub-acute, when mastitis develops and milk production declines. The milk has a characteristic yellow-green colour. There is sometimes a more severe sub-acute form with mastitis and hot, swollen joints. This joint swelling can occur in males and non-lactating females. Sometimes there is an eye infection as well. Mortality may reach 15 per cent. In the acute form there is a high fever and emaciation; milk production stops and the goat will die within one week. Contagious agalactia is controlled through good hygiene, disinfection, and separation of infected goats. Treatment with antibiotics is not recommended, because it can result in the treated goat becoming a carrier. An effective vaccine is available in some countries.

6.5.7 Diseases of the eye and skin

Fleas and lice

Fleas normally affect only kids, and usually poorly fed kids. They may irritate the kids, causing them to scratch themselves repeatedly; they will also suck blood. The net result is that kids will not grow and thrive. Lice can commonly be found on adults. Most of the acaricides listed in Tables 6.13 and 6.14 will kill fleas and lice, but they should be administered very carefully to young kids, which are very sensitive. Powdered acaricides are safest for kids. Thorough cleaning and treatment of housing may also be necessary to prevent re-infestation.

Goat pox

Goat pox is caused by the same virus as sheep pox. It can be severe in kids. Early signs are a clear nasal discharge, standing with an arched back, fever, and standing hair. One or two days later many small nodules will appear all over the body, clearly visible on the less hairy parts of the body. Eventually scabs will develop on the lumps and last for 3–4 weeks. Mortality can be as high as 80 per cent, usually from the development of pneumonia. There is an effective vaccine, which should be given annually. If goat pox is suspected, it should be reported to the local government veterinary office.

Malignant oedema

Malignant oedema is a particularly bad infection of a wound. The wound may be a simple cut or a wound from castration. The tissue around the wound starts to die and rot through the invasion of Clostridial bacteria. The goat may die within two–three days, depending on the severity of the infection. Early treatment with penicillin, tetracycline, or sulpha drugs can effect a recovery. There are vaccines against clostridial infections.

Melioidosis

Melioidosis is a bacterial disease that was thought to occur only in South-east Asia but has now been reported in Africa, Australia, and Europe. The symptoms are vague, and the disease is hard to spot. There may be an intermittent fever and coughing, with or without a nasal discharge. The eyes may become watery as well. Sometimes joints become swollen and there may be abscesses in lymph nodes, lungs, and other organs. Nervous symptoms may also be seen. There is no effective treatment. Control is difficult to achieve, because there are often symptomless carriers where the disease is endemic. The lymph-node abscesses can make it difficult to differentiate melioidosis from caseous lymphadenitis. Infected goats can be identified conclusively by blood tests or cultures. If it has entered a large flock, culling infected goats may be considered, and even culling any that have been in contact with infected stock.

Pink eye

Various organisms can infect the eye. In most cases the infection will clear up by itself, but infected goats should be kept separate from the rest of the flock when possible, because many of the organisms are highly infectious. The first signs of infection include a watery eye, swelling of the eyelids, and dislike of bright sunlight. Later the centre of the eye may become cloudy. In most cases this white patch on the eye will clear up, but sometimes it will ulcerate, resulting in blindness in that eye. Antibiotic eye ointments will, in most cases, speed up recovery. Alternatively, oxytetracycline given under the skin (subcutaneously — s.c.) should help the goat to recover. If pink eye develops into a serious problem in the flock, it is simplest to treat all affected goats and those in contact with them with a course of long-acting oxytetracycline.

Ringworm

Ringworm is a fungal disease of the skin. The first signs are rough circular areas on the skin, often on the head and neck. The hair will fall out, usually in a roughly circular pattern. Ringworm is not a serious problem, but care should be taken, because it can affect humans. Special fungicides, such as 'Defungit', can be purchased to control ringworm; there are simpler alternative treatments, such as washing the affected areas with iodine (2–7 per cent) two–three times a week. Another treatment suggested is to make a paste from the anthelmintic thiabendazole and rub it into the affected area. Ringworm must be differentiated from mange, because different treatments are required; see 6.4.2.

Streptothricosis

Streptothricosis, also known as dermatophilosis, is a bacterial skin disease of goats, found particularly in the humid tropics. Large spots appear, mainly on the head, ears, and legs. The hair becomes matted with the clear fluid oozing from the spots. The spots tend to merge into large scabs. The bacteria causing the infection may enter the skin through long periods of wetting, which softens the skin, or through biting flies, ticks, or wounds. Treatment involves giving large doses of antibiotics (penicillin, streptomycin, or long-acting tetracyclines). Control is achieved through controlling factors which predispose the goat to infection, such as ticks or exposure to rain.

Warts

Goats appear to be rather prone to warts. Warts are most likely caused by a virus which enters the skin through a scratch or wound. There appear to be three main types: those affecting the head (and gradually spreading over the body); those affecting the lymph nodes (which can lead to tumours); and those that affect the feet, leading to foot rot as a secondary infection. Warts grow slowly; most goats shed their warts after about six months. Warts appear to be most common during drier seasons.

Warts can be cut, burned, or frozen off; but if this is inexpertly done, the warts will spread and become a major problem, even causing death. It is normally best to leave them alone. Treatment with 10–20 per cent salicylic acid ointment in a stable base such as Vaseline has been found to be effective. It is best to apply the ointment at least twice at an interval of 3–4 days. It is important to provide good nursing in order to prevent secondary infections of the wounds. Maggots may develop in the wart lesions. Systemic antibiotics such as oxytetracyclines may prevent secondary infections of lesions. A predisposing factor for warts is exposure to sunlight. A wart can lead to carcinoma and eventually to skin tumours. The main complications are foot warts, which may lead to foot rot and severe lameness and the formation of tumours.

Warts are controlled by isolating affected goats and avoiding physical injuries. The use of a vaccine has been reported as successful in some cases. It is made by grinding up a wart and suspending it in saline solution (8 grammes of salt in one litre of distilled water), adding oxytetracycline, and injecting it **into** the skin, **not under** the skin.

Wound dressing

If a goat is wounded, the wound should be cleaned with either a saline solution (salt and water) or a dilute antiseptic such as Savlon. Make sure that all foreign material is removed and that the wound and wound edges are clean. The use of forceps and cotton wool ensures cleanliness but may not always be possible. Ideally the wound should be left uncovered to dry and heal. An antibiotic spray or antibiotic powder should be applied to the clean wound. Insect-repellent, applied around the edges of the wound, may prevent development of maggots in open wounds.

6.5.8 Diseases of the nervous system

Listeriosis

Listeriosis, or circling disease, shows three forms. One affects the brain, causing the circling symptoms; the second one may cause abortion; and the third, which is rare, causes blood poisoning. In the form that affects the brain the goat will die quickly, normally within 48 hours. Affected goats show lack of coordination, circling behaviour, high fever, and partial paralysis of the face, such as drooping eyelids, mouth, or ear. Intravenous injections of penicillin or tetracycline antibiotics in the early stages may be helpful, but most will die. Isolation of infected goats is important.

Listeriosis may come from poorly made silage. The organism can be passed in the milk of infected goats, and the disease is transmissible to humans.

Rabies

Rabies may, rarely, affect goats if they are bitten by a rabid dog or vampire bat. Urban scavenging goats are, perhaps, more liable to rabies infection than rural goats. There is no treatment and the disease is always fatal. The main cause for concern is transmission to humans through handling a goat with rabies. It is always a fatal disease in humans. The main symptoms are confusion, standing apart from other goats, and eating unusual objects such as wood or metal. The goat may have saliva dripping from its mouth, and staring eyes. Laboratory diagnosis is necessary to confirm the disease. People should exercise extreme caution when handling any goat that shows any sign of nervous symptoms. Avoid contact with saliva and other body secretions, and wash hands immediately after handling the animal.

Scrapie

Scrapie is caused by a virus-like organism; it is mainly a disease of sheep, but it can affect goats. It is now widespread in the tropics through the export of affected sheep from Europe. It has a very long incubation period, two–four years, so it is seen only in mature adult goats. There is no treatment and the disease always causes death two–six months after the first signs. Symptoms appear very slowly; they include general nervous signs, a wobbly walk, and dull hair. As the disease progresses, the goat will show the characteristic sign of trying to scratch itself at the base of the tail. This itching will creep up the body. If the goat is scratched, it will indicate its pleasure by twitching its lips. The only form of prevention is to purchase goats from scrapie-free flocks. Once established in a flock, the disease may be impossible to eliminate without destroying the whole flock.

Tetanus

Tetanus is a well-known disease of humans and animals. It is caused when a bacterium (*Clostridium tetani*) enters the body through a wound. Signs of tetanus may appear one–two weeks after a goat is wounded. The legs become stiff and the animal stands with straight legs. The whole body becomes stiff when the goat is frightened; the nostrils flare open; and the eyelids droop. There is no effective treatment, and most goats die. There is an effective vaccine. Tetanus is associated with some routine management procedures such as open castration, so animals should be vaccinated before these procedures are carried out.

6.5.9 Diseases of nutrition and metabolism

Grass tetany

Grass tetany, or grass staggers, occurs when the forage consumed has low levels of magnesium. It may occasionally occur if goats are grazing very fast-growing pastures. Goats with grass tetany show nervous signs at first which can look like milk fever (see below). They may tremble and be unable to stand. Treatment involves the use of drugs containing magnesium.

Milk fever

Milk fever is caused by an acute shortage of calcium in a doe just before, or just after, kidding. It is quite rare. The doe will become very weak, perhaps unable to walk, and may have difficulty delivering her kid. She may have an abnormally low temperature. This disease should be considered an emergency. In a severe case, if left untreated, the doe may enter a coma and die. Treatment involves the slow intravenous injection of calcium borogluconate (25 per cent). An injection of 50–100 ml should be given cautiously, as the heart may be affected. Milk fever is rare in goats in the tropics, but may occur in high-yielding dairy goats.

Mineral deficiencies

Table 6.15 presents the symptoms of the most important mineral deficiencies, together with the main source of the mineral to correct the deficiency. Mineral deficiencies are rare in most goats grazing in the tropics, if they are able to select a wide range of feed. Localised mineral deficiencies do occur, such as the well-known deficiencies in copper, zinc, manganese, and cobalt in plants grown on the soils of the Rift Valley in East Africa. If they are known to occur, the appropriate supplements should, ideally, be fed. However, in practice it is often hard to do so. Common salt should be offered regularly, particularly in very hot climates.

Vitamin deficiencies

Table 6.16 lists the most important vitamin deficiencies and their symptoms likely to encountered among goats in the tropics. Young, growing animals have a much higher demand for vitamins and minerals and are therefore more likely to exhibit signs of their lack. Provided that it is supplied with the necessary ingredients, the goat itself can successfully synthesise many vitamins.

Poisonous plants

There are several plants that are reported to poison goats if eaten. In most cases goats appear to know which plants are poisonous and avoid them, unless they are very hungry. The most common plants reported to poison goats are as follows.

Table 6.15 Mineral-deficiency symptoms

Mineral	Deficiency symptoms	Source of mineral
Major minerals		
Calcium	Deformed bones (rickets) Retarded growth Milk fever	Milk, green feed, fish/bone meal, limestone
Phosphorus	Rickets, stunted growth Soil eating, deformed bones, low milk yield, poor fertility	Milk, cereals, fish/bone meal
Magnesium	Weight loss, excitability	Bran, cottonseed/linseed cake
Sodium	Loss of appetite, slow growth	Common salt, fish/bone meal
Sulphur	Salivation, baldness	Protein in feeds
Minor minerals		
Cobalt	Weight loss, weakness	Vitamin B_{12}
Copper	Anaemia, weight loss, poor appetite, nervous signs	Seeds
Iodine	Goitre, poor hair, birth of dead kids, poor growth and fertility	Fishmeal, seaweed, iodised salt
Iron	Anaemia, poor appetite	Green forages
Manganese	Difficulties in walking, deformed forelimbs, poor fertility	Rice/wheat bran
Selenium	Weak muscles, difficulties in walking	Vitamin E
Zinc	Stiff joints, salivation, swelling of feet, low libido	Cereal grains

- Lantana (*Lantana camara*): a common ornamental species in the tropics which often escapes from gardens and colonises large areas if left unchecked. It is not liked by goats, except during severe dry periods, when it may be consumed. Large quantities have to be consumed before any symptoms are shown. The plant is reported to make the skin sensitive to light (photosensitisation) and may cause severe diarrhoea, even resulting in death.

- Castor bean plant (*Ricinus communis*) contains the poison ricin in the leaves and stems as well as the bean.

Table 6.16 Vitamin-deficiency symptoms

Vitamin	Deficiency symptoms	Source of vitamin
Vitamin A	Poor appetite, weight loss, night blindness, poor hair coat	Browse, leafy hay, sweet-potato vines
Vitamin B_1	Blindness, nervous signs	Synthesised in rumen, supplied from brewer's yeast
Vitamin B_{12}	Weight loss, weakness	Synthesised in rumen, supplies cobalt to rumen
Vitamin D	Weak, deformed bones	Synthesised by skin, obtained from hay, fish meal
Vitamin E	Weak muscles, difficulties walking, poor fertility	Grains, leaves of green forage

- Solanaceae family, including the Thorn Apple, Sodom's Apple, etc. are all poisonous but are rarely eaten.

- Mimosine is found in many legumes, including leucaena, which is toxic to most goats if consumed in large quantities (greater than 50 per cent of the diet). There are goats in some countries, such as Indonesia and Hawaii, that are very tolerant of high levels of mimosine in the diet. A procedure has been developed to inoculate mimosine-intolerant goats with rumen micro-organisms from tolerant goats, enabling them to consume high levels of mimosine-rich legumes.

- Cassava has a high level of hydrogen cyanide in the skin which can poison goats. Cassava should never constitute more than 50 per cent of the diet.

The sudden death of a goat from an unknown cause is often attributed to poisonous plants, for want of any other cause. In reality poisonous plants only rarely kill goats. Evidence of the suspected plant should be looked for in the rumen contents while carrying out a post-mortem examination. It should be a large part of the rumen contents to make a convincing case for poisoning.

Pregnancy toxaemia

Pregnancy toxaemia may occur in goats in the tropics that are very poorly fed during pregnancy and which are carrying twins or triplets. The uterus expands as the foetuses grow, reducing the capacity of the doe to consume a large quantity of forage. The multiple foetuses themselves also make a high nutritional demand on the doe. If the forage is of very low quantity, she is in double trouble: she has a critical shortage of energy and will have to mobilise whatever body reserves she has. This rapid mobilisation of body reserves at the end of the pregnancy results in the production of ketones as a by-product; these are toxic in large numbers. The main symptoms are depression, weakness, poor balance, and eventually inability to stand. If the condition is caught in the early stages, good feeding with a grain concentrate will help. If it is caught late, the doe is most likely to die in a few days. Intravenous glucose, together with good feeding, may save her, but the chances are slim.

6.5.10 Diseases of the liver

Rift Valley fever
Rift Valley fever (RVF) is a viral disease, transmitted mainly by mosquitoes but occasionally by ticks. It is found only in Africa. The disease usually appears in occasional epidemic waves. Usually the first sign is abortion. In younger goats the signs are a fever, unsteady walking, vomiting, and a profuse nasal discharge. Milk production drops and sometimes stops altogether. Mortality rates are high among kids, but lower in adults. There is no treatment. Control is through the control of the mosquito and the housing of goats in mosquito-proof houses.

6.6 Treating and investigating diseases

6.6.1 Treatment and nursing of sick goats

Sick goats, like sick people, need special care and attention if they are to recover. All too often, unwell goats are neglected and treated like the rest of the flock. The stress to a sick goat from having to go out grazing long distances, or not having access to clean water, may make the difference between death and recovery. Any goat that is ill, particularly if it has a fever, should be allowed to stay at home in a cool, quiet place. It should have access to green feed and clean water. Goats are not good patients. They tend to sink into a depression from which it is often difficult for them to recover. Psychological support and encouragement will help them to recover.

How to give injections
Pneumonia is the main disease for which non-professionals might need to give an injection of antibiotics. If using reusable plastic or nylon syringes, sterilise them and reusable needles by first cleaning them in soap and water and then boiling them in water for 15–20 minutes. Disposable needles and syringes are more convenient, but are expensive. Before injecting into any site, clean it with alcohol or an antiseptic. There are three sites for injection.

- **Intramuscular (i.m.)** is the most common injection method. Use a 18-gauge needle, 2–3 cm long, to inject antibiotics deep into a large muscle. In small, young goats a smaller 20-gauge needle should be used. The best site is the neck muscle just in front of the shoulder, or the fleshy part of the shoulder itself. Hit the muscle two or three times with your fist to accustom the goat to the procedure and prevent it from clenching its muscle as the needle enters. This can lead to muscle stiffness and discomfort. The needle should be inserted quickly, straight into the muscle. Before injection, draw out the plunger slightly to check that the needle has not entered a blood vessel. If blood enters the syringe, withdraw the needle and try again in another place. No more than 5 ml of drug should be administered in one site.

- **Subcutaneous (s.c.)** injections are given under the skin, usually in the skin just behind the shoulder or in the neck. A short needle, 1–2.5 cm, should be used. Pull out a fold of skin and insert the needle at an angle towards the body of the goat.

- **Intravenous (i.v.)** injections are given into a vein. This may be needed in an emergency, in order for antibiotics to enter the bloodstream as quickly as possible. Intravenous injections should, ideally, by given by a veterinary professional.

6.6.2 Procedure after death

If a goat dies, it is helpful to carry out a simple post-mortem (after death) examination to try to find out the cause of death. This may be important in identifying infectious diseases and preventing their spread to other goats in the flock. Many farmers cut open the carcass of animals which die and look inside, and this is good practice. It is also useful if extension staff are able to carry out a simple post-mortem examination and learn how to record systematically what is seen. Extension staff should teach farmers to look out for the key signs of specific diseases and report them when seen.

In order to carry out an effective post-mortem, it is important that the size, colour and texture of normal organs are known, so that any abnormalities can be observed and recorded. Visits to a slaughterhouse, or to butchers who slaughter goats will enable extension staff to become quickly familiar with the appearance of the organs of normal goats.

How to do a post-mortem
First find a convenient site, away from the owner's house and other livestock, and in a place where the dead goat can subsequently be burned or buried at a depth of at least one metre. You must be aware of the potential risks of contaminating the

area around the post-mortem site. Never perform a post-mortem near any water supply, or close to grazing areas. Dig a small hole beside the carcass, into which organs and fluids can be placed.

Ideally, post-mortem examinations should be carried out wearing rubber gloves. Alternatively thin plastic bags can be used to cover your hands. However, in the field they may not be available. If they are not available, check your hands for any cuts or bruises. If you have any cuts, do not perform a post-mortem. Get someone else to open the carcass and examine the organs while you watch.

Obtain a detailed case history from the owner of the goat (see 6.2.3). This, combined with an examination of the outside of the carcass, will help to direct your attention to the organs most likely to be involved in the disease described.

Ideally you should have someone to record the findings of the post-mortem as you describe them.

Post-mortem diagnostic key

1. **Observe the dead goat.** If there are any dark bloody discharges from the mouth, nose, or anus, then **DO NOT OPEN IT,** as it may have died of **anthrax**. Anthrax is a very dangerous disease. If the body is opened, the whole surrounding area may become contaminated.

2. **Touch the body to check for any gas under the skin.** Does it crackle under the skin? If yes, there might have been **clostridial** infection, such as **malignant oedema**. Check the body for any external abnormalities. Check for ticks. How severe is the infestation? If there are any ticks, take samples. Check all legs for **foot rot** and **wounds**.

NOTE: If the body is stiff, swollen, or bloated, **DO NOT OPEN IT,** because too long a period has elapsed after death to be able to determine the cause of death. Do not bother to carry out a post-mortem on a goat that has died more than 12 hours before, because the internal organs will have already started to decompose.

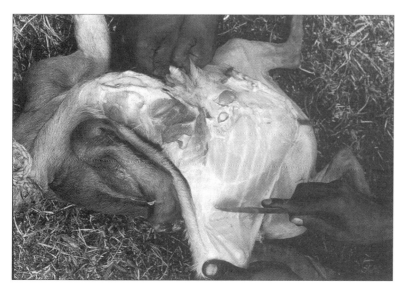

3. Lay the body on its back or side and cut the skin in a line along the centre of the abdomen and chest. Remove the reproductive organs (testicles or udder). Pull the skin back. Bend back top foreleg and hindleg.

4. Open the body by cutting the ribs along the line of the backbone and cutting the ribs along the chest and removing the rib cage.

5. Tip the body up and look at the fluids. Are they bloody or yellowish?. Do there seem to be a lot of fluids? If yes, suspect **enterotoxaemia**.

6. Remove the whole digestive tract without opening it, by tying the top and bottom ends of the tract with string, so that the contents of the tract do not spill out. If you do not have string, you can tie the intestine itself in a knot. Remove the tract and keep it for later, with the liver and the spleen.

7. Check the heart for fluids inside the outer membrane of the heart. If there are lots of fluids, then **heartwater** might the cause of death.

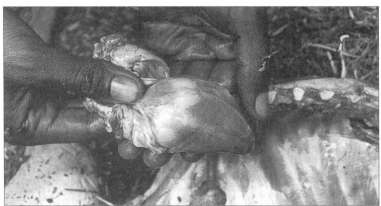

8. **Cut the top of the trachea and remove it with the lungs** and keep them for later.

9. **Look for the kidneys**, which will be in some fat at the back of the abdominal cavity. Extract the kidneys from the fat, remove and keep them.

10. **Check the bladder.** Open and observe the colour and quantity of urine. Check inside the bladder for any haemorrhage, dots of blood, or lines of blood. If yes, suspect **poisoning.**

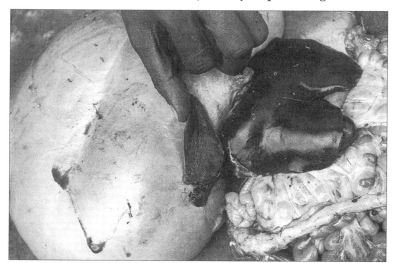

11. **Look for the spleen** attached to the rumen, close to the liver. Check the length and edge of the spleen. Is it sharp or blunt? A normal spleen is firm, with sharp edges. Feel the consistency. If the spleen is enlarged and soft with a blunt edge, then the cause of death was possibly **anaplasmosis**. If the spleen is very swollen and lymph nodes are swollen, suspect **trypanosomiasis**.

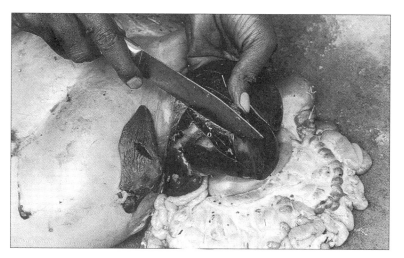

12. **Check the liver** for size and consistency: hard, springy like dough, or fragile? Cut across the length in 2–3 places and press. If **liver fluke** are present, dark-coloured fluke will pop out. Run a knife blade on the surface of the liver to feel for any spots of dead (necrosed) tissue. If there are greyish/yellow areas, these may be the migratory tracts of liver fluke.

If the liver and spleen are very enlarged, and if the gall bladder is distended with thick, dark green bile, then suspect **babesiosis**. If it is a kid and the liver is pale and yellow with grey patches, or if it is an adult and the liver is red/brown with dead patches, then suspect **Rift Valley fever**. To confirm, check intestines for haemorrhage. **Note:** Rift Valley fever is dangerous and can infect people.

13. Check the lungs for consistency. Feel each lung for hardness, nodules, and cysts.

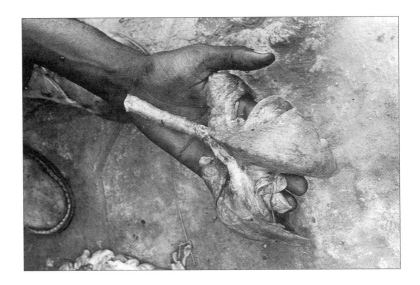

Open the trachea and continue cutting into the lung. Check for foam, worms, and blood. Adult worms in the bronchi indicate **lungworms**.

Cut a small piece of lung and put it in a cup of water. If the lung is normal, it will float; if diseased, it will usually sink.

Cut across the length of the lung, press, and see if there is any foam. If there is much straw-coloured fluid, then suspect **contagious caprine pleuropneumonia (CCPP)**. If there is clear fluid and the lower part of the lung is red/purple, then suspect **pasteurellosis**. If there are abscesses in the lung which are oozing pus, then suspect **melioidosis**.

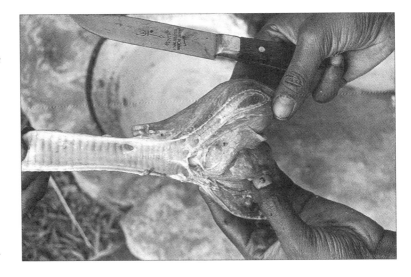

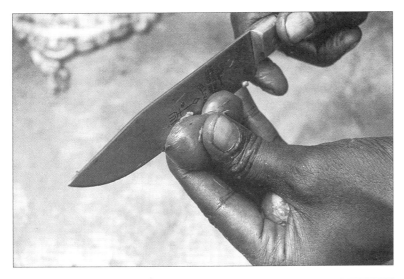

14. Check the kidneys.
The kidney will normally
start to putrefy 12–24
hours after death.
However, if the kidney
putrefies within six
hours after death,
suspect **enterotoxaemia**
(pulpy kidney).

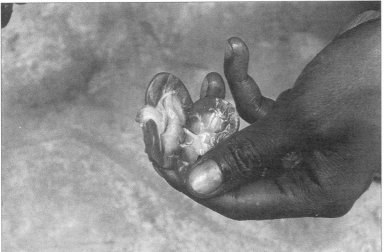

**15. Check the digestive
tract.** First observe the
whole tract for any dark
patches.

Small intestine: If there is a dark patch, open in that area; if it appears normal, open randomly. Cut open and remove the contents into a container. Cut along the length and check for any attached worms.

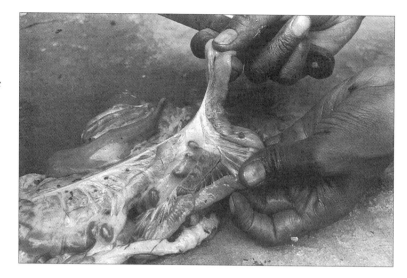

Check the inside wall for any blood lines. If they are present, suspect **enterotoxaemia**. Check the contents for any worms. In some cases you may not be able to see the worms with the naked eye. Watch for a wave-like motion in the contents of the small intestines. This is due to the movement of parasites. If the contents are bloody and nodules are present on the intestinal surface, suspect **coccidiosis**.

Large intestine: As for small intestine, but carefully check for blood lines: the so called 'zebra markings', which are common in **peste des petits ruminants (PPR)**. If the large intestine is filled with liquid faeces, and there was evidence of severe dehydration, suspect **colibacillosis.** If there are obvious haemorrhages, particularly in the caecum and colon, and enlarged internal lymph nodes, then suspect **Nairobi sheep disease**.

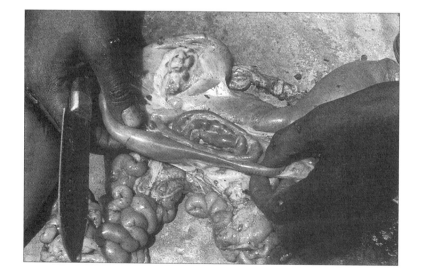

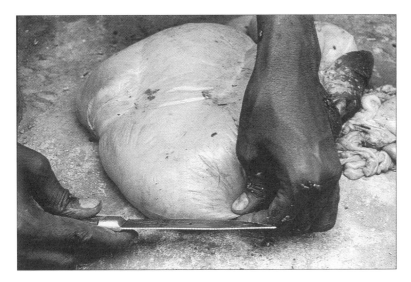

Rumen: Cut the rumen along its greatest curve. Remove the contents. Look for worms attached to the wall (small red oval-shaped worms when full of blood). They indicate **Paramphistomum** and are not important.

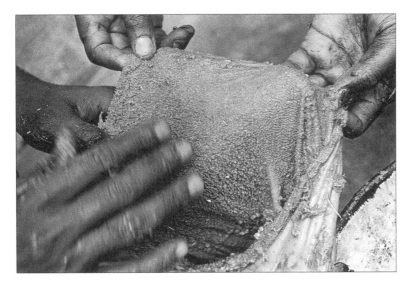

Check the inside wall; if it rubs off easily, then **acidosis** might be the cause of death. Check contents for foreign materials (plastic bags, metal objects, etc.); for smell (a beer-like, fermenting smell indicates **acidosis**); for appearance (if frothy, suspect **bloat**).

Check the contents of the **reticulum** for foreign material such as nails, plastic bags, wires, etc.
Check the contents of the **omasum** for foreign material.

Abomasum: Put contents into a container and wash the flaps of the wall into the container. Look at the wall for blood spots, blood lines, or blood. Look for small white worms with a red spiral pattern attached to the wall; these are probably **Haemonchus contortus**. If you can see many worms, there is a major worm problem.

All post-mortem photographs were taken by Jᴇɴɴʏ Mᴀᴛᴛʜᴇᴡꜱ

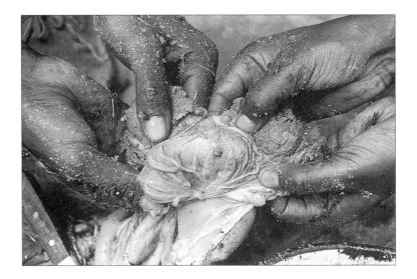

16. After the post-mortem the body should not be eaten, but ideally should be deeply buried or burned.

Taking samples during a post-mortem

If you have access to a good veterinary laboratory, any organ found not to be normal should be preserved as a sample and taken to a veterinary laboratory for further investigation. When taking samples, always take both the affected part and a normal part of the organ. Samples should be preserved in 5 per cent formalin, or frozen. If this is not possible, they can be preserved in a strong saline solution. They should reach a laboratory within 12 hours. Clearly label the sample, and send it to the laboratory with a copy of the post-mortem examination record.

6.7 The organisation of goat health care

In most countries in the tropics, the veterinary services are over-stretched and tend to be concentrated in the richer, more fertile areas. It is hard for poorer countries to provide a veterinary service to all livestock producers. Many governments have realised that they cannot afford to continue providing a subsidised veterinary service, so they are starting to privatise their service. Goats are more often kept by marginal farmers and by pastoralists, in areas where veterinary services are scarce. Even the services that do exist are more concerned with cattle and buffaloes than with sheep and goats. Few veterinarians receive any special training on the diseases of goats, or are encouraged to carry out research on the problems of goat health. For all these reasons it is of fundamental importance in any goat-development programme that owners themselves are trained to prevent the important diseases and to cope with the major health problems as they arise. Some problems will require the assistance of veterinary professionals if available, and the government veterinary service will always have an important role in controlling infectious diseases through the regulation of stock movement, vaccination, testing herds and flocks, and regulating drug use. The current trend appears to lead towards an increase in the use of private veterinary practice for basic clinical treatment; this trend may leave many marginal goat farmers with even fewer veterinary services than they had before.

Many governmental and non-governmental organisations have found it helpful to supplement the existing veterinary service and establish a more decentralised health-care system, involving the community themselves in looking after the health of their livestock, rather than relying on outside services. In order to achieve this, farmers are trained to be what may be called paravets, community veterinary assistants, basic veterinary workers, or vet scouts. The objectives of this training are:

- to improve the community's access to essential veterinary drugs and services, and so maintain the health of their goats;
- to encourage the paravets to train farmers and pastoralists in the basic health care of their goats;
- to improve disease surveillance through the timely reporting of disease outbreaks in the community.

The paravets should, ideally, work within the existing veterinary system, whether that is a government service or veterinarians operating in private practice. Before paravets are trained, discussions must be held with the relevant authorities, to ensure that they are accepted and will be able to function effectively. There may be regulations governing the use of certain scheduled drugs, such as antibiotics and trypanocidal drugs. Ideally the paravets would have close links with government veterinary staff and might initially be supervised by them.

Paravets may be trained to serve the needs of a defined group of goat owners, such as members of a goat group or cooperative. In the short term, paravets have a useful role in improving the health care of goats. In the long term, the most important role of the paravets is to train their fellow farmers and pastoralists to carry out simple procedures and use basic drugs.

6.7.1 Training of paravets

Selection of trainees

Ideally, the trainees should be selected by the community itself. They should be willing to serve the community, and be responsible and respected members of the community. They should be successful livestock keepers themselves. Paravets may be men or women. Women have been found to be very effective paravets for goats. They should be settled members of the community who are prepared to serve for a reasonable period and are not likely to leave soon after training has been completed. It is not essential that they are able to read or write, although it is a bonus if they can. Illiteracy should not prevent candidates who are otherwise suitable from being trained. Ideally, at least two trainees per community should be trained, so that if one is sick, or leaves the community, one will still remain. Often school-leavers are selected for training, because they are literate. However, unless their paravet role offers them a living, they are unlikely to be interested in serving the community for a long period.

Duties of the paravet

The paravet should, at a minimum, be able to deworm, spray, treat wounds, and castrate goats. They should be able to detect important diseases and report outbreaks to the local veterinary officer. They should also be able to train their fellow farmers in maintaining the health of their stock. In certain circumstances, trainees could be taught to use antibiotics and trypanocidal drugs, provided that the range of drugs and their dosages are small. Each country will have its own legislation governing injectable drugs, and these regulations must be followed.

Training method

The training does not have to be very sophisticated, but should be very practical. There should be an initial training period of, say, 5–7 days. It is important that the training sessions are simple, short, practical, and participatory. 'Hands-on' experience is very important in developing skills and building up confidence. The training should take place in the community itself. There is no need, and it is undesirable, to take trainees away from their community for residential training. The most important element in the training is obtaining enough goats to expose the trainees to as many different diseases and conditions as possible in the time available, so giving them as much experience as possible. It is helpful to gather together trainees in one village and call goats to come and be treated; this is a very effective way of seeing many cases. Different villages can be visited each day of the course.

To assist illiterate trainees, simple pictorial treatment-guides and price-lists can be prepared, to serve as a reminder and assist in recording payments received for the different services given.

At the end of the training, a small graduation ceremony should take place, at which the paravets are presented with a certificate of attendance and their set of drugs and equipment. In this way they are identified within their communities as people with special skills and resources.

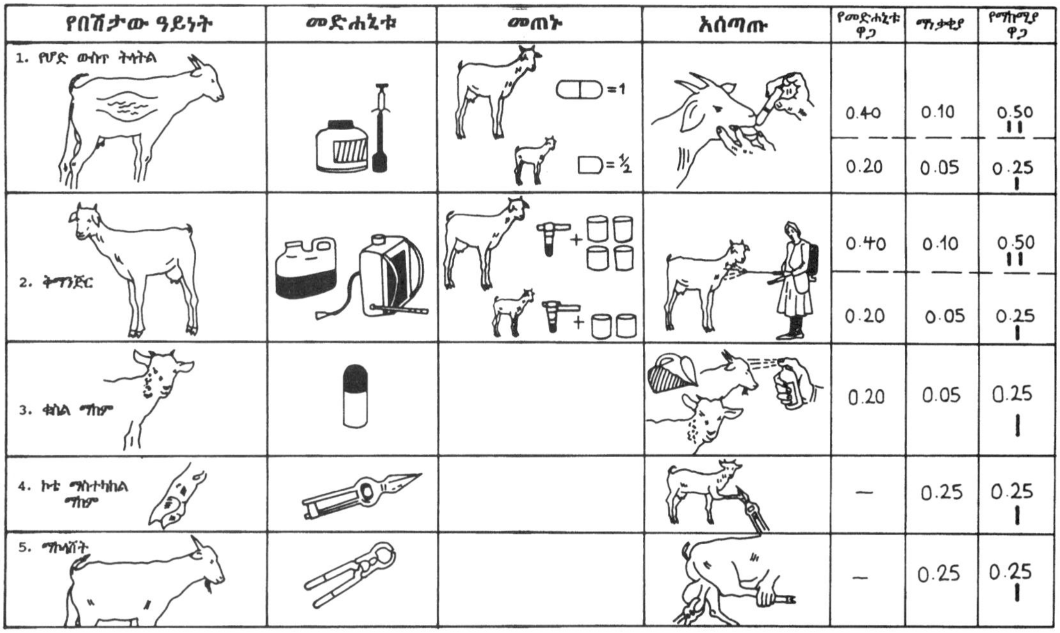

Figure 6.23a (above) A pictorial guide to treating goats, used in Ethiopia

Figure 6.23b (below) A pictorial chart to record treatment given

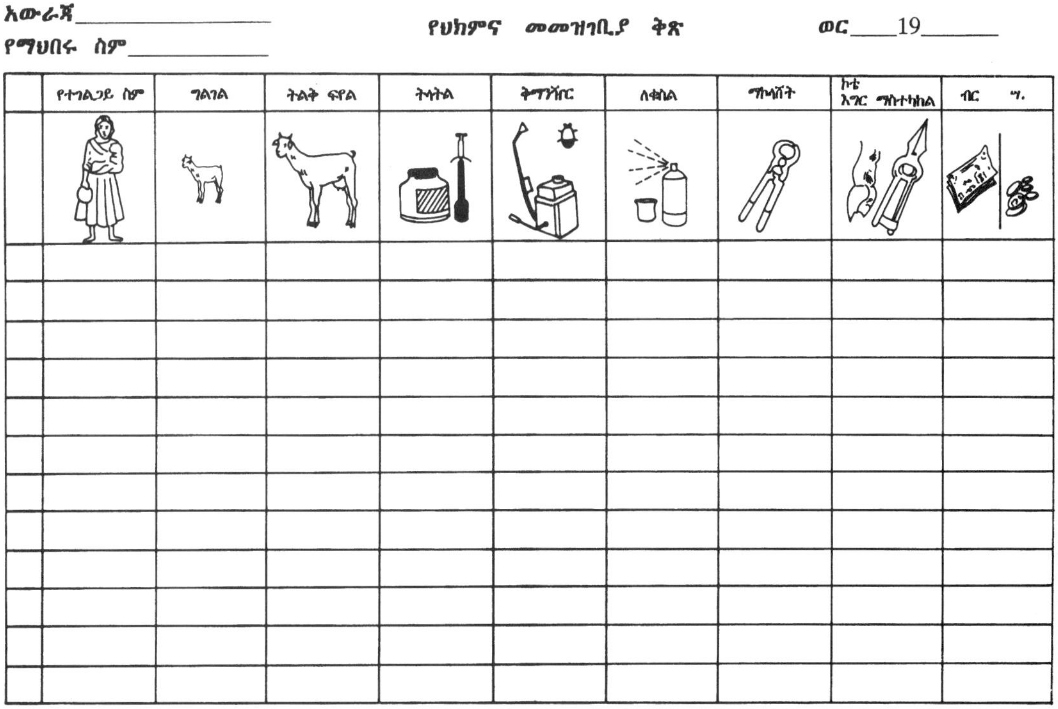

After the initial training course, government veterinary staff should closely supervise the newly-trained paravets. A follow-up course should be organised after, say, three months, to allow feedback and discussion of problems encountered. Refresher courses should also be arranged, probably every year, to maintain standards and teach the use of any new drugs that may become available.

Course content

The content of the training should vary according to the major diseases of the area. There is no point in including obscure diseases that are rarely seen. Emphasise the importance of prevention, rather than efforts to cure an already sick animal.

- Animal diseases and management
  Recognising sickness
  Care of young, pregnant, and lactating stock
  Kidding problems

- Examination of a sick animal
  Taking a history
  Observing clinical signs, including temperature, to identify infections

- Internal parasites
  Common internal parasites
  Effects on animal and clinical signs
  Post-mortem on purchased animal to demonstrate internal parasites
  Treatment
  Strategic control in relation to rainfall pattern

- External parasites
  Common external parasites (ticks, lice, and mange)
  Effects on animal
  Transmission
  Treatment
  Control

- Digestive problems
  Causes
  Treatment

- Lameness, wounds, and fractures
  Foot rot
  Dressing wounds
  Abscesses

- Infectious diseases
  Common infectious diseases, including CCPP and PPR
  Isolation

    Reporting
    Vaccination

- Trypanosomiasis (in appropriate areas)
    Clinical signs
    Transmission
    Treatment
    Control

- Care of sick animals
    Feed and water
    Rest
    Isolation

- Procedures
    Deworming
    Spraying
    Dressing wounds
    Castration
    Hoof-trimming
    Measuring medicines and estimating weight
    Administering medicines
    Care of drugs and instruments
    Restraint of animals

- Planning a year of goat health-care
    Vaccination
    Drenching
    External parasite control
    Routine measures (foot-trimming, castration, etc.)

Drugs and equipment required

After training, the paravets should be supplied with basic drugs and equipment in a convenient bag or box. Basic equipment might include:

Anthelmintics	Knapsack sprayer
Flukicide	Thermometer
Acaricide	Burdizzo castrator
Terramycin spray	Injectable Terramycin
Savlon	Foot trimmers
Cotton wool	Syringe 10 ml (for measuring)
Ophthalmic ointment	Record book
Fungicide	Balling gun for anthelmintic boluses
Antibiotic powder	Dressing forceps

    The content of the set should vary according to the prevailing diseases of the area and the appropriate control measures that paravets can take. Ticks are not a problem in many areas, so the knapsack sprayer would not be required in all places.

Provision must be made to resupply the paravets with drugs when they have exhausted their supplies. This may be done by an external donor or government veterinary department, by purchasing from a commercial drug shop, or by a community-established revolving fund for the purchase of drugs. It is important to be realistic about the long-term sustainability of the supply of drugs. Recovering the full cost of the drug is the only realistic way of ensuring the long-term sustainability of the programme. In many countries, drugs are in short supply or — if available — are very expensive. Paravets should not start using drugs that they cannot subsequently obtain.

Recording methods

The records kept must have a particular purpose, which will depend on the organisation of the paravet programme. Records can be kept to monitor disease incidence and drug use, and to keep accounts for a revolving drug-fund. The records can also monitor the activity of the paravets themselves. Simple records can be kept by even illiterate farmers.

6.7.2 Organisation, monitoring, and evaluation of paravets

Paravets can operate in several different ways. They can function as part of the government veterinary service, being supervised and supplied with drugs by them. Alternatively they can operate privately, obtaining drugs from the private sector and selling them and their services to client farmers. They are likely to be trained by government veterinary staff, with some NGO or other external support. They will then be supervised by government veterinary staff and are likely, in the short term, to receive drugs from some external source. Paravets may start as virtual volunteers, receiving some remuneration by charging a small mark-up on the cost-price of the drug. However in the long term it is too much to expect them to remain as volunteers. The continuing sustainability of the programme cannot be ensured unless drugs are charged at their full cost. The price charged by the paravets should provide sufficient incentive for them to continue working. Some are likely, at some point in their lives, to find their duties a burden and stop working, while others may develop their own 'practice' and become professional paravets.

The government veterinary staff and the community should be involved in supervising paravets and ensuring that drugs are used properly. In some places, the government veterinary service prefers paravets to sign an agreement, indicating that they will administer only certain authorised drugs and carry out certain specified activities. An example of the agreement is shown in the box opposite.

I am a member of [Name] Goat Group.

I have received training in deworming, spraying, foot-trimming, wound-dressing, and castration.

I have received the following drugs and equipment from [Name] Goat Group to treat goats belonging to the group members:

Anthelmintics	Knapsack sprayer
Acaricide	Balling gun
Terramycin spray	Thermometer
Savlon	Burdizzo
Cotton wool	Dressing forceps
Ophthalmic ointment	Foot trimmers
Record book	Bag

I will work in the future under regulations set by the Veterinary Department and the needs of the community. If I do not keep this agreement, I will return all drugs and equipment to [Name] Goat Group. If I fail to return this equipment, I understand that I may be pursued under the law.

....
Paravet   *Leader of Goat Group*   *Veterinary Dept.*

Drug shops and revolving funds

If paravets are to provide a sustainable service, they must have easy access to a reliable supply of the important drugs they need. There may already be local veterinary drug shops, from which they can buy their supplies. If there are no drug shops, owners of general stores might be trained and encouraged to stock a small selection of basic veterinary drugs. Alternatively, credit may be given to a trained paravet to start a small drug shop, or the goat group or cooperative may set up their own. These drug shops can also play a useful role in monitoring the performance of the paravets. The shop-keeper or attendant must be trained as a paravet, so that he or she can give reliable advice to any farmers coming directly to the shop.

In some countries where drugs are scarce, there may be a black market in certain drugs. If black-market drugs are available, paravets must be trained in their correct use, so that they can educate their fellow farmers. Farmers and pastoralists must be encouraged and trained to use all drugs properly, and paravets can play a vital educational role.

Example of paravet organisation: the 'Wasaidizi' of Kenya

In Meru, central Kenya, the Intermediate Technology Development Group (ITDG), supported by Oxfam (UK and Ireland) and working with the Catholic Diocese of Meru, started a community-based animal health-care project. They trained both men and women farmers to be 'Wasaidizi wa mifugo', or 'helpers of livestock', providing basic health services to farmers in the area. They quickly became known simply as Wasaidizi. ITDG also helped several individuals to start small veterinary drug shops. After seven years of operation, some paravets are earning a small income from the services they provide. The owners of the drug shops, who were also trained as Wasaidizi, found that they could not make a good enough living from selling only drugs, so now they stock some grocery items as well. They report that increasingly farmers are coming directly to the drug shops to buy their drugs, having been trained in their use by the Wasaidizi. The drug-shop owners have developed contacts with drug wholesalers in Meru town and are able to negotiate their own discounts. The drug shops are vital to the long-term sustainability of the Wasaidizi in this area. *Source: Grant (1992)*

Further reading

Grant, S. (1992) 'Helpers of Livestock: The Wasaidizi of Kenya', Development Projects in Arid Lands No. 3, Oxford: Oxfam

Hall, H.T.B. (1985) *Diseases and Parasites of Livestock in the Tropics* Intermediate Tropical Agriculture Series, London: Longman

Hansen, J. and B. Perry (1990) 'The Epidemiology, Diagnosis, and Control of Gastro-intestinal Parasites of Ruminants in Africa', Nairobi: International Laboratory for Research on Animal Diseases

Mathews, J.G. (1991) *Outline of Clinical Diagnosis in the Goat*, London: Wright

Matzigkeit, U. (1990) *Natural Veterinary Medicine: Ectoparasites in the Tropics*, Weikersheim, Germany: AGRECOL/Josef Verlag

Smith, M.C. and D.M. Sherman (1994) *Goat Medicine*, Philadelphia: Lea and Febiger

Thedford, T.R. (1983) *Goat Health Handbook*, Arkansas: Winrock

CHAPTER 7

Management of reproduction

Introduction

Reproduction is one of the main factors which determine the
overall productivity of the goat enterprise. It is important that goat
keepers are able to manage the reproduction of their goats
according to their own objectives, the availability of feed, and the
demands of the market. Reproduction dictates not only the rate of
expansion of the flock and the number of excess stock for sale, but
also the availability of milk for home consumption and sale. It
should be possible for goat farmers to exert enough control to
determine when their goats start breeding, how often they breed
and, if required, what season they give birth.

In order to manage reproduction successfully, it is important to
understand the basic physiological processes underlying it.

7.1 Reproduction in the goat

7.1.1 Female reproduction

The reproductive organs of the female goat are shown in Figure
7.1. The female's eggs (ova) are produced in the ovaries and
transported into the oviducts, where fertilisation occurs. The
development of the ova, and timing of their release for fertilisation,
are controlled by hormones.

The ovaries are the two essential organs of reproduction in the
female. The ovaries produce the ova, as well as the hormones
oestrogen and progesterone. The oviducts, also known as
Fallopian tubes, pass from the horns of the uterus to the ovaries,
where they end in a funnel-shaped structure. These tubes carry
one or more ova from the ovary down to the uterus. The uterus is
lined with a mucous membrane. Once an ovum has been fertilised,
the doe supplies oxygen and nutrients through this membrane to
nourish the developing foetus. The vagina extends from the neck
(cervix) of the uterus to the vulva, which is the external part of the
reproductive tract.

Puberty is the period when the reproductive organs of a young
animal become functional. In females this is the age at which

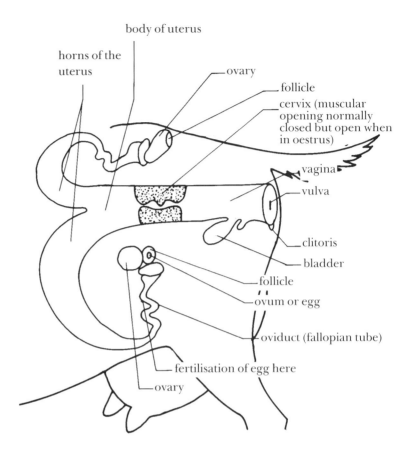

*Figure 7.1 Female
reproductive organs*

oestrus is first shown and the young female will allow a male to mount and mate her. In goats this occurs at about 7 months, but may vary from 3 to 12 months. The age at which puberty occurs will vary according to breed (smaller breeds are earlier, larger breeds are later); nutrition (poor nutrition will delay it); health; and the presence/absence of a sexually mature male (the sight, sound, and smell of a male will encourage sexual maturity).

From puberty onwards, females experience repeated sexual cycles, called oestrus cycles. This cycle will normally continue, unless interrupted by pregnancy, or suppressed during the early stages of lactation (lactational anoestrus) or if the goat is poorly fed and experiences nutritional stress (nutritional anoestrus).

Oestrus cycles are regulated by hormones. In goats the cycle takes about 19 days to complete, but this may vary between 17 and 21 days. The site of the developing egg (Graafian follicle) releases oestrogen, which induces the doe to come into oestrus.

The main signs of oestrus are bleating, wagging the tail, seeking out a male (if present), standing to be mated, swelling of the vagina, and discharge of mucus from the vagina.

The oestrus cycle culminates in ovulation, when a mature egg (ovum) is released into one of the oviducts. The collapsed Graafian follicle is then known as the corpus luteum, which in the event of fertilisation and pregnancy will secrete the hormone progesterone to maintain pregnancy. The ovum remains viable in the oviduct for 10–12 hours. If the ovum is unfertilised, it will degenerate and die, passing out of the oviduct into the uterus, where it may be reabsorbed, or lost through the vagina.

In temperate areas of the northern and southern hemispheres, oestrus occurs only when the day-length decreases after the summer months. This is a natural way of ensuring that goats are mated in the autumn and give birth in the early summer, when pastures are at their best. This restricts goat farmers in temperate countries to one breeding season per year. On commercial farms, farmers have developed ways of artificially breeding outside this natural season.

In the tropics and sub-tropics, where day-length varies little, theoretically oestrus can occur throughout the year. However, in practice most farmers do encounter a period of anoestrus, triggered by nutritional stress, for example in the dry season.

In tropical breeds of goats, there is a relatively high incidence of multiple births: twins, triplets, and occasionally quadruplets. This is due to the release of more than one ovum at ovulation. Ovulation rate, the number of eggs released at ovulation, is determined by the number of follicles developing in the ovary. This, in turn, is determined partly by genetic factors, the breed of the goat, but also by the body condition and age of the doe. A well-fed mature doe is more likely to produce twins than a poorly fed doe. This has led to the practice of 'steaming up': feeding does particularly well for one to two months before mating. In this way there is a higher chance of multiple births.

7.1.2 Male reproduction

The reproductive organs of the male goat are shown in Figure 7.2. They consist of two testes, suspended by the spermatic cord in the scrotum. The sperm and the male hormone testosterone are both produced in the testes, which hang outside the body inside the scrotum. The location of the testes, outside the body, maintains their temperature 4–7°C lower than the rest of the body. This is important for normal sperm production. The penis is the male organ of copulation. The end of the penis (prepuce) protrudes outside the body. In order to provide extra length during copulation, the penis of the goat has an S-shaped curve behind the scrotum, enabling considerable lengthening of the penis during copulation.

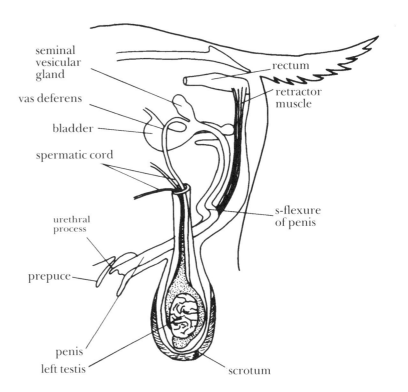

*Figure 7.2 Male
reproductive organs*

Puberty is reached in male goats at about seven months of age, but successful matings have been reported from bucks as young as three months. Male kids may even show sexual behaviour, such as mounting each other, within a few days of birth.

7.1.3 Mating and fertilisation

The buck responds to the signs of oestrus shown by the doe. Apart from behavioural signs, odours (pheromones) are released by the doe, stimulating the buck to sexual excitement. The main signs of male sexual excitement are pursuing the doe, pawing her with the front legs, curling back of the upper lip, and usually a loud snorting sound. The doe is ready to be mated when she stands for the buck to mount her. Once oestrus has been detected, copulation takes place. At ejaculation, sperm are deposited into the vagina, from where they are transported through the uterus and into the oviducts by the muscular contractions of these organs. Sperm may be able to fertilise an ovum for 24–36 hours after ejaculation, although there is some ageing of the sperm during this period, which reduces fertility.

7.1.4 Age at first mating

The age at which female goats should first be mated will vary according to breed and feeding. It is important that the young female is well grown before she is expected to become pregnant and rear a kid. If she is mated too young, she herself will be stunted and it is unlikely that she will ever reach a good mature body-weight which will give her the capacity for a long and productive life. Young breeders are very likely to abort and may be unable to produce enough milk for the kid; this will lead to nutritional stress and a high probability that the kid will die. However, feeding and looking after an unproductive female is a burden for farmers.

A doe should never be mated before one year old. Ideally she would have one pair of permanent incisors, i.e. be aged about 14–17 months, before first mating. Exceptions to these rules would occur only in intensive systems, where goats have been well fed and are able to develop early.

It is best if bucks are not used for mating before one year.

7.1.5 Intersex goats

Occasionally intersex (or pseudo-hermaphrodite) goats are born with a mixture of male and female sexual organs. In goats the dominant gene for polledness (having no horns) is linked to the gene for intersex. If polled males mate with polled females, there will be a high chance of some of the offspring being intersex. Affected goats are genetically females, but they may show great variation in external sexual organs, from virtually male to virtually female reproductive organs. All intersexes are infertile. They may be kept for fattening, but are of no breeding value, and should be culled if feed is scarce.

7.2 Mating management

7.2.1 Detecting oestrus

If fertile males are kept continuously with fertile females, the males will detect the occurrence of oestrus and will mate repeatedly with females in oestrus. The natural detection of oestrus, and natural mating, is by far the most effective method of ensuring successful mating. It is usually when people interfere that problems arise!

If the farmer does not own or cannot borrow a breeding male and so is not able to keep one continuously with the breeding females, there are several important steps which must be taken to ensure a successful mating. Firstly, the signs of oestrus must be observed. In situations where goats are kept close to the farmer's family, perhaps even share the owner's house, or are in a nearby house, it should be possible to notice any changes in behaviour. If the female starts bleating, wagging her tail, and perhaps riding other goats, these are sure signs of oestrus. Oestrus often starts late at night, so signs might be observed early the following morning. Once oestrus is noticed, the farmer must make arrangements for the doe to be taken to the buck, or *vice versa*. The farmer is unlikely to know the exact time at which oestrus started and so is not able to predict the time of ovulation, the optimum time for mating. Once shed, the ovum will be viable for only 10–12 hours; the sperm has a longer period of viability: 12–24 hours. To ensure a good chance of fertilisation, the sperm must overlap with the ovum when both are viable. Because the sperm has a longer period of viability than the ovum, it should be in place in the reproductive tract before ovulation takes place, so it is ready for the descending egg. The best time for mating is shown in Figure 7.3.

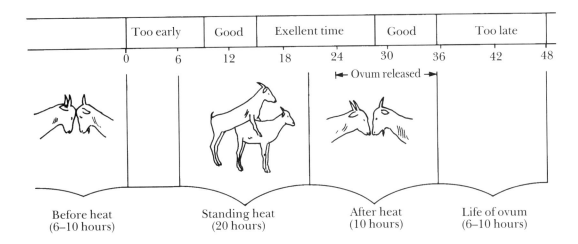

Figure 7.3 When to mate?

In large flocks it may be desirable that a selected buck mates with some particular does: in a breed-improvement programme, for example. It may not be easy for farmers to spot each doe in oestrus. In these circumstances, it may be useful to have what is known as a 'teaser buck'. The teaser buck is run with the flock continuously and used to detect the occurrence of oestrus. However, he is not allowed to mate. Mating may be prevented by the use of an apron, or by performing a vasectomy. A vasectomy is a surgical operation to sever the spermatic cords; it does not affect the sexual desire of the buck, but does render him infertile. In very large flocks that are not supervised when grazing, the teaser buck may be fitted with a raddle harness with a coloured block that leaves a mark on the doe during mating. This raddle harness can also be used if fertile bucks are introduced into a flock, to show when, and by which buck, a doe is mated.

7.2.2 Manipulation of breeding

For various reasons, goat-keepers may want to control the time of mating. This may be in order for kids to be born at a favourable time of year when feed is plentiful, or it may be to ensure that milk is available at a certain time of year. For example, in many pastoral societies goats provide milk to their owners at the end of the dry season, when cows have dried up, but goats are able to make use of the first flush of browse growth. In more intensive systems, farmers may want to breed their goats to take advantage of seasonal changes in the price of goats, or goat products.

There are several methods to control mating and the season at which kids are born.

- **Separation of males from females**: this requires the year-round separate management of males and females, introducing males into the flock at the time desired for mating. For most farmers in the tropics, this method of breeding control is suitable only for goats that are housed for most of the year; otherwise there would be a large labour demand to look after two grazing flocks.

- **Buck apron**: the buck wears an apron made of leather, canvas, or other suitable material when it is not required for mating (Figure 7.4). This apron is either removed, or twisted round during the time of mating.

- **Buck penis string**: a string is looped at one end around the testicles and at the other around the prepuce of the buck, so that, if the buck extends his penis, it is forced to deviate to the

Figure 7.4 Use of a buck apron to prevent conception
CHRISTIE PEACOCK

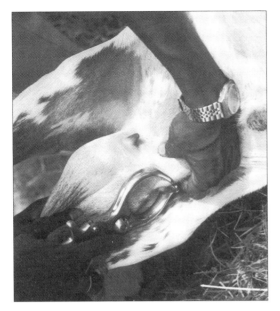

right or left, making copulation impossible. The string must be removed for successful mating.

- **Castration**: unwanted breeding males may be made infertile by crushing their spermatic cords, using a rubber ring or a special metal pincer known as a Burdizzo castrator (Figure 7.5). Rubber rings should be used only on very young kids. The surgical removal of testicles should be carried out only by skilled people in clean conditions. There are usually traditional methods of castration, involving two pieces of wood and a hammer or stone. Because they often only partially castrate the buck, the Burdizzo castrator is the recommended method.

Castration is one method of ensuring that poor-quality males do not breed. In some countries it is also used to reduce the odour of the meat from males; it will also increase both the fat content of the final carcass and the goat's growth rates, by reducing the energy spent on sexual activity and fighting.

7.2.3 Planning breeding seasons

It is important to consider carefully the implications of adopting a seasonal breeding policy, and the reasons for doing so. If the reason for seasonal breeding is to take advantage of a season of good grazing for dams and kids, then you need to consider whether that season is reliable. In marginal areas, where rainfall is unreliable, aiming for the majority of kids to be born during a particular season can be risky.

In large flocks, a kidding season can place heavy demands on available labour. If many kids are born within a short time period, much labour will be needed to look after the kids at, and after, birth. This labour may not be available, because of competition with other farm work.

Figure 7.5
Top: Castration using a Burdizzo castrator
Bottom: A Burdizzo castrator

Christie Peacock

7.2.4 Artificial insemination

Artificial insemination (AI) is a procedure whereby the sperm from a male goat is collected and used to inseminate a female goat artificially. The sperm may be used fresh or can be frozen and stored for long periods. Semen may be inserted through the cervix using a speculum, or inserted into one horn of the uterus using a surgical procedure.

The Maasai in Kenya try to control the season at which their sheep and goats give birth by using a leather apron. There are two rainy seasons and most flock owners try to arrange for the majority of births to occur during, or just after, the short rains in November. The owners remove the aprons at the beginning of the dry season, in June, when the goats' body condition is at its best. When a doe is observed standing to be mated, the owner holds her, slips the buck's apron round, and holds the doe while she is mated. After mating the apron is replaced. In practice, there are births all the year round, but as many as 60 per cent of births may take place in November.

The Maasai believe that, if kids are born during the short rains, their dams will have good feed and so produce ample milk for their kids. The kids are then reared during a short dry season and are naturally weaned during the long wet season, March/April. In theory this strategy makes sense and will ensure good survival rates of the kids. However, in the arid environment in which the Maasai live, the rains are notoriously unreliable. If the short rains do not occur, then the majority of the kids are born at the end of a very long dry season and their chances of survival are very poor. High mortality rates can be expected. Seasonal breeding control appears to be quite risky in semi-arid and arid environments.

The main theoretical reasons for using AI are listed below.

- It provides an opportunity for the rapid improvement of breeds by using semen from high-quality bucks which farmers could not afford to buy for themselves.
- It is one method of importing new genes, even breeds, into a country, while reducing the risk of importing diseases, and without the problems associated with handling live goats.
- It allows the use of outstanding bucks after their death.

While there are many good theoretical reasons for using AI, running a successful AI programme is not easy and requires many resources for its success. A supply of semen, skilled staff, technical equipment, and good transport and communications, as well as highly motivated farmers, are needed for a successful AI programme. If semen is to be collected 'in country', a well-equipped laboratory will be needed, together with highly trained laboratory staff. AI programmes should not be considered unless these conditions exist, or the resources are available to make these conditions exist. It may be possible to run a goat AI programme alongside a cattle AI programme, making use of the same laboratory and technicians.

7.2.5 Embryo transfer

The embryo transfer (ET) technique is a method of surgically introducing a fertilised embryo from a superior buck and dam into a goat of poorer genotype. The recipient goat becomes a stand-in or 'surrogate' mother to the developing embryo, eventually giving birth to the fully-developed foetus in the normal manner. ET requires highly skilled staff and sophisticated equipment. It might be successfully used under research-station conditions, but should otherwise not be considered.

7.2.6 Oestrus stimulation and synchronisation

In order to inseminate a batch of goats at one time, either naturally or artificially, it is possible to artificially induce oestrus to take place simultaneously in a group of does. Small sponges, impregnated with a synthetic progesterone hormone, are inserted into the vagina. They are removed 16–18 days later. The does will show signs of oestrus two–three days after the removal of the sponges. This approach may be used on research stations or large commercial farms when using AI.

Oestrus can also be stimulated by using the so-called 'buck effect'. Females which have been kept apart from bucks, out of the sight or smell of a buck, can be stimulated to come into oestrus by introducing a buck. This technique can synchronise oestrus in a batch of female goats with a fair degree of success.

7.3 Reproductive problems

Reproductive problems are often difficult for a farmer or extension agent to investigate. However, it is usually possible to identify whether the problem is one of management or whether it has a physiological cause. Problems of reproduction management can be identified and normally overcome. However, if deeper physiological problems are suspected, for example difficulties of a hormonal nature, access to an appropriate laboratory, able to do hormonal assays, will be required, in order to make a definitive diagnosis. Such a facility is unlikely to be available.

Figure 7.6 sets out a series of questions that might be asked when investigating the reasons why a doe is not kidding, or why the reproductive rate of a flock is poor.

The first question to ask is: *Is the doe showing signs of oestrus?* It is important to check whether oestrus is being detected properly. In flocks where males are not run continuously with females, oestrus detection can be a problem, unless the owner is very alert.

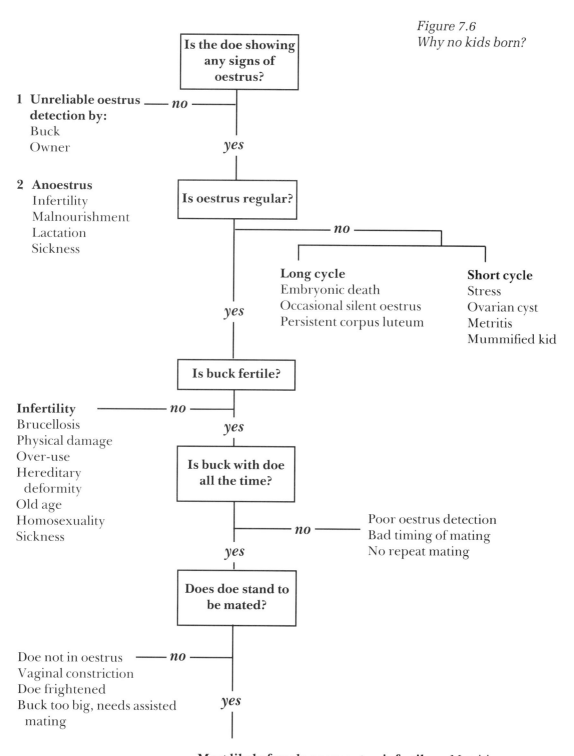

Figure 7.6
Why no kids born?

Is the doe showing any signs of oestrus?

1 **Unreliable oestrus detection by:** —— *no* ——
  Buck
  Owner

yes

2 **Anoestrus**
  Infertility
  Malnourishment
  Lactation
  Sickness

Is oestrus regular?

—— *no* ——

Long cycle
Embryonic death
Occasional silent oestrus
Persistent corpus luteum

Short cycle
Stress
Ovarian cyst
Metritis
Mummified kid

yes

Is buck fertile?

Infertility —— *no* ——
Brucellosis
Physical damage
Over-use
Hereditary
  deformity
Old age
Homosexuality
Sickness

yes

Is buck with doe all the time?

—— *no* ——
Poor oestrus detection
Bad timing of mating
No repeat mating

yes

Does doe stand to be mated?

Doe not in oestrus —— *no* ——
Vaginal constriction
Doe frightened
Buck too big, needs assisted
  mating

yes

Most likely female pregnant or infertile — Metritis
Vaginitis

Those most closely involved with the goats, possibly women and children, should know when the doe is in oestrus, but this should not be automatically assumed. It is necessary to check this, and also to check that the buck responds normally to females. Homosexual bucks may not do so (see below).

Females may be experiencing normal cycles, but may not show overt signs of oestrus. Any of the following factors may cause **anoestrus**.

• **Poor condition:** poor nutrition over long periods, resulting in severe weight loss (10–20 per cent of body weight), can cause the doe to stop showing sings of oestrus; this is known as 'nutritional anoestrus'.
• **Lactation**: in the early stages of lactation, does may not show signs of oestrus. This is known as 'lactational anoestrus'.
• **Sickness**: if the doe is very ill, she may not show signs of oestrus.

Alternatively the doe may not be cycling at all, owing to some infertility problems, and so is not able to show any signs of oestrus.

If the doe is showing signs of oestrus, the next question to ask is *Is oestrus regular?* Try to record when oestrus occurs. Sometimes oestrus cycles are very short (6–10 days) or very long. Long cycles may be caused by any of the following factors.

• **Embryonic death**: the death of the embryo in the uterus.
• **Anoestrus**: occasional anoestrus, possibly due to malnutrition or disease.
• **Hormonal disturbance**: a hormonal disturbance resulting in a persistent corpus luteum.

Causes of short cycles are listed below.

• **Stress**: when the doe is stressed, for example during transportation, the corpus luteum may prematurely regress, causing a short oestrus cycle, perhaps as short as seven days.
• **Ovarian cyst**: cysts on the ovary produce oestrogen, which may shorten the oestrus cycle to 3–7 days.
• **Metritis**: infection of the uterus after kidding may result in short oestrus cycles.
• **Mummified kid**: if a kid becomes mummified in the uterus, it can serve to stimulate repeated short oestrus cycles.

If oestrus is being regularly shown, but there are still problems, the next question to ask is *Is the buck proven to be fertile?* Males may be infertile for a number of reasons.

• **Brucellosis:** infection with brucellosis in males can result in orchitis (swollen testicles), which can make the buck temporarily infertile, or permanently sterile.

- **Physical damage**: any physical damage to the penis or testicles can render the buck sterile. Also lameness or other physical problems can make the buck unable to mount a female.

- **Over-use**: bucks should not be expected to serve successfully more than one or two females per day. If a buck is run with a batch of females that come into oestrus close together, he may attempt to serve them, but the sperm quality will fall with each doe served. By the third or fourth doe of the day, the buck may be effectively infertile.

- **Hereditary condition:** occasionally a buck is born with deformed reproductive organs, causing him to be sterile.

- **Age**: when bucks grow weak through age, they may no longer be able to mount and mate a doe successfully.

- **Homosexuality:** males reared exclusively with other males in the absence of females can develop homosexual behaviour patterns, and will not respond to females in oestrus.

In some systems of production the buck and doe may both be fertile, but the buck may not be kept with the doe all the time, and may even have to be borrowed from a distant neighbour. The next question to ask is *Is the buck with the doe all the time?* If the answer is no, then there may be problems either in detecting oestrus, or in mating at the correct time in relation to ovulation. If the doe has to be taken to be mated to a distant buck, it may not be possible for her to be mated twice at the recommended interval of 12 hours.

Does the doe stand to be mated? Standing to be mated is the true sign of oestrus; however, even if the doe is in oestrus (check this), she may be too small to support the weight of the buck. It is common in cross-breeding programmes for the doe and buck to need assistance at mating. The doe may have to be supported while the buck mounts, in order to achieve successful copulation.

If the answer to all the previous questions is yes, but the doe is still not breeding properly, then it is time to consider the possibility that the doe is infertile.

Females may be effectively infertile, either not showing signs of oestrus, or simply not ovulating at all, for one of the following reasons.

- **Pregnancy:** if the reproductive problem reported is a recent one, consider the possibility that the doe is currently pregnant.
- **Previous metritis:** metritis, infection of the uterus, may occur after kidding and can leave the doe infertile.
- **Hereditary condition**: hereditary deformities do occur, but are rare.
- **Age**: eventually females become too old to breed.

7.4 Pregnancy

7.4.1 Normal pregnancy

If a doe that has been mated does not show signs of oestrus (does not return to service) 17–21 days after mating, she is most probably pregnant. This is not an infallible method of diagnosing pregnancy, because the doe may experience anoestrus, or may have an unusually long oestrus cycle, for some reason. However, non-return to service is, in most cases, the only practical method of pregnancy diagnosis. In the last six weeks of gestation, the foetus can sometimes be observed moving and may be felt by firm pressure deep into the lower part of the abdomen.

The more sophisticated methods of pregnancy diagnosis, such as ultra-sonic scanning or testing milk for progesterone, have little real value to farmers in the tropics.

Gestation lasts about 150 days, but may be more or less than this by a few days. Once the doe is known to be pregnant, small adjustments to routine management can help to ensure that there is a successful pregnancy. Ideally the level of feed should increase during pregnancy, and the quality of the feed should be increased, as described in 5.6.1. Pregnant does should not be stressed in any way. Stress, often due to transportation or rough handling while dipping, can lead to spontaneous abortion.

7.4.2 Causes of abortion

Spontaneous abortion is probably slightly more common in goats than in other domestic livestock. The most common stage of gestation for abortion to take place is at 90–115 days. Goats are more susceptible to spontaneous abortion than other domestic animals, because the foetus is dependent on the corpus luteum for the hormonal control of its development. If this is disturbed in any way, the foetus will be aborted. The main causes of abortion in goats were described in 6.3.9.

7.4.3 Kidding

Kidding is triggered at the end of gestation by a series of hormonal controls. Contractions of the uterus push the foetus through the relaxing cervix. The membranes around the kid remain attached to the foetus while it is being born. If kidding is prolonged for any reason, the kid can still obtain oxygen through the umbilical cord. The first signs of imminent kidding are an enlarged vulva and restless behaviour; the udder may become slightly enlarged. The vast majority of kiddings proceed normally and do not require assistance. Often they occur while the doe is out grazing. She will normally seek a quiet place, away from other

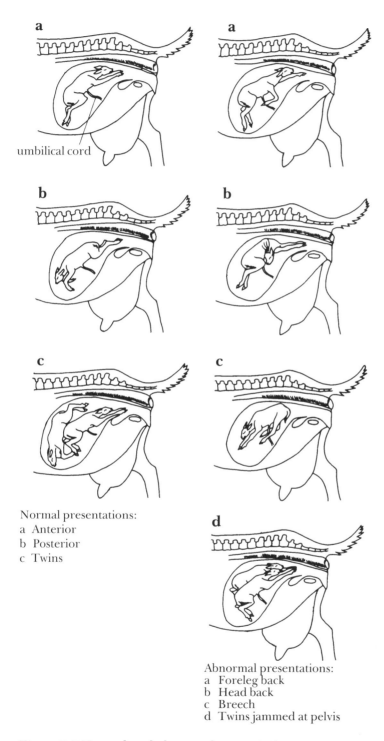

Normal presentations:
a Anterior
b Posterior
c Twins

Abnormal presentations:
a Foreleg back
b Head back
c Breech
d Twins jammed at pelvis

Figure 7.7 Normal and abnormal presentations

goats, lie down, and give birth. The water bag, preceding the foetus, will protrude from the vulva and burst; the kid(s) will follow soon afterwards. The herder must be alert to goats that may kid while out grazing. The new-born kid will not be able to keep up with the rest of the flock and will need to be carried home.

7.4.4 Difficult kidding (dystocia)

Occasionally a doe will experience difficulties while giving birth and may become so weak in the process that she needs assistance. The correct procedure is first, if possible, to wash your hands in soap and water. Ensure that the doe is lying on her side. Try to identify the parts of the kid showing at the vulva. How many feet are there? Can you feel a head or a tail? If you suspect that there may be more than one kid, be very careful. It is easy to get the kids' legs muddled up and pull a leg from one foetus with the leg of another. Feel to the top of the leg, if possible, and make sure that the legs are coming from the same body. Make sure you know which bit of which kid's anatomy you are holding before pulling. If necessary, push the kid back into the uterus and try to encourage a better position. When you do pull, pull at same time as one of the doe's contractions; work together, pulling downwards, in the same-shaped curve as the doe's back. Figure 7.7 shows the normal and abnormal ways in which kids may be presented. Always be very careful not to tear the vagina, which will result in the death of the goat.

An experienced veterinarian may be able to perform a Caesarian section, and remove the kids by surgery.

7.4.5 After kidding

Immediately after kidding, the doe will naturally start to lick the new-born kid clean. The stimulation of the licking is very important to revive the kid after its birth sufficiently for it to stagger to its feet and suckle. The sucking of the first milk, colostrum, is vitally important for the kid's future health. It is from its mother's colostrum that it acquires antibodies to protect it during the early period of its life. Make sure that the kid sucks milk within six hours of birth.

After checking that the kid is breathing normally, and has drunk some colostrum, it is very important that the doe and kid are left quietly together after birth, particularly for first-time kidders. It is during this period immediately after birth that the doe and kid bond together.

If the kid was born very weak, it may need some assistance to revive it. Clear the mouth and nostrils of any mucus. Swinging the kid by its hind legs to stimulate breathing helps, and also vigorously rubbing its body and pumping the chest. Even if a kid shows few signs of life, keep trying to revive it for several minutes. Do not give up too quickly.

7.4.6 Problems after kidding

Prolapse of the uterus may occur if the doe has to strain very hard during kidding and pushes out the uterus during or after the birth. Unless there is an experienced veterinarian immediately available to sew the uterus back in place, there is nothing that can be done and the goat should be killed.

After a normal birth the placenta falls out of the vulva within three hours. However, occasionally the doe may have a **retained placenta** after kidding. Unless speedy action is taken, the cervix will close, trapping the placenta inside the uterus, where it is likely to cause a severe infection which may lead to the death of the goat. A course of antibiotics should be given.

Normally after kidding there is a reddish discharge from the vulva for up to 14 days. However, if the discharge is dark red and sticky, there may be an infection of the uterus known as **metritis**. A course of antibiotics normally results in full recovery; however, if chronic metritis develops, the doe may be rendered infertile.

7.5 Measures of reproductive efficiency

Reproduction is the engine of the flock, ensuring that goats are able to generate enough replacements for themselves, expand the flock, and supply excess stock for sale. The reproductive rate of both individual goats and the flock as a whole is an important determinant of the overall success of the flock. Chapter 3 described methods for gathering information about farmers' goats, including information on reproductive performance. Some data can be collected from one visit to the flock, but most aspects of reproduction need long-term monitoring studies. However, it is important that reproductive problems are spotted as early as possible and action taken to remedy the situation.

Some measurements used to assess individual reproductive performance are given below.

* The frequency with which individual does produce kids (**parturition interval**).
* The number of kids born per doe (**litter size**).
* The number of kid deaths up to weaning (**pre-weaning mortality rate**).
* The number of kid deaths after weaning (**post-weaning mortality rate**).

In addition, consideration must be given to the question of whether there are any females that are *not* reproducing.

Some measures of reproductive performance of a whole flock may express the number of kids born either from the breeding females that were actually mated or from the potential breeding females, i.e. including infertile females. These indicators may include the number of kids born per number of breeding females per year (**kidding rate**).

An index that includes an estimate of pre-weaning mortality is:

*   Number of kids weaned per number of breeding females per year (**weaning rate**).

Further reading

Dunn, P. (1990) *The Goatkeeper's Veterinary Book* (2nd edition), London: Farming Press

Evans, G. and W.M.C. Maxwell (1987) *Salamon's Artificial Insemination of Sheep and Goats*, Sydney: Butterworths

Hunter, R.H.F. (1982) *Reproduction of Farm Animals*, London: Longman

Matthews, J.G. (1991) *Outline of Clinical Diagnosis in the Goat*, London: Wright

Mowlem, A. (1992) *Goat Farming* (2nd edition), Ipswich, UK: Farming Press

Smith, M.C and D.M. Sherman (1994) *Goat Medicine*, Philadelphia: Lea and Febiger

CHAPTER 8

Breeds and breed improvement

Introduction

The aim of goat farmers is to improve the productivity of their goats in order to achieve better the purposes for which they are kept. Productivity can be improved by two approaches:

- Improving the **management** of goats, so that their genetic potential can be expressed as fully as possible. This is achieved through technical improvements such as improving the quality and quantity of feed given, reducing the incidence of disease, improving the rate at which goats breed, or any of the other technical options described in this book.

- Improving the **genetic potential** of goats by selecting the best goats for future mating (**selection within the breed**), or by introducing new genetic material (**cross-breeding with another breed**).

Although professional animal breeders may be needed to design detailed breeding plans, there are many simple improvements that extension staff can suggest, with or without the advice of animal breeders.

8.1 Principles of breed improvement

It is important for extension staff to understand the basic principles of how genetic changes occur within livestock populations, so that they can understand the characteristics of the tropical breeds with which they work, and help farmers to improve the genetic characteristics of their goats, when appropriate.

The genetic make-up, or genotype, of any goat is determined by the genes passed on to it by its parents, which in turn received their genes from their parents, and so on, back to the original ancestors of the goat. Genetic changes, both good and bad, within any population such as a flock, village, or district can be brought about through the mating of individuals which may occur randomly, or through human intervention. Positive change, or breed improvement, may occur through goat-breeders' selection of superior individuals for mating. These two steps of selection and mating are the basic tools of breed improvement.

8.1.1 Variation

Most characteristics of production, such as milk production or growth rate, known as traits, are determined by a combination of genetic and environmental factors. A characteristic, such as the weaning weight of a kid, is determined by a combination of factors: the dam's milk production, whether the kid was born as a single or twin, and the kid's original birth weight. Each of these individual factors, in turn, is also determined by genetic factors and by environmental factors, such as feeding and disease incidence.

For any particular trait within a population there will be some variation, because goats are genetically unique, and each goat lives in its own unique environment. This variation is the raw material of breed improvement; an example is shown in Figure 8.1. The main tool that goat keepers, extension staff, and professional animal breeders use to make changes to this variation is selection. The objective of any breeding programme, whether at the level of the flock, village, or national population, is to improve the mean performance of a trait, or a number of traits, and reduce the degree of variation.

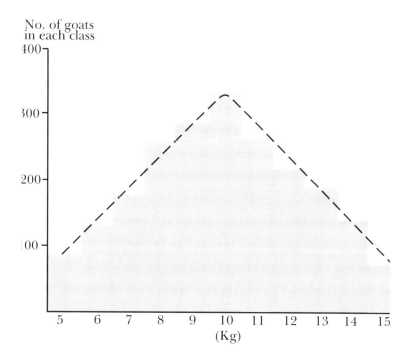

Figure 8.1 Histogram showing variations in weaning weights

8.1.2 Selection

Natural selection by the environment and selection by human goat-keepers have occurred for generations in goats. During breed improvement, the owner selects superior individuals to be the parents of the next generation, and does not select others. Individuals not selected may be removed from the population through culling; or males may simply be castrated.

8.1.3 Genetic progress

There are three factors which control the genetic progress made in a trait through selection.

1 **Heritability** describes the likelihood of passing on a characteristic from the parents to the offspring. If a trait has a heritability of 50 per cent, it means that it is highly heritable; and, if the parents have this trait, there is a good chance that it will be passed on to their offspring. Coat colour is a simple trait with a high heritability. Growth rate is a more complex trait than coat colour, but is quite heritable; so if parents with superior growth rates mate, there is a good chance that this superior growth will be passed on to their offspring. If heritability is low, say 10 per cent, then little parental superiority will be passed on.

Table 8.1 Heritabilities of some characteristics in goats

Trait	Heritability (%)
Weaning weight	30-50 (high)
Milk yield per lactation	20-30 (medium)
Multiple births	15-25 (low)

2 **The selection differential** expresses the degree of superiority of the selected parents over the rest of their generation. If there is a great deal of variation, it is possible to select only the very best individuals for mating, and, provided that the heritability of the trait is high, the offspring will be considerably better than the average of the previous generation (Figure 8.2).
3 **The generation interval** is the time interval between generations. It affects the rate at which genetic progress can be made. Genetic progress can be made more quickly the shorter the generation interval, because selection pressure can be put on a population more often than in species with longer intervals. So faster genetic progress can be made in goats than cattle.

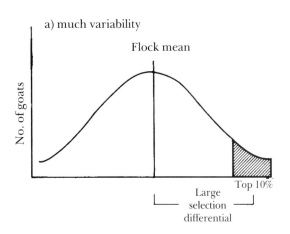

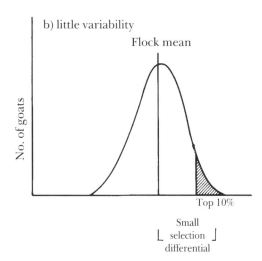

Figure 8.2 Selection differential

It is clear that quite rapid genetic progress, through selection, can be made in a trait with high heritability, if larger selection differentials can be applied to a population with a short generation interval.

8.1.4 Relationships between traits

Many traits in goats can be improved. If one trait is improved, another is often also improved; in this case the traits have a positive correlation. An example of a positive correlation is that which is found between weaning weight and weight at 12 months. Sometimes there is a negative correlation, when an improvement in one trait of production will result in a loss in another. An example of these relationships between traits might be that an increase in birth weight, increasing the kid's chances of survival after birth (positive correlation), might decrease the ease with which the kid is born, resulting in a higher incidence of dystocia and lower survival at the time of birth (negative correlation).

It is important to be aware of correlations known to occur between traits, because they can be used by breeders to plan better breeding programmes.

8.1.5 Identification of superior stock for selection

It is obviously important to be able to identify accurately which goats are superior for the characteristic(s) being improved. Selection by eye for body size, udder size, body shape, or other physical characteristic has been used for generations, but this method is not necessarily accurate when judging the economic traits of milk production or growth. The recording of performance is the most accurate basis for selection, but this can often be hard to organise in the tropics. Often more than one trait is of interest, and they may be correlated in some way, so an index is constructed, incorporating all the traits of interest. Goats are then chosen according to this selection index, rather than on the basis of a single trait. For accurate selection, accurate recording of the performance of relevant goats is vital. However, the performance of goats does not depend only on genotype. There are environmental factors to consider. Factors such as management standards, season of birth and weaning, and the difference between years can all affect performance. This must be accounted for in any selection programme.

Selection of individual goats for mating can be made on the basis of the following factors.

- **Performance testing**: individuals are selected on the basis of their own performance. This is useful if the trait is highly heritable and can be measured in both sexes (growth rate, for example). Performance testing is probably the most practical approach to selection for goats in the tropics.

- **Progeny testing**: goats are selected on the basis of the performance of their own offspring. This is useful when the heritability of the trait is low, or where the trait can be measured only in one sex (milk production, for instance) or can be measured only after slaughter (carcass characteristics). To carry out a successful progeny-testing scheme, the use of Artificial Insemination (AI) (see 7.2.4) is required, in order to have a large enough number of offspring from which to record. The need for AI means that progeny testing has limited value for the improvement of goat production in most countries in the tropics.

- **Pedigree selection**: goats are selected on the basis of the performance of their parents and grandparents. This method might be used if there is no information on the performance of the goats themselves, perhaps because the trait is related to the sex of the goat or can be observed only at a later age (milk production, for example). Pedigree selection requires accurate information on the performance of the ancestors of the goats in question. This information is unlikely to exist for goats in most countries in the tropics.

- **Collateral selection**: goats are selected on the basis of the performance of their close relatives. If there are several relatives, their performance is measured, to provide information which can be a guide to indicate the performance of the individual in question. Goats are quite prolific, so the performance of all close relatives should be scrutinised, whenever possible, before selection is made.

8.1.6 Mating plans

After selecting the goats to be mated, the second tool of breed improvement is to decide how to mate them. There are two methods: mating within the breed (**pure-breeding**), and mating outside the breed (**cross-breeding**).

Mating goats of the same breed will not improve that breed unless one or more of the parents selected is superior, and is mated to pass on a reasonably heritable trait. The performance of goats must be accurately recorded and rigorous selection procedures followed.

Mating individuals of one breed with those of another breed possessing some desired characteristics is known as 'cross-breeding'. Cross-breeding brings new genetic variation into the goat flock and can dramatically improve the performance of goats.

8.1.7 Cross-breeding

Cross-breeding is one method of quite quickly improving the performance of goats in one or more traits, while retaining many of the advantages of the local breed. There are many situations in the tropics where a better goat is an intermediate type that is still adapted to the tropical environment but has the improved breed's potential for higher production. Cross-breeding should be undertaken only in situations where the levels of management have been improved sufficiently to take advantage of the cross-bred's potential. The necessity of a link between the cross-breeding programme and an extension programme to improve management is discussed in 8.4.2, where practical methods of breed improvement are described.

Genetic gains from cross-breeding come from two sources:

- A combination of the superior adaptation of the tropical breed with the better productivity of the improver breed. This effect is purely additive, adding some of the characteristics of one breed to the other.

- If the goats mated are genetically distant from each other, a phenomenon known as **heterosis** may be observed. Heterosis can be positive and negative. Positive heterosis is when the offspring, known as the F_1 generation, is better than the mean of its parents; this is known as **hybrid vigour**. The offspring may be known as a hybrid, or cross-bred, and can be greatly superior to the worst parent. This characteristic of heterosis can be very beneficial in animal breeding, but it can be hard to maintain, because when the offspring themselves go on to

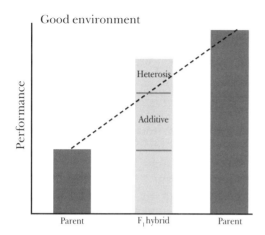

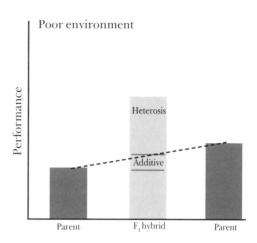

Figure 8.3 Heterosis in good and bad environments

mate, the genetic difference will not be so great, and some of the hybrid vigour will be lost in the next generation (F_2).

The effect of heterosis can be greater in a harsher environment than in a more favourable environment. This is because the improver breed may not perform very well in a difficult environment, indeed may be little better (or even worse!) than the local breed. However, the cross-bred often shows remarkable performance, even under stress, and may surpass both parents. This is as a result of heterosis. In a better environment, the improver breed will be able to perform closer to its potential and will be far superior to the local breed, and to the cross-bred. The cross-bred may perform little better than the mean of the two parents, indicating that heterosis is making little contribution to overall improvement, but that the additive effect is.

In any cross-breeding programme, the problem always arises of what to do after the first cross? There are two main approaches: to try to maintain high levels of heterosis, or to upgrade the local breed through repeatedly mating it with the superior breed.

High levels of heterosis can be maintained by:

- the continuous production of F_1 stock, known as **terminal crossing** (a very expensive and inefficient method of improving production);
- alternately mating tropical and improved breeds, known as **criss-cross mating**. The local breed is first mated with an improver breed and then mated with its own breed. At equilibrium, two thirds of the heterosis of the F_1 is maintained. This system is flexible, but requires access to two breeds of goats and their appropriate use.

Figure 8.4: Criss-cross mating

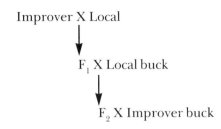

Improver X Local

F₁ X Local buck

F₂ X Improver buck

- Production of a synthetic breed. Synthetic breeds may be made through the reciprocal crossing of several breeds and the rigorous selection of the offspring. This is a complicated approach to breed improvement, which requires good management over a long period of time. Few countries in the tropics would have the resources to undertake the development of a synthetic breed and could do so only with high levels of external support.

The Kenya Dual Purpose Goat (KDPG) Breed

Individual farms in western Kenya are becoming too small to support a dairy cow, so a dual-purpose goat breed was proposed, to supply milk and meat to households on these small farms. The USAID-funded Small Ruminant Research Project, begun in Kenya in 1980, believed that the local Small East African breed of goat had limited potential for improvement through selection, while pure temperate breeds of goats would not survive on these farms. It was felt that a structured cross-breeding programme was not feasible for smallholder goat farmers in Kenya, so the development of a new synthetic breed of goat was proposed.

Four breeds — two temperate (Toggenburg and Anglo-Nubian) and two tropical (Small East African and Somali) — were chosen to make up the new breed. Each temperate breed was mated with each tropical breed to produce four types of F₁ cross-breds. Each cross-bred was then mated with each of the three other cross-breds, to produce a F₂ generation, having 25 per cent of their genes from each of the four breeds. These four-way crosses were then mated together to produce large numbers of this synthetic breed. Rigorous selection procedures were then applied to these four-way crosses, to produce a stable and superior breed, known as the Kenya Dual Purpose Goat (KDPG).

The development of the KDPG breed has taken over 14 years to reach the stage of producing a small number of superior KDPGs for distribution to farmers. This is a long time for farmers to wait. All breeding has been carried out on a large breeding station, and has required a high level of professional skills, as well as good flock-management. This has been very expensive to supply.

8.1.8 Grading up

Probably the most practical approach to cross-breeding in the tropics is to place less emphasis on maintaining levels of heterosis and to base improvements on the additive effects of one breed on another. 'Grading up' is the gradual improvement of a breed through repeated matings of the local breed with an improver sire. It is accepted that after four matings the local breed is a member of the pure improver breed. However, grading up local breeds to virtually 100 per cent improver is rarely desirable, and it is usually more appropriate to stop at some point in the up-grading process and stabilise at a suitable blood-level. This might be at 50 per cent or 75 per cent improver blood-level. Sires of the desired blood-level are used from then on. This system is simple to implement, and management can be graded up in step with the genetic improvements.

8.1.9 In-breeding

There are many fears associated with in-breeding, no doubt mainly because of cultural taboos in human societies against marriage between close relatives. In-breeding can become a problem in a population for two reasons: firstly, because it can throw up occasional physical deformities in offspring (an example in goats is the occurrence of an undershot jaw), and secondly (and more seriously) because 'in-breeding depression' may result in a reduction in the size, fertility, and possibly survival of each succeeding generation.

Farmers can take simple steps to prevent the build-up of in-breeding in their flock and any depression in performance from in-breeding. These are suggested in 8.3.2.

8.1.10 The application of bio-technology in goat breeding

Rapid developments in bio-technology in recent years have considerably expanded the range of tools available to breeders to improve livestock breeds more efficiently. It is now possible to study the individual genes of goats, describe them, and identify which parts control which characteristics. Breeders are close to being able to incorporate specific characteristics, such as disease resistance, or milk-fat content, into individual animals. This genetic engineering is still in its infancy but is, potentially, a very powerful tool.

The genetic analysis of goats can also identify the genetic distance between individuals, types, and breeds. This can help in classifying indigenous goats into breeds, or types, and can also be used to predict the degree of heterosis between two parental strains of goats.

8.2 Tropical goat breeds

8.2.1 The development of tropical goat breeds

The basic principles of genetic change and breed improvement have been described, and it is now possible to relate these principles to the tropical breeds of goats which are found in the field. A consideration of how these forces of change have acted on goat populations will help to improve our understanding of their characteristics.

The breeds of goats found in the tropics have been reared there for hundreds or thousands of years. The breeds that now exist are the result of hundreds of years of pressure by the tropical environment, through natural selection, combined with some selective breeding by owners. As a result, tropical goats are well adapted to surviving in tropical environments with high temperatures, poor-quality feeds, limited water, and a high disease challenge. The environment does not allow these goats to perform at a high level of production, and they rarely have the potential to do so. Rather, their important characteristic is the ability to survive under rigorous conditions, with sufficient production to reward the efforts of their owners.

There are several hundred different breeds of goat in the world, which all originated from the basic goat stocks domesticated in the Middle East and Central Asia over 10,000 years ago. Over the years, as goats developed, physical changes in colour, size, and shape differentiated goats into distinct breeds. Most of these breeds have developed in relative geographical isolation. New blood may have entered goat populations when human populations moved during trade, wars, and ethnic migrations, when it is likely that some cross-breeding occurred. Looking at the breeds that now exist, we can see that there are locations containing populations of goats of relative uniformity; these might be called breeds. However, the mixing of stock around the boundaries of these areas, through trade or movement, has led to many intermediate, less distinguishable, goats, which are often referred to as 'types' or 'sub-types'. Many goats are referred to as a 'non-descript type', simply because nobody has made the effort to describe and name them. In most countries in the tropics, little effort has been put into the systematic description, classification, and evaluation of goats, so the potential of most tropical goat breeds and types remains only poorly known.

Most goats in the tropics serve multi-purpose functions for their owners. There have been few breed-improvement programmes to develop them for more specialised economic functions, such as for producing milk or meat.

Although the environment has probably played the major role in developing the breeds of goat we know today, the societies that have kept goats have their own preferences and have exerted some influence of their own. This influence can be both positive and negative. Positive selection has been reported among the Somali pastoralists who have selected for single births and against twins.

Somali goat-breeding in East Africa

The Somali pastoralists of East Africa, who keep large flocks of very distinctive white goats, report that they do not like their goats to twin. They select against twinning in their own flocks. When purchasing new breeding females, the first question they ask is whether it has ever had a twin birth; they will not buy it if it has. The reasoning behind this is that the Somalis live in a very harsh environment and rely on milk from their goats. If the lactating doe is trying to rear twins, there will be little milk left over for her owners, and two kids may be put at risk. If she has to look after only one kid, there is more milk for the owner and a good chance for the kid to survive. As a result of this selection policy, practised for generations, the Somali goat breed rarely gives birth to twins.

Negative selection for growth is believed to take place in flocks where males are sold or culled young — for example, among the Afar pastoralists of Ethiopia and Eritrea.

Afar goat-breeding in Ethiopia and Eritrea

The Afar are pastoralists who live in one of the harshest environments in the world. They keep large flocks of goats for milk, grazing the arid borders of the Danakil desert. Grazing is so scarce that they cannot afford to keep any unproductive goats. They kill most male kids, not required for breeding, within one week of birth. Breeding males, therefore, are selected when very young, when there can be no objective reason for making the selection, except on the basis of the performance of their ancestors. It is therefore likely that the best males are not always kept for breeding, and in reality some negative selection pressure may be exerted in Afar flocks.

Other pastoralists, in less harsh environments, may keep males for longer periods, but are likely to sell the fastest-growing males earlier, before they can breed and pass on their fast growth to future generations. The slower-growing males remain in the flock for longer, and therefore have a greater chance of passing on their genes.

It is clear that all past selection by goat-keepers has been at the level of the flock. There have been no cases reported of villages, or other groups, cooperating to improve the genotype of their goats.

However, in virtually all societies where goats are kept, new goats may enter the flock through purchase, loans, gifts, or even theft; thus superior individuals may have been introduced into the flock, and in the process improved it.

In very small flocks of goats (1–10), there is very little opportunity for farmers to apply any selection pressure within their own flocks. All they are able to do is to reduce the negative effects of in-breeding by the regular introduction of new stock.

It is clear that the forces of natural selection, together with the intervention of keepers who select and cross-breed their goats, have acted on goats in the past to produce the breeds which we have today. Extension staff have to start with the local breed kept by farmers in the area in which they are working. They must first understand the particular characteristics of the breed kept by the farmers with whom they work, before considering any course of breed improvement.

8.2.2 The characteristics of tropical breeds

Thousands of years of development, in so many different environments by different ethnic groups, have resulted in goat breeds with a wide range of characteristics.

- **Size**: goats may range from the tall, leggy, desert goats such as the Jamnapuri and Sudan desert breeds to the small West Africa Dwarf and Black Bengal goats. Size is partly related to nutrition, but genotype also plays a part.

- **Colour**: colours may range from the pure white Somali goat, through patchy coat colours, to the pure black of the Black Bengal.

- **Coat type**: most tropical goats have a short thin coat, adapted to reflecting radiation and keeping the goat cool. However, in some colder environments hairy coats have developed, as in the Kashmiri (Pashmina) goat, found in northern India, Tibet, and Mongolia.

- **Growth**: growth is generally slow, partly reflecting the poor nutrition of most goats in the tropics, but also their genotype. Nutritional studies in the tropics show a generally poor response to improved nutrition by tropical breeds of goats.

- **Milk production**: some selection by owners has taken place for milk production. Milk yields per day are generally rather low at 200–1,000 ml per day, and lactation length is short at 3–5 months. This partly reflects the environment in which the goats are reared for milking, as well as their own inherent capability.

- **Prolificity**: most tropical breeds of goat regularly give birth to twins, and triplets are not uncommon.

- **Disease resistance**: most goats manage to build up their own resistance to the common diseases of the area in which they are kept. There is great variability, both within and between breeds, in resistance to disease. Breeders are starting to look at the possibility of breeding resistance to certain diseases into future generations.

- **Water use**: tropical breeds of goat have adapted to using water efficiently in their physiological processes.

- **Survival**: survival rates are generally quite good, although survival from birth to weaning can be poor in the harsher environments.

These characteristics create both advantages and disadvantages among tropical goat breeds (see Table 8.2).

The best-known tropical breeds of goat are listed in Table 8.3, together with their locations and the main features of the breed. Extension staff are most likely to be confronted with a breed of goat that is not in this list, and perhaps has only a local name, often associated with the area in which the goat is found, or the ethnic group keeping them. The characteristics of these 'non-descript' types should first be investigated before any consideration is given to their genetic improvement.

8.2.3 Conservation of goat genetic resources

Recently there has been interest in conserving the variety of breeds of domestic livestock. In developed countries, the genetic base of domestic livestock has become very narrow, with very few breeds farmed, and few sires used. Much genetic variability, the raw material of breed improvement, has been lost. In the tropics there is concern that the indiscriminate cross-breeding of indigenous breeds with imported breeds will result in the replacement of the indigenous breed altogether, or at the least some diluting of it. There is often talk of 'genetic pollution', and the debate can become quite heated. Often it becomes an issue of national pride, rather than one for rational consideration. Developing countries, striving to improve the welfare of their population, must make use of all appropriate technology, including new breeds, where suitable.

There is no doubt that preserving genetic diversity, for either immediate or future use, is important. We can never know when we may need to incorporate new genetic material into existing stocks for some productive use. The conservation of what we have is necessary for future generations. However, for developing countries the questions arise of who should be responsible for this preservation, and how it should be done?

The Food and Agriculture Organisation of the United Nations (FAO) is coordinating the global conservation of domestic

Table 8.2
The advantages and disadvantages of tropical goat breeds

Advantages

Ability to survive with little care
Some disease resistance

Disadvantages

Low milk yields
Slow growth rates
Limited response to improved management

Table 8.3 The major goat breeds of the tropics

Name	Location	Characteristics	Uses
Africa			
Nubian	East Africa	Tall, long ears, convex nose	Good milk production
Somali	East Africa	White, short coat, no twins	Milk, meat in harsh conditions
Afar	Ethiopia, Eritrea	Leggy, curved horns	Milk, meat in harsh conditions
Small-East Africa	East Africa	Small, multi-coloured	Meat
Sudan Desert	Sudan	Long legs	Meat
Red Sokoto	Nigeria	Dark red, medium size	Skins, meat
West African Dwarf	West and Central Africa	Very small, prolific, adapted to humid tropics	Meat
West African Longlegged	West Africa	Tall, fine hair, many colours	Meat, milk, skins
Bantu	Southern Africa	Small, multi-coloured	Meat
Boer	South Africa	White, stocky, long ears	Meat, milk
Middle East			
Angora	Turkey	Long thick hair	Mohair
Black Beduin	Syria	Black, long hair, long ears	Milk, meat
Damascus	Cyprus, Syria	Red/brown, hairy	Milk
South America			
Criollo	Central America, Caribbean	Black, brown, thin coat, short ears	Meat, milk
Moxoto	NE Brazil	White/cream, black face, belly stripes	Meat, skins
South-East Asia and Pacific			
Katjang	Malaysia, Indonesia	Black, brown, small	Meat
Ettawah	Indonesia	Large, long ears	Milk
Fiji	Fiji	Small, short hair	Meat
South Asia			
Barbari	India, W Pakistan	White, red spots	Milk
Beetal	India, W Pakistan	Red/tan, white spots, long ears	Milk
Black Bengal	India, Bangladesh	Small, black	Meat, skin
Cheghu	Kashmir, Tibet	White, long thick hair	Milk, fibre, meat, transport
Gaddi	N India, Pakistan	Large, white thick hair	Hair, meat, draught power
Jamnapuri	India	Large, long ears, convex nose	Milk, meat
Kamori	Pakistan	Black, hairy	Meat, hair
Kashmiri	N India, Tibet	Large, thick hair, white or black	Pashmina fibre
Malabar	India	Many colours	Milk
Sirohi	India	Small, many colours, short hair	Meat, milk

Source: adapted from Devendra and McLeroy (1982)

livestock breeds. It is encouraging the establishment of herds and flocks of different pure breeds. Genetic material can be preserved for 10–15 years as frozen semen, and embryos can be frozen and stored. The establishment of breed societies in developing countries should be encouraged, so that they can be charged with the task of conservation.

Goats lag far behind other species in their identification, description, and classification, which are all prerequisites for conservation. We need more knowledge about the characteristics of indigenous breeds of goats, so that they may be preserved for use by future generations. As yet there is little 'threat' to indigenous breeds of goats from cross-breeding and there is no reason to deny farmers the chance of improving their lives through cross-breeding where appropriate. It should be the responsibility of concerned authorities to undertake genetic conservation, but not at the expense of individual farmers.

8.3 Practical methods of breed improvement for individual farmers

Breed improvement can take place at different levels in a goat population, from an individual's or village's flock to the goats of a district or nation. Individual owners should always try to improve their flock, whatever size it is.

8.3.1 Improvement of individual flocks

What can an individual owner do to improve the genetic potential of his or her flock of goats? If the flock is large, more than 100 goats, an owner would be able to make genetic improvements through selection within the flock, together with careful selection of new stock to counteract the negative effects of in-breeding. In smaller flocks there is little scope for selection, so the approach should be to try to counteract the negative effects of in-breeding, or up-grading through cross-breeding.

The farmer or pastoralist embarking on a programme of selection must be clear about his or her objectives. It is necessary to be able to measure the characteristic in question, in order to select goats for mating, and cull those not performing well. The farmer must also be able to measure progress in the trait. It would be possible for individual pastoralists, with large flocks of more than 100 goats, to select within their own flocks, and it has been pointed out that some selection does already take place. It may also be possible for farmers to purchase improved bucks for mating.

For farmers with smaller flocks, clear guidelines for breeding and culling within a flock are needed, to ensure that in-breeding is not building up and depressing production.

8.3.2 Guidelines on breeding and culling

Wherever possible, the best bucks in the flock should be selected and used for service. Farmers are likely to have their own criteria for judging how good a buck is and his likely effect on his offspring. Good bucks should be retained in the flock for one–three years, provided that their mating is controlled, to avoid high levels of in-breeding. In order to reduce in-breeding, a buck should never be allowed to mate with his full sisters (same father, same mother); his daughter; or his grand-daughter.

If new bucks cannot be bought, so the flock is 'closed', one buck should be selected each year to be the breeding buck for the year. He should serve for one year and then he should either be culled or some breeding-control device, such as an apron or string, should be applied to him.

A superior buck can be used for longer than one year if the owner separates the flock into groups, using the buck for one year before moving him to another group, and so on. However, this separation may be difficult for the owner to manage.

Another option is for an owner to cooperate with others and exchange bucks every one or two years, or rotate them regularly among a small group.

8.4 Practical methods of breed improvement for groups and governments

Before embarking on large-scale breed-improvement pro-grammes, first consider the environment in which the improved goats are to be kept. It is a waste of resources to improve the genetic worth of livestock, if the environment in which they are kept remains unchanged. Any up-grading of the genetic worth of goats must be preceded, and accompanied, by the up-grading of management. Only consider breed improvement after efforts have been made to improve management.

However, once management levels have been raised, they should not outpace the genetic value of the goats managed. There is a limit to which the performance of tropical breeds of all livestock can be improved, solely through improved management. Tropical breeds do reach a production ceiling, above which they cannot rise through improved management alone.

Much greater genetic gains can be made if owners group together in some way, either to exert some selection pressure on their larger, combined flock, or to make use of a superior breed by sharing the cost of an improved buck among many members.

Government and NGOs have a role in assisting goat-keepers to organise breed improvement for themselves, or developing improved stock on some sort of breeding station. A government or an NGO might run a programme to improve the goats of, say, a district. At a national level, government organisations should always be striving to improve the genetic potential of the national population, while also taking responsibility for preserving the nation's genetic diversity for future use.

It is very important that the objectives of the breed-improvement programme are clearly defined, and are in agreement with the objectives of the target farmers. Clearly define the traits to be improved, and define what constitutes an improvement. Remember that traits can be both positively and negatively correlated, so one owner's improvement may be a disadvantage to another owner. Increasing body size inadvertently, by improving milk production (positive correlation), may not be attractive to goat-keepers with limited access to feed.

Figure 8.5 outlines the questions to consider when deciding on the approach to breed improvement. Work through these questions carefully before deciding on any course of action.

8.4.1 Selection within a breed

There have been very few organised selection programmes for goats in the tropics. This reflects the general neglect of goats in these countries, rather than any lack of potential. There is much unrealised potential in tropical goat breeds that could be released by a relatively simple selection programme.

Selection programmes should be considered if:

- the trait to be improved is highly heritable, such as growth rate;
- there is a large population with great variability from which to select;
- a long-term commitment can be made by those involved;
- accurate records can be kept;
- the environment is harsh.

Because it is possible to apply more selection pressure in a large population with greater variability than in a small one, the larger the flock, the greater the progress that is likely to be made. There are few large flocks of goats in the tropics, except those kept by pastoralists or at government institutions. However, larger flocks can be created if owners with small flocks get together and collaborate in a group selection programme.

Selection programmes do not make large or quick improvements in production. They require a long-term commitment from those involved, whether donors, government agencies, or owners. Accurate records of the performance of goats in the target population are needed for a successful selection programme. If this cannot be organised, real progress is unlikely, and selection should not be considered.

Figure 8.5 *How to decide the method of breed development*

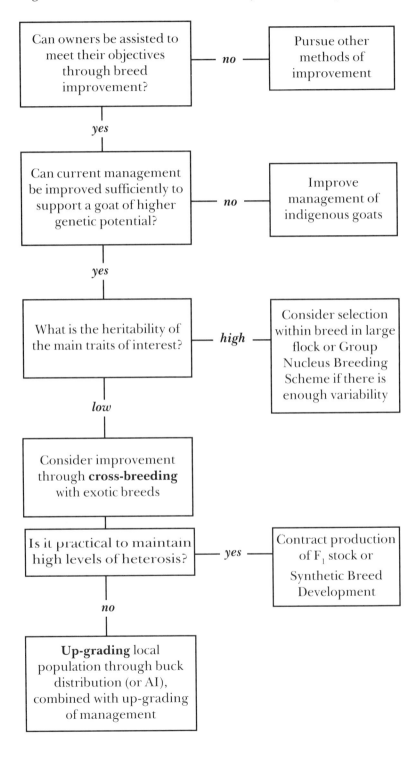

Selection is an appropriate strategy for goats kept in harsh environments where management can be improved only a little, and cross-bred goats are unlikely to perform well. In this case, strong emphasis must be placed on selection for both performance characteristics and characteristics of survival which indicate good adaptation.

Selection in group breeding schemes

The principles of group, or cooperative, breeding schemes are very simple. Members agree to cooperate to set up a nucleus flock of their best goats to produce their replacement breeding males. Interest in group breeding schemes has increased recently and they are now widely used for sheep in Australia and New Zealand, and for goats in some Scandinavian countries and also in India.

These are the basic steps to setting up a group nucleus breeding scheme.

1 Members meet and agree the objectives of the breeding scheme, its structure and organisation. Each owner must make a long-term commitment, for a minimum of ten years, to the programme and must fully understand that slow, steady improvements are to be expected.

2 Terms of membership of the scheme are clearly set out. A useful guide is that, if a member contributes four does to the nucleus flock, he or she receives one buck in return. The location and management of the flock must be determined. It is best if the flock is located close to the members' farms and in a similar environment to that to which they are expected to return. Selection must take place under the conditions in which the selected goats are expected to perform. This will ensure that the adaptation characteristics of the tropical breed, particularly disease resistance, are not lost. The management of the nucleus flock should closely match the general management of all cooperating members. The physical location of the flock, how it will be supported, whether external funds are required, the advice that may be needed, and day-to-day management must all be considered.

3 The group members contribute the foundation stock for the nucleus flock. Ideally they would record the performance of their goats in their own flocks, so they had enough information about the traits of concern to enable them to select the very best females for the group flock. Otherwise, judgement will have to be by eye, which is not satisfactory. This selection of the foundation stock, known as 'screening', is a very important step. It determines the starting point of the central, or nucleus, flock to which selection pressure is applied. If the very best goats are contributed, the flock will have a good start; if the goats offered

271

are of poor quality, then the starting point for selection will be low, and the nucleus flock may even be worse than the average of the contributing flocks!

Genetic gains are maximised when the number of nucleus does is at least 5–10 per cent of the total number of does involved in the scheme. However, the situation is more complicated if the flocks owned by members are very small. If a member is able to contribute only one or two females to the nucleus flock, he or she will be entitled to receive an improved buck only every fourth or second year. When small flocks are involved, the nucleus flock should represent a much higher proportion of the total target flock, say 10–20 per cent. Alternatively, numbers could be gradually built up over one–five years.

The critical parameters to consider are the number of bucks produced per year and how long they will serve in the members' flocks, i.e. how often they need to be replaced on-farm.

4 Once the members of the group have contributed their best does to the nucleus flock, rigorous selection procedures, on the traits of interest, are applied to this central flock. In return for contributing their best females, members will receive back superior bucks for mating within their own flocks. Quite rapid improvement in the average performance of the nucleus flock can be made in the first one–four years. Whether this improvement makes any impact on the flocks of the members will depend on the rigour of the initial screening which determined the initial quality of the nucleus flock.

Every year some does will die, or become old, and will have to be replaced. The very best buck and does should be kept in the nucleus flock. The next-best bucks can be distributed to members, and the worst bucks and does should be culled. These culls can provide a valuable source of income to help support the costs of running the nucleus flock.

It must be decided if the nucleus flock will remain 'open' and take in good females every year, or be maintained as a 'closed' flock, selection being applied only to the females which pass the original screening. Provided that the recording of on-farm performance remains accurate, the best gains are made if the nucleus flock is open. Half the nucleus doe replacements come from the flock itself, while the other half come from the flocks of group members, who must continue to give their very best does.

The beauty of group breeding schemes is that they are very flexible and can vary in size, objectives, and organisation. They could operate at the level of a village, district, or nation. In tropical countries it is probably best if group breeding schemes are designed to operate close to the members of the group, so that

1 A group of 30 pastoralists decide to get together and set up a nucleus breeding flock. The average flock size owned by the members is 60, making a target population of 1,800 goats. The nucleus flock should be 90–180 goats, so each member must contribute 3–6 of their best females. In return, each member will be able to receive a selected buck every year. If the flock is only 90 goats, and the members want a buck every year, little selection pressure will have been applied, the bucks will not be superior, and they will make little impact on the target flocks. If the flock either is larger, say 180 (10 per cent of the target flock), or members receive a buck only every second year, greater selection pressure can be applied, because more poor-quality bucks can be culled from the nucleus flock, and the bucks selected and distributed will be better, making a bigger impact on the target flocks. The length of service of the buck in the members' flock, together with the male:female ratio, will determine the members' need for bucks.

2 A group of 50 farmers make a decision to collaborate in a group breeding scheme, but their flocks are very small. The average size is only 6, making a target population of 300. The nucleus flock theoretically should be 15–30, but little selection pressure could be placed on such a flock and the members would receive a buck only every 4–7 years. This is unlikely to be attractive to them. A bigger nucleus flock is obviously needed, but how can it be created without the members having to give an unacceptably large proportion of their small flocks to the nucleus? In this situation, the nucleus flock would have to be built up slowly over 3–5 years, until it was large enough for reasonable selection pressure to be applied to it, and for the members to derive real benefits from it.

they feel involved in the screening, selection, and redistribution of improved bucks. Owners are naturally reluctant to part with their best stock and may be persuaded to do so only if they participate thoroughly in the management of the breeding unit. Returns from breed improvement through selection are notoriously slow to be realised, and members may become impatient if they have given up their best females to the nucleus but see no benefit for a long time. However, if they are involved in the programme from the start, they will understand the procedures better.

Group breeding schemes can also form a focus for encouraging matching technical improvements. The group might serve as a

273

Figure 8.6 Cooperative breeding scheme

Structure of group breeding scheme

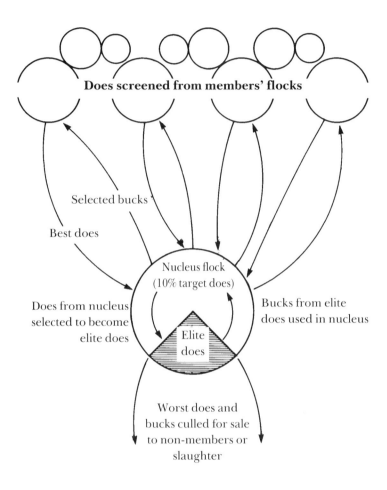

Does screened from members' flocks

Selected bucks

Best does

Nucleus flock
(10% target does)

Does from nucleus selected to become elite does

Bucks from elite does used in nucleus

Elite does

Worst does and bucks culled for sale to non-members or slaughter

cooperative, assisting members to purchase drugs and equipment, and perhaps to market their goats and products.

It is best if group breeding schemes have an income-generating component, for example through selling culled stock, or supplying drugs, to make them sustainable in the long term. Genetic gains are relatively slow through selection programmes, perhaps of the order of an average of 3–4 per cent per year, depending on the trait. Major improvements will be realised after 10–20 years. This demands a long-term commitment to the programme by all those involved. This may not be possible to achieve through donor-funded projects, which are normally of only 5–8 years' duration. If the group can generate sufficient income to support the flock, and increase the incomes of the members, the breeding objectives of the programme are more likely to be fulfilled.

Selection on government breeding stations

Selection can be made in a large goat flock at a government farm. Selected bucks could be sold to goat-keepers. However, not surprisingly, government staff usually find it difficult to purchase the best goats from farmers and pastoralists. They are naturally reluctant to sell their best stock, even for a premium price. As the initial screening of stock is so important in determining the genetic quality of the flock, government organisations should not consider this approach to breed improvement unless they are confident of obtaining really good breeding stock.

8.4.2 Cross-breeding methods

Cross-breeding can quite rapidly improve the performance of goats, provided that the management of the cross-breds is of a high level. Cross-breeding has been the most common method of improving milk production in dairy cattle in tropical countries. However, in some countries, the crossing of local and temperate cattle, when management has not been improved, has led to many cross-breeding schemes performing below expectation. Some disappointing results in certain countries have led to a reaction against cross-breeding, which has fallen into disrepute among some people. Many academics now advocate selection as the only method of breed improvement for developing countries. This is unfortunate. Under the right conditions, cross-breeding has a lot to offer farmers in developing countries, and it is not fair to goat-keepers who have improved their management to deny them access to superior stock.

Cross-breeding should be considered if:

- the trait to be improved has a low heritability, such as milk production;
- the current management of local goats is good, or there is an effective extension programme that is improving management;
- the environment has the potential to allow real improvements in management;
- quick results are needed.

Cross-breeding should be considered only if the cross-breds are going to live in an environment that allows them to express their improved potential and perform well. Otherwise it is a waste of resources. To get real benefits from cross-breeding, the environment should have the potential for improvement.

One major advantage of cross-breeding which is rarely considered is the effect it can have on an extension programme. The cross-bred goat is a new animal, it may look different, it can certainly perform differently, and so it quite quickly captures the interest and enthusiasm of goat keepers. This can be a vital boost to extension programmes and, in the process of breed improvement, it can motivate owners to adopt the improved management strategies simultaneously being promoted. The two forces of change — improved management and breed improvement — can stimulate each other. The new cross-bred goat needs good management in order to perform well, and owners must provide it through adopting better feeding strategies, such as forage development, and better health care. Once the cross-bred is performing well under good management, it can be further up-graded in blood-level or breed, and management should be up-graded again. This step-wise improvement in management and then breed should be a continuous process, until a combination is reached that suits the owner, family, and flock (Figure 8.7).

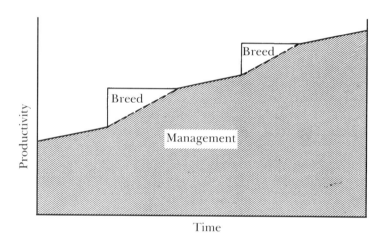

Figure 8.7 Breed and management improvement

The principles of cross-breeding were described in 8.1.7. The mating plans made must take into account the practical reality of the situation to be improved, and the practical means of introducing new genes into the target population. The main issues to consider are:

- the blood-level suitable for the environment;
- the level of heterosis it is possible to create and retain;
- the method of introducing new genes into the target population;
- the costs of production and delivery of new genes.

Mating plans for cross-breeding

The level of sophistication of the breeding plan will depend on the circumstances under which it will have to be carried out in the field situation. A criss-cross mating plan requires a high level of understanding among the owners involved, and a quite complex recording system. It is probably better to compromise some heritability for simplicity and to take an approach of up-grading local goats to a blood-level that functions well in the target environment. After grading-up to a suitable blood-level, mating between goats of that blood-level will be simple for farmers and pastoralists to continue by themselves. Some selection can be undertaken at that blood-level to improve performance. For an up-grading programme, all that is needed is a steady supply of bucks or semen. Once large numbers of grade goats are within the target population, they can be used to maintain the population, and trading in grade goats among owners can help to avoid in-breeding.

Choice of improver breed for cross-breeding

In selecting the improver breed to use in a cross-breeding programme, consider the following factors:

- environment
- desired production characteristics
- desired adaptation characteristics
- past experience
- ease of access to new breed
- cost of new breed.

What are the characteristics of the local breed that need to be improved, and how can they be improved without losing the survival characteristics of the breed? Has there ever been any past experience of using new breeds in your country? Was the experience good or bad? In most cases, the practical considerations of access to the breeding stock and cost will over-ride other considerations. Simply because Europe, the USA, and Australia have well-organised livestock-export companies and regular flights to tropical countries, most goats used for cross-breeding are temperate breeds.

The characteristics of breeds of goats that might be used for genetic improvement are described below. Improver breeds may be divided into improved tropical breeds and temperate breeds (Table 8.4).

Improved tropical breeds

Jamnapuri: also known as the Ettahwah, this is the largest breed of goat in India. It is mainly brown or black, with long ears and a convex face. Adult weights of 65–75 kg are common. Twinning rates are quite high, at 1.2–1.4. The Jamnapuri can be considered a dual-purpose breed, but is usually used to improve milk production. Average daily yields of 1–3 litres are possible. It has been used to grade-up goats in South-East Asia, particularly Indonesia, where its influence on the Katjang goat may be widely observed.

Table 8.4
Some goat improver breeds

Tropical	Temperate
Jamnapuri	Anglo-Nubian
Boer	Toggenburg
Damascus	Saanen
Beetal	Alpine

Boer: the improved Boer goat has been developed through selection programmes in the local Boer type in South Africa. It is a very stocky, well-muscled goat, which has been used to improve the meat characteristics of local goat breeds. The Boer is mainly white, often with a red/brown head and neck. It is quite short, with long ears and a convex face, and has a short neck and thick bones. It is a prolific breed, with a kidding rate of 1.5. The Boer goat has been exported from South Africa to Europe, the USA, and Australia, from where it can be obtained.

Damascus: the Damascus goat is undoubtedly related to the Nubian family of north-east Africa. It is found in Cyprus, Syria, and Lebanon. The Damascus goat is normally red/brown in colour, and is sometimes known as the Red Damascus. It is predominantly a dairy breed and can produce up to 4 litres of milk per day under intensive management. It is quite prolific, producing 1.4–1.8 kids per kidding. The potential of the Damascus goat as an improver breed in the tropics has not been investigated, but it is probably worth doing so.

Beetal: the Beetal goat is an important milk producer in India, Pakistan, and Bangladesh. It is similar to the Jamnapuri, but slightly shorter. It has long ears and a convex face. It is normally red/brown in colour with white spots. It is thought to be hardier than the Jamnapuri. It is valued for its milk production, producing 1–2 litres per day. It is more prolific than the Jamnapuri, with 1.0–1.8 kids per kidding. The Beetal breed is worth considering as an improver breed in harsher environments.

Improved temperate breeds
Anglo-Nubian: the Anglo-Nubian breed was developed in Britain about 100 years ago. Two tropical breeds — the Zairiby from southern Egypt and the Jamnapuri from India — were taken to Britain and crossed with the local British goat. After selection, the breed stabilised into the form now seen. It is a tall goat, with long ears and a markedly convex nose. The colours are very variable, including brown, black, black and white patches, fawn, and grey. Mature body weights can be high: 50–70 kg in females and 60–80 kg in males.

The Anglo-Nubian's tropical ancestry has given it some residual tropical adaptation which has made it very successful in breed improvement in the tropics. It is a useful breed to improve both milk production and growth rates. Although milk yields are not as high as the dairy breeds originating in Switzerland, its hardiness and good adaptation to tropical environments make it an ideal breed with which to start any breed-improvement programme. The Anglo-Nubian has a relatively high milk-fat content (4.5 per cent), making its milk highly valued for butter and cheese-making.

Toggenburg: the Toggenburg breed originated in Switzerland and is now quite widespread in Europe and the USA; it has been used for breed improvement in some parts of the tropics. Toggenburgs are normally brown or fawn, usually with white stripes on either side of the face, and a white muzzle. The lower part of the legs and the rear of its rump are a paler colour than the rest of the body. The breed originally had long hair, mainly on the rear of the body, but this is being selected against and short hair is now more common. Mature body weights of 45–55 kg in females and 55–65 kg in males are common.

The Toggenburg has been bred for milk, but cross-breeding it with tropical breeds will undoubtedly improve growth rates as well. The breed has been able to adapt to tropical climates, and has been introduced into Kenya, Tanzania, the Caribbean, Venezuela, and South Africa.

Saanen: the Saanen is perhaps the best known of the dairy breeds of goat. It originated in Switzerland but, like the Toggenburg, has since spread throughout Europe, the USA, Australia, and New Zealand. In most countries there has been some separate development of the breed, making one country's Saanens slightly different from another's. Saanen goats are large and normally white, occasionally light fawn. They often have black spots on the skin, which can be seen on the udder or nose, but rarely show on the hair, which is short. They are mostly polled and, as a result, intersex goats are quite common. This feature is reducing in incidence through more careful breeding, and now horned Saanen goats are increasing in number. The face is straight, and occasionally concave. Well-bred Saanens have very good dairy conformation, with big well-hung udders and a pronounced wedge shape. Mature body weights of 60–70 kg in females and 70–80 kg in males are typical.

The Saanen breed has mainly been developed for milk production and is the highest-yielding goat in the world. Yields ranging from 825 to 3,850 litres per lactation have been reported. At its best, a Saanen milking doe can match a mediocre dairy cow. The Saanen responds well to good management, but is perhaps less able to withstand the rigours of the tropics. Its light skin colour makes it susceptible to strong sunlight and so it has performed well in the tropics only when housed. Nevertheless, it has been imported into many countries in the tropics including India, Malaysia, the Caribbean, Nigeria, Venezuela, and South Africa. The Saanen breed should be considered as an improver breed only when management is at a very high level; otherwise its huge potential for improvement will be wasted.

Alpine: the Alpine breed, like the Saanen, has been developed in separate populations in each country in which it has been imported. There are now French, Swiss, German, and British Alpine lines of

Figure 8.8 Goat breeds

Anglo-Nubian
JENNY MATTHEWS/OXFAM

Toggenburg
CHRISTIE PEACOCK

Boer
TREVOR WILSON

this breed, each with slightly different characteristics. The coat of the British Alpine is short, and coloured dark brown to black, with light stripes either side of the face. The mature body weight is 50–60 kg in females and 55–65 kg in males.

The Alpine has been bred for milk production, but will also improve growth rates. It is relatively hardy and has been found to be a useful improver breed in the tropics. It has been introduced to India, the Caribbean, Burundi, and South Africa.

Angora: the Angora goat is an outstanding breed for mohair production. The breed is thought to have originated in Central Asia, but was found in its present state in Turkey in the sixteenth century. Angora goats have thick wavy coats. The hair grows 12–15 cm long. The value of mohair has resulted in the breed being imported into many countries in Europe, the USA, Eastern Europe, India, Australia, and South Africa. There are now two million Angora goats in South Africa, where selection has produced Angoras with the highest fibre-yields in the world.

Angora goats have been used to up-grade the fibre production of goats in Australia, India, and Pakistan. Their main weakness is a very high incidence of abortions.

Importation of goats for cross-breeding

Importing goats from a foreign country is not easy. It needs careful planning at all stages, from identifying the source of the goats, arranging transport, receiving the animals, looking after them on arrival, and making the best use of them in a well-planned breeding programme. Importing goats is expensive, and great care is needed to make the best use of these valuable stock.

Goats in the temperate regions of the northern and southern hemispheres are seasonal breeders. In the northern hemisphere they kid in January–April. Most male kids are not wanted and so are destroyed at birth. It is important to reserve males well ahead of the kidding season, so that sufficient numbers can be reared for export. Transport costs usually double the purchase price of the goats. It is cheapest to transport them in an airliner livestock-container, if available. This is cheaper per head than constructing a special crate, and makes handling on arrival much easier.

Each importing country will have its own regulations concerning the health of the goats to be imported. Careful inquiries should be made to determine the exact procedures that should be followed in the recipient country. Most countries require a veterinary officer to inspect the goats immediately before departure; some also demand that extensive tests are carried out to prove that the goats are free of major diseases, such as contagious agalactia (never recorded in the UK) and caprine arthritis encephalitis (CAE)/maedi visna, brucellosis, scrapie, and infectious reproductive diseases. Tests can be very expensive and can add considerably to the final cost of the goats. The original health certificate travels with the goats and must be handed over to the importer, together with the original airway bill. The importer must sign a document, stating that the goats have been received in good order. Once this has been signed, insurers are no longer liable for any claims made against them. The exporter should also supply certificates describing the pedigree of each goat. This is vital in planning any breeding programme.

Once goats have been ordered, careful preparations should be made to receive and quarantine them. In most countries there is a lot of paperwork to complete before the goats can be released. A suitable truck should be available and the necessary permits obtained to allow it to enter the tarmac area and get close enough to the aeroplane to off-load the goats easily. There should be grass, hay, or sand in the back to make it comfortable and safe for them to travel. They will be very tired on arrival and will need to lie down on some comfortable material. The side should be high enough to keep them secure. It is better if they can be kept in quarantine for at least their first night, somewhere not too far from the airport, so they can rest before travelling on to a more distant place. The stress from travelling can be a predisposing cause of many diseases, particularly respiratory problems.

Most countries have their own quarantine regulations, which should be strictly followed. If there are no regulations, follow proper procedures anyway. Make sure that the goats are isolated and their health monitored for the first six weeks. These procedures should be clearly seen to be followed by the relevant authorities. In this way there can be no recriminations against the importer, should anything unusual occur after importation.

Some loss of weight after arrival is inevitable, with a change in diet and climate. Every effort should be made to find feeds that are liked, so that the goats are eased into consuming new feeds. Lack of appetite and weight loss in the presence of appetising feeds indicate a disease problem which must be identified. The health of the goats should be monitored for any changes, and speedy remedial action taken.

Organisation of cross-breeding
There are several methods of organising cross-breeding to introduce new genes. It can take place on special breeding farms or in villages through bucks or artificial insemination.

Breeding farms
If high levels of heterosis are considered important, goats can be cross-bred on a government-owned or privately owned farm or station. A large number of breeding females can be kept on the farm, with a few bucks of the chosen improver breed, for the production of F_1 cross-breds with high levels of hybrid vigour. F_1 males and females can be produced in this way for sale to farmers, for cash or on credit. The F_1 females may be distributed either

'open' (not pregnant) or 'in kid' with a kid of another blood-level. If they are released open, they can leave the breeding station at a younger age than if they are retained for mating. This can considerably increase the rate of production of the farm.

A small flock of the pure improver breed can be kept on the breeding station to breed replacement stock for the farm, so that repeated importations are not needed.

Farmers with good management skills can breed cross-breds on contract, making a profitable enterprise for them.

Breeding stations have been used by governments all over the developing world for selection or cross-breeding. They have generally performed rather badly and have been notoriously difficult to manage efficiently. This makes the cost of each F_1 very high, and their production has normally had to be subsidised in some way. Furthermore, breeding stations never truly represent the management environment in which the cross-breds are expected to perform. Stations often have management levels, including health care, much higher than the recipient farms. If this is the case, goats may be bred without the immunity necessary to survive on farms after distribution. Alternatively, the station management is so poor that the breeding flock performs so badly that few cross-breds are produced per year, making them very expensive and the station very inefficient.

The use of breeding stations to produce F_1 females has traditionally been the main method of introducing new genes. However, this use of females is a very expensive and slow method of disseminating new genetic material. It is much quicker and more efficient if the prolific breeding of improver males can be exploited more widely through the use of bucks or, possibly, through AI.

Buck stations

It is important to make the best use of the prolific mating ability of expensive improver bucks. Bucks can be used for breeding at the village level. They may either be sold for cash or on credit to individuals, or sold or loaned to groups of owners, who may combine to obtain the buck. It might be justifiable for an individual with a large flock (more than 30) to purchase a buck for his or her exclusive use; otherwise it is better if goat-keepers can cooperate in the use of the buck and so spread the costs.

Cross-breeding in the environment in which the cross-bred will live has the added advantage of producing hybrids with naturally acquired immunity to the common diseases of the area. This is of great value.

If the buck is to be shared among several owners in a group, there are a few key principles to follow:

- The conditions under which the buck is received by the group must be clear. It is best if any one buck stays in one site for no

*Organisation of buck
stations in Ethiopia*

> Anglo-Nubian bucks were loaned freely by an NGO project to groups of women farmers in Ethiopia. The buck was looked after by one family, elected to do so by all members of the group. Members brought their does to be mated to the home of the buck-keeper. Each group agreed its own terms to pay the buck-keeper for looking after the buck. In some groups, the members take turns cutting feed for the buck. In other groups, the members provided labour to help the buck-handler during busy times such as weeding or harvesting. Another alternative is a cash fee, which perhaps provides a greater incentive to the buck-keeper to promote the use of the buck.
>
> Many buck-keepers found that feeding a buck was a great burden and could do it for only a few months before passing him on to another family. Others took great pride in the condition of their buck, and villages rivalled each other to give the best care to their buck.

more than 12–18 months, to avoid in-breeding. If the buck is loaned to a group by a project, it must be clear that the project is able to recover the buck and exchange him for another after some agreed period. An annual membership fee, which guarantees a buck to the group, is a useful arrangement. If the buck is sick, or has served for a long period, he can be removed and replaced.

- The buck should be looked after by one family, who are responsible for ensuring that he receives enough feed, and are responsible for his health and alerting relevant people if he becomes sick.

- All members of the group should have equal access to the buck. If houses are very dispersed, this may mean moving the buck occasionally, so that all have easy access.

- The buck should not be expected to serve more than two–three does per day. Any more than this will exhaust him, and fertility rates will drop. If he is sick, he should not serve at all.

- The buck should be kept in a good house, and receive good feed and attention. There should be enough space for mating in the buck pen, and assistance should be given in mating whenever necessary. Ideally females should stay for 12 hours, or return after 12 hours to receive the second, recommended mating.

Once farmers have gained some experience of keeping cross-breds, some of the most successful may move on to produce a

Farmers in the densely populated highlands of Burundi keep small flocks of 2–6 goats. The intensity of land cultivation means that most goats are kept at home and food is cut and carried to them. 'Projet Caprin Ngozi', funded by the German government, started in the Ngozi district of Burundi in 1980. The objective of the project was to intensify production and improve the milk production of local goats, so that farmers would have excess milk to sell. A small milk-processing and cheese-making factory was built, and an efficient milk-collection system established.

The project decided to improve milk production through crossing local goats with Alpine goats imported from France and Germany. At first the project set up a goat-breeding station for the production of F_1 stock for distribution to farmers. However, they quickly realised that the capacity of the station was not sufficient to meet the huge demand for cross-breds. Instead the station became a farm for breeding pure Alpine goats for distribution to farmer-managed buck stations. Pure Alpine bucks were placed in a network of buck stations managed by groups of farmers. Farmers brought their does for service, and very quickly large numbers of cross-breds were bred in the villages of Ngozi. At its peak, 8,000 cross-breds were produced per year from 52 buck stations.

Farmers were impressed with the performance of the cross-bred and wanted to up-grade their goats further. They back-crossed their F_1 stock to the Alpine breed to produce a F_2 of 75 per cent Alpine blood. Farmers realised that under their management it was best to stop up-grading at 75 per cent. They now maintain blood-levels at 75 per cent, while at the same time keeping some pure local goats as an insurance, in case the cross-breds have any problems.

pure line of the improver breed, for their own use and for sale. This will ensure the long-term, local supply of pure-bred stock.

The use of artificial insemination (AI) in cross-breeding programmes

Artificial insemination of goats has in the past been used only on research stations, government breeding stations, or large-scale commercial goat farms. There has never been a successful goat AI programme for smallholder farmers or pastoralists in the tropics. Although there are many good theoretical reasons for using AI, the practical problems associated with its use appear insurmountable in most countries. The running of a sustainable AI programme seems difficult. Using AI in a small area, with a few trained and highly motivated farmers and AI technicians, probably has the best chance of success. This might be part of the early stages of a grading-up process and, if managed well, could quickly introduce many genotypes into a population, giving farmers a wide range of genetic material with which to breed in the future.

AI programmes could also exploit the facilities of AI programmes for cattle. For this to be successful, there must be a strong demand from goat farmers for the service, and AI technicians must be well trained in both techniques.

Further reading

Dalton, D. C. (1981) *An Introduction to Practical Animal Breeding*, London: Granada

Devendra, C. and G. B. McLeroy (1982) *Goat and Sheep Production in the Tropics*, London: Longman

Mason, I. L. and V. Buvanendran (1982) *Breeding Plans for Livestock in the Tropics*, Rome: FAO

CHAPTER 9

Management of large goat farms

9.1 Introduction

This book is concerned mainly with smallholder and pastoral production of goats. However there are circumstances in which a larger number of goats than are normally kept by smallholders or pastoralists might be managed in a more intensive manner. Large goat farms might include government, or NGO, goat farms for breeding, teaching, and research; and commercial goat farms.

Organisations might start large goat farms to supply breeding stock to farmers. The goats distributed from the farm might be cross-breds, or stock improved through a selection programme. A goat flock might be kept at an agricultural college farm for teaching purposes, enabling students to have practice in the handling and management of goats. Finally, research institutions, with a goat-research programme, might maintain a large flock of goats to breed goats for experimental purposes.

Sometimes large goat farms are used to demonstrate 'modern' goat farming. However, the value of a large goat farm for demonstration purposes is very limited. There is no value in showing smallholder or pastoral goat-keepers a large goat farm with expensive housing, infrastructure, and equipment, and a large staff. There is little they can learn from such a farm and it will only create aspirations which cannot be met.

It is inevitable that large goat farms will be managed differently from flocks kept by neighbouring farmers. This has important implications. If goats bred on large farms for distribution are managed better than those on surrounding farms, they will not develop the immunity to disease which they need after distribution and may not survive. Selection programmes must select stock in the environment in which they will eventually be kept. However, often the reverse is true: large government-run goat farms are rather badly managed, and goats are distributed from a poor environment into a more favourable one.

In addition to the institutional functions of large farms, more commercially minded farmers in the tropics are increasingly keen to keep larger numbers of goats, more intensively, in order to make a profit from the sale of milk, and/or stock for slaughter or breeding. Often they do not have experience of the management of larger farms, and usually underestimate the management requirements.

There may be many different objectives for keeping larger numbers of goats, but their management, for whatever purpose, presents particular problems. Experience has shown that goats require special care when large numbers are housed, fed, and managed together. There are several disease complexes, such as respiratory and parasitic problems, associated with the intensive management of goats, and special precautions have to be taken.

This chapter offers brief guidelines on setting up a goat farm, the annual planning of the farm, and its daily management. Readers should refer to the appropriate chapters of the book for technical details.

9.2 Setting up a goat farm

9.2.1 Definition of objectives

It is important to define the objectives of the farm very clearly at the start, as this will to some extent dictate the management strategy of the farm (Table 9.1). Setting up a purely commercial farm, under tight financial control, is slightly different from starting a government farm with a grant or allocation from the government budget.

Table 9.1 Influence of farm objective on management system

Type of objective	Emphasis in management system
Breeding	High-quality foundation stock Batch breeding Detailed breeding plan Good recording systems
Teaching	Variety of breeds Range of equipment Range of management systems
Research	Specialist buildings and pens Good recording systems
Profit-making	Low-cost infrastructure Simple management system Few staff to reduce labour costs Good financial management

Establishing an institutional farm for breeding, teaching, or research will usually be done with a lump-sum grant, either directly through the government budget, or, more likely, with a grant from an external donor. A realistic budget must be prepared to allow for the construction of sound infrastructure. Government goat farms usually receive an annual budget for their management and this subsidises, to some extent, the products of the farms. These products might include breeding stock for sale to farmers, research outputs, and access by students to learn about goats. Non-profit making objectives should not be an excuse for inefficient management, but they often are.

9.2.2 Assessment of resources

Consider the resources available for developing the farm, and design a management system that makes the most efficient use of them. Table 9.2 considers some of the essential resources, and the influence they can have on the management system.

Table 9.2 Effect of available resources on management system

Resources

Land
Flock size will be affected by size and type of land, including current fodder production
Is any land irrigable for forage?
Are the rights to land long-term or short-term?

Climate
Rainfall, temperature, and humidity will affect house design

Goats
Availability of foundation stock

Finance
Funds available for farm development and recurrent costs
Timing of finance

Access to inputs
Feed supplements, drugs, equipment, forage seed, fertiliser, irrigation equipment, building materials, fencing

Personnel
Goat-management skills and experience of available staff
Skills and availability of veterinary personnel

9.2.3 Flock-management system

The flock-management system of the farm will be determined by its objectives and resources. This will dictate the groups in which the goats are managed: breeding females, breeding males, suckling kids, weaners, fatteners, or experimental groups; how the goats are fed: grazing (which requires a shepherd or fencing), seasonal grazing/seasonal housing, cut and carry feeding; the level of health care; the type of housing and the breeding systems followed: seasonal, continuous, or in batches.

9.2.4 Farm layout and infrastructure

It is important to make a plan of the land available for the farm, in order to plan its overall layout. Consider what infrastructure is required and how best to arrange it for easy management of the flock. Is all the infrastructure needed immediately, or can it be developed over time?

The infrastructure on a large goat farm might include the following features.

- Buildings:
  housing for breeding males
  kidding pens
  kid boxes
  milking parlour and milk-handling area
  isolation pen for sick goats
  post-mortem/slaughter room
  office/recording room, with lockable drug cupboard
  feed and equipment store
  hay barn
- Experimental pens, including feeding-trial pens
- Water troughs
- Dip bath/spraying area
- Handling pens
- Weighing equipment and pens
- Burial pit
- Manure pit
- Exercise yards
- Fencing

9.2.5 Housing

It is important to consider the function of the house to be constructed. With the management system adopted, what sort of housing do the goats require? Will they be housed all the time and will feed be cut and carried to them? If so, they will need more space, an exercise yard, good feed racks, and water. If the goats will be housed only at night, the house design can be more simple, and they can be housed in the groups in which they are herded for grazing during the day. When building a house for goats, consider the purpose of the house, the site, materials, and labour available (see Table 9.3).

Table 9.3 Factors affecting goat-house design

Consider	Effect on house
Purpose:	
Permanent housing	Pen ($1.5m^2$/goat) + exercise yard, feed racks, water
Night housing	Pen ($1.0–1.5m^2$/goat)
Permanent buck pens	$3m^2$/buck + exercise yard
Kidding pens	$3m^2$/doe
Site:	
Land ownership	If ownership is permanent, build a more permanent structure. If site is on a short-term lease, build cheaper structure.
Aspect	If hot climate, site house away from sun to reduce day-time temperatures. If cool climate, house should face the sun to dry inside during day.
Prevailing wind direction	If wind is cool, site house sheltered from it.
Drainage	Build on well-drained site; or raise floor of house.
Rainfall	Heavy rainfall requires good roof.
Temperature	High temperature requires good ventilation, achieved through roof design and low walls.
Humidity	High humidity requires good ventilation.
Materials:	
Availability	Locally available materials are usually cheapest; future repairs will be easier.
Cost	Projected length of service.
Durability	If long life required, use more durable materials.
Labour:	
Skilled, locally available craftsmen	A more sophisticated construction

Main house

Decide whether the goats will be housed throughout the day, in which case they will need more space inside the house, as well as an exercise yard with easy access from the main house. They will also need feed racks and access to water. If the goats will go out grazing during the day, returning to the house at night only for protection

Figure 9.1 Goat -house layouts

a) permanently housed

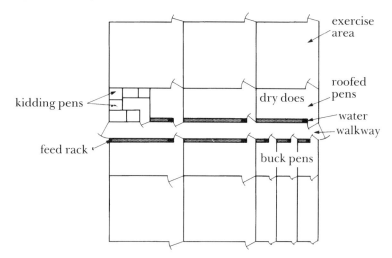

exercise area

roofed pens

kidding pens

dry does

water

walkway

feed rack

buck pens

b) housed at night only

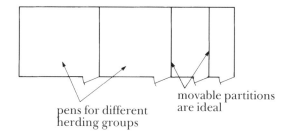

movable partitions are ideal

pens for different herding groups

and not to feed, then they will need slightly less space, and a simple design will suffice. Two suggested house layouts are shown in Figure 9.1.

Ventilation

Goats are very susceptible to respiratory diseases and must therefore have good ventilation. In order to maintain fresh air in the house, and to eliminate contaminated air, the house must be designed to allow air to circulate. This is achieved when hot air rises and escapes from the house, ideally through the roof, which in turn draws fresh air into the house through side openings. This ensures the regular change of air that is needed to avoid respiratory problems (Figure 9.2).

It is very important to design a house with good ventilation from the start. Once it is built, it is hard to modify a house to improve its ventilation. In the belief that goats are desert animals, there is a tendency to over-protect them, building structures with high walls and no air vents in the roof. This must be resisted. The

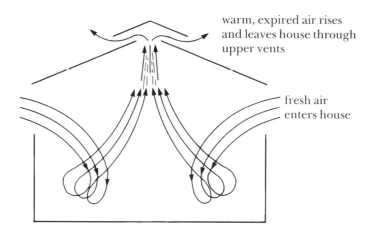

warm, expired air rises
and leaves house through
upper vents

fresh air
enters house

*Figure 9.2 Principles of
good ventilation*

air must smell fresh and clean at all times. Any smell of ammonia
indicates poor ventilation and an unhealthy environment.

In most conditions in the tropics, goats will not need any walls;
or, if they do, they require only a low wall at the sides of the house.
The roof should be waterproof and designed to allow the release of
contaminated air. It should either slope, or have air vents, or have
ventilation in the centre of the roof.

Floor

The main types of floor to consider are earth, concrete, or wooden
slats. They each have advantages and disadvantages. The floor of
the house should be designed so that it is easy to keep it clean and
dry. A concrete floor is easy to clean, but, without bedding, is a
cold, hard surface and therefore not always desirable. An earth
floor is often adequate, provided it is well drained. Sand, or light
sandy soil, is often adequate; it can be swept clean every day and
more sand put down at regular intervals.

A raised, slatted, wooden floor is ideal, but can be very
expensive. If the floor is slatted, the urine and manure will fall
through and can be collected below, keeping the floor clean and
dry. The spaces between slats must be wide enough to allow
manure to fall through, but not wide enough for a goat's legs to be
trapped. A gap of 1.5–2.0 cm, about the width of a matchbox, is
about right. Wooden slats will need to be regularly replaced, as the
urine will rot the wood and cause gaps to develop. The floor
should be raised high enough to allow staff easy access to collect the
waste underneath.

Milking shed

The milking shed should be a quiet, calm, easily cleaned
environment, where it is easy to milk. When goats are milked by

*Figure 9.3 Milking
platform*

hand, it is easiest if they are raised on a platform with a small feed-rack. Simple wooden platforms are quite adequate (Figure 9.3).

Isolation pens
It is very good practice to have an isolation pen where sick goats can be kept apart from the rest of the flock to avoid cross-infection. Ideally the pen would be quite separate from the main goat house and grazing areas, to avoid any chance of air-borne infections. It should be made from materials that are easy to clean and disinfect after the death, or recovery, of the sick goat.

Post-mortem/slaughter room
A simple post-mortem/slaughter room is useful; it should be constructed next to the isolation pens. Ideally it would have a concrete floor, side bench for post-mortem examinations, drainage system and soakaway, water, and a central hook to lift carcasses for butchering.

Burial pit
A deep pit should be dug, far away from the goat flock, where infected carcasses can be disposed. Carcasses should either be burned, or deeply buried and covered with soil. Wild animals must be prevented from gaining access to the carcass and spreading infected material.

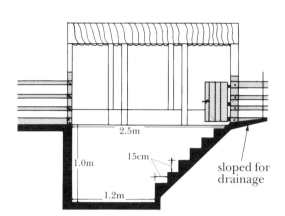

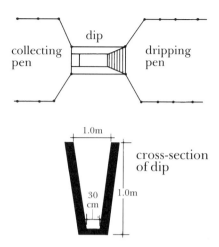

Figure 9.4 Dip-bath design

Dip bath

In situations where large numbers of goats need to be regularly dipped to control external parasites, a cement dip bath should be constructed (Figure 9.4). The dip should be built away from the rest of the farm and should have a soak-away drain or septic tank to dispose of the waste dip-wash, without contaminating adjacent pasture and water sources. Ideally it would be constructed close enough to a source of water to allow the easy filling of the trough. However, if the water-source is a well, be careful not to contaminate the well water itself with waste dip-wash.

Handling pens

Goats may need to be handled regularly and it is much easier for staff to handle and sort them and carry out a job if the animals can be confined in suitable pens. Handling pens are useful for sorting goats for mating/culling/sale/distribution; handling before weighing; and handling before dipping/vaccination/foot trimming.

Office and stores

A simple office, close to the goat house, makes record-keeping easier. The office can serve as a focal point of the farm, where records, reference books, and valuable equipment are kept. It is handy to have a store near the office, where bulky supplies and equipment such as feed and tools can be stored securely. It is an important management practice to keep good records of the stocks of materials in the store, so they can be replenished in good time, and to devise an effective method of controlling their use.

It is good to have a few simple visual displays about the farm in the office, such as number of stock by age/sex/breed, etc., for staff, students, and visitors. Lists of does due to kid can also be displayed, so that they can be checked regularly.

Figure 9.5 Water-trough dimensions

40cm

150cm

55cm

9.2.6 Equipment

Feed racks

Goat-farmers have tried for years to design the perfect goat-feeding rack. Everyone has a particular design and different materials available. The principles outlined in 5.5.3 should be followed. Allow enough space for all the goats: a width of about 30 cm per animal is adequate. If there is not enough space, the weaker goats will be squeezed out of the rack by their stronger fellows, and will not eat properly.

Feed troughs

Simple wooden boxes, raised off the ground, are adequate to feed dry supplements, such as rice bran, grain, or oil cakes. If feed is offered wet, a waterproof container (such as an old oil drum, neatly cut in half, a plastic bucket, or specially constructed metal trough) must be used. Allow about 30 cm per goat. If there is not sufficient trough space, feed goats in batches, to ensure that all have an equal chance to feed.

Water containers

Ideally, water troughs would be made from cement-covered bricks or hollow blocks, with a drainage plug to assist cleaning. They should not be so high that the goats have to perch on the top to drink, or so low that kids get in and foul the water (Figure 9.5). Match the trough with the size of your goats. A trough with piped water and float valve, to allow self-filling, saves a lot of work.

Kid boxes

Kids do not have a functioning rumen and so do not generate much heat to keep themselves warm. Young kids are very

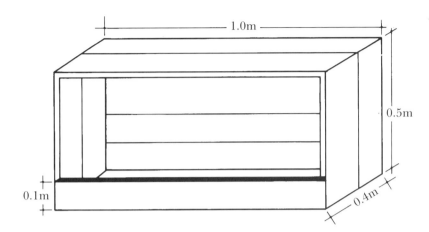

Figure 9.6 Kid-box design

susceptible to draughts and cold and must be kept warm, but also well ventilated, at all times. In many parts of the tropics, temperatures can fall considerably at night and kids will need help to keep warm. If they are kept with their mothers at night, each family in a separate pen, the mother will keep her kid(s) warm enough. If they are kept with other kids and their mothers, they may not necessarily be warm enough, and if they are cold they have a tendency to lie on top of one another, and may even be trampled on or suffocated by older goats. To avoid these problems, and keep kids warm, dry and safe, it is best to construct a kid box of some sort. A design for a kid box is given in Figure 9.6. The box should be constructed from a warm material, such as wood or bamboo. Ideally it would have some suitable bedding, such as straw or dry grass. Other traditional methods can be used, such as a large up-turned basket.

Figure 9.7 Weighing crate

Weighing crate

Farms that need to weigh several hundred goats regularly will need a weighing crate with suitable handling pens, to save staff time and grazing time. A swing gate at the end of the pen can help in sorting goats on the basis of weight. This might be useful in selection programmes or on fattening farms that sell when a target weight has been reached.

9.2.7 Purchase of foundation stock

When setting up a goat farm, all the goats will have to be purchased. The quality of the foundation stock will, to a great extent, determine the overall performance of the farm in the years to come. For this reason, care should be taken to obtain the best breeding goats possible. This is not always easy. It is particularly difficult to obtain high-quality breeding females, because owners are naturally reluctant to sell them. Female goats sent to market are usually infertile, repeat aborters, or poor mothers. It is only in extreme circumstances that farmers or pastoralists will sell good females. For this reason, it is difficult to buy females through normal channels, and special arrangements should be made. If the farm is intended to benefit members of the surrounding community through production of cross-breds, for example, community leaders should be involved in setting up the farm so that they can approach owners to sell their stock. A premium price should reward goat-keepers for selling their very best stock.

Commercial farmers will probably have to build up their stock numbers gradually, by purchasing from large, busy markets where there is a good choice and they are able to select the best goats on offer.

New goats may bring diseases, or disease vectors, to the existing flock. For this reason, all new stock should be drenched for internal parasites, dipped if necessary, vaccinated, and given a thorough health check. Ideally they would be isolated from other stock for two–three weeks for observation of their health, but this may not be possible to arrange. New stock should be tagged and a record opened for them, in which all known information about them is recorded for future reference.

Some females will probably be pregnant when purchased. In the original plan you should allow time to assess the status of breeding females and, if necessary, time to deliver their kids before they enter any planned breeding programme.

9.2.8 Staff recruitment

The successful care of livestock demands constant attention to detail and a high level of commitment from all staff. Goats require attention at weekends and often need tending at night. Carelessness means that sick goats are not noticed, drugs are not administered properly, kids are not fed properly, and events are mis-recorded. The levels of husbandry skills of staff attending goats and their thoroughness will be some of the main factors affecting the performance of the farm. It is important to recruit staff with the attitude, skills, and dedication required to look after goats well.

Sometimes management of institutional farms is assigned to a committee of experts. This is unsatisfactory. Management by committee leads to delays in decision-making which can be disastrous. Sharing responsibility among several people means that no one is ultimately responsible, and husbandry standards will tend to slip. There must be one person acting as manager/supervisor who is responsible for the overall management of the farm. The manager may take advice from different specialists, but must ultimately be responsible for the whole farm. The manager should, ideally, have some experience of goat husbandry; but, if this is not the case, should at least have experience of the successful management of large numbers of some other species. The manager should be responsible for preparing the annual plan for the farm, with outside assistance, if necessary, and for supervising the day-to-day activities on the farm, assigning responsibilities and checking that they are carried out properly. In addition the manager should be responsible for ensuring that all necessary inputs, drugs, feed, etc., are ordered and in stock, and that records are properly maintained. The manager is ultimately responsible for the performance of the flock. This task is made considerably easier if the staff reporting to the manager can be trusted to carry out their work in a competent and reliable manner.

The farm workers should have experience of some aspect of livestock husbandry. Although they will be assigned to different responsibilities (kid management, milking, buck management, etc.), they should be able to cover for each other when necessary. Certain tasks require more skill and patience than others (attendance at kiddings, care of young kids, etc.), and staff with suitable skills should be recruited and assigned to these more skilful jobs. It is sometimes helpful to build a financial incentive into the wages paid, to encourage high standards. Staff can be paid individually for what they have achieved, such as paying the kid rearer for the number of kids successfully weaned, or the number of does conceiving. Alternatively a bonus can be paid to all the staff at the end of the financial year, according to the overall performance of the farm. If it is hard to pay staff in cash, they may be rewarded with culled stock, or manure, or perhaps an option to buy good-quality stock at a subsidised price.

It is important that the farm is regularly attended by a competent veterinarian, or veterinary assistant, who is on-call to the farm. Very large farms may even justify the full-time employment of veterinary staff. They should be able to treat sick goats, advise on preventative health measures, and undertake simple diagnostic procedures. Ideally these staff would be based fairly close to the farm, so that they can be called out at night or at weekends.

All staff working on the farm should be trained in simple goat health-care; the curriculum suggested in 6.7.1 might be used for this training.

9.2.9 Records and record-keeping

Records can be kept for many purposes. It depends on the objectives of the farm. Do not keep unnecessary records. Use simple formats that record the performance of the farm sufficiently to monitor flock productivity and inputs, in order to improve flock performance. Consider what information is needed, and how it can be obtained without disrupting the work-routine excessively. Assign competent staff to keep the records, and up-date them regularly. Be clear who will collate and analyse the records, how it will be done, and how often they should be analysed. Records might be kept of some or all of the following:

* mating
* feeding
* health, including disease incidence, treatment, outcome
* drug use
* vaccination
* daily labour attendance
* temperature/rainfall
* weight records (weekly, bi-weekly)
* milk yields
* kidding.

Records kept in the goat house itself should be transferred every day to more permanent records in the office. In the office there should be an individual record for each goat on the farm. This record might be kept on a card, sorted numerically by tag number, or in a large hard-covered book or file. Computers are becoming more widespread and there are now specially designed software programmes to record information from large herds or flocks. An example of a livestock database management programme is the Livestock Information Management System (LIMS) from the International Livestock Research Institute (ILRI in Addis Ababa). Other database programmes are coming on to the market all the time.

There is no real need for a computer on a farm. Computers are useful for processing large quantities of data very quickly, but for day-to-day management they are unnecessary. Do not consider a computerised data-management system unless you have a large number of goats, and have staff able to manage the computer and learn its operation efficiently. Otherwise a great deal of effort can be put into learning computer programmes, wasting valuable staff time and leaving other tasks neglected. Always keep a hard copy of all records. Computers break down and are mis-managed, and diskettes can get lost or damaged. Valuable records should always be kept in duplicate.

9.3 Annual planning

In order to run a goat farm efficiently, it is important to make an annual plan, indicating the timing and frequency of different activities. This will help the manager to procure equipment, drugs, vaccines, and additional staff in good time, without delaying important farm operations. It is likely that any annual plan will be modified from time to time as circumstances change, but it is helpful to have a plan as a starting point.

It is useful to have a calendar of activities laid out on a large sheet of card that can be attached to the office wall for all to see (Table 9.4).

Consider how all the different classes of stock will be fed through the year. Make a flock projection for the year and calculate how much feed is required to support the projected flock at different times of year. Is there enough feed of the right quality? Will feed have to be conserved, or bought into the farm? What feed supplements are available locally?

Health
What prophylactic health measures will have to taken and at what seasons? What vaccinations should be given and when? Are there enough drugs and vaccines available, or will they have to be purchased? Where can they be bought?

Breeding
Decide on your mating policy and make mating plans for the year. Will goats be bred in certain seasons, or continuously mated as they become ready? Consider the option of batch mating versus continuous mating. Which suits the farm and staff best?

How will oestrus be detected? Will staff have to observe it, or will a raddled or vasectomised buck be used? Does mating have to be assisted? Who will record matings?

How many goats will be culled? On what basis will they be culled?

Labour
The quality of the staff recruited to work on a goat farm is perhaps the single biggest determinant of the overall performance of the flock.

Daily tasks
Consider the separate batches of goats maintained on the farm and the labour required to look after them on a daily basis. Allocate responsibilities clearly.

Table 9.4 Example of a calendar of goat-farm activities

Activity	Year 199_											
	J	F	M	A	M	J	J	A	S	O	N	D
Feeding												
Grazing management	▓	▓	▓	▓	▓	▓	▓	▓	▓	▓	▓	▓
Forage development and maintenance												
Weeding				▓								
Irrigation	▓										▓	▓
Forage conservation												
Equipment required									▓			
Labour required									▓			
Purchase and storage of feed supplements		▓			▓		▓					
Health												
Vaccination	▓						▓					
Drenching		▓										
Dipping	▓	▓	▓	▓	▓	▓	▓	▓	▓	▓	▓	▓
Drug purchase	▓											
Breeding												
Mating plans			▓	▓								
Culling										▓		
Labour												
Daily	▓	▓	▓	▓	▓	▓	▓	▓	▓	▓	▓	▓
Seasonal			▓	▓					▓			
Occasional												
Training				▓								
Buildings and infrastructure												
Maintenance				▓	▓							
Construction			▓									
Marketing and distribution												
Hardening-off before distribution									▓			
Transporting goats											▓	
	J	F	M	A	M	J	J	A	S	O	N	D

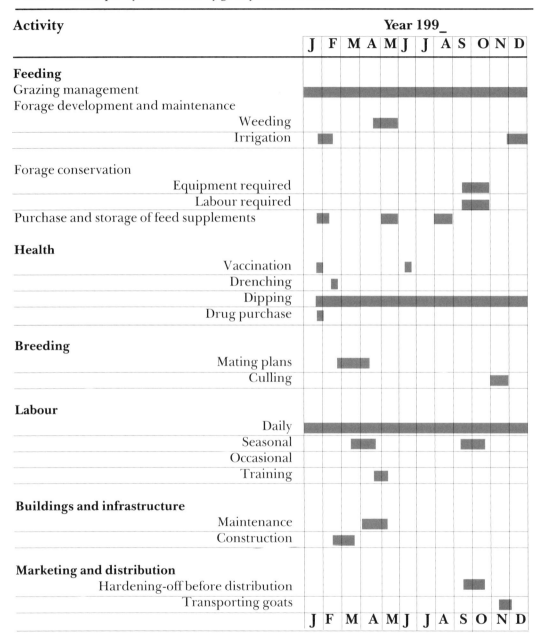

Seasonal tasks

There are likely to be seasonal jobs such as forage harvesting and building maintenance, when labour may have to be employed in addition to the regular labour force.

Occasional tasks

In addition to the daily labour requirement, there will be tasks such as dipping, drenching, and weighing, for which there will be a high demand for labour. Can this demand be met from the daily labour force by rearranging their normal work pattern, or are additional staff required?

Training

All staff should receive good supervision and regular training as a matter of routine. Training may take the form of specialised courses in particular aspects of goat production or regular weekly or monthly training sessions. On recruitment of staff, assess their existing skills and consider what additional knowledge and skills they need in order to work more efficiently. Training is also one method of motivating staff.

Buildings and infrastructure

Buildings require regular maintenance; time, money, and labour should be allocated for this purpose. Building and infrastructure maintenance can be done during slack periods when labour is free from other jobs.

Marketing and distribution

When and where will goats be sold or distributed? Is there a target market time and/or place? Should goats for sale be fattened before market? If goats are for distribution, do they need particular vaccinations before distribution?

Transporting goats

How will goats get to market or to their point of distribution? Will they be trucked or trekked? Most tropical breeds of goats will need about 0.3 m² of lorry space each. Always try to give transported goats bedding for the journey, because they normally lie down and can be damaged when bumping on rough roads. If it is a long trip, they should be allowed stops every six hours for feed and water. Always make sure that goats are driven carefully, particularly if they are being transported in large numbers. Sudden braking can push goats on top of each other, crushing those in the front. Bad driving can cause high mortality rates.

   If valuable goats have to be transported long distances, they can be given an injection of long-acting antibiotics (such as Terramycin LA) to prevent stress-induced diseases.

Budgeting

One of the most useful economic tools to help a farm manager to plan a farm is to prepare a cash-flow budget. This is worth doing, on both commercial and institutional farms. The cash-flow budget is prepared simply by subtracting the money spent from the money received. This can be calculated for a one-year period or for longer periods. It is perhaps more useful if each year is broken up into quarterly or monthly periods. Cash-flow budgets can be helpful in planning the running of a farm, or projecting the cash flow over a short-term or medium-term period of farm development. They can assist the farm manager's planning when repaying borrowed money.

Table 9.5 sets out the arrangement of a simple cash-flow budget of a dairy-goat farm. At the end of a period, the manager can compare the actual receipts and expenditure with the estimates made in the plan. If there are any differences, action can be taken to improve the situation before any harm is done. Action can be taken quickly if the budget for the planned cash flow and the analysis of the actual cash flow are made regularly for short periods, such as quarters.

Table 9.5 Example of a cash-flow budget for a farm of 100 milking does

Item	1st quarter ($)	2nd quarter ($)	Year 199_ 3rd quarter ($)	4th quarter ($)	Total ($)
Receipts					
milk sales	3,000	3,600	4,000	3,800	14,400
sale of fattened males	—	—	—	2,000	2,000
sale of culls	—	—	500	—	500
Total receipts	**3,000**	**3,600**	**4,500**	**5,800**	**16,900**
Payments					
feeds costs	200	200	300	200	900
mineral licks	10	10	15	10	45
drug costs	20	20	30	20	90
equipment	150	—	—	—	150
housing repairs	—	—	100	—	100
labour	600	600	600	600	2,400
marketing costs	—	—	50	150	200
new capital investment	—	2,000	—	—	2,000
interest	150	150	150	150	600
Total payments	**1,130**	**2,980**	**1,245**	**1,130**	**6,485**
Net cash flow	**1,870**	**620**	**3,255**	**4,670**	**10,415**
Loan repayment	1,500	1,500	1,500	1,500	6,000
Balance	**370**	**-880**	**1,755**	**3,170**	**4,415**

9.4 Daily management

The daily routine management of the goat farm should be simple and clear to all staff. It is most important that each member of staff is clearly allocated his or her responsibilities and is competent to carry out those duties efficiently.

Routine checks

First thing in the morning when entering the goat house, or pen, goats should be observed for signs of sickness; signs of oestrus and/or mating; and signs of labour or recent kidding.

Allocating the responsibility for these routine checks is important, but all staff must be trained to identify and report any of these events, and take any immediate action that might be necessary. If the health check is not made by a member of the veterinary staff, the veterinary personnel responsible should be alerted when a goat is thought to be sick. If there is a night guard on duty, he should give a report on the events of the previous night.

During the day all staff should get into the habit of observing goats for sickness, oestrus, mating, labour, and kidding, and observe the land for broken fences and the state of the pasture and the water supply. Constant vigilance by all staff should be encouraged and rewarded.

House cleaning, feeding, and watering

Goat houses and pens should be cleaned regularly and disinfected when appropriate.

Decide where each group will graze and for how long. Will they be out all day, or return in the middle of the day? Will any supplement be fed? How much and how often? Ideally, goats should have constant access to water both in the house and while out grazing. In practice, this is not always easy to arrange for a large number of goats, so they may have to be watered once, or twice, a day — on their way to and from grazing perhaps.

Regular jobs

It is likely that every day there will be at least one routine husbandry task to do, such as drenching, dipping, weighing, vaccination, hoof-trimming, or ear-tagging. Develop a simple and efficient method of tackling the job that disturbs the goats the least and does not take up valuable staff time. Continually analyse the method used and try to improve it.

Constant attention to detail by competent motivated staff is the key to success. Keeping large numbers of goats healthy and productive is not easy and requires considerable dedication from all those involved.

Further reading

Abbott, J.C. and J.P. Makeham (1979) *Agricultural Economics and Marketing in the Tropics*, London: Longman

Coy, D.V. (1982) *Accounting and Finance for Managers in Tropical Agriculture*, London: Longman

Mowlem, A. (1992) *Goat Farming* (2nd edition), Ipswich, UK: Farming Press

Skea, I. W. (undated) *Keeping Goats in Kenya*, Nairobi: Ministry of Livestock Development

Wilkinson, J.M. and B.A. Stark (1987) *Commercial Goat Production*, Oxford: Blackwell Scientific

CHAPTER 10

Processing and marketing goat products

Introduction

Any improvements made in the productivity of goats should be exploited as fully as possible. Once a surplus to the family's requirements has been produced, attention should be paid to the handling, processing, and marketing of goats and goat products. Goats can produce a huge range of products which, if processed at home, or by a group of farmers or pastoralists, can increase the owner's income. Products include:

- milk and milk derivatives
- meat and carcass products
- butter
- cheese
- skins
- fibre
- manure

Improving the processing of these products can increase the value of the product; balance out seasonal fluctuations in supply through processing and storage; improve human health; and increase the income earned by farmers from their goats. Farmers should carefully consider the costs of any processing equipment, the extra labour required, and the costs of marketing the product, and match these to the higher price of the product sold. In most cases, if there is the possibility of processing products at home, it is worthwhile to do so.

Processing milk and meat is one way to make use of surplus production. Perhaps in the wet season there is plenty of milk and milk products, while in the dry season there is a scarcity, and the price rises. Farmers have a choice of either trying to produce them during the dry season, which may be very difficult, or of processing the surplus for storage and later consumption or sale.

There are diseases which can be transmitted from goats to humans through milk and meat. Farmers must always be encouraged to improve the way they handle products, to reduce the risk of disease to their own families and to other consumers of their products.

10.1 Milk

Table 10.1
Goat-milk composition

Goat type	Fat (%)	Crude protein (%)
Tropical	3-6	3-5
Temperate	2-4	3-4

Milk is a valuable source of protein (including essential amino acids), fat, calcium, iron, phosphorus, and vitamins (including the important Vitamin A). With proper milking and handling practices, milk can be a highly nutritious food. It is especially valuable for growing children. The small size of the fat globules in goat's milk makes it easier to digest than cow's milk. Some children who are unable to digest cow's milk can happily drink goat's milk. Milk composition varies with breed, nutrition, stage of lactation, and age of the goat. Table 10.1 indicates the composition of goat's milk.

Unfortunately, milk is an ideal medium for the growth of bacteria. This means that great care must be taken at all stages, from goat to mouth, to avoid contamination of the milk with dirt that contains micro-organisms, and to reduce the growth of the bacteria that naturally occur in milk.

The wide range of vegetation consumed by goats can sometimes lead to milk tainted with a particular smell and flavour. Temperate breeds may emit a smell from musk glands in the head of sexually active males, so the odour is normally limited to the breeding season. Most tropical breeds are sexually active all the year round, but most are virtually scentless. If they release a smell at all, it is not as potent as in temperate breeds. The tainting of milk is almost entirely caused by the presence of a buck close to the place of milking. If temperate breeds are being used, tainting can be reduced by milking away from bucks and covering the milk container immediately after milking. Musk glands are also present in females and some emit a mild smell, but this is unusual.

10.1.1 Milking practice

The release of milk by a goat is an involuntary reflex in response to a set of external stimuli. These stimuli include the presence of the kid and the action of suckling by the kid. This reflex, to 'let down' milk, can be conditioned to occur under a set of particular circumstances. This is why a settled routine will help the goat to let down her milk under the artificial conditions of milking. If goats are to be milked, they should be milked regularly, once or twice a day. Irregular milking can lead to low yields and a much greater chance of mastitis developing (see 6.4.9). Ideally the same person should milk the goat, at the same time and in the same place every day. The establishment of a quiet, settled routine will help the goat to be relaxed and let down her milk. Changes to the routine will unsettle the goat, reducing milk yield.

If only a few goats are milked, it is best to give them a little food during milking, to settle them. The kid(s) should be present at milking, to encourage the doe to let down her milk. Farmers must decide how much milk there is in the udder, how much of it should be milked, and how much can be drunk by the kid. Some farmers may decide to let the kid suckle one teat, while milking the other at the same time. In order to reduce mastitis, the kid should be allowed to suck the milked teat after milking; this ensures that the teat canal is properly emptied, reducing the risk of later infection. Goats that are only suckled by kids and never milked have a very low incidence of mastitis. It is good to alternate the teats used for suckling and for milking.

It is vital that any milk for human consumption is as clean and uncontaminated as possible. The milker must observe the following precautions.

- Wash his or her hands.
- Clean the teats with warm soap and water, but only if clean water is available.
- Check the milk for mastitis, looking for any clots or blood. If mastitis infection is being treated with antibiotics, the milk must not be consumed by humans during the day of treatment and for seven days afterwards.
- Milk into a clean container, ideally a clean metal container.
- Milk away from the presence of a buck.
- Avoid any contamination from faeces, urine, or feed.
- After milking, cover the container and remove the milk from the vicinity of the goat as soon as possible.

The ideal milking technique would closely mimic the natural sucking of a kid. The base of the teat should be gripped between thumb and forefinger, the remaining fingers creating a ripple of gentle pressure down the teat, pushing the milk down the teat canal and expelling the milk in regular, even squirts. The teats should not be pulled, as this can damage the teat canal and invites infection. When milking very small teats of first-time kidders, pulling the teat may be necessary, but should be done gently.

10.1.2 Milk handling

All milk for human consumption must be pasteurised. Milk can transmit the following health problems to people: brucellosis, tuberculosis, and diarrhoea and abdominal pains.

Milk can be pasteurised by heating it to boiling point and keeping it there for one minute. Pasteurisation will not only make the milk safe to drink: it will also lengthen the time for which it can be stored. Pasteurised milk can be stored for two–three days in a cool place (less than 10°C). The warmer the storage temperature, the shorter the storage life.

In some cultures, milk containers, often made from gourds, are smoked and then burnt wood, notably the African olive (*Olea africana*), is rubbed inside them. This preparation is believed to reduce contamination and gives the milk a characteristic smoky taste. This treatment will not reduce the bacterial content of the milk, but the strong taste produced will make the fresh milk more acceptable to drink for a longer period.

Many cultures in Africa and India allow the milk to sour naturally, and may either consume it as sour milk, or use the sour milk as the starting material to make butter, ghee, or cheese.

10.1.3 Milk collection, processing, and marketing

In areas where there is a tradition of milk production, there are also likely to be traditional systems of trading surplus milk with neighbours, or in rural or urban markets. Milking is normally the responsibility of the women of the household, and it has often been found that they have traditional systems of cooperation with neighbours to market milk in more distant and lucrative markets. These systems should be investigated before any intervention to improve milk marketing is suggested.

In countries with a national system of cow's-milk collection, such as Kenya, it might be possible to market goat's milk through the existing system. The Kenya Cooperative Creameries, for example, will mix goat's milk with cow's milk, to a maximum of 5 per cent of the total.

In situations where there is no traditional system, or only limited markets, a system of milk collection and marketing might be organised as part of a project intervention. Milk could be collected fresh and pasteurised in a central plant, or further processed into more valuable products such as butter, cheese, or yoghurt. The scale on which the collection and processing and marketing take place will depend on several factors:

- the supply of milk, including seasonal fluctuations in supply;
- the market demand for goat's milk and milk products;
- transportation available for both collection and marketing;
- potential profitability of collection, processing, and marketing;
- the technical capability of those involved.

The functions of marketing organisations are discussed in 10.6.

10.1.4 Milk products

Figure 10.1 outlines how milk can be broken down into its components and converted into different products. Only the main products relevant to goats are described.

Figure 10.1 The conversion of milk into its products

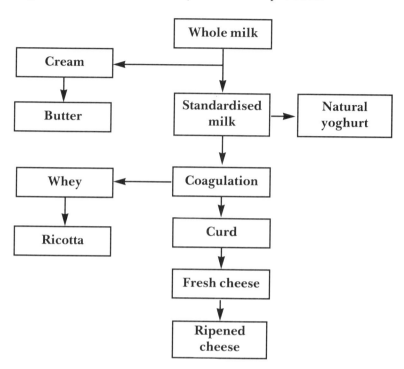

Condensed milk

Making condensed, sweetened milk is one simple method of storing fresh milk for future use. The principle is to reduce the moisture content of the milk by 20–30 per cent and then add sugar until the milk reaches a thick consistency. A large saucepan of milk should be brought to the boil and then simmered for one hour, until moisture has been boiled off. Sugar should be added at the rate of about one third of the volume of the milk. The sweetened condensed milk can then be stored in a sealed container, such as a clean tin with a lid. Condensed milk can be stored in this way for 6–8 months. It can then be used in tea or coffee, or in other cooking.

Yoghurt

Yoghurt is made when milk is soured by certain selected bacteria, and not by other bacteria. Raw milk should be heated nearly to boiling point for three minutes. It should be cooled to about 45°C, when a small quantity of a starter, such as previously made yoghurt, is stirred into the milk. The milk should then be left, undisturbed, to sour at a temperature between 30°C and 45°C. Yoghurt incubated at 40°C–45°C takes 3–6 hours to set; at 30°C–40°C it takes 15–24 hours. The temperature will determine the time it takes for the bacteria to grow and pleasantly sour the milk. The correct temperature will feel warm to touch, neither too hot nor too tepid.

Butter

Butter is a very valuable commodity in many societies; it may be used in cooking, for human beautification, and in some societies as a medicine. Converting milk to butter is an important method of adding value to milk and increasing the income earned from goats. Most societies which make butter have their own traditional methods of doing so. These methods are often very labour-intensive and inefficient; usually they require women to spend hours in churning milk, to recover a small amount of butter. Goat's milk, from tropical breeds, has a high fat content, making it very suitable for butter-making. Many societies add goat's milk to cow's milk to increase the fat content of the milk and increase the butter yield. In order to produce one kilo of butter, 25 litres of milk must be churned. There is seldom enough goat's milk from one farm alone to consider making butter from it

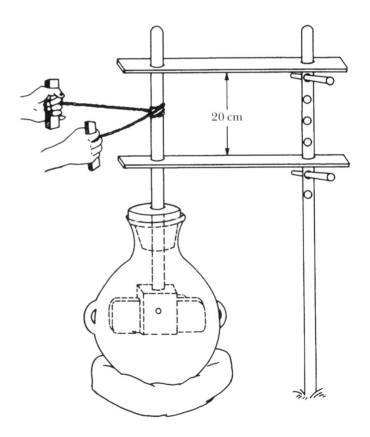

Figure 10.2 ILRI butter churner

exclusively. A group of goat farmers might consider getting together and contributing milk to a butter-making enterprise.

Butter can be made from whole fresh milk, cream, or sour whole milk. The milk or cream is agitated, often in a large earthenware pot, until butter grains form. The pot is then rotated slowly, until the grains join together into one lump, sloshing about in the buttermilk. The lumps of butter are then picked out and kneaded together in cold water. Salt may be added to help to preserve it. Some societies flavour the butter with herbs or spices, which helps to increase its storage life. Others further process the butter into ghee, or clarified butter, which is simply butter that has been heated to reduce the moisture content. Butter should be stored in a sealed container at a cool temperature. The buttermilk, left over after butter-making, can be used to make cottage cheese.

Traditional methods of butter-making can be improved through the construction of a simple paddle churner, or the purchase of a specially constructed butter churner. Specialised equipment can be purchased, perhaps on credit, by a group of farmers who contribute their milk. Improved equipment will reduce the time spent churning, relieving women of a burden, and increase the yield of butter obtained from milk.

Cheese

Hundreds of types of cheese are made around the world. Northern and southern European countries have developed many types of goat's milk cheese, and the recipes for some have spread outside Europe. Few countries in the tropics traditionally make cheese, and even fewer make cheese from goat's milk. This reflects local traditions and the small quantities of milk produced by most goats in the tropics, rather than any lack of potential. India and Central and South America are the main areas in which goat's cheeses are produced. The high fat-content of goat's milk makes it very suitable for cheese-making, and some delicious cheeses can be made.

In the countries where cheese is traditionally made from cow's milk, it is worth encouraging farmers to try making their traditional cheeses from goat's milk, when they have produced sufficient milk to do so. Where goat's milk cheeses are made, the process can often be refined to improve the quality of the product. There may also be potential to organise larger-scale cheese-making and improve packaging and marketing.

In situations where cheese has never been made and is not traditionally consumed, there must be very good reasons for introducing the practice. These may include the following factors:

- lack of access to a market for fresh goat's milk;
- surplus milk production;
- some farmers motivated to learn cheese-making;

- the existence of an accessible market for cheese, or a potential market which can be developed.

Most traditional cheeses are soft cheeses of some sort. Greater skills, more equipment, and a greater volume of milk are needed to make hard cheese. About 7.5 litres of milk are needed to produce one kilo of fresh cheese, but over 10 litres are needed to make a kilo of hard cheese. The harder cheeses often become popular with urban residents as they become richer and are able to afford them. It is good for poorer farmers to take advantage of the increase in wealth of urban dwellers and sell them valuable products, provided that the farmers get a fair price for their products.

A goat-cheese factory in Burundi

As part of a dairy-goat project funded by the German government in Ngozi district of Burundi, a milk-collection system was set up to provide a guaranteed market to producers and supply goat's milk to a small cheese factory. The factory made soft and hard cheese. A small cheese shop was opened in the town and a few cheeses sold to middle-class residents. More cheeses were transported to Bujumbura city, where they were sold to wealthy Burundians and expatriates. A few cheeses were exported to Germany as a novelty product.

It is beyond the scope of this book to describe the procedures for making the different types of cheese. Special equipment is needed and skills must be acquired before cheese-making is begun on a large scale. Help must be obtained from experts in the field. A few of the simplest recipes are given below for people to try making cheese for the first time. Have a go and see if you like the results!

Soft or cottage cheese
Heat two litres of milk (fresh or sour) in a saucepan and bring it to the boil, stirring all the time. Remove it from the heat and, while stirring, add eight teaspoons of lemon or lime juice, or vinegar, drop by drop. Curds will form. Strain the curds through a clean cotton cloth with a fine mesh, until all the moisture (whey) has dripped through and the curds remain. The curds can be flavoured with salt, spices, or herbs and put into a small pot. Two litres of milk will make about 250 g of fresh cheese. This sort of cheese should be consumed within one–two days.

Ricotta
The whey from the making of soft cheese can be made into ricotta cheese. Heat two litres of whey until a cream-like substance rises to the surface. Add three cups of milk and heat it until very hot.

Then stir in 3.5 teaspoons of vinegar or lemon juice. Keeping the mixture hot, stir it quickly until the curd rises to the surface. Remove the curd and drain it through a cloth for a few hours. Ricotta can be salted and stored for a few days.

10.2 Meat and carcass products

Most goats in the tropics are either killed at home for use by the owner's family, friends, and relatives, or sold alive at a livestock market for subsequent slaughter. Few goats are slaughtered in recognised slaughterhouses, so their contribution to most nations' meat supply is usually grossly underestimated. Being small in size, goats are easy to slaughter for home use, or conveniently slaughtered by a butcher for sale in his shop during the day.

In most developing countries, virtually every part of the carcass is consumed or used in some way. For this reason, the Western concept of dressing percentage — a measure to describe the proportion of the carcass that is edible — is irrelevant. Very often the highest prices per unit of weight are paid for the portions that are, perhaps, less appealing to Western palates. In parts of Africa, raw blood is highly prized, and the goat's head may be valued to make a medicinal soup, common in East Africa.

In most countries, goats are valued for the medicinal properties thought to be possessed by different parts of the carcass. The basis of this belief is the goat's consumption of a wide variety of plant species in its preferred diet. There has been virtually no scientific research to establish the validity of these widely held beliefs.

10.2.1 How to kill a goat

Every culture has its own method of killing goats. Methods vary according to the state of consciousness of the animal at death and how it is bled. Methods of slaughter may broadly be divided into three kinds.

- **Ritualistic or religious slaughter:** this requires the goat to be conscious at the time it is bled. Muslim (Halal), Jewish (Kosher), and Sikh (Jhatka) methods are basically similar in practice, but each has its own ceremonial procedures.

- **Traditional slaughter:** there are many traditional methods of slaughter which have no religious connotations. For example, the Maasai pastoralists of East Africa value fresh blood and will suffocate the goat by placing a hand over the mouth and nostrils, while an assistant holds it down. This is a very slow death. After death the jugular vein is slit open lengthways and a flap of skin pulled out to catch the blood, from where it is drunk.

- **Humane slaughter** means that the goat is unconscious at the time of bleeding. Unconsciousness is induced by mechanical or electrical means. The goat's death is painless.

Each culture has a different attitude towards the animals it keeps. Many people in Western countries are concerned that the animals they consume are treated kindly during production and killed in a humane manner. Other countries may value their animals equally or even more, but do not ascribe feelings to them in the same way that Western societies do. Cultural considerations aside, farmers must be aware that the welfare of the livestock they keep affects the animals' health and productivity, and that a quick painless death is an appropriate end to an animal that has served its owner well. However, we must be realistic: unless there is legislation to confine the slaughter of goats to recognised slaughterhouses, using humane methods of slaughter, it is very difficult to make any changes to the method by which goats are killed.

If a gun is not available, the following method of killing a goat is humane and efficient.

- Hold the goat securely. Stun it by a sharp blow to the centre of the forehead. Use a small heavy instrument, such as a hammer.

- While the goat is still stunned, use a sharp knife to cut its throat from ear to ear, making sure that the windpipe and blood vessels are severed.

- Allow the body to bleed. Although the goat is dead, nervous reflexes will cause its body to jerk for a few minutes after death.

- When the body is quiet, it can be hung up by its hind legs and skinned, and the carcass cut in the local manner.

10.2.2 Preservation of meat

Most goats slaughtered in the tropics are consumed almost immediately. Their small size makes them ideal to slaughter for a family and a few friends, at a time of family celebration or a religious holiday. However, there may be occasions when the carcass of a goat is too much to consume in one–two days and it would be helpful to store meat in some way. In the absence of refrigeration, there are two main methods of preserving meat:

- **Air drying**: strips of lean meat are cut and hung in the open air until thoroughly dried. The resulting dried meat, sometimes known as 'biltong' or 'pemmican', can be kept for several months in this way.

- **Deep frying**: several pastoral groups in Africa deep-fry meat until it is dry and crisp. Stored in a sealed container, goat's meat preserved in this way has been reported to last for several years.

10.3 Skins

For many countries in the tropics, the sale of semi-processed hides and skins forms a valuable, sometimes major, source of foreign exchange. Several countries produce goat skins and products of great value, such as Moroccan kid leather, quality leather from Red Sokoto goats in northern Nigeria, and 'Bati' quality leather from Ethiopia. Most tanning is still carried out by the country which imports the skin. European leatherware manufacturers prize high-quality goat skin for the manufacture of gloves, shoes, and other products. The main types of leather made from goats' skins are Glacé, or glazed, kid leather, Semi-chrome leather, Patent leather, Full-chrome suede garment, Full-chrome goat Nappa, and Chamois leather. Tanning skins and manufacturing leather products from them can increase the value of the skins by four or five times. As a result, several developing countries now ban the export of semi-processed skins, insisting that they are processed in-country. It is obviously more profitable if these products can be made in the country of origin, but the quality of products must be high to compete in the world market. There are many countries in the tropics which are developing their own leather industries, notably India, Pakistan, Bangladesh, Nigeria, and Ethiopia.

For the individual owner, the skins of goats slaughtered at home can be used in countless ways for making clothes, bags, beds, thongs, and various containers. It is often too useful at home to be sold. If skins are sold, they are more valuable if they have been preserved in some way, to prevent deterioration.

10.3.1 Preservation of skins

Skins naturally contain bacteria which, on the death of the goat, will multiply, putrefying the skin. In hot humid conditions, this process of rotting will quickly spoil the skin. The first stage in the preservation of fresh skins is known as *curing*. There are two simple methods of curing.

- **Air-drying**: The wet skin can either be pegged out on the ground or tied to a frame and dried upright. It is important to avoid any damage to the skin and to try not to spoil the edges through clumsy pegging or tying. In climates that are not too humid, skins can be cured in one–two days.

- **Salt curing**: The fresh skin is cleaned of any blood or dirt, and washed with clean water. It should be laid out with the inside facing upwards. About 40 per cent of its weight in salt is then sprinkled on to it, until it is covered in an even layer. The salt will serve both to reduce its moisture content and to prevent bacterial development. The skin can be folded with the salted side inside and kept in this way for long periods before tanning.

Factors affecting skin quality

There are many diseases of goats that will damage the skin and affect its quality and price. They include goat pox, streptothricosis, ticks, mange, ringworm, and warts.

10.4 Mohair and cashmere

Goats produce several types of hair fibre, depending on their breed and to some extent on their environment. There are three main types.

- **Mohair** is the hair of the Angora goat. The Angora produces fair-coloured long hair in either waves or ringlets, 12–18 cm long. Mohair is used to make fine cloth, carpets, and other products. Mohair production is now a specialist activity and has developed into a sophisticated industry. The International Mohair Association sets international standards, grading mohair fleeces according to fineness. In some countries, the fleece can be shorn twice a year. Shearing must take place in a clean environment, so that the mohair is not contaminated with other fibres. Any contamination will immediately downgrade the whole fleece, or — even worse — the whole bale in which it is packed.

  A few countries in the tropics, including India, Lesotho, and Madagascar, have begun upgrading local goats for mohair production through cross-breeding with Angora bucks.

- **Cashmere (Pashmina)**: many breeds of goat produce the very fine soft cashmere undercoat that is so highly valued internationally. There are no specific cashmere goat breeds, but many breeds in the colder regions of China, Mongolia, Tibet, and Northern India are considered cashmere types. These goats may yield 200–300 g of high-quality cashmere fibre per year. The cashmere fibre is grown by the goat for insulation, so when temperatures rise, they are naturally shed. In most countries the fibre is carefully combed out by hand, but other, labour-saving methods of harvesting are being investigated.

- **Common goat hair:** many breeds of goat are naturally hairy, with long coarse hair, which can be clipped and used. For example, Tauran goat keepers in northern Iran clip their goats and use the hair to weave coarse cloth for making tents. Skins of goats with long hair are often used to make warm clothes.

10.5 Manure

Goat manure is a valuable product and in some areas, such as Java, may be traded and given a cash value. The quantity and quality of manure depends on the quantity and quality of the diet consumed. As a rough guide, a goat is likely to produce 1–2 per cent of its weight as dry matter (DM) of manure per day. Therefore a 30 kg goat might produce 300–600 g DM manure per day, depending on the feed intake and digestibility of the diet. Table 10.2 indicates the typical composition of goat manure.

Table 10.2 Composition of goat manure

Moisture (%)	Nitrogen (%)	Phosphorus (%)	Potassium (%)
40-60	1.0-3.0	0.2-0.8	0.4-0.8

The quantity and quality of manure that can actually be collected and used will vary according to the system in which goats are kept. In housed systems, it may be possible to collect urine in addition to the solid waste, enriching the value of the combined waste material. Urine is particularly rich in nitrogen and potassium. In raised goat houses, urine can be caught underneath the house, soaking into waste feed and bedding, and combined with manure to make a rich fertiliser. Wet goat wastes are approximately 66 per cent solid waste and 33 per cent urine. In systems where goats are grazed, only the dry manure can be swept up and collected from areas where goats are penned at night, limiting the amount of waste collected and its quality.

There are two main uses for goat manure and urine: soil fertiliser and fish-pond fertiliser.

10.5.1 Soil fertiliser

Manure used to fertilise crops may be applied to the soil fresh; or mixed with waste feed and bedding; or stored with, or without, additional organic material. The breaking down of organic material through the action of bacteria is known as *composting*. The addition of manure to organic matter such as waste feed, fruit skins, and crop wastes can considerably improve the fertilising quality of the compost. The soil will benefit from the release of nutrients, and the build-up of organic matter will improve the structure of the soil. However, the storage of manure can lead to considerable losses of nitrogen, and exposure of manure to air leads to the volatisation of ammonia. These losses are greater at higher temperatures, under windy conditions, and the larger the surface area exposed. The bacteria that break down the organic material also require nitrogen for their growth, which results in further losses. In addition, nitrogen can be leached out of manure by rain. If manure can be composted under conditions that reduce these losses, such as in a covered pit, then it is probably worth composting manure. Otherwise it is probably best to use the manure fresh.

There are also many pastoral systems in West Africa, and northern Pakistan and India, where goat flocks may seasonally graze crop-stubble, indirectly returning valuable nutrients to the soil.

10.5.2 Fish-pond fertiliser

There are many different systems of fish production into which livestock may be integrated. Common systems in South-East Asia include the housing of chickens, ducks, and pigs directly over, or next to, ponds containing a polyculture (mixture) of fish. The manure, urine, and high-quality waste feed fertilise the pond to supply nutrients for a rich phytoplankton, or algal, growth, which is consumed directly by fish such as tilapia (*Oreochromus niloticus*) and carp, such as Silver carp (*Hypophthalmichthys molitrix*). In addition, the phytoplankton feed zooplankton, which are consumed by other fish species, such as the Bighead carp (*Aristichthys nobilis*).

There are few traditional systems of fish production that integrate ruminants; but, with the increasing intensification of ruminant livestock production, particularly for dairying, new systems could develop. The traditional housed goat and sheep systems of Indonesia, Malaysia, and Philippines could immediately be integrated with fish culture, requiring little change in the management of either system. Conversely, fish farmers might consider starting goat farming as an additional source of cash income for their families. Some experiments indicate that the total income from a pond can be more than doubled by the addition of goats.

Goat manure should not be considered a high-quality pond input. Fertilising the pond with goat manure alone will not produce high yields of fish. However, it can serve as a basal fertiliser, supplemented with a higher-quality source of nutrients such as purchased chemical fertilisers, or with manure from intensively fed chickens. Or the farmer may decide that the low yields obtained from the pond are worthwhile.

Total fish yield depends on many factors, among them the stocking rate and the general water quality, including phytoplankton growth and the amount of dissolved oxygen in the water. The faster that phytoplankton multiply, the more oxygen they need for their growth; this reduces the oxygen available for fish. In extreme cases, fish can die through over-manuring of ponds. A balance has to be found between manure loading and

Recommendations for a goat/fish farm

As a rough guide, recommendations for a small enclosed pond of 200 m² are as follows.

- Fish stocking rate is 200–400/pond
- Goat manure loading rate is 1–2 kg DM/day, which can be obtained from 4–8 goats.

It is recommended that fresh manure is used.

The ratio of dry matter to fish weight gain is about 5:1.

the oxygen demands of the fish. The ratios of organic matter, nitrogen, phosphorus, and potassium also affect the growth of phytoplankton, and thus zooplankton, and water quality. Water quality can be assessed by observing the pond early in the morning. A well-fertilised pond should be a rich green colour. A rough guide is to immerse an arm in the pond up to the elbow: if the hand can be seen, there are not enough algae in the pond and more inputs should be added; however, if fish are gasping at the surface of the pond, there are low levels of dissolved oxygen in the pond, and manure should not be added.

A goat farmer with both crops and a fish pond must decide which will receive manure from the goats. There are a number of questions to consider.

- Is there enough waste to make a significant contribution to the pond?
- Can other fertilisers be purchased for the pond or field?
- What are the relative costs and returns from fertilising the field crops, compared with fertilising the fish pond?

The farmer may have to compromise and perhaps use the liquid waste and some solids for the pond, and the remaining solid manure for the crops.

Example of a goat/fish enterprise

A farmer has a fish pond of 200 m², stocked with 200 tilapia fingerlings. There is a goat house over the pond, receiving manure and urine from goats which are fed a high-quality diet of leucaena and sweet-potato tops, supplemented with rice bran.

If there are six adult goats weighing 30 kg each, the total DM production per day is 2.7 kg DM.

This will produce about 0.5 kg fish per day.

321

10.6 Marketing goats and goat products

It is obviously important that any goat or goat product for sale, whether it is milk, skins, or live animals, should earn the farmer a good price. Goat products which have been produced traditionally will have a 'traditional', informal market. There are few State-run or private marketing organisations for goat products in the tropics. This is because most goat products are either consumed at home or are traded in villages, or perhaps in district centres.

Careful consideration must be given before any interventions are made to improve the marketing of goat products. Local marketing systems are constantly evolving in response to changing circumstances, and they usually function best when not interfered with. From the goat-keeper's point of view, marketing is only partly for the sale of the goat or product. It also serves a social function: people meet not only to buy and sell but also to eat, drink, and chat together. If owners are selling directly to consumers, the balance between supply and demand will normally create a fair price. If the owner is selling to a trader, provided there are many traders, operating independently, and vendors have access to reliable information about prices, there is no reason to suppose that the owner is offered anything but a reasonable price. Farmers and pastoralists are in a weak position when, due to circumstances beyond their control, such as a drought, they are forced to sell their goats and have to take whatever price is offered.

Interventions in markets should not be considered except in the following circumstances.

- There is a very significant increase in production and the market cannot absorb it, which causes the price to fall.
- A new product is being introduced and there is no existing market.
- There is an advantage to individual goat-producers if they cooperate and market a larger volume of products together.

It must be decided whether the intervention will be for a short or long time period. Interventions might be designed to overcome a short-term marketing problem, allowing the normal market to adapt to the problem. Setting up a longer-term, even permanent marketing organisation might, in some circumstances, be desirable.

Marketing interventions might take one or more of the following forms.

- **Collection of goats or goat products**: collection may be from the farm itself or from some central collection point, to which farmers bring their products.

- **Processing products**: processing might include pasteurising milk, making cheese, making butter, slaughtering goats, and sorting fibres.

- **Grading products**: grading may be important in fibre production, or for the sale of live goats, particularly for export.

- **Packing products**: packing may be for easier transportation, for example baling mohair fleeces, or for the final consumer, such as packing cheese or butter for retail sale.

- **Promotion of new products**: if a new product has been made, for example goat's milk yoghurt, it may need to be advertised and promoted in some way. This does not mean billboard advertisements! It might take the form of inviting neighbours round to a house of a woman who is making cheese or yoghurt for the first time, for a free tasting.

- **Transporting goats or products**: transporting goats or goat products can be costly. It helps if owners get together to rent or buy a bicycle, scooter, van or truck; if goats or products are collected together and transported to a more distant market where prices are higher; and if they are sold on a contract to a slaughterhouse or butcher's shop, or other retail outlet.

- **Selling goats or products**: producers who group together in some way will have more bargaining power with buyers than if they negotiate separately. If they can offer a reasonable price and a regular supply, they can probably negotiate a good contract with the buyer.

Organisations that might serve some or all of these functions are listed below.

- **Producers' groups, associations, and cooperatives**: groups of farmers might get together and form an informal (or more formal) group, in order to improve the marketing of their goats and/or products.

- **Private companies** may make a contract with producers to buy a product at an agreed price, quality, and frequency. This arrangement can be beneficial to both parties.

- **Government organisations**: an existing government marketing organisation, such as one dealing in milk, might agree to help with the marketing of goats' milk. Alternatively a government might decide that goats are important enough to need their own marketing organisation.

- **Non-governmental organisations** might help to set up a producers' marketing organisation.

Further reading

O'Conner, C. (1993) *Traditional Cheesemaking Manual*, Addis Ababa: International Livestock Research Institute (ILRI)

Dubach, J. (1989) *Traditional Cheesemaking*, London: Intermediate Technology Publications

Ebing, P and K. Rutgers (1991) *The Preparation of Dairy Products*, 2nd revised edition, Agrodok 36, Wageningen: AGROMISA

Little, D. and J. Muir (1987) *A Guide to Integrated Warm Water Aquaculture*, Sterling: Institute of Aquaculture, University of Sterling

O'Mahony, F. (1988) *Rural Dairy Technology*, ILCA Manual No. 4, Addis Ababa: ILRI

Sinn, R. (1985) *Raising Goats for Milk and Meat*, Arkansas: Heifer Project International

CHAPTER 11

Goat-improvement programmes

11.1 Introduction

So far, this book has described both the common problems of goat production in various systems and the methods that can be used to identify the specific problems in particular systems. The technical aspects of improved goat production have been described in some detail. It is now time to consider how to put these technical improvements into a plan of action in the field.

11.2 Goat-improvement strategies

Goats have many different functions in the rural economy. Developing and extending their use can benefit many social groups. There are two main approaches to the use of goats in development.

- **The improvement of existing systems of goat production**: improving some existing system of goat production is, of course, the most common approach. Chapters 2 and 3 showed the importance of identifying the system concerned and investigating the specific problems of keeping goats in that system, before improvements are attempted.

- **Stocking/restocking people who do not own goats**: extending the ownership of goats to people who do not own them may have a major impact on the lives of families and can be used to help some of the poorest to take a step out of poverty.

11.2.1 Improvement of existing systems

The approach to improving existing systems of goat production should be one of stepwise progress, in keeping with the owner's objectives. After identifying the owner's reasons for keeping goats and defining with the owner what would be an improvement, technical or economic improvements can be designed.

In donor-funded projects, a 'package' of improvements is often promoted, the argument being that the individual technical innovations proposed are linked to other innovations and will not perform properly unless they are adopted by producers simultaneously. An example of such a linkage might be the promotion of supplementary feeding, combined with an anthelmintic drenching regime. The supplementary feeds will not be used efficiently by the goat, if it is supporting a heavy load of internal parasites. Technically a 'package' approach makes sense. However, in reality owners seldom adopt new technology in strict accordance with the recommendations given by scientists and extension staff. They tend to pick up new technology in a piece-meal way, adopting and adapting it as they are able and as it suits them. It may be that, in the example above, the owner can see and appreciate clear improvements resulting from drenching, but not from the use of the supplementary feed. He or she may become interested in supplementary feeding at some later date.

Dairy goat project: Ethiopia

In order to improve local goat production in the highlands of Ethiopia sufficiently to introduce a cross-bred milking goat, a stepwise approach to improvement was taken by the FARM-Africa Dairy Goat Project. Small farms in the highlands suffer from a chronic shortage of animal feed. The Dairy Goat Project started by introducing the growing of forage crops in strategies which did not take any land away from food-crop production. The project then trained women to be paravets and improve the health of local goats through the use of anthelmintics, vaccination, and tick control. The women soon showed varying levels of management skills and varying levels of adoption and adaptation of the technology being promoted. Once the level of local goat management by some of the women was good enough, cross-bred goats were introduced, two–three years after the start of the project, and performed very well. Some women, however, were learning the value of drenching their goats, while others were still struggling to establish some forage successfully.

There is no shortage of technical options for goat improvement to be incorporated into an extension programme. It is often said that little is known about goats and that more research needs to be done. Although it is true that less is known about goats than about other domestic livestock, many technical improvements can be made with the knowledge currently available to us. What is often lacking is not the technology but the means of appropriately introducing it, and sustaining it, within any community. Technology should not be divorced from the method of organising it: the two are intimately linked.

Options for improving the feeding of goats

Use existing feeds more efficiently:
  careful selection
  appropriate treatment: wilting, chopping
  correct presentation: rack/net/tied bundle; mixture; frequency; cleanliness
  frequent/continuous access to water
  supplementation with energy/protein/minerals
  scarce feeds targeted to the most needy goats.

Improve the quantity and quality of feeds through the year:
  conservation and storage
  forage-crop growing.

Options for improving the health of goats

Improve nutrition	Close supervision of kids
Improve housing	Foot care
Vaccination	Identify and treat diseases
Control parasites	Drug shops

Primary health care through use of paravets

Options for improving the reproduction of goats

Improve nutrition
Improve oestrus detection
Improve access to males

Options for improving the genetic potential of goats

Selection of the best males and best females
Buck exchange/rotation to avoid in-breeding
Selection programmes on stations
Up-grading through cross-breeding (on-station F_1 production, buck stations, artificial insemination)

Options for improving goat-product processing and use

Group milk collection, processing, and marketing
Improved butter churner
Condensed milk
Simple cheesemaking
Meat preservation: air dry/deep fry
Skin preservation: dry/salt

The technology options available have been described in detail in the relevant chapters and are summarised in the box on the previous page. It is important to be aware of the need for fine-tuning the techniques, so that they work properly in particular districts, villages, and farms. Most of this fine-tuning will be done by the producers themselves, who will pick up and adapt technology to suit their own particular circumstances. This is a continuous process, as circumstances (weather, prices, owners' objectives, family sizes) are constantly changing. Producers may need some help with some of the adaptation. For example, if drenching of goats is carried out for the first time, monitoring the faecal egg count for a one-year period will help to show how effective the drenching regime is, and whether it should be adapted in any way.

The methods of organising the introduction and support of technology in any community are listed in the box on this page, and are discussed in 11.4.

Organisational options

> **Use existing organisations or establish new goat group to**
> *supervise credit repayments and reallocation of credit*
> *manage a drug supply*
> *supervise paravets*
> *supervise buck stations and 'rotation' of bucks*
> *assist in recording/monitoring performance*
> *organise an accompanying savings association*
> *assist in group collection and processing, e.g. butter or cheese*
> *assist in group marketing*
> *manage a communal grazing resource*
> **Basic training course**
> **Specialised training courses**

11.2.2 Stocking/restocking people with goats

Supplying goats to people who do not currently own them is a very attractive way for a donor-assisted project to make an immediate and significant impact. There are two main approaches here. First, extending goat ownership within a community, often to the poorest members, by providing finance, normally in the form of credit for the purchase of goats, either local or improved. Second, restocking pastoralists or farmers who have lost their goats, and thus their livelihood, during a drought, disease epidemic, or warfare.

The role and management of credit for goat-keepers, together with guidelines on restocking pastoralists, are discussed in 11.6.

11.3 Participatory planning
11.3.1 Introduction

Chapter 3 described the methods that might be used to identify the specific problems of goat production in an area, in order to design a programme of action to improve production. The process of identifying improvements, considering how they might be implemented, consulting all individuals and organisations who would have to be involved, negotiating the allocation of responsibilities, obtaining the finance (if required), and phasing the activities are the elements of planning.

Who should be involved in planning? It seems obvious that all those who would be involved in the eventual programme of action should be involved in its planning. However, in reality, this rarely occurs. Far too many development plans are made by outsiders who live at a physical and cultural distance from the situation to be improved. This seems absurd, because there is a much greater chance of developing an effective improvement programme if all those to be involved participate, right from the start, in all stages of the planning process. Participation is the basis for success.

It is important to understand that planning is a continuous process. The traditional distinctions made between planning, implementation, and evaluation are artificial separations of what is, in reality, one on-going activity. At some stage a plan has to be made, normally to secure funding, but this plan should be constantly reviewed and revised in the light of experience.

11.3.2 The planning process: alternatives analysis and participation analysis

Planning starts when initial contact is made between one or several communities and a governmental or non-governmental agency. There must be an initial period of listening to, and learning from, the community, during which rapid methods of assessment are used to make a preliminary analysis of the situation. This period of assessment should not be too long: farmers or pastoralists expect to see some action. Experience has shown that, after an introductory period, an initial period of joint action, often called a *pilot phase*, deepens the relationship between producers and extension staff. This will build up trust between all the parties involved, and will inevitably bring new information to light; the result will be better plans. Learning by doing is an important component of the planning process.

The course of action to improve goat production evolves thorough discussion and constant consultation among all those to be involved. Section 3.2.13 described how a group could use the tools called problem analysis and objectives analysis to think about the problems of goat production in their area. These tools will normally reveal several, often interlinked, problems which can be solved through several alternative courses of action. There comes a point when the group must decide which of the alternative courses of action they are going to follow; this is known as *alternatives analysis*. There are usually many factors which affect the final choice, including:

- the interest of the community
- the capability and resources of the donor/implementing agency
- the policy of the government
- the costs and likely benefits.

Using the example of low milk production employed in the problem and objectives analysis, it is clear that there are several alternative ways of achieving the main objective of increased milk production. One, or more, of the four means of increasing milk production could be tackled. For example, the health of goats could be improved, through reducing the parasite burden by improving the supply of anthelmintics, and training owners in their economic use. Alternatively, the feeding of goats could be improved by developing high-quality forage crops to be fed as a protein supplement. If the resources are available, both health and nutrition could be tackled. If the agency involved is concerned only with animal husbandry, it might be difficult for it to become involved in improving the water supply; but it might encourage an appropriate agency to tackle this problem. Some NGOs have the capacity, themselves, to improve water supply. Improving the breed characteristics might be too difficult for a small agency to consider, but a large government programme, or a well-funded NGO, might consider breed improvement.

During the planning process, it is also important to gauge the strengths and weaknesses of the individuals and organisations concerned; this is sometimes known as *participation analysis*. Make a list of all organisations, individuals, and interest groups who are, or might become, involved in the proposed action. Next, consider what each party's interests are, and what their fears are. Assess the strengths and weaknesses of each group and the possible implications of the chosen course of action. Consider how to make best use of participants' strengths and interests, how to allay their fears, and either avoid their weaknesses or strengthen their capabilities.

It is important to identify what each party is capable of doing and what they could do with better resources. Then enter a process of negotiation to allocate specific responsibilities to them. Consider what is expected from the community itself. What will be the contribution of local people? What do they expect in return? What is the role of community leaders? What is the

Figure 11.1 Alternatives analysis

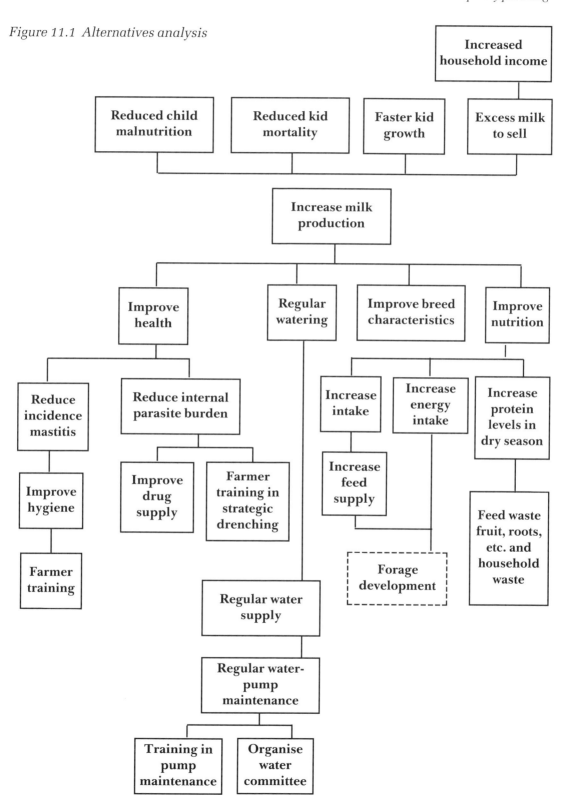

Planning a goat project in Kenya

> The Ministry of Agriculture, Livestock Development and Marketing (MALDM) invited an NGO to start a goat project in a densely populated, marginal farming area of Kenya. After a short reconnaissance visit by a small team representing the government and the NGO, a Rapid Rural Appraisal was made over a period of six weeks by a livestock specialist and a socio-economist. Extensive discussions were held with farmers, individually and in groups, to identify the problems they experienced in keeping goats and their interest in overcoming these problems. By the end of the RRA, a report was written and a good picture emerged of the problems of goat production, and the areas and people who would benefit most from project interventions. A project proposal was written and external funds sought, in order for the NGO to implement the project jointly with the MALDM.

extension service expected to provide? What resources would help them to do this better? What service will the local farmers' organisation, such as a co-operative, supply?

Once responsibilities for different aspects of the project have been assigned, consider whether a legally binding agreement is required, or whether an informal agreement is adequate. What will happen if one party is unable to fulfil its obligations? Will this have a major or minor effect on the outcome?

Developing a government goat-improvement plan: Sikkim, India

> The Food and Agriculture Organisation (FAO) of the United Nations received a request from the Department of Animal Husbandry and Veterinary Services of the government of Sikkim for assistance to develop goat production in the state. Sikkim is a small mountainous state in the north-east of India. It has received very little outside assistance for the development of its agriculture. It was decided that there was very little information available on goat production in Sikkim, beyond the understanding that goats were tended by women, and that it would be an opportunity to assist women with their chickens as well. A small team of consultants ran a training course on RRA methods for department staff and carried out a RRA exercise with them, to start to identify goat-production problems. This was used as a starting point for a longer, monitoring study, designed to yield sufficient information to write a long-term plan for the development of the goat and chicken resources of the state.

11.4 Writing a plan

At some stage, a plan will have to be written down for others to read and assess. If external funding is being sought, it will have to be written in the form of a project proposal. Donors often have a standard format for the proposal, which must be followed scrupulously, before they will consider funding any project. Even if external funds are not required, it is still important to write down the proposed plan of action, to show to all those who will be involved. This will form the basis for any agreement, possibly a legal agreement, under which the project operates within the community. A project proposal should have the elements described below.

11.4.1 Objectives

The objectives for undertaking the proposed activities must be clearly stated, because it is against these that the project will ultimately be evaluated. The objectives might be revised later, but they will be the guiding force behind the start of the project.

It is sometimes helpful to state objectives at two levels. General, or wider, objectives might be statements such as: 'to improve the welfare of goat farmers in X District by increasing the incomes they receive from their goats'; or 'to increase the stability and sustainability of family incomes through improving goat production'.

More specific objectives should then be stated, such as 'to increase the milk production of goats owned by 1,000 farmers through improved management and breeding'; or 'the development of cut-and-carry feeding of goats in X District through the establishment of forage strips and back-yard pasture'; or 'to reduce the pre-weaning mortality rate of kids through improved health care by paravets'; or 'the breeding of 200 cross-bred goats per year for distribution to farmers in X District'. A project will probably have several specific objectives which it is trying to achieve simultaneously.

11.4.2 Physical context

There should be a description of the climate (rainfall, temperature, humidity, frost incidence), topography, soils, vegetation, land use (agriculture, communal grazing areas, forests), and infrastructure (water points, roads, markets, slaughterhouses, etc.).

11.4.3 Socio-economic context and the target population

The current economic activities of the people of the area should be described (agriculture, trading, manufacturing, employment opportunities), together with some assessment of current annual incomes, size and distribution of land-holdings, land-tenure arrangements, and access to communal resources (grazing, water, forests).

Current community organisations, producers' organisations, and co-operatives should be mentioned and their functions described. Existing extension services, other development agencies (government and NGO), and their programmes and their potential involvement in the proposed programme should be described.

The current sources of agricultural inputs — seed, drugs, fertilisers, credit, breeding stock, etc. — should be described. The marketing system for livestock and livestock products, and current prices, must also be described.

11.4.4 Statement of current situation and problems

There should be a clear statement of the current methods of keeping goats in the target area. The problems associated with goat-keeping must be described, together with a description of how these problems were identified. A report from a Rapid Rural Appraisal might be attached to the proposal as an annex.

A description of the sorts of farmer, or pastoralist, who are likely to benefit from the proposals should also be made. Are you trying to help the poorest families, or will the slightly richer families be more likely to adopt the proposals? Define the target group for whom the proposals are made.

11.4.5 Project activities and organisation

The plan must clearly state exactly what will be done, and by whom. The allocation of responsibilities between all those involved must be clear, to avoid misunderstandings. What is expected from men and women farmers or pastoralists, from extension staff, from community leaders and community organisations, credit banks, the project agency, commercial companies, and producers' groups must be negotiated and must be clear to all concerned. Project proposals often form the basis for a legal agreement between agencies and government organisations, so the expectations and responsibilities of all parties involved must be clearly stated.

It should be the aim of any development agency to achieve sustainable improvements in goat production, which must mean that either existing rural institutions take up new responsibilities as part of the project, or that new institutions are created, which become responsible for activities started under the project. Either way, responsibilities will inevitably shift as the project develops; but their initial allocation should be clear.

The project proposal must clearly describe the activities that will be carried out, under headings such as the following.

- **Extension programme:** the activities carried out with farmers and pastoralists must be described. Will producers be visited individually, or will they form producers' groups? How often are extension staff expected to visit individuals/groups/villages? What will they do during their visits?

- **Training**: what training is required by different individuals and organisations involved in the programme? What sort of training is needed by farmers and families, and by extension staff? Is specialist training needed by veterinarians, credit-fund managers, breeding specialists, or forage specialists? Who will do the training? Where will the training take place? How often and for how long? How many people will be trained?

- **Infrastructure development**: what infrastructure needs to be built? Who will build it: the community or the government or the development agency? How will it be funded: jointly with the community, or wholly by a donor agency? What materials will be used? What are the costs and availability?

- **Research:** is any research needed to assist the implementation of the project? Who is able to do this research: can project staff, or should specialists be brought in? What equipment will be needed? Is it available, or will it have to purchased?

- **Public awareness/education**: is there a need to run a special public-awareness campaign? How will it be organised? Through schools, community meetings, churches, mosques, women's groups?

- **Monitoring**: what information needs to be collected to assess the performance of the project? Who will collect it? How often? Who will analyse it? How often will it be reviewed? Monitoring is discussed further in 11.7.

- **Reporting:** regular reports should be written, to record the progress of the project. Donors have their own reporting requirements, which must be strictly followed. However, even if an external donor is not involved, reports should be written to review performance and record events before they are forgotten. Reports are the history of the project and are a valuable resource. They should not be written too often, or they become a burden: monthly is too often; but they should be written regularly enough to keep people up-to-date with events: every six months is reasonable. The project proposal must state how often reports will be written. Reports should be written honestly. When writing reports for donors, there is a temptation to over-emphasise achievements and play down problems that have caused delays. Be careful! Later on, if the project is reviewed by the donor, the reports will form the basis for charting the project's progress. If real problems have not been reported, it is hard to cite them later as a reason for not meeting a target objective.

11.4.6 Project period, phasing of activities, and targets

The period covered by the project proposal will vary according to the purpose for which it is written. Normally the period would fall in the range of 1–10 years and would most likely last for 3–5 years. It must be remembered that improvements in livestock production will take time to achieve. Although it is perhaps quicker to make improvements in goat production than, say, in cattle production, some improvements — particularly in breeding — will take a long time.

There should be a calendar indicating the proposed timing of activities. It is inevitable that the timing of activities will be described in detail for the first year and in less detail with each succeeding year. Activity calendars should be reviewed every year and modified in the light of current circumstances.

Output targets to be achieved each year should be set at a realistic rate, considering the resources likely to be available, to encourage achievement, rather than to create a burden to discourage project staff and participants. Targets often become a burden if staff believe that they must be met at any cost. Donors will naturally want to know the number of people they will be assisting through the project and the likely scale of benefit received by each person involved. Set reasonable, achievable targets that do not become a burden to staff.

11.4.7 Inputs required

The calendar of activities, together with targets, will indicate the type, timing, and quantities of inputs needed for the project to function. The organisation responsible for obtaining these inputs must plan carefully, to ensure that they are available on time. Delayed procurement is often the cause of delays in implementing the whole project. This is particularly true if items have to be imported into the country — which can be a slow and costly process. A few useful addresses of (mainly UK-based) companies which supply livestock inputs are given in the Appendix.

Inputs required might include the following.

- **Staff:** if staff have to be recruited, it is important that suitable staff are in place at the start of the project. The process of staff recruitment can take a very long time, and can considerably delay the important early stages of a project.

- **Forage seed:** forage seed can often be obtained through local agricultural offices, or in small quantities from research stations, universities, and colleges. There are several international organisations that will supply very small quantities of seed for small trial plots; their addresses are given in the Appendix. Larger quantities for an extension programme may have to be procured from a reputable seed company. There are several good seed companies in Australia which sell tropical forage species.

- **Drugs:** drugs can often be obtained locally, but the quality of locally manufactured drugs must be checked, where possible. There have been reports of ineffective drugs reaching the market in tropical countries. Drugs procured from an internationally reputable company should be effective. If drugs are imported, allow plenty of time for delivery, and make sure that the company specifies the exact drug, its method of presentation (liquid, powder, or bolus), its container size, and its date of expiry.

- **Goats:** the purchase of good-quality goats from local markets can take time (see 11.6.7). The procedures for the importation of goats have already been described in 8.4.2. Make sure that time is allowed in the plan to purchase goats if they are needed in the project.

- **Vehicles and spare parts:** if staff need vehicles, make sure they are appropriate to the terrain, the likely distances to be covered, and the abilities of the user, and that they can be easily maintained and repaired locally.

- **Equipment:** what equipment will be needed? Can it all be purchased locally, or will some of it have to be procured from overseas? Do you know a supplier? Is there a locally available alternative to the overseas product?

- **Training:** can all necessary training be carried out by project staff and collaborators, or will an outside expert be needed? Do you know of such an expert? If a more formal training course is envisaged, is the course 'in country' or overseas?

- **Extension materials:** consider the training materials that will be needed. What sort are appropriate to use: pamphlets, flip-charts, slides, film strips, videos, etc.? Will they have to be specially developed; if so, by whom? Where will they be produced? Can it be done locally? What languages will be used?

- **Finance:** money will be needed for infrastructural developments and any operating costs. Will cash be needed to establish
  a credit fund, or purchase stock from contract farmers?
  Consider the source of finance and how it will be managed.

11.4.8 Making predictions about the future

It is important both for those preparing a goat-improvement plan
and for the potential funders to think through the likely
consequences of the proposed improvements. This should be
done for the individual farmer or pastoralist, and might also be
carried out at a broader level, for example for a village flock.

Start by considering the biological effects of the improvements
on the flock, and then consider what this means in terms of
increased products, and ultimately money and security.

Table 11.1 Projected flock structure (before project)

Age/sex categories	Year 1	Year 2	Year 3	Year 4	Year 5
Flock structure					
Adult females	10	11	13	15	18
Adult males	1	1	1	1	1
Weaner females	3	4	5	6	7
Weaner males	3	4	4	5	6
Kids females	4	5	6	7	8
Kids males	4	4	5	6	7
Total	**25**	**29**	**34**	**40**	**47**
No. dead					
Kids	4	4	5	5	7
Weaners	2	2	3	3	4
Adults	2	2	3	3	6
Total	**8**	**8**	**11**	**11**	**17**
No. sold					
Adults	1	1	1	1	1
Weaners	2	3	3	4	5
Total	**3**	**4**	**4**	**5**	**6**

Parameters:
Age at first kidding = 18 months
Kidding interval = 365 days
Number of kids per kidding = 1.2
Pre-weaning mortality rate = 30%
Post-weaning mortality = 20%
All females retained in flock
One buck retained for breeding per year, previous buck culled

11.4.9 Flock projections

Let us consider the effect of health and management improvements reducing pre-weaning mortality from 30 per cent per year to 15 per cent per year, and post-weaning mortality from 20 per cent per year to 10 per cent per year. What is the effect on the flock? Tables 11.1 and 11.2 present the development of a flock of 10 breeding females over a five-year period. The first table reflects the current performance of the flock with high mortality rates. The second table shows the dramatic improvement in flock development if mortality rates are reduced by half. The number of weaners available for sale is roughly double, and the flock size has dramatically increased in number, and thus in value. The parameters used must always be shown, together with the management strategy assumed. When

Table 11.2 Projected flock structure (after project)

Age/sex categories	Year 1	Year 2	Year 3	Year 4	Year 5
Flock structure					
Adult females	10	12	16	20	25
Adult males	1	1	1	1	1
Weaner females	5	5	6	8	10
Weaner males	4	5	6	8	10
Kids females	5	6	8	10	13
Kids males	5	6	8	10	12
Total	**30**	**35**	**45**	**57**	**71**
No. dead					
Kids	2	2	3	4	5
Weaners	1	1	1	2	2
Adults	1	1	2	2	3
Total	**4**	**4**	**6**	**8**	**10**
No. sold					
Adults	1	1	1	1	1
Weaners	2	4	5	7	9
Total	**3**	**5**	**6**	**8**	**10**

Parameters:
Age at first kidding = 18 months
Kidding interval = 365 days
Number of kids per kidding = 1.2
Pre-weaning mortality rate = 15%
Post-weaning mortality = 10%
All females retained in the flock
One buck retained for breeding per year, previous buck culled

calculating flock structures for small flocks, round up, or down, to the nearest whole number.

11.4.10 Partial budgets

Once the likely biological improvement in production from an intervention has been calculated, the costs of achieving this improvement should be estimated. First consider the owner's objectives and whether the benefits gained meet these objectives. Then consider the cash costs and benefits. A simple calculation of the net benefit, in terms of cash income, of the current and future goat enterprise will indicate whether the benefits of improving production are likely to outweigh the cash costs. A simple table, like Table 11.3, will reveal the cash benefits of the proposed health and management interventions.

The interventions proposed do more than increase cash income through supplying more young males for sale. Reducing mortality rates has dramatically increased the number of goats owned, increasing the flock size from 30 to 71 in five years. This is an improvement of 136 per cent over what would have been the final flock size without the intervention. This expansion of the flock has increased the security of the family, giving them more goats to sell in times of trouble; it has increased the future earning power of the flock; and it will provide many future benefits to the family. Finally, within most societies, the increase in flock size will have increased the esteem with which the family is held within the community.

Table 11.3 Goat-enterprise budget for 10-doe flock

Before project Item	$	After project Item	$
Variable costs		**Variable costs**	
Vaccination	10	Vaccination	10
		Veterinary drugs	50
		Mineral lick	5
Total	**10**	**Total**	**65**
Income		**Income**	
Sale of weaners	250	Sale of weaners	450
Sale of adult culls	75	Sale of adult culls	75
Total	**325**	**Total**	**525**
Net benefit	**315**	**Net benefit**	**460**
(Total income less variable costs)			**(+46%)**

The increase in flock size and income will, of course, have been achieved not only through simple cash expenditure on drugs and minerals, but will have required increased labour and skills, greater supervision, perhaps the construction of a larger house using local materials and family labour, as well as other, less quantifiable, costs. In addition, we should consider the effects of any changes in input or output prices on the overall profitability of the new system. Will the interventions increase the risk faced by the owner? Is this acceptable, or is it putting the owner in jeopardy? These matters must all be considered and discussed with producers, when considering any intervention and making a plan.

11.4.11 Expected benefits and number of beneficiaries

A plan for external funding must explicitly state the number of families which will benefit from the proposed interventions and try to quantify the benefits they will receive. The flock projections, estimates of increased productivity (milk production, etc.), and partial budgets for different situations will help to establish the expected increases in meat, milk, and cash. These can then be combined with an estimate of the number of families which can reasonably be expected to participate in the project.

In addition to the quantified benefits, there should be a statement of some of the unquantifiable benefits derived from the project. These might be increased knowledge about goats through the monitoring or research components; improved awareness of goats among policy makers, school children, and others; improved public health through better hygiene in milk handling; and improved status for women in the community through their involvement in a goat programme.

11.4.12 Environmental impact

It is important to be aware of the effects of people and their way of life on the environment. Donor agencies are increasingly concerned that their projects should not have any detrimental effects on the environment, and, wherever possible, should have a beneficial impact. Furthermore, the widely held misconceptions about goats and their supposedly negative effect on the environment mean that it is essential to have an explicit statement concerning the environmental impact of any proposed goat project.

The sorts of environmental concern that should be addressed are whether the project will increase the numbers of goats, and thus increase the pressure on the available grazing resources. How will the goats be managed? Is it possible to encourage forage development (beneficial to the environment) and the cut-and-carry feeding of goats? Is there any chance of widespread agreement among producers to exercise control of livestock using communal grazing areas?

11.4.13 Other side-effects of proposals

It is good to state what other likely side-effects the project might have. Many of these side-effects cannot be predicted and will come to light only after the project has been operating for some time. However, it is important for those who will implement a project to think about both the good, as well as potentially bad, side-effects of the actions they are planning. In particular, the following questions should be considered.

- **Labour requirements:** does the proposed intervention involve more work? If so, by whom? Will they have time to carry out their existing tasks as well as the new jobs?

- **Gender:** will the intervention change any of the current roles and status of men and women? Will it improve the quality of life for men, women, and children? If one member of the family benefits from the project, will the benefits be shared among the family or retained by the individual for personal use?

- **Culture:** does the intervention expect any change in the culture of those involved? For example, in some societies people are not used to drinking goats' milk. Will it be accepted?

11.4.14 Budget

It important to prepare a clear and realistic budget, whether external funding is required or not. Consider whether all the resources are available or not in order to carry out the programme of work successfully. It is distressing for all concerned if work is started and cannot be completed because of lack of resources.

External donors normally require a budget to be prepared in a particular format. A simple example is given in Table 11.4. Costs are separated into funds spent on capital items such as vehicles, farm development, and the purchase of bulky items such as large equipment and goats. Costs that recur every year, such as staff salaries, vehicle running costs, and purchase of drugs and stationery, should be presented separately.

It is usually helpful if capital and recurrent costs can be presented separately for each activity of the proposal. If this is done, donors can immediately see how their funds are going to be spent and, if desired, shift more resources to a preferred activity from another, less preferred one.

Table 11.4 Sample budget format for project proposal

Item	Year 1	Year 2	Year 3	Total
Capital				
Extension				
Goat purchase				
Vehicle purchase				
Training				
Audio-visual equipment				
Breeding				
Farm development				
Equipment				
Total capital costs				
Recurrent				
Extension				
Staff				
Vehicle operating costs				
Drugs				
Forage seed				
Equipment				
Stationery				
Breeding				
Staff				
Drugs				
Equipment				
Training				
Staff				
Extension materials				
Monitoring				
Staff				
Stationery				
Administration				
Staff				
Stationery				
Total recurrent costs				
Total budget required				

11.5 Methods of implementation

11.5.1 Introduction

At the start of the implementation of any development initiative, it is important to develop points of contact and channels of communication with the local community and with those directly involved in the programme. It is assumed that the communities with whom the project was designed are aware of their role and the benefits they are likely to receive during the course of the project. However, it is very hard to provide enough extension staff to work closely with individual families. Contact with individuals is very important, but it is unrealistic to base an extension programme on one-to-one contact.

For effective implementation, there must be:

- a channel to supply and manage inputs;
- a forum for the exchange of ideas;
- a training forum.

It is most likely that some sort of organisation of farmers or pastoralists, formal or informal, will be used as the main point of contact. It is much more efficient, and appropriate, for producers to learn from each other, and it is a more efficient use of the time of extension staff if they can train groups, rather than individuals. The appropriateness of any technology that requires regular, lengthy contact between an extension agent and an individual owner has to be questioned.

There is often debate about the need for, and role of, contact farmers. The well-known training and visit (T and V) system of agricultural extension relies heavily on extension staff working exclusively with contact farmers, who pass on agricultural messages to their 'follower' farmers. This is a very formalised extension system, which allows little scope for feedback and for extension staff and farmers to diverge from the official programme. In reality, extension staff will always get to know a few of the more enthusiastic farmers or pastoralists, upon whom they will increasingly rely as their main contacts with the local community. These enthusiastic men or women will be the ones who quickly take up new ideas, who regularly attend meetings, and want to attend training courses. Their motives are, naturally, mixed between seeking advantage for themselves and their family and wanting to help their less able neighbours. Some development agencies formalise this relationship and employ these leaders as community workers, who earn a small salary, and in turn visit their neighbours on behalf of the project and, perhaps, help to organise meetings. This can be an extremely cost-effective method of maintaining contact with the community. However, over-stretched extension staff may quickly find that their only contact with the community is through these leader farmers, who may not represent the views of the whole community and may tend to monopolise the staff and resources of the project for themselves.

11.5.2 Farmer/pastoralist organisations

Farmer, or pastoralist, organisations can take many forms, from informal neighbourhood groups to legally recognised co-operatives. These organisations can serve one or more of the following functions:

* as a channel for inputs, including credit;
* for processing products;
* for marketing products;
* as savings associations;
* as forums for discussion;
* as forums for training;
* as welfare organisations;
* as lobbying groups.

Each country has its own legislation governing the status of producers' groups, or associations, and the necessity for legal recognition, registration with authorities, reporting, accounting, etc. In some countries, producers' organisations are used more for political purposes than genuinely to assist their members; they may even be used as a channel for the collection of taxes.

A project first has to decide whether, in order to achieve its purposes, it is able to work through existing organisations, or whether it is necessary to start a new one. Existing groups are seldom orientated towards goats and goat development. But it is preferable in most cases to try to work through, and adapt, existing structures wherever possible. This will improve the chances of the long-term sustainability of the intervention. However, if there are no appropriate organisations with which to work, new ones might have to be established.

A 'goat group' might be set up to serve one or more of the following functions:

* to supervise credit repayments and reallocation of credit;
* to manage a drug supply;
* to supervise paravets;
* to supervise buck stations and 'rotation' of bucks;
* to assist in performance recording/monitoring;
* to organise an accompanying savings association;
* to assist in product collection and processing, e.g. butter or cheese making;
* to assist in group marketing;
* to manage a communal grazing resource.

The status of the group might start by being quite informal; but, as production increases, the group could develop into a more formal organisation, serving the functions of a co-operative for goat producers. All groups, of whatever status, should be democratic and accountable bodies. If groups start accepting credit on behalf of their members, more formal arrangements may have to be initiated. Each country will have its own legislation regulating these informal groups and they must, of course, always function within the law.

11.5.3 Training

One of the main purposes of a producers' organisation is to become a forum for the frank exchange of ideas and information, among producers and between the community and the agency assisting them. These organisations can provide the structure through which training takes place.

The effective training of farmers and pastoralists is likely to be critical to the success of the goat-improvement programme. Training may take several forms:

• a basic farmer-training course in improved goat-management;
• specialised training in a new skill, such as cheesemaking;
• training of selected individuals in specialist skills, such as paravet techniques.

Designing appropriate training programmes for producers requires a careful assessment of their existing knowledge, and consideration of how to help them to acquire the new knowledge they need.

Methods

Many different methods have been used to train farmers and pastoralists, from a residential training course away from home to an informal demonstration within the community. Training sessions might take place at the regular meeting of a group, or during a specially organised training course. Training can be in small neighbourhood groups, or larger village groups. As a general rule, training should be informal, practical, and brief; it should take place in a familiar setting; and it should be fun.

Farmers are unlikely to be comfortable or to learn well when confined in a formal classroom. Make the training friendly and informal. Participants could bring some food and drink to share.

Learning by doing is always better than just listening and learning. Whenever possible, use real objects: real goats, actual equipment. Encourage people to handle them and to practise the new skill for themselves.

Farmers and pastoralists are busy people who have no leisure to attend long courses or long training sessions. Like most people, they will quickly become bored in a long session, unless the subject matter is particularly interesting. Keep the sessions brief.

It is very hard for farmers and pastoralists, especially women, to leave their homes to attend a residential course. A shady spot under a tree is usually a suitable place to learn, or in the home.

Make the training as interesting and enjoyable as possible; there is much more chance that the lessons will be learned and remembered. Acting short sketches has been used with great success.

11.5.4 Extension materials and other forms of communication

The choice of extension materials depends on whether you are trying to transmit a training message to a target group, or simply to gain publicity for a new project or programme. In the latter case, the best way to convey simple messages to large numbers of people is through posters and the organs of the mass media: radio, television, and newspapers.

There can be no doubt that the best materials to support training are real goats, equipment, forage plots, etc., which can be seen, touched, and examined. However, it is not always possible to arrange this, and visual aids may have to be used instead. There are many different visual aids available, and they vary in cost and effectiveness. It is important to consider the sort of message you want to communicate, the target audience, and the cost; not least you should consider how to make the materials appropriate to the local culture. Here is a summary of the advantages and disadvantages of various kinds of visual aid.

Posters

A well-designed, attractive poster can effectively present a simple message. However, many posters designed to convey an extension message are dull, complicated, and poorly drawn and designed. Most of them try to say too much. Keep posters simple and eye-catching, and use them only to convey one simple message. Try to print them on good-quality paper, or they will soon deteriorate, especially out of doors.

Pamphlets

Small pamphlets with a simple text and drawings can be a helpful method of distributing information fairly cheaply. Obviously, producers must be literate in order to benefit from any text. Pamphlets are a useful method of providing the sort of information that needs to be kept for future reference. They can take the form of photocopied and stapled sheets, or be professionally printed and bound.

Figure 11.2
A flip-chart in use

Flip-charts

An experienced extension agent, with an extrovert personality and basic presentation skills, should be able to present fairly complicated information in a manner that is attractive and memorable. However, not all extension staff have the necessary skills and confidence. Less experienced staff will run more effective, interactive meetings with the aid of pre-prepared flip-chart presentations, written up on A3-sized paper (or even bigger), supported by clear, detailed accompanying notes.

More sophisticated equipment

Overhead transparencies, film strips, and video films can present information in an extremely attractive and memorable way. Unfortunately, of course, they require electricity. If mains electricity is not available, you might be able to use a small, portable generator, or large batteries charged by solar power.

An overhead projector can be a useful visual aid in training, provided that the transparencies are prepared in a clear, simple manner. In a darkened room, the image can be projected on to a screen or white bed-sheet.

A limited number of film strips about goats are available. Or you could make your own: it is quite simple to put together a series of slide transparencies, photographed in the project area, to present a message. This can be especially powerful if the slides feature people in the audience! There are projectors that can run off solar power and are small and light enough for extension staff to carry around (see the Appendix).

Video films may be purchased commercially (though there are very few concerning goats), or they can be specially made, by professionals or amateurs. Such a production can be very time-consuming and expensive, but video films are the most powerful of all types of medium for communicating a message.

Mass media
Mass media such as radio, TV, or newspapers offer a very useful method of presenting a simple message to a large number of people. Mass media channels might be used during a disease epidemic, such as an outbreak of CCPP: radio transmissions might be used to encourage farmers to vaccinate their goats.

Visits
It is often useful to arrange for a small group of selected producers to make a visit outside their home area in order to see something new for themselves. They might visit a large goat farm to see new breeds or new techniques, or visit other producers who are having some success with a new technology. 'Seeing is believing', and visits can have a profound effect on people's thinking.

Goat shows
A gathering where owners exhibit their goats in public can generate a great deal of interest and provide valuable publicity. Invite senior professional extension staff, or research staff, or respected local producers to act as the judges; involve local leaders, perhaps religious leaders if appropriate, in presenting the prizes. Classes might include best milking doe, best buck, best castrate, best forage, etc. Think of classes appropriate for the conditions. Give small prizes to as many people as possible. Prizes might include milk cans, hoof-trimmers, or other agricultural tools.

11.6 The role and management of credit

11.6.1 Why do producers need credit?

Credit is normally given to help people start a new enterprise or expand an existing enterprise. Receiving goats on credit may be the only way that some farmers or pastoralists will be able to start keeping goats. If families do not have enough savings, or if they generate little income from which savings can be made, or possess few capital items to sell, credit in some form remains the only way they can start to own goats. In addition, goat producers who want to up-grade their stock may require credit for the purchase of an improved buck or doe. Credit can be a valuable way (indeed, for some, the only way) to gain access to new technology.

When the case for giving credit is being considered, it is important, at the outset, to decide whether the new goat enterprise is likely to be viable and productive and whether the borrower is able to repay the loan without getting into long-term debt. You should also be sure that the area is suitable for goat production and that the goat enterprise does not place too large a burden on the family receiving it. For new goat-keepers, credit is not enough. Some form of training and extension will be necessary at the start to ensure the proper care of the goat. If someone wants credit for improved stock, then he or she is likely to know about goat-keeping but may not be aware of the special management requirements of the improved animal; in this case too, extension will be required.

11.6.2 Likely sources of credit for goat purchase

There may be a government institution such as an agricultural credit bank which provides credit for livestock; or a commercial bank might agree to lend money for goat purchases. However, the work involved in administering a loan for the relatively small purchase price of one or two goats may make these institutions reluctant to lend for goat credit. In order to borrow money from such formal institutions, some form of collateral security is required: proof of ownership of land or capital items equivalent to the value of the loan requested. The collateral is pledged to the lender, as a guarantee for the loan. It can be difficult for poor people, particularly women, to provide collateral.

Ethiopia: women in Laftu try to get goat credit

The Ministry of Agriculture started a women's goat group in Laftu, Eastern Hararge, and registered over 50 names of the poorest women in the village who wanted to receive two local goats each. In order for the application to be considered by the local branch of the Agricultural and Industrial Development Bank (AIDBANK), the local extension staff had to prepare a 20-page technical proposal to AIDBANK, to enable them to consider its feasibility. This proposal had to be supported by letters from the district and regional Ministry of Agriculture offices. A visit was made to the group by a loan officer to discuss the proposal with the women and extension staff. It was found that the husbands of several of the women had outstanding debts with the bank; until these were repaid, their wives could not receive credit. Although it was pointed out that, at the time of their husbands' taking the loan, women were not legally able to receive credit, the AIDBANK insisted that the wives were equally liable for the outstanding debt and so were not able to take a new loan for themselves. Finally, once the terms of the loan were set at 12 per cent interest + insurance, the women decided against taking the loan, because it seemed too expensive.

The Grameen Bank of Bangladesh was established to give credit to the landless, or those with very small farms. A small loan is given to a group of five for any productive enterprise. To start with, only two members of the group receive a loan. The other members of the group act as guarantors of the loan. No further credit is given to other members of the group until the first two recipients have made successful repayments for at least two months. After successful repayment by the first two recipients, two more members of the group receive their loan, and the same procedure is followed to allow the final group member to receive credit. In this situation, collateral was impossible to offer; instead, the pressure which members of the group exerted on each other ensured that repayments were made. The bank's repayment rates of 98 per cent are very high, demonstrating the success of using group liability in place of a guarantee. The Grameen Bank has been used as a model for other countries.

Borrowing by individuals from a formal lending agency may also be difficult for illiterate people, who may be expected to fill in forms and produce letters of support from people in their community. Often there are simply too many hurdles to overcome for the sorts of people who may benefit. The requirement for collateral is hard for marginal producers, tenant farmers, landless labourers, and urban residents to comply with. This is the reason why local-level organisations, such as co-operatives or farmers' associations, are set up to help their members obtain credit from larger lending institutions.

Producers' organisations take many different forms, ranging in size from large farmers' co-operatives down to groups of 4–5 farmers who may run their own group guarantee scheme. The co-operative or farmers' association acts as an intermediary and guarantor for the loan, borrowing from a bank at the official rate of interest and lending to its members at a few per cent more, in order to cover their costs. However, it can be difficult for the very poorest to participate even in this set-up. Special arrangements may have to be made by projects and programmes established to reach the poorest.

11.6.3 Terms and conditions

In situations where a development agency is setting up its own credit programme, careful consideration should be given to the conditions under which loans will be given. The terms should be discussed with the community and agreed by them. If credit terms are too difficult, producers will not accept them or, if they do, may not be able to meet the repayment schedule and may become indebted. If the terms are too easy, people will be discouraged from taking the responsibility of the loan seriously. Borrowers who do default should be penalised, to discourage irresponsibility and the development of a culture of non-repayment.

A community committee should be established to select suitable recipients. Repayment schedules should be discussed with the borrower in detail, and a grace period and repayment rates agreed. It should be clear under what circumstances (drought or disease, for instance) repayments may be delayed and for what periods. In the case of very poor borrowers, flexibility and kindness should be exercised if the family encounter a problem outside their control. Penalties and procedures in the case of default must be discussed and agreed.

The terms agreed should be written in a contract, for future reference. The contract should be signed and witnessed. If the borrower is illiterate, the contract should be carefully read out and a mark made to indicate agreement. The borrower should be given a copy.

Repayment of a loan to purchase a goat can be made in two ways:

- repayment in cash, either in small regular instalments, or in a lump sum on the sale of a goat, or at crop-harvest time;
- repayment 'in kind': repaying a weaned kid to the lender for sale, or repaying a weaned kid (female) to another family.

11.6.4 Repayment in cash

Repayment of a loan in cash is the method of repayment accepted by banks and other formal lending institutions. The loan is received in cash and repaid in cash, normally with some interest. If the interest rate is less than the rate of inflation in goat prices, then repayment in cash is preferable, for the farmer or pastoralist, to repayment in kind. Repayments may be requested annually or may be allowed in small regular instalments. Some farmers may find it easier to repay a larger lump sum after the annual harvest, for example. Others find it easier to repay in small amounts, perhaps with money obtained from some petty trading activities. Repayments made from benefits derived directly from the goat may take some time to materialise. If the goat is female, she will have to be mated and give birth and the offspring will have to be sold before any income is received which can be used to repay the original loan — unless some milk can be sold. This may take at least one year, and probably more. If the loan is short-term credit for fattening male goats, repayment is relatively straightforward and can be made at the end of the fattening period, when the fattened goat is sold. Producers need to think carefully about where they are going to get the cash to repay a cash loan, and must be realistic about when they can repay it.

Repayment in cash is often relatively difficult for communities to manage themselves. It is essential that accurate records are kept; this requires standards of literacy and book-keeping which may not exist within the community. It is normally essential that a bank account is opened — a difficult procedure in some countries. Handling relatively large sums of cash also requires honesty if the scheme is to succeed. The possibility of corruption exists and may be very tempting. When community-managed credit schemes are set up, they are usually designed to establish some sort of revolving fund. A lump sum is obtained by a co-operative or farmers' association, which is on-lent to individuals. Once individuals have repaid their loan, the money can be used again and lent to new individuals. In theory the money can revolve forever. In practice, unless the funds are very well managed, they tend to revolve away and disappear! People default or delay repayment, some funds are stolen, and the original fund gradually shrinks.

11.6.5 Repayment in kind

For families where cash is very scarce, repayment in kind, returning a kid, is a very attractive option. Repayment in kind is also much easier for the community to manage themselves, because it is not essential for the fund's managers to be literate, and there is very little chance of corruption. There are often traditional practices for giving or lending livestock which can be used as a basis for credit programmes.

If the current interest rate is greater than the current rate of inflation in goat prices, then repayment in kind is attractive for farmers. Schemes involving repayment in kind are ideal ways for NGOs to reach and help the poorest. They are perhaps harder for government extension systems to promote and manage. There are many different methods of organising repayment in kind. The principle is simply that, for any goat received, a goat should be returned.

Repayment in kind should be started on a relatively small scale, involving no more than 10–30 members per group initially. Because of the nature of the repayment method, the original number of members will quickly double and then quadruple, and so on. This, of course, is a very attractive feature for donors, because the injection of a small amount of money into a community can have a widespread impact. Through people helping each other, close ties can be formed within the community, which can be of lasting benefit. However, there comes a point when everyone in a community who wants one has received a goat, or the scheme becomes so big that it is

Repayment in kind: some examples

1 A doe is received by a member of a group and the first kid kept by the owner. The second kid is returned. If it is a female, it is passed on to another member of the group. If it is male, it is sold and the money either used to buy a female goat or used by the group for another purpose, such as topping up the group's savings, or to buy veterinary drugs.

2 A doe is received and the first female kid is returned and on-lent to a new member of the group. If the doe does not produce any female offspring in the first two years, a male kid is taken and sold. The money is used for the group, as above.

3 A pure exotic doe is lent to an individual who has access to an exotic buck. The borrower keeps the pure-bred kid and passes on the doe to another member of the group.

unmanageable. At some point the on-lending of goats must end. If it is a small group activity, the group should decide when to stop repayment in kind. Perhaps the group is developing some other activity and could use funds generated from the sale of the last round of repayment goats for some other group activity. Perhaps the members need the money to buy veterinary drugs or an improved buck.

11.6.6 Insurance

It is always best to insure a loan when possible, to ensure that the borrower is not thrown into debt if the goat dies or is stolen, and so is unable to repay the loan. The insurance premium should be calculated according to the probability of the goat's dying or otherwise being lost to the owner. Ideally some cost of administering the insurance should also be included in the premium calculation, but it may not be. There are two ways of insuring goats: via a commercial or government insurance company, or through a self-insurance scheme.

Commercial or government insurance companies may not have any experience of insuring goats; they may need to be persuaded to do so and may need help to obtain information on mortality rates, in order to calculate a premium. The goat should be insured for the whole period of the loan. Normally insurance companies, like lenders, will insist that the goat is permanently identified in some way. The identification will then need to be produced at the time of making any claim for the death of the goat. Insurance companies vary in their claims procedures. Some may require a death certificate signed by a local government veterinarian, certifying that the goat died of natural causes and not through neglect. This may not be easy to obtain if the farmer lives far from a vet.

If a farmers' co-operative or association is administering the loan, it might be simplest if they run their own insurance scheme. An annual cash premium is paid to the association, which accumulates the funds for purchasing replacements for any goats which die. Realistic premiums should be calculated, so that the fund is not exhausted. It should be made clear that, if there is an outbreak of an epidemic disease which causes abnormally high mortality rates, the association or co-operative cannot be liable in this case.

11.6.7 Purchasing goats

Most organisations which lend funds for the purchase and insurance of goats will require them to be purchased under some sort of supervision by a responsible authority, such as the extension staff of the local Ministry of Agriculture. Goats will normally have their health checked before they can be insured. Certain guidelines should be followed, to ensure a fair and proper purchasing procedure.

Normally there is little choice but to purchase from local markets. There are advantages in this: the borrower will participate in selecting the goat; the goat will not have any problems in adapting to its new home environment and is unlikely to introduce any new diseases. The purchasing group would consist of the borrower, a representative of the lending organisation (bank, co-operative, association, NGO), and a local veterinarian.

If there is not a convenient market, or if local market prices are particularly high, purchasing from a more distant market may have to be considered. It may be difficult to transport several borrowers to the market, in which case a representative of the borrowers should be elected and should purchase on their behalf. Arrangements will then have to be made to transport the goats back from the market. If goats are bought in this way, it is fair to allocate them by drawing lots.

The sort of goat to buy depends on the purpose of taking the loan. If it is to establish a small breeding flock, young healthy females should be bought. A buck should be bought only if sufficient breeding males are not available near the borrower's home. If the loan is for fattening, immature males should be bought.

A female with one pair of permanent incisors (15–18 months), or a female with milk teeth which has been weaned for some time (12–15 months), would be ideal foundation breeding females. Older females are usually sold for a reason, frequently infertility or poor mothering ability; be careful not to buy an older female with a poorly developed udder: this is a bad sign.

Figure 11.3 A doe with a good wedge shape and a well-hung udder
JENNY MATTHEWS/OXFAM

A good doe should have a 'wedge' shape when viewed from the side, having as much depth as possible in front of the hind legs, giving her a triangular look: deep in the hindquarters, narrowing towards the front. Check the teeth, not just for age, but also for wear and any irregularities. Make sure there are no obvious problems with the udder, such as supernumerary teats (small teats attached to the side of the main teat) or any sign of mastitis, if she has kidded.

The vet should make a physical inspection to check for obvious diseases or wounds: the eyes (for infections), nose (discharge), feet (foot rot), swelling under the jaw (internal parasites), skin (mange mites or ticks), coats (is it dull or shiny and healthy?), and general appearance (dull/listless or full of energy?).

Often prices fluctuate with seasons or cultural holidays. Try not to buy just before a major holiday, when prices are high. The arrival of a group of buyers, including, perhaps, a government official, may make traders in the market raise their prices artificially high, thinking they are selling to the government.

After purchase, the following procedure should be observed.

- The goat should be identified with an ear-tag or other means of identification. (At this point, it is useful to write a physical description of the goat, so there is no doubt about its status if the tag is lost in the future.)
- The animal is drenched for internal parasites, and vaccinated against major diseases (this may be a condition for insurance).
- Ideally a blood sample should be taken and the goat, if it is to be used for breeding, checked for brucellosis. This may be difficult to arrange.
- The borrower should pay the insurance premium at this point, before receiving the goat.

Buying a goat from a market is always risky. After purchase, the goat may show signs of disease or some sort of incapacity. In females it may be found that they regularly abort and that is, perhaps, the reason why they were sold in the first place. As a rule, if a goat aborts twice, it should be sold for slaughter and replaced.

11.6.8 Group development and training for credit management

It is clear that the proper management of funds is of fundamental importance to the success of any credit programme. The mismanagement of credit funds, repayments, and insurance is the most common reason for the failure of credit programmes and a consequent loss of confidence in them by producers, extension staff, and donors. It is therefore of great importance that effective systems of management are in place from the start; that producers and fund managers are properly trained in the skills necessary to manage the credit properly; and that a relevant organisation regularly supervises and monitors the scheme.

Training of goat-keepers and/or extension staff for effective credit management might range from basic literacy/numeracy skills to computer training, depending on their initial levels of skill. At the most basic level, a small-scale credit programme for a small group of farmers can prompt them to recognise the need to learn to read and write. Many NGOs have set up functional literacy programmes in order to train group leaders in literacy, so that they can keep simple records, write letters, operate a bank account, and write simple reports to their donors. It is important that the capacity of the group is developed to make use of organisations outside their community, better manage their own affairs, and directly improve their livelihood through the use of the credit received.

Think carefully about the training needs of those involved in a credit programme. If you control funds, allocate a proportion of credit funds for training, as a routine procedure. In this way the funds will be better used and mismanagement reduced.

11.6.9 Gifts of goats

Is it ever right to give goats away to farmers or pastoralists? Under what conditions might this be considered? The advantage of giving away goats is that gifts are much simpler to organise than loans, which require constant follow-up to ensure that they are repaid and reallocated correctly to new families. For destitute families, in desperate conditions, the gift of some goats might make the difference between life and death. However, it must be clear that they are able to look after them properly and are not going to sell them immediately for cash to buy food. If they do this,

357

it would have been much simpler to give them cash or food in the first place.

The main reason not to give goats is that, if they are widely and regularly given, it can create a culture of dependency within the recipient community. This is not a good basis for the solid, sustainable economic development for which we strive.

11.6.10 Restocking pastoralists

The restocking of pastoralists with goats after a disaster, natural or otherwise, has been a particularly important role for goats in recent years. It is a specialised form of goat credit, or gift, and so is described separately here.

Experiences of restocking in Africa over the last 10–15 years have been reviewed by Oxby (1994). She has set out clear guidelines on restocking, which are summarised below.

Restocking is an appropriate strategy during the early stage of recovery after a disaster. After a drought, epidemic, or war, pastoralists will typically congregate around a settlement such as a feeding camp, irrigation scheme, or food-for-work scheme. The land around the settlement will quickly become over-grazed by their remaining stock. Restocking should be considered only for pastoralists who are willing and able to return to the pastoral way of life, away from the settlement centres where they have sought assistance. Goats are a suitable species for pastoralists familiar with them, because they are relatively cheap and reproduce quickly, so they can soon be 'traded-up' in exchange for larger cattle or camels.

Restocking should be achieved through the purchase of goats from richer pastoralists for redistribution to poorer families; in this way the total stocking rate of the whole area is not disrupted. Normally it is not possible to restock a family with enough livestock to meet all their food needs, so restocking must be viewed as a supplement to what is already owned; it would, ideally, be sufficient to tip the balance, and return the family to a nomadic way of life. For this reason it has been found that destitute families, with no livestock of their own, cannot benefit from restocking programmes which are unable to provide them with enough livestock to return them to full self-sufficiency. For this reason, the key to a successful restocking programme is the selection of families who are in a position to benefit from the restocking package on offer, and time and resources must be devoted to the selection of suitable families.

How many goats to give? Inevitably there will be limited financial resources and/or a limited number of goats available to be purchased. Therefore it will not be possible to provide a complete recovery package to all who may need it. It is for this reason that restocking should be viewed as supplementing existing livestock with enough animals for families to leave the settlement and return to the nomadic way of life. It must be appreciated that pastoralists have traditional ways of assisting their needy relatives. Livestock are often loaned to families in need, and so restocking families should be viewed as a supplement to these traditional welfare systems, and to any alternative sources of income. The total combination of different sources of livelihood must be viable, not just the restocking package itself. Most restocking packages range from 25 to 70 goats per family. Packages are provided per family, not per head, as it is time-consuming for agency staff to try to find out how many people are genuinely dependent in a family.

Target groups who might be specially selected to benefit from restocking might include food-for-work recipients and women-headed households, especially after war, if they have sufficient labour. Restocking young widows may make them more eligible for remarriage, opening up another route to return to the pastoral life. Allocating goats to women is often appropriate anyway, because they traditionally look after goats and are responsible for feeding children with their milk. In addition, women are often less likely to receive traditional livestock loans from relatives.

Families may be selected, and goats purchased, by a committee representing the beneficiaries, local leaders, and the agency financing the purchase. Selecting near-viable households may prove to be such a sensitive issue that it is sensible to have a wide spectrum of opinion, and then to cross-check the choices made by the committee. Mature female goats should be given together with adequate bucks, which may take time to buy. This delay can mean that partially restocked flocks are forced to remain near the settlement, which is not desirable. It is best if a family can be completely restocked in one allocation, so that they can move away from the settlement immediately.

The conditions under which the livestock are received must be clear right from the start. These must be discussed with all concerned. Are they a gift or a loan? If they are a loan, what are the repayment terms and conditions? Some restocking programmes give a loan in cash for pastoralists to buy their own stock, and repayment in cash is expected. Others give the loan in kind and expect the repayment in kind. Harsh repayment conditions will undermine the recovery of the family, while gifts can lead to the development of an irresponsible attitude. Some past projects have based the restocking conditions on the terms enforced in traditional livestock loans.

The sale or slaughter of any livestock received is usually prohibited until loan conditions have been fulfilled. This is hard to enforce if the family is not viable and has to sell stock in order to stay alive. This emphasises the need for careful selection. If goats will immediately be sold to buy grain, it is probably simpler to give grain in the first place. Some restocking programmes do supply grain for a limited period and may even supply a pack animal, such as a donkey, to carry the grain away from the settlement centre. Grain distributions should not be too frequent, or families will not be able to move very far from the settlement, thus defeating the purpose of the restocking programme. Ideally they would be decentralised as much as possible.

Regular health-care is often a condition of receiving livestock. Frequently herders are trained as paravets, and vaccination may be offered through the programme.

To evaluate the effects of the restocking programme, flocks should be monitored every 6–12 months. At this time repayments can be made to agency staff, who are in a position to evaluate the effect of repayment on the family's viability. Some flexibility may be needed, to give families every chance to make a full recovery to the pastoral life, which is the purpose of restocking.

11.7 Evaluation of goat-improvement programmes

11.7.1 Introduction

Although this book is called *Improving Goat Production*, its concern is to improve goat production in order to improve human welfare. We should never forget the importance of defining, and continually redefining, what constitutes an improvement in any situation, and trying to measure whether this improvement has in fact been achieved. If it is not being achieved, and human welfare is not improved, then either modifications must be made to our actions, or we should cease them altogether.

There is a tendency for the job of monitoring project progress and evaluating project achievements to be done by outsiders, usually representatives of the donor. Their evaluation is often seen as investigative and threatening, leaving project staff and their collaborating farmers feeling defensive about their efforts. This is very unfortunate. While donors obviously need to check that their money is being spent as it was supposed to be, and there has been no dishonesty, it is project staff and beneficiaries who have the greatest interest in checking that their joint efforts are not wasted. Monitoring and evaluation should therefore be seen as an integral, and continuous, part of project life, involving producers, extension staff, development agencies, and donors on equal terms. An atmosphere must be created whereby all concerned feel able to make a frank evaluation of their efforts, achievements, and failures. We often learn more from failure than from success. Systems must be in place for this to happen.

Monitoring, therefore, has two main functions: to improve project implementation, and to provide the background information for effective evaluation.

All goat programmes will have both quantifiable and unquantifiable outputs, and both must be monitored in order for them to be evaluated. It is important that those collecting data have a real interest in, and need for, the information that comes from the data. This will ensure that the data are regularly and accurately collected. There is a tendency to collect too much data, which then become a burden for the collectors; too much information is difficult to analyse and so cannot be used to improve implementation.

11.7.2 Quantifiable information

Table 11.5 lists the basic minimum information that should be collected on outputs that can be quantified. This information might be recorded by the farmers or pastoralists themselves, or by extension staff. Ideally it would be recorded before any project interventions have been made, in order to describe the situation at the start of the project. Any changes in these parameters can be recorded over the life of the project.

Monitoring records must be simple and easy to maintain. They should be regularly analysed; the results should be presented to the community and discussed by them at regular reviews. This will

Table 11.5 Basic monitoring information required for quantifiable outputs

Topic	Minimum monitoring information
Credit	Rate of credit disbursement Credit repayment rates
Productivity	Births, deaths Milk production (daily yield, lactation length)
Health	Deaths (cause if possible) Sickness (cause if possible) Paravet treatment book
Nutrition	Growth rates, milk production
Forage	Number of seedlings distributed and surviving
Marketing	Number and price of goats sold Amount and price of milk sold

allow quick reactions to changing circumstances and should feed back into the implementation process, helping staff and beneficiaries to improve their operations.

Quantitative records will form the basis by which any donor will also assess the overall costs and benefits of a project, and they should assist in the design of more efficient projects.

11.7.3 Qualitative information

Besides the hard data collected on the performance of goats, it is important to make a more qualitative assessment of interventions. Farmers may have improved their goats' performance, but has it had a detrimental effect on some other part of their lives? For example, cut-and-carry feeding may have improved the diet of the goat, and its productivity, but the extra labour needed is being taken away from another activity. What do farmers — men, women, and children — think about this? Planting forage on every square metre of land available may have improved feed supply, but has it reduced the family's recreation area? Does the meat from a cross-bred goat taste the same as that from local goats? Is it better or worse?

In addition to these qualitative side-effects of improved production, we should remember that the participation of the family in the project will affect their lives in other ways. Many projects place a strong emphasis on social development, rather than exclusively on economic development. Social development projects are often concerned with empowering farmers, increasing self-reliance, and increasing their involvement in the development process. For example, goat projects are often used as a way of channelling assistance to the poorest in a community. It is hoped that the beneficiaries will, for instance, increase their incomes, or milk supply — but in addition that their status in society will be improved. Perhaps they have been elected to a village committee, or have been able to make a contribution to a community project, which they would have been unable to make before. Likewise, goat projects are often focused on women, because they are usually responsible for looking after goats. Project interventions may encourage women to take up new roles in their society. For example, in some societies it might be unusual for women to attend meetings, manage credit funds, speak in public, or take products directly to market. An increase in self-esteem and personal confidence is not something that can be easily measured and evaluated, and yet it is of inestimable worth to the individual. In order to try to evaluate these aspects of development, in the context of the local culture, we must listen to all concerned and give people the opportunity to express themselves.

Further reading

ALIN (1993) *Restocking in Kenya*, Dakar, Senegal: Arid Lands Information Network (ALIN)

Cammack, J. (1992) *Basic Accounting for Small Groups*, Oxford: Oxfam (UK and Ireland)

Elliott, N. (1996) *Basic Accounting for Credit and Savings Schemes*, Oxford: Oxfam (UK and Ireland)

Feuerstein, M. (1992) *Partners in Evaluation*, London: Macmillan

MacDonald, I. and D. Hearle (1984) *Communication Skills for Rural Development*, London: Evans

Marsden, D. and P. Oakley (eds) (1990) *Evaluating Social Development Projects*, Oxford: Oxfam (UK and Ireland)

Oxby, C. (1994) *Restocking: A Guide*, Edinburgh: VETAID

Werner, D. and B. Bower (1991) *Helping Health Workers Learn*, Palo Alto: Hesperian Foundation

Glossary

abomasum the fourth of four compartments of the stomach.

abortion the termination of a pregnancy before its natural end.

abscess an enclosed collection of pus caused by an infection.

acaricide a chemical that kills ticks.

acute of disease, appearing suddenly, lasting a short time with severe symptoms.

alley farming growing annual crops between rows of trees.

anaemia lack of red blood cells in the blood, shown by pale mucous membranes.

anaesthetic a drug which prevents the feeling of pain.

anoestrus period when the obvious signs of oestrus are not shown because of poor nutrition or lactation.

anthelmintic a drug which kills internal parasites.

antibiotic a drug which controls bacterial infections.

antibody a naturally produced substance that circulates in the blood and protects against infections.

anus the opening of the rectum through which undigested food (faeces) passes.

arthritis inflammation of a joint.

artificial insemination (AI) the introduction of male sperm into the reproductive tract of a female by means of a tube.

bacteria very small living agents which cause infections.

browse the leaves and stems of trees and shrubs eaten by goats.

buck male goat.

caprine to do with goats.

carcass the body of a dead animal.

castration making a male animal sexually inactive by removing its testicles or making them shrivel and die.

cervix the neck of the uterus.

chromosome the part of the nucleus of a cell that contains the genetic material or DNA.

chronic of disease, lasting a long time.

clinical to do with the practical study of a sickness.

colostrum the first milk produced after birth, containing antibodies.

contagious spreading by contact.

corpus luteum the structure remaining after ovulation. In pregnancy it persists to produce progesterone.

cross-breeding the process of mating different breeds or types for the purpose of improving one of them.

culling the process of removing unwanted animals, usually of poor quality, from a flock.

dam mother.

diarrhoea the frequent passing of liquid faeces.

discharge the passage of liquid from the body.

disinfectant a chemical which is used to kill bacteria.

disposable designed to be used once and thrown away.

DM dry matter

doe female goat

drenching giving a liquid by mouth, often an anthelmintic.

dry matter (DM)the part of the feed, not containing water, that contains its nutrients.

dystocia difficulty giving birth.

drench a liquid given by mouth to an animal, usually an anthelmintic.

ejaculation the release of sperm during mating.

embryo a young animal or foetus, developing in its mother, during its very early stages before the legs and head are clearly visible.

endemic regularly found in a region.

enteritis inflammation of the intestine, causing diarrhoea.

epidemic the occurrence of a disease at a much higher rate than normal.

exotic introduced from outside.

F_1 the name given to the first generation after a cross between parents.

faeces undigested food that passes out of the body through the anus.

fever a high body temperature.

foetus a young animal developing inside its mother before birth.

gangrene death of tissue.

genotype the genetic composition of an animal.

gestation the period of pregnancy. About 150 days in goats.

Graafian follicle the group of cells containing the mature ovum.

heritability the degree to which a characteristic is passed on from parents to offspring.

heterosis the difference between the offspring and the mean of the parents. Can be positive or negative.

hybrid vigour arises when there is positive heterosis and the offspring is better than the mean of the parents.

Glossary

immunity	protection within the body against disease-causing agents.
indigenous	naturally occurring in an area.
in-breeding	the mating of two closely related individuals.
infection	invasion of the body by disease organisms.
infectious	able to cause an infection.
inflammation	a response of the body to injury, characterised by heat, pain, redness, and loss of use.
intersex	a goat born with a mixture of male and female sexual organs.
intramammary	into the udder.
intramuscular	into the muscle.
intravenous	into the vein.
lactational anoestrus	when signs of oestrus are not shown because the doe is lactating.
larva	the early form of a parasite.
legume	a plant able to trap nitrogen from the atmosphere and fix it as protein, e.g. pigeon pea or leucaena.
libido	the sexual urge.
lymph nodes	swellings in the body that act as filters for harmful organisms.
mucous membrane	a surface tissue of the body covered and lubricated with mucus, e.g. inside the skin surrounding the eye.
mucus	a shiny liquid which covers some body surfaces (mucous membranes) e.g. inside the eyelid, mouth or nose.
nutritional anoestrus	when signs of oestrus are not shown because the doe is poorly fed.
oedema	a collection of fluid in tissues.
oestrogen	hormone which induces oestrus.
oestrus	period when the doe is receptive to mating. Sometimes known as 'season' or 'heat'.
orchitis	inflammation of one or both testicles.
ovum	unfertilised egg. Plural is **ova.**
ovary	female organs where ova develop.
oviduct	tube (Fallopian tube) running from the ovary to the uterus.
ovulation	time at which ripe ovum is released into the oviducts.
perennial	a plant which lives for three or more years.
phenotype	the way an animal's genetic composition is seen in physical characteristics.
pheromones	a chemical substance produced by one animal that affects the behaviour of another, e.g. substances produced by a buck that stimulate oestrus in a doe.

pneumonia	inflammation of the lungs.
polled	without horns.
post-mortem	after death.
prophylactic	preventative.
puberty	the age at which a young animal becomes sexually active.
pus	thick liquid, yellow or green, with or without blood, produced at sites of infection.
rapid rural appraisal (RRA)	methods used to make a quick assessment of the problems of a rural community.
rumen	the large first stomach of ruminants that allows them to digest fibrous feeds.
ruminant	any animal with a rumen, which enables it to digest fibrous feeds.
salivation	the production of liquid (saliva) from the mouth.
scab	the dried crust forming over a wound.
scrotum	the skin bag containing the testicles.
serum	the liquid that separates from blood after it has clotted.
spermatic cord	the structures by which the testicles are suspended in the scrotum.
strategic	carefully selected to have maximum effect and be economical.
subcutaneous	under the skin.
symptom	a sign of abnormality indicating disease.
systemic	widespread throughout the body.
testicle	the male sexual organ contained in the scrotum.
toggle	a small growth dangling from the neck of some goats, also known as tassels or wattles.
trait	a characteristic of an animal.
undersowing	planting a crop underneath another one.
uterus	a Y-shaped organ and the site where the embryo is nurtured.
vagina	organ connecting the uterus with the outside, into which sperm is inserted during sexual intercourse.
vasectomy	operation whereby the male is made sterile but retains its sexual desire.
vector	a carrier, especially an insect, which carries an infective agent from one animal to another.
vulva	outside opening of the vagina.
wattles	a small growth dangling from the neck of some goats, also known as tassels or toggles.

Useful addresses

Export of breeding goats from UK

Agricultural Export Services,
Caudle Farm,
Caudle Green,
Cheltenham, GL53 9PR
UK
Tel/Fax: +44 1285 821659

Goat societies

International Goat Association,
216 Wachusett St,
Rutland, MA 01543,
USA
Fax: +1 508 886 6729

Publishes the *Small Ruminant Research Journal*

British Goat Society,
34-36 Fore Street,
Bovey Tracey,
Newton Abbot,
Devon, TQ13 9AD
Tel: +44 1626 833168

Publishes a monthly journal for members

Dairy Goat Journal,
W2997,
Markert Rd,
Helenville, WI 53137

Monthly newspaper obtained by subscription

United Caprine News,
PO Drawer A,
Rotan, Texas 79546,
USA
Tel: +1 817 579 5211
Fax: +1 817 579 2606

Monthly newspaper obtained by subscription

Heifer Project International,
PO Box 808,
Little Rock,
Arkansas 72203,
USA

Produces useful newsletter, 'Heifer Project Exchange'

Film strips on goats and forage and solar-powered projection equipment

World Neighbors
5116 North Portland Avenue,
Oklahoma City, OK 73112
USA
Tel: +1 405 946 3333

Veterinary drug supplies

Veterinary Drug Co. plc,
Common Road,
Donnington,
York, YO1 5RU,
UK
Tel: +44 904 488444
Fax: +44 904 488208
Telex: 57588 VETDRU G

Channelle Veterinary Ltd.,
Loughrea,
Co Galway,
Ireland
Tel: +353 91 41788
Fax: +353 91 41303
Telex: 50857 BURK EI

Veterinary and livestock equipment

Alfred Cox (Surgical) Ltd.,
Coulsdon,
Surrey, CR3 2XA
Tel: +44 181 668 2131
Fax: +44 181 668 4196
Telex: 947946 COXSURG G

Temperate and tropical forage seeds

HR Marketing Ltd.,
11-13 Bentham Street,
Adelaide,
South Australia 5000,
Australia
Tel: +61 8 2310640
Fax: +61 8 2310642

Can supply large quantities of high-quality seed

SETROPA,
Postbus 203,
1400 AE Bussum,
Holland,
Tel: +31 2152 58754
Fax: +31 2152 65424

International Livestock Research Institute (ILRI),
PO Box 5689,
Addis Ababa,
Ethiopia
Tel: +251 1 613215
Fax: +251 1 611892
Telex: 21207 ILCA ET

Will supply small quantities (50 g) of forage seed for trials

Weighscales

David Ritchie (Implements) Ltd.,
Whitehills,
Forfar, DD8 3EE
Scotland
UK
Tel: +44 0307 62271
Fax: +44 0307 64081

Index

abomasum (4th stomach)
  acidity as defence mechanism
    154
  digestion in 74, 75, 76
  in kids 79
  post-mortem treatment 226
abortion 18, 169, 248
  brucellosis 200
  causes 170
  chlamydial abortion 170, 206
  predisposing factors 169
  symptoms 170
abscess lancing 198, 199
Acacia albida 69
Acacia mellifera 151
Acacia nubica 151
Acacia tortilis 69, 150, 151, 152
'Acaprin' 189
acaricides 191
  carbamates 193
  formamidines 193
  organo-phosphates 193
  pyrethrins 193
acetic acid 75
acid detergent fibre (ADF) 74
acidosis 163, 203-4
  post-mortem identification 225
Acorus calamus 194
Afar goats 263, 266
Africa
  agro-pastoral systems 10-11
  mixed farming
    highland 13-14
    humid 11-12
    sub-humid 12-13
  pastoral systems 9-10
aging by dentition 35-6
agro-pastoral systems 10-11
Akabane disease 167, 208
Albendazole 183
alfalfa 68, 100, 102-3
allethrin 193
alley farming 110

see also forage strips
Alpine breed 277, 279, 281, 285
Amblyomma variegatum (ticks)
  188, 193
America: extensive systems 17-18
Amitraz 193
ampicillin 201
anaemia
  causes 166
  packed cell volume (PCV) 60,
    173, 174
  predisposing factors 164
  symptoms 166
Anaplasma ovis 190
anaplasmosis 166, 188, 190, 221
  post-mortem identification 221
  symptoms 190
Anglo-Nubian breed 277, 278-9,
  280
Angora breed 266, 281, 318
anoestrus 245, 246
anthelmintics 133, 179-82
  application methods 181
  common 181, 183
  lungworm treatment 185
  resistance to 181-2
  under-dosing 182
anthrax 164, 207
  post-mortem danger 207, 219
  vaccines 207
Aristichthys nobilis 320
artificial insemination 242-3
  cross-breeding using 285-6
Asia
  extensive systems 16
  mixed farming
    humid (irrigated) 14-15
    humid/semi-humid (rain-fed)
      15-16
assessment methods, high-cost
23
  body condition 53, 55

continuous monitoring 55, 56
disease *see* disease, assessment
  methods
farmer participation 49
Farming Systems Research
(FSR)
  22
feed monitoring *see* feed
  monitoring
flock inventory 56
flock structure 51
identifying individual goats 51,
  53
laboratory analysis 46, 47
management monitoring 62-3
marketing studies 63
milk measurements 55, 57-8
monitoring studies 46-63
recording frequency 48-50
RRA methods 48
sample site selection 47-8
sample size 48
setting objectives 48
setting up study 49-51
visit frequency 49-50
weighing 50, 53, 54
assessment methods, low-cost
  22-46
causal chains 42
community consultation 44, 46
direct observation 41
disease calendars 27, 29
feed calendars 26-7, 28
flock structure 38
group discussions 25-6
identification of improvements
  30
identification of problems 21-2
interviews *see* interviews
maps and walks 41-2
objectives analysis 42, 44, 45
problem analysis 42, 43
problem tree 42, 53

predisposing factors 163
symptoms 165
'Synanthic' 183
synthetic breeds 260
'Systamex' 183
systems of farming *see* farming
systems

tahu processing, waste by-
products
146
tall fescue 100, 104-5
tannins 69
tapeworms (cestodes) 172, 176-7
taro 11
tattoos 51
teeth problems 166
teff 13
'Telmin' 183
temperate breeds
see also individual breeds
improver breeds 278-81
temperature of goat, 158, 159
tepary bean 102-3
Tephrosia vogelii 194
tetanus 168, 213
tethering 13, 14, 18, 116
dairy goats Ethiopia 147-9
tetrachlorvinphos 193
tetracycline 195, 197, 201
Tetrahydropyrimidines 183
Tetramisole 183
Thiabendazole 183
'Thibenzole' 183
Thiophanate 183
Thorn Apple poisoning 216
tick-borne diseases
anaplasmosis 166, 188, 190, 221
babesiosis 166, 188, 189-90, 221
heartwater 10, 168, 188-9, 193,
220
Nairobi sheep disease 163, 164,
170, 188, 189-90, 224
ticks 10, 29, 165, 166, 188
acaricides 191
Amblyomma variegatum 188, 193
control 191, 192-4
see also dipping
lameness and 167, 202
physical damage caused 188
'Py-grease' 191
Rhipecephalus appendiculatus 189-
90
sampling 60
tilapia (fish) 320

tobacco 194
Toggenburg breed 277, 279, 280
toxoplasmosis 170
training 346-7
paravets 228-31
traits
see also breed improvement;
genetics
heritability 255
positive and negative correlation
256, 269
relationship between 256
to be improved 269
variation 254
transhumance 13, 16, 149-52
transportation 303, 323
tree crops 11, 19
tree legumes 18, 100, 102-3,
116-17
back-yard pasture 105-6
cuttings 124
forage strips 109
nutritive values 88
seedlings 121
seeds 119-21
tree lucerne 100, 102-3, 109
tree nurseries 121
community nurseries 122-3
individuals 123-4, 149
schools 122-3
women 122, 124
trees 68-9
seed pods 69, 150
seedlings 121-2
tannins 69
trematodes 172, 177
Trichostrongylus spp. 172
Trichuris spp. 172
Triclabendazole 183
Trifolium pratense 102-3
Trifolium repens 102-3
'Trodax' 183
tropical breeds
advantages and disadvantages
265
characteristics 262, 264-7
by breed 266
conservation of genetic resources
265, 267
development 262-4
flock-level improvements 263
improver breeds 277-8
major breeds 266
multi-purpose functions 262
new stock 264

non-descript type 262
trypanosomiasis 11, 13, 166, 169,
170, 207
post-mortem identification 221
symptoms 207
treatment 207
tsetse fly vector 207
tsetse fly 166, 207
tuberculosis, pasteurisation
requirement 309
tylosin 195

udder problems 169, 171
Undegraded Dietary Protein
(UDP) 77-8
undersowing 112-13, 148
annual crops 112-13
functions 112
perennial crops 113-14
shade tolerance 113-14
urban goat keeping 19-20
urea
absorption 76
chemical treatment of straws
129-30
urine 319
clinical observations 157

vaccination 10, 11, 12, 13, 16, 195,
196, 200, 207, 305
'Valbazen' 183
Van Soest feed analysis 74
ventilation of housing 292-3
verano stylo 102-3
vetch 100, 102-3, 109, 113
Vicia dasycarpa 102-3
video films 348-9
Vigna sinesis 102-3
visits 349
visual aids *see* extension materials
vitamin deficiencies 167, 214
sources of vitamin 4, 215
symptoms 215
vitamins 72
volatile fatty acids (VFA) 75

warts 165, 171, 211-12
carcinomas and tumours 212
maggots in lesions 212
water
containers 296
cooling by evaporation 72
feeding time lost 95, 151
kids 140
lactation 139

385

Oxfam (UK and Ireland) publishes a wide range of books, manuals, and resource materials for specialist, academic, and general readers.

Oxfam publications are available from the following agents: for Canada and the USA: Humanities Press International, 165 First Avenue, Atlantic Highlands, New Jersey NJ 07716-1289, USA; tel. (908) 872 1441; fax (908) 872 0717; for southern Africa: David Philip Publishers, PO Box 23408, Claremont, Cape Town 7735, South Africa; tel. (021) 64 4136; fax (021) 64 3358.

Available in Ireland from Oxfam in Ireland,
19 Clanwilliam Terrace, Dublin 2; tel: 01 661 8544

For a free catalogue, please write to
Oxfam Publishing, 274 Banbury Road, Oxford OX2 7DZ, UK.